SOULHAPPY

Compiled by Kobi Yamada

Designed by Steve Potter and Jenica Wilkie

COMPENDIUM™
INCORPORATED

live inspired.

THIS BOOK IS DEDICATED TO THOSE HAPPY SOULS
WHO HAVE A WAY OF BRIGHTENING THE DAY.

ACKNOWLEDGEMENTS

These quotations were gathered lovingly but unscientifically over several years and/
or were contributed by many friends or acquaintances. Some arrived—and survived
in our files—on scraps of paper and may therefore be imperfectly worded or attributed.
To the authors, contributors and original sources, our thanks, and where appropriate,
our apologies. –The Editors

WITH SPECIAL THANKS TO

Jason Aldrich, Gerry Baird, Jay Baird, Neil Beaton, Josie Bissett, Laura Boro, Melissa
Carlson, M.H. Clark, Tiffany Parente Connors, Jim & Alyssa Darragh & Family, Rob
Estes, Pamela Farrington, Michael & Leianne Flynn & Family, Sarah Forster, Dan
Harrill, Michael J. Hedge, Liz Heinlein & Family, Renee Holmes, Jennifer Hurwitz,
Heidi Jones, Sheila Kamuda, Michelle Kim, Carol Anne Kennedy, June Martin,
David Miller, Carin Moore & Family, Moose, Josh Oakley, Jessica Phoenix & Tom
DesLongchamp, Janet Potter & Family, Joanna Price, Heidi & José Rodriguez, Diane
Roger, Alie Satterlee, Kirsten & Garrett Sessions, Andrea Shirley, Jason Starling, Brien
Thompson, Helen Tsao, Anne Whiting, Heidi Yamada & Family, Justi & Tote Yamada &
Family, Bob and Val Yamada, Kaz & Kristin Yamada & Family, Tai & Joy Yamada, Anne
Zadra, August & Arline Zadra, and Gus & Rosie Zadra.

CREDITS

Compiled by Kobi Yamada
Designed by Steve Potter & Jenica Wilkie

ISBN: 978-1-932319-10-1
©2009 by Compendium, Incorporated. All rights reserved. No part of this publication may be
reproduced or transmitted in any form or by any means, electronic or mechanical, including
photocopy, recording, or any storage and retrieval system now known or to be invented without
written permission from the publisher. Contact: Compendium, Inc., 600 North 36th Street, Suite 400,
Seattle, WA 98103. Soul Happy, Compendium, live inspired and the format, design, layout and coloring
used in this book are trademarks and/or trade dress of Compendium, Incorporated. This book may be
ordered directly from the publisher, but please try your local bookstore first. Call us at 800-91-IDEAS
or come see our full line of inspiring products at www.live-inspired.com.
5th Printing.
Printed in China

Happiness is not in our circumstances, but in ourselves. It is not something we see, like a rainbow, or feel, like the heat of a fire. Happiness is something we are. John B. Sheerin

How do we nurture our souls? By revering our own life. By reaching for the best within ourselves. By taking chances and stretching our boundaries. By leaping into the unknown. By going places we've never been. By having faith and staring down our fears. By embracing our uniqueness. By doing things for the fun of it. By slowing down, so the important things can catch up. By breathing in wide-open spaces. By walking in nature's wildness. By appreciating each day, moment by moment. By learning to live it all, not only the joys and triumphs but the pain and struggle. By giving more than we take. By being there for others. By making a difference. When we are living a life we love, our souls are singing and dancing.

authenticity

Of all things which we have, next to the gods,
our souls are the most divine and most truly our own.

PLATO

abundance

For every beauty there is an eye somewhere to see it. For every truth there is an ear somewhere to hear it. For every love there is a heart somewhere to receive it.

IVAN PANIN

faith

It may be that when we no longer know what to do, we have come to our real work, and when we no longer know which way to go, we have begun our **real journey.**

WENDELL BERRY

energy

When you put yourself wholeheartedly into something, energy grows.
It seems inexhaustible.

HELEN DE ROSIS

serendipity

One cannot divine nor forecast the conditions that will make happiness; one only stumbles upon them by chance, in a lucky hour, at the world's end somewhere, and holds fast to the days, as to fortune or fame. WILLA CATHER

relationships

The world connects
not by molecules.
It connects through
ideas, hopes, faces,
dreams, actions,   BARRIE SANFORD GREIFF
stories, and memories.

harmony

At the heart of each of us, whatever our imperfections, there exists a silent pulse of perfect rhythm, which is absolutely individual and unique, and yet which connects us to everything else.

GEORGE LEONARD

gratitude

...it is not joy that makes us grateful; it is gratitude that makes us joyful.

BROTHER DAVID STEINDL-RAST

purpose

Whatever the soul knows how to seek,
it cannot fail to obtain.

MARGARET FULLER

wisdom

We should cultivate the ability to say no to activities for which we have no time, no talent, and which we have no interest or real concern. If we learn to say no to many things, then we will be able to say yes to things that matter most.
Roy Blauss

enthusiasm

Oh for the wonder that bubbles into my soul. D.H. LAWRENCE

focus

If you pay attention at every moment, you form a new relationship

to time. In some magical way, by slowing down, you become more

efficient, productive, and energetic, focusing without distraction

directly on the task in front of you. Not only do you become

immersed in the moment, you become that moment. Michael Ray

essence

In rivers, the water that you touch
is the last of what has passed
and the first of that which comes;
so with present time.

LEONARDO DA VINCI

inspiration

Great ideas…come into the world as gently as doves…
if we listen attentively, we shall hear, amid the uproar…
a faint flutter of wings, the gentle stirring of life and hope.

ALBERT CAMUS

potential

We are boundless creatures.

KOBI YAMADA

Knowledge

I do not know what I may appear to the world; but to myself I seem to have been only like a boy playing on the seashore, and diverting myself now and then finding a smoother pebble or a prettier shell than ordinary, whilst the great ocean of truth lay all undiscovered before me.

SIR ISAAC NEWTON

genius

Neither a lofty degree of intelligence nor imagination nor both together go to the making of genius. Love, love, love, that is the soul of genius.

WOLFGANG AMADEUS MOZART

adversity

When we face
the worst that
can happen in
any situation,
we grow. When
circumstances
are at their
worst, we can
find our best.

ELISABETH KUBLER-ROSS

courage

God, give me guts.

ELI MYGATT

hero

History provides abundant examples of people whose greatest gift was in redeeming, inspiring, liberating, and nurturing the gifts of others.

SONYA RUDIKOFF

No one is useless who has a friend, and if we are loved we are indispensable.

ROBERT LOUIS STEVENSON

 balance

We know the truth,
not only by the reason,
but also by the heart.

BLAISE PASCAL

Wellness

When the body is weak, it takes over command. When strong, it obeys.

JEAN-JACQUES ROUSSEAU

rest

There is precious little hope to be got out of whatever keeps us industrious, but there is a chance for us whenever we cease work and become stargazers.

H.M. TOMLINSON

wonder

No sight that human eyes can look upon is more provocative of awe than is the night sky scattered thick with stars. LLEWELYN POWYS

restore

A person should hear a little music, read a little poetry and see a fine picture every day in order that worldly cares may not obliterate the sense of the beautiful which God has implanted in the human soul.

JOHANN VON GOETHE

comfort

Every now
and again
take a good
look at
something
not made
with hands—
a mountain,
a star,
the turn of
a stream.
There will
come to you
wisdom and
patience and
solace and,
above all, the
assurance
that you are
not alone in
the world.

SIDNEY LOVETT

quiet

We need to find God, and he cannot be found in noise and restlessness. God is the friend of silence. See how nature—trees, flowers, grass—grows in silence; see the stars, the moon and the sun, how they move in silence…. We need silence to be able to touch souls. MOTHER TERESA

listen

There are sounds to seasons.
There are sounds to places,
and there are sounds
to **every time** in one's life.

ALISON WYRLEY BIRCH

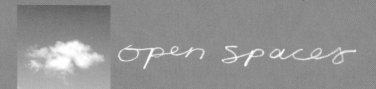

open spaces

I said in my heart, "I am sick of four walls and a ceiling. I have a need of the sky. I have business with the grass."

RICHARD HOVEY

nature

Forget not that the earth delights
to feel your bare feet and the winds
long to play with your hair.

KAHLIL GIBRAN

 *play*

Always leave enough room in your life to do something that makes you happy, satisfied, or even joyous.

PAUL HAWKEN

laughter

From there to here, from here to there, funny things are everywhere.

DR. SEUSS

appreciation

Delight in the little things.

RUDYARD KIPLING

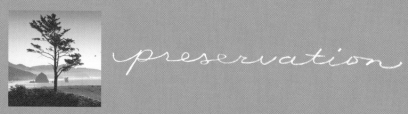

preservation

Our task
must be
to widen
our circle of
compassion,
to embrace
all living
creatures
and the
whole of
nature in
its beauty.
ALBERT EINSTEIN

peace

Ultimately, we have just one moral duty: to reclaim large areas of peace in ourselves, more and more peace, and to reflect it towards others. And the more peace there is in us, the more peace there will be in our troubled world.

ETTY HILLESUM

love

The day will come
when, after harnessing
space, the winds, the
tides and gravitation,
we shall harness for
God the energies of love.

PIERRE TEILHARD DE CHARDIN

And on that day, for the
second time in the history
of the world, we shall
have discovered fire.

beauty

Anytime we catch a glimpse of soul, beauty is there; anytime we catch our breath and feel "how beautiful!" The soul is present.

JEAN SHINODA BOLEN, M.D.

Gift/Inspiration/Self-help

ISBN 1-932319-10-7

5 1 4 9 5

5 1 4 9 5

7 49190 01951 4

9 781932 319101

* * * * *

A NATURAL HISTORY
OF
NEW YORK CITY

* * * * *

BOOKS BY JOHN KIERAN

THE STORY OF THE OLYMPIC GAMES
776 B.C. – 1936 A.D.

THE AMERICAN SPORTING SCENE

POEMS I REMEMBER
editor

FOOTNOTES ON NATURE

AN INTRODUCTION TO BIRDS

AN INTRODUCTION TO WILD FLOWERS

AN INTRODUCTION TO TREES

JOHN JAMES AUDUBON
with Margaret Kieran

AN INTRODUCTION TO NATURE

JOHN KIERAN'S TREASURY OF GREAT NATURE WRITING
editor

A NATURAL HISTORY OF NEW YORK CITY

Snow Geese above New York City

* * * * * * * * * * * *

A Natural History
of
New York City

A Personal Report after
Fifty Years of Study & Enjoyment
of Wildlife within the Boundaries
of Greater New York

BY JOHN KIERAN

Illustrated by Henry Bugbee Kane

HOUGHTON MIFFLIN COMPANY · BOSTON
THE RIVERSIDE PRESS · CAMBRIDGE

* * * * * * * * * * * *

To my wife
Margaret Ford Kieran
who helped beyond words

Foreword

CANDOR COMPELS the confession that this book was not my own idea. It was suggested by my friend Paul Brooks, Editor-in-Chief at Houghton Mifflin, for what seemed to be two good reasons, to wit:

1. Few persons suspect the variety of wildlife that persists in an area populated by millions of human beings; and

2. More than a few would enjoy this wildlife if they were told when, where, and how to find it.

On that basis I began this book that has taken five years in the writing. It is, essentially, an account of fifty years of enjoyment of the wildlife in a single great city but it might well have been written by any of a hundred other persons on the wildlife of a hundred other large cities scattered over the globe. It is limited to New York City because I was limited to New York City. I was born there, went to school there, worked there for forty years, and, of necessity, had to confine most of my outdoor explorations to brief excursions in my own neighborhood.

Even this limited area has been more than I could cover with any degree of thoroughness. There are many things in it that have escaped my eye and many others that have remained beyond my grasp. In the following pages I have touched on some of the easily observed divisions of plant and animal life that occur within the city limits, but not a single division has been plumbed to its depths. It would have been impossible to do so in a book of this kind. One limiting factor is the author's ignorance. Another is the reader's patience.

Any person interested in wildlife in any form will find the museums of his city a source of vast information as well as endless entertainment. New Yorkers are particularly fortunate in having on the premises such institutions as the American Museum of Natural History, the New York Botanical Garden, the Bronx Zoo, the Brooklyn Institute of Arts and Sciences, the Staten Island Institute of Arts and Sciences, and the resources of the many public parks spread over the five boroughs of the city. The youngsters of New York have this fertile ground to explore as a preparation for wider searches in more distant fields.

Within the boundaries of this book, then, and with the aid of real authorities in various divisions of natural history, I have done the best I could to offer a general survey of the different kinds of wildlife that are still to be found within the geographical boundaries of the City of Greater New York. Among those to whom I owe a deep debt of gratitude for expert advice and guidance in the writing of various chapters are the following:

> T. Donald Carter, Associate Curator of Mammals, American Museum of Natural History
> Dr. Ralph W. Dexter, Department of Biology, Kent State University, Kent, Ohio

Carl Kauffeld, Curator of Reptiles, Staten Island Zoo

Joseph Monachino, New York Botanical Garden, Bronx Park

John T. Nichols (deceased November 10, 1958), late Curator of Fishes, American Museum of Natural History

Dr. Frederick H. Pough, Consulting Mineralogist, New York City

Edwin Way Teale, author and naturalist

Farida A. Wiley, Honorary Associate in Natural Science Education, American Museum of Natural History.

Miss Wiley and these kindly gentlemen were most helpful in making corrections and suggesting amendments to the text of the different chapters. The final versions, however, were not subjected to the scrutiny of their expert eyes before the manuscript went to the printer, which means that they are absolved of any responsibility whatever for the ultimate result. Such errors as may appear in this book are all my own. I hope that there are not too many.

JOHN KIERAN

Contents

* * * * *

A NATURAL HISTORY
OF
NEW YORK CITY

* * * * *

Chapter 1

History

In 1524 the Italian navigator Giovanni Verrazano and his crew in the caravel *Dauphine*, cruising along the North American coast, turned into the outer reaches of New York Harbor, the section called the Lower Bay. With the craft at anchor, the captain put off in a small boat with a few men who rowed him northward between what he referred to as "two prominent hills"—now The Narrows—into the Upper Bay, which he described as "the mouth of a very great river." Then Verrazano and his men returned to their ship and sailed away. So far as is known, they were the first Europeans to visit this particular region. The native inhabitants were Indians of Algonquin stock who lived largely by hunting and fishing, adding to their tables the edible wild fruits and roots and some few cultivated crops, chief of which was Indian maize or corn. In 1525 one Esteban Gómez, a Portuguese explorer, appears to have poked around the bay and perhaps there were other unrecorded intruders in the decades that followed. There exists a map of New York Bay printed by Johan Cossin in Dieppe, France, in 1570.

All this, however, is mere chronology. No one of these men had anything to do with the founding of the city, nor did the visits of sixteenth-century explorers have any effect on the plant or animal life of the region. The history of New York City began with the arrival of Henry Hudson and his crew in *De Halve Maen* (or *The Half Moon*) on September 2, 1609. Hudson had been sent out by the Dutch East India Company to look for the legendary "Northwest Passage" to China and India and was far to the south of where he should have been, under his sailing orders, when he came up the New Jersey coast and turned at Sandy Hook to anchor in the Lower Bay that September day of long ago. He liked what he saw from his anchorage and he decided to explore the region. He sailed his ship up Verrazano's "very great river" as far as the point where Albany now stands. He even reached the future site of Troy in a small boat. Then he returned to his ship, sailed down the river, cleared the harbor on October 4, and was homeward-bound to report to his owners that he had discovered a fine harbor, a wide river, and a pleasant region offering prospects of a good fur trade with the natives.

The home port of *De Halve Maen* was Amsterdam. The ship reached it safely and so did the captain's report. But not the captain. On the voyage home the ship touched at Dartmouth, England, and there Hudson, as an English navigator, was restrained by the port authorities from going any farther in a Dutch vessel. A year later he sailed an English ship into what is now Hudson Bay, spent the winter locked in the ice with ship and crew, and in June, 1611, was set adrift in a small boat with eight others by mutineers who seized the ship and sailed off with it in open waters. Hudson and his companions never were seen alive again, nor was any trace of them ever found. Thus perished in the Arctic wasteland a man whose name truly is "writ in water," imperishably so in Hudson Bay, on the desolate shore of which he found an unmarked grave, and in the Hudson River, whose lordly flow carries the shipping of the greatest port in the world to the open sea.

The Dutch East India Company did nothing official about Hudson's report for nearly five years, but in the interim some independent adventurers who heard the news sailed into New York Bay to try their fortunes. One of the early invaders was Adriaen Block, a trader who sailed his "yacht" — a Dutch term — up the East River and was surprised to find it widen into Long Island Sound. It was Block who gave the name of "Hell Gatt" to the narrow passage in the East River where the meeting of the tides causes the turbulence for which it is noted. There were other independent traders in the area but they left no traces on the pages of history. The Dutch East India Company sent out an expedition in 1614 and established a trading post called Fort Orange at what is now Albany, preferring that to a site at the mouth of the river. The actual founding of what became New York City occurred in 1615 when the New Netherland Company, a subsidiary of the Dutch East India Company chartered to make four voyages within a three-year limit, built a storehouse on the lower tip of Manhattan Island. Around this storehouse the huts of traders sprang up. This was the inconspicuous beginning of the city and for some years there was no change in the scene. There was just the storehouse and the rude huts of a few hardy men who bartered with the Indians for furs.

In June, 1623, the home government set up the whole area as a province of the Dutch West India Company, and in 1624 the company made a determined effort to colonize the region by sending out thirty Walloon workers, of whom eight settled on Manhattan Island and the remainder continued up the river to Fort Orange. In 1625 the company received from its new province 5295 beaver skins and 463 pelts of other fur-bearing animals to the total value of 35,825 guilders, a guilder

being worth about 40 cents.   The following year the company
sent out more colonists and a Director-General who negotiated
the most famous real estate deal in history.   The Director-
General was Peter Minuit and he bought the whole of Manhattan Island from the Indians for an assortment of beads,
trinkets, and bolts of cloth worth 60 guilders, or 24 dollars.
The assessed value of the taxable real estate on Manhattan
Island in 1958 was $8,072,910,419.

Having thus satisfied the Indians and taken quasi-legal title
to the island, Minuit named the little settlement Fort Amsterdam and made it the seat of government of the province, meaning all the territory claimed by the Dutch in that part of North
America.   By 1628 the fur trade had been increased to a total
of 6951 beaver skins and 734 pelts of other animals to the value
of 61,075 guilders; and in that same year the Reverend Jonas
Michaelius, the first minister of the gospel to preach on Manhattan Island, wrote to a friend in the Netherlands: "The
country produces many species of good things which greatly
serve to ease life; fish, birds, game and groves, oysters, tree
fruits, fruits of the earth, medicinal herbs and others of all kinds."

Now the settlement had taken root and was beginning to flourish.   The fur trade at Fort Amsterdam steadily increased and
the surrounding countryside was yielding to cultivation.   A
map drawn by an unknown hand in 1639 shows "plantages"
and "bowerij" spread out over what is now Manhattan, the
Bronx, Brooklyn, Staten Island, and part of New Jersey, and the
names of the owners of the cultivated strips — the "plantages"
and "bowerij" — are marked in script at each location.   At
this point the human history of the colony was beginning to
have an effect on the natural history of the region.   Some of
the settlers had brought with them from the Netherlands such
domestic animals as horses, cows, sheep, swine, ducks, geese,
pigeons, poultry, and household pets of various kinds.   They
also brought shrubs, roots, slips, seedlings, and seeds from the
old country to plant in their fields and gardens in the New

World. It has been estimated that 40 per cent of the plant life in New York City and vicinity is of European origin. Along with the plant and animal life from the Old World there came, to be sure, a considerable number of unwanted or un-noticed European insects and many more were to follow in later years. As the human population of Manhattan Island increased, the wild-animal population — at least of the larger species — began to dwindle. With every settler owning a rifle and with no game laws in existence, most of the resident deer and bear of the region either moved out or were soon killed off.

That was a purely local change: the surrounding territory was as wild as ever it had been. Under date of May 23, 1654, one Nicasius de Sille, writing to Maximiliaen van Beeckerke at The Hague of conditions at New Amsterdam, stated that

> the rivers are full of good edible fish which is very cheap; three large sea crabs for a stuiver; also fried venison fat as mut-ton. Oysters we pick up before our fort . . . some so large they must be cut in two or three pieces. The weeds consist mostly of strawberries, catnip and blackberries . . . the Indians bring us wild geese, turkeys, partridges, wild pigeons, ducks and various birds and animals. In the way of fish we have perch, sturgeon, bass, herring, mackerel, weakfish, stone bream, eel and various other kinds of which I do not yet know the name.

In a postscript he added: "Boat held up by rumors of war with England. There are no sparrows here* but wild pigeons fly thick as sparrows in Holland this time of year and eat straw-berries and cherries in our gardens. They are shot by the thousands. They taste like partridge."

The Jacques Cortelyou plan of New Amsterdam in 1660 shows that the settlement by that time had grown into a com-pact little town that stretched across the lower tip of Manhat-tan Island from the Battery as far north as Wall Street, so named because there actually was a wooden palisade erected

---

*Evidently a reference to the absence of the European House or "English" Sparrow at the settlement.

across the island at that point to keep the inhabitants safe from any surprise attack by Indians or English or French forces to the northward. Those were the days when the great Peter Stuyvesant, stout-bodied, stouthearted and short-tempered, noted for his wooden leg with its silver band, was in his troubled glory as Director-General of the Province of New Netherland and the titular ruler of New Amsterdam. For good reasons and bad, he was in and out of hot water through most of a term of office that began on May 11, 1647, and ran on with much bickering and some real broils until 1664, when he received the shock of his belligerent life in the form of news from abroad.

The news was that, by royal decree dated March 22, 1664, Charles II of England had granted to his brother James, Duke of York, the right and title to Nantucket, Martha's Vineyard, Long Island, and all the mainland from the Connecticut River to Delaware Bay — which included, of course, the whole Province of New Netherlands claimed by the Dutch — with authority to "encounter expulse repell and resist by force of Armes as well by Sea as by land and all wayes and meanes whatsoever all such Person or Persons as without special lycence of our saide deare brother, his heires or Assignes shall attempt to inhabite within the several Precinctes, Lymitts of our said Territories and Islands."

Stout Stuyvesant and the worthy burghers of New Amsterdam were trapped. They had no sufficient store of arms or ammunition with which to defend either the town or the province when an array of armed English ships dropped anchor in the harbor in the late summer of 1664 and the commander threatened to cannonade the town unless it was surrendered. The doughty Director-General was for holding out as long as they could but less belligerent burghers begged him to give in before they were all killed and the town burned down over their dead bodies. To their pleas and the superior forces of the English, Stuyvesant yielded. On September 8, 1664, he

formally surrendered to the Right Honourable Colonel Richard
Nicolls of His Majesty's forces. Colonel Nicolls and his troops
took possession not only of the town but the whole Province of
New Netherlands in the name of James, Duke of York. And
New Amsterdam became New York without a struggle.

There were at that time about a thousand inhabitants of
Manhattan Island. Only the lower end, from the Battery to
Wall Street, had docks and wharves and straight or curving
streets with rows of shops or houses along them. Beyond Wall
Street were the "plantages" and "bowerij" of the 1639 map
that were linked by country lanes. Except for scattered farm-
houses and patches of tilled ground, most of the island still
remained almost as it had been when the Indians alone roamed
the area. The Nicolls map, completed in 1668, shows many
brooks and streams that ran from high ground on the island
into the East, Harlem and Hudson Rivers. The Saw Kill, for
instance, ran from what is now Park Avenue into the East
River at about 75th Street. Montagne's Brook ran from what
is now 120th Street and Eighth Avenue in a zigzag course to
empty into the East River at about 107th Street. It even had
an island in it between Lexington and Third Avenue and
bridges over both branches of the creek for north and south
travel. Minetta — or Manetta — Brook wandered through the
Greenwich Village area and, though it long ago disappeared
from the face of the earth, a householder of the region com-
plained only recently that it was coming up again through his
cellar.

In 1670 there was published *A Brief Description of New York,
with the Places Thereunto Adjoyning, called The New Netherlands,*
the author being Daniel Denton, who in 1644 left Stamford,
Connecticut, to settle in what is now the Jamaica section of
the city on Long Island. Of his surroundings he wrote:

> For wilde Beasts there is Deer, Bear, Wolves, Foxes, Raccoons,
> Otters, Musquashes and Skunks. Wild Fowl there is great store

Harbor Seals and cormorants

of, as Turkies, Heath-hens, Quails, Partridges, Pidgeons, Cranes, Geese of several sorts, Brants, Ducks, Widgeon, Teal and divers others. There is also the Red Bird and many sorts of singing birds . . . On the South-side of Long Island in the Winter lie store of Whales and Crampasses. Also an innumerable multitude of Seals, which make an excellent oyle.

Of the trees, shrubs and flowers he found in the area he mentioned, among many others, the following:

Oaks White and Red. Walnut-trees, Chestnut-trees, which yield a store of mast for swine . . . and also Maples, Cedars, Saxifrage,* Beech, Birch, Holly, Hazel with many sorts more . . . Purslaine, White Orage, Egrimony, Violets, Penniroyal, Alicampane, besides Saxaparilla very common . . . Mulberries, Posimons, Grapes great and small, Huckelberries, Cramberries, Plums of several sorts, Rasberries and Strawberries, of which last is such abundance in June that the Fields and Woods are died red.

The quaint spelling is easy to swallow but those teeming strawberries so numerous that the fields and woods were "died red" have to be taken not with the customary sugar and cream but just a grain of salt. However, Daniel Denton was merely speaking well of his home territory, which is an amiable weakness at the worst. Travelers also spoke well of New York and vicinity in those early days and some of them put it in writing.

*He meant Sassafrass.

Among such travelers were two Labadist preachers, Jasper Danckaerts and Peter Sluyter, who wandered about the area in 1679 and 1680 and published an account of their travels under the title *Journal of a Voyage to New York, and a Tour of Several of the American Colonies.* Of Staten Island they wrote that it was hilly and the middle part uninhabited but the lower sections near water were fine places because of "salt meadows" and the ease with which fish were caught and oysters were gathered. They reported about one hundred families on the island, mostly Dutch and French Walloons, with a few English. They mentioned that they had inspected "Oude Dorp" and "Nieuwe Dorp" and had seen "fine creeks well provided with wild turkeys, geese, snipe and wood-hens." Somewhere along the shore they saw the rotting remains of thousands of fish set down as "marsbancken," now called "Mossbunkers" or Menhaden and still occasionally drifting ashore in great numbers to provide a malodorous removal problem for the city authorities.

Of how a person leaving Manhattan Island could go dry-shod to the Bronx, the travelers wrote of the Harlem River: "They can go over this creek at dead low water, upon rocks and reefs, at a place called Spyt den duyvil." The reference, of course, is to the Spuyten Duyvil of today, which brings up the point that in the literature and on the maps of the colonial period we find strange spellings for names with which modern New Yorkers are familiar in a different guise. The Danckaerts and Sluyter journal, for instance, contains references to such localities as "Breukelen," "Guoanes Bay," "Correlaers hoock," and "Nieuwe Haarlem," all easy enough to locate on a modern map, but they might leave a reader at sea with regard to the offshore island they touched at on their voyage home — "Maertens Wingaert." We know it now as Martha's Vineyard.

In 1748 a noted naturalist visited New York. That was Peter Kalm, Swedish scientist and Professor of Oeconomy at the University of Abo in Swedish Finland. He was the first European naturalist to collect and study the fauna and flora of North America. Kalm had intended to visit Siberia on a collecting expedition but the great Linnaeus, who was eager to include the plants and animals of the New World in the enormous catalogue of species on which he was then working, persuaded his pupil and friend to change direction and head for North America. That was how Peter Kalm came to be in New York in the autumn of 1748 and to write:

I found it exceedingly pleasant to walk in the town, for it seemed quite like a garden; the trees which are planted for this purpose are chiefly of two kinds, the Water Beech or Linnaeus's Platanus occidentalis are the most numerous . . . the Locust Tree or Linnaeus's Robinia pseudacacia . . . there is likewise lime trees and elms but they are not by far so frequent. Tree frogs, Dr. Linnaeus's Rana arborea, are so loud it is difficult for a man to make himself heard. Homes shingled with White Fir Tree (Pinus strobus) are as good as Pennsylvania roofs of White Cedar (Cupressus thyoides).

Of course, Kalm wrote in Swedish and the excerpt here is from the translation by John Reinhold Forster that was published in three volumes in London in 1770 and 1771 under the title *Travels in North America*. Perhaps Kalm's writings lost something — or gained something — in the translation. In any case, Benjamin Franklin, being in London on business for the colonies a bit later, came upon Kalm's work in translation and penned the following comment in a letter of March 5, 1773, to David Golden of New York:

Kalm's account of what he learned in America is so full of idle stories which he picked up among ignorant people, and either forgetting whom he had them of, or willing to give them Authenticity, he has ascribed them to persons of Reputation who never heard of them until they were found in this book. And where he really had accounts from such persons, he has varied the Circumstances unaccountably so that I have been ashamed with some mention'd as from me. It is dangerous conversing with strangers who keep journals . . .

This seems a little severe, considering that Kalm, though he may have been a gullible traveler, was a good naturalist and did noble work as a pioneer in North America. He gathered a notable collection of material that was duly delivered to Linnaeus to classify and name. As a partial reward for the zeal Kalm displayed and the hardships he endured on the trip, Linnaeus named a genus of North American plants for him, calling it *Kalmia*, and in this group we find one of the most beautiful of our native flowering shrubs, the Mountain Laurel, the *Kalmia latifolia* of the botanist.

The letter of complaint that Franklin wrote concerning Kalm was mild in tone compared to the famous letter he wrote three years later from Philadelphia to a printer named Strahan in London who was also a member of Parliament, a missive dated July 5, 1775, and ending:

You and I were long friends; — You are now my enemy, — and I am

Yours,

B. FRANKLIN

In short, the American Revolution was afoot. At that time the population of New York was approximately 20,000 but at the end of the war — due to two bad fires during the British occupation and the departure of thousands of Tories with the British troops — it was down to little more than half that number. The inhabitants were still crowded at the lower tip of Manhattan Island. What is now Canal Street was a suburban region. Greenwich Village was out in the country beyond. To Harlem and back was a day's ride by coach or on horseback. But with the coming of peace the town grew rapidly because of its favorable location for trade by land and sea. By 1790 the population was up to 33,000 and by 1800 it was a little over 60,000. Immigrants from Europe arrived in increasing numbers each year. The opening of the Erie Canal on November 4, 1825, and the beginning of railroad transportation a decade later further stimulated the growth of the city. By 1840 New York had a population of 300,000 and terrific growing pains, the worst of which was not eased until August 8, 1842, when good clear Croton water began to flow through the pipes of the city's new water supply system.

A great day, indeed! From 1790 until 1842 the story of the water-supply problem and the consequent public health problem was a tale of terror. There was lack of water for drinking, for cooking, for bathing, and for washing clothes. There were chickens in every backyard and pigs roaming most of the streets. Sewage-disposal and garbage-disposal methods were crude in the aristocratic districts and nonexistent in the poorer neighborhoods. Fires spread unchecked among wooden structures for lack of water. There were recurring epidemics of yellow fever, typhoid, cholera, and other diseases. In some of these epidemics hundreds died daily. The arrival of Croton water saved the day — and the years ahead — for New York City.

Now the population could increase without discomfort and the city expand with safety. In 1860 the inhabitants of Manhattan Island numbered more than 800,000 and in 1874 the territorial limits of the city were extended beyond the Harlem River to take in part of what is now the Bronx but was then a segment of Westchester County. In 1895 another chunk of Westchester was annexed to stretch the city limit to its northern line of today along the Yonkers–Mount Vernon border. In 1898 Brooklyn, Staten Island, and the great bulk of Queens County were enfolded to create the metropolis chartered as The City of Greater New York, though nobody ever calls it that and few of the 7,795,471 (census of April, 1957) residents of the city today know that such is the official name of their home town.

What enables New York City to function as a great industrial center is its subway system. What enables its inhabitants to live in comfort, decency, and good health is its water-supply system; capable of delivering more than 1,200,000,000 gallons of clean and potable fresh water every day within the city limits. The vast network of aqueducts that drains hundreds of miles of distant watershed areas was planned and carried out in the interest of public health, domestic convenience, industrial use, and municipal cleanliness, but the program produced a by-product deeply appreciated by local amateur naturalists. As part of the city water-supply system, there are reservoirs in every borough. These reservoirs serve as feeding areas and refuges for ducks, gulls, and other waterfowl, and more than a few rarities have been sighted on such waters.

This matter is close to my heart because it was through the fact that the rear attic window of our house overlooked the waters of the Jerome Reservoir in the Bronx that I became acquainted with two noted ornithologists and was admitted to membership in the Linnaean Society of New York. It was during the winter of 1913–1914, at which time I had developed a lively interest in birds, that I began to take notice of ducks congregating on the reservoir. I saw them first from the rear window of the attic room in which I slept. I immediately armed myself with field glasses and went out to inspect the ducks at closer range by peering at them through the iron picket fence surrounding the reservoir. I remember that the first bird I brought in focus turned out to be a White-winged Scoter and, looking back, I recall seeing Canvasback, Redheads, Goldeneyes, Common Mergansers, and, in all, fourteen different species of waterfowl on the reservoir that winter.

Standing in front of a cageful of North American warblers in the Bird House at the Bronx Zoo one cold day, I met three elderly men who, from their talk, evidently were much interested in birds. I told them about the ducks on the reservoir and they were so much stirred by the news that we left the zoo together and plodded westward through the snow to the reservoir, where the ducks were duly seen as advertised. One of these men was a proofreader for the New York *Daily Mail*, a newspaper long since defunct, and under the pseudonym of "The Pelham Observer" he contributed occasional nature notes to a column on the editorial page of the paper. In telling of the ducks on the reservoir, he mentioned me by name as his guide on the expedition. It was the first time that my name ever appeared in print and I was naturally impressed by it.

Incited by the public notice in the newspaper, two men from the American Museum of Natural History appeared on the scene the following Saturday afternoon and found me watching the ducks as usual. The men were Ludlow Griscom and Charles H. Rogers, who were then growing up as ornithologists under the great Frank M. Chapman at the museum. After they had checked on the ducks, they set off to prowl the Van Cortlandt Park region and I was invited to go with them, a privilege I properly appreciated. They made repeated visits to the reservoir during the winter and each time I seized the opportunity to tag along on their further travels and glean something from their store of knowledge of ornithology. Impressed by my enthusiasm and my faithfulness in keeping good watch on the reservoir ducks, Dr. Rogers suggested that I attend the meetings of the Linnaean Society of New York, a scientific group that met on alternate Tuesdays at 8 P.M. in one of the smaller rooms in the old building of the American Museum of Natural History. I attended as a guest for some months and then, nominated by Charles Rogers and seconded by Ludlow Griscom, I was elected a member of the society late in 1914 and have been a member ever since.

I was naturally awed by the noted professional ornithologists and the keen amateurs among whom I found myself in these gatherings of long ago. The regular attendants at the meetings included that wonderful old gentleman Dr. Jonathan Dwight, the ultimate authority on gull plumages, Waldron DeWitt Miller, who never let a bird visit New Jersey without making note of it, Charles Urner, poet, printer, philosopher, expert on owls, and a most delightful companion indoors or out, genial Walter Granger, who had been to the Gobi Desert, and John Treadwell Nichols, Lincolnesque in stature and appearance and equally Lincolnesque in wisdom and kindliness, an ichthyologist by profession but a keen birder on the side and perhaps the best man in the field on the shore birds of North America. Of course, Charles Rogers, who was to rise to eminence as an ornithologist at Princeton, and Ludlow Griscom, who was to become Curator of Ornithology at the Agassiz Museum at Harvard, were faithful in attendance and now and then we had such wanderers as Roy Chapman Andrews, back from Mongolia, William Beebe, up from the ocean depths, Robert Cushman Murphy, returned from Peru, or James P. Chapin on furlough from the Belgian Congo. Being in the room with such men was inspiring; listening to them was an

education. *Ter quaterque beati* were they in my eyes — and
in my heart.   I owe them much and here publicly acknowledge
a debt far greater than I ever can pay.

The joining of the five boroughs to form the City of Greater
New York and the extraordinary rise in population in the last
half-century changed the appearance of the area completely.
Where there had been lawns, hedges, gardens, meadows,
groves, and even farmlands, there were now paved streets and
solid blocks of apartment houses.   One would think that such
an incursion of humanity and its steel, concrete, and asphalt
appurtenances would almost completely erase the wildlife of
the invaded territory and, to a certain extent, this has happened.   Where an orchard has disappeared to make way for a
huge factory, we no longer can find the wildlife that once
flourished there — the orchard community of plant and animal
life, the birds, mammals, insects, trees shrubs, flowers, and
grasses.   But the curious thing is that the destruction or elimination of plant and animal life in the area through the blanket-

Meadow Mouse

ing of the ground by buildings and pavements is largely a matter of quantity and not of kind. Let us say that four-fifths of what was once open ground or open water in the area is now covered with steel or concrete or some such substance generally incompatible with animal or plant life; the fact is that the remaining one-fifth of the open ground or open water will contain practically all the kinds of plant and animal life that once filled the whole area, but by no means the same quantity. In short, if you cover with buildings or pavement 999 former meadows and leave one meadow untouched, the chances are that you will find all the different kinds of meadow life of the region in the one tract left untouched. The larger mammals may be driven off, but the Meadow Mice will remain. On the outskirts of the city there are still areas of greenery that offer hospitality to birds, insects, and small mammals. There are more than 28,000 acres of public park land within the city limit. New York's rivers and bays and ocean front are the seasonal haunt or permanent home of many different forms of wildlife. Let the population of the area increase and multiply as it may, let men build and pave to their heart's content, there will always be many kinds and untold numbers of wild things in the great city.

Chapter 2

Geology

In the Book of Job we find the Voice out of the whirlwind inquiring:

> Whereupon are the foundations thereof fashioned? Or who laid the cornerstone thereof?

A query beautifully put, and a quotation pat to our purpose in this chapter, which is to look into the matter of the foundation upon which New York has reared itself to unsurpassed heights. It is a cold, hard and somewhat reassuring fact that the tall towers of Manhattan, the skyscrapers that give the city its famous skyline, are built upon and anchored to bedrock of sturdy character and truly ancient lineage. The geologists tell us that this city by the sea is perched upon a sunken, eroded and glaciated mountain ridge of long ago. Three uptilted strata of metamorphic rock, with some later igneous intrusions, provide a firm foundation for the heaviest kind of structure in most sections of the city.

The older geologists had it that the three uptilted strata form-ing the backbone of the region were Pre-Cambrian, meaning that these rock formations were "of the order of" possibly 1,000,000,000 years old, which is about as far back as we can go on this planet and still be on fairly solid ground. But fur-ther studies by members of the staff of the Department of Geol-ogy at Columbia University — right on the premises, so to speak — have led to the conclusion that one of the strata, and the most important one because it's the Manhattan Schist that upholds the architectural eminence of the city as well as Col-umbia University itself, is of mere Paleozoic origin, possibly Ordovician by birth and therefor of the tender age of 380,000,000 years or so. The two strata whose Pre-Cambrian origin still remains unchallenged are the Fordham Gneiss (pronounced *nice*) and the Inwood Dolomite (or Kingsbridge Limestone, as some call it).

The fundamental rock formation of the area is the much contorted Fordham Gneiss that comes down through Con-necticut and Westchester County to be the backbone of the high ground in the Bronx. This includes the Riverdale–Spuyten Duyvil ridge on the west, the region best described by such local names as Fordham Heights, University Heights, Morris Heights, and High Bridge in the middle, and the Grand Concourse ridge that runs almost the length of the borough. The gneiss dips under the Harlem River waters and reappears only as a few rocky islets in the East River and in one spot — where the Court House stands — in Long Island City. How-ever, it remains the underlying layer of the whole city area, as you will find if you dig deep enough.

The next layer above the Fordham Gneiss, though it appears beside it because of the uptilt of the strata, is the Inwood Dolo-mite of limited area and little importance in city affairs. It occurs as a layer from 150 to 500 feet thick in the bed of the Harlem River and adjacent low regions at the northern end of Manhattan Island. Its only noteworthy emergence on a higher

A balancing rock

level is as a ridge climbing gently northward from Dyckman Street west of Broadway to reach a modest apex in the section known as Marble Hill on the north side of the Harlem River Ship Canal. The exposed sides of the cut made for the ship canal give subway riders and railroad commuters of that region a chance to view a cross section of the limestone ridge.

Now we come to the third layer, which is the younger but more important Manhattan Schist that runs the full length of Manhattan Island from the Henry Hudson Bridge at Spuyten Duyvil all the way to the Battery. It also extends under the flat sections of the East Bronx and crops out here and there as islands in the East River, but these are minor matters compared to its function as the firm foundation for skyscrapers that have made the city famous around the world. It occurs as a long narrow ridge of rock with a jagged profile that is highest at the northern end of the island. The general trend from there to the Battery is a downward slope but there are sharp variations in elevation along the way.

The layer starts at a fair height in Isham Park at the northern tip of Manhattan Island but, less than a mile to the southward, there is a cross-break in it represented by the Dyckman Street gap. On the south side of that gap loom the twin bluffs of Fort George and Fort Washington, the highest points on the island. These are the tips of two spurs jutting northward from common high ground at 181st Street. Between them is a brief valley of Inwood Dolomite whose less durable substance accounts for the hollow between the great spurs of schist. Broadway takes advantage of the gentle slope to meander down that valley toward Dyckman Street.

The ridge is still high at 168th Street where Medical Center stands on solid rock. Autoists on the West Side Highway see the exposed western face of this formation as a sheer cliff overhanging the motor parkway from the George Washington Bridge to the Dyckman Street gap. On the east the exposed face goes by the name of Coogan's Bluff, where it looms above the Harlem River and looks down on two enclosures famous in the sports annals of the city, the Polo Grounds just below it and the Yankee Stadium across the river. The bluff takes its name from "Old Man Coogan," a colorful character who owned much of the area a century ago and twice ran for mayor of New York City, once as a Labor candidate and once as an independent. His wife, who survived him many years, turned out to be a character in her own right. By the terms of her husband's last will and testament she gained ownership of the land on which the Polo Grounds stadium had been erected and thus the famous "Giants" of baseball history, who disported themselves on the diamond there from 1891 until they moved to San Francisco in 1958, were her tenants. On the first day of the month for many years the little old lady appeared at the downtown offices of the Giants on West 42nd Street to receive in her own hand the check for the rent of the Polo Grounds real estate. When she finally grew too feeble to walk to the baseball office, she sent a messenger for the check. To the day of her death she didn't trust the mails.

The rock formation remains high as far south as the campus of the City College on St. Nicholas Heights and then slopes to the 125th Street gap before rising again to Morningside Heights, where the student allegiance is to Columbia University. From there the trend of the ridge is slowly downhill with a broad leveling off through midtown Manhattan. This runs southward with little change as far as the north side of Washington Square, where it suddenly plunges hundreds of feet and doesn't come close to the surface of the ground again until Chambers Street in the downtown area is reached. This great gap in Manhattan's rock profile is filled with glacial till for the most part.

Incidentally, this rock dip explains why the skyscrapers of Manhattan appear in two groups, the "downtown" and the "midtown" groups. In between, the rock is so far below the surface that it is, for all practical purposes, unavailable under current construction methods as a foundation for a modern skyscraper. This is also the explanation of the famous Canal Street that bisects the area. All through the colonial period this was a region of tidal flats, marshes, and river inlets. There were times when the tides ran so high that the waters of the Hudson and the East River reached through these marshes to meet and mingle and make two islands out of Manhattan instead of one. It was to remedy this nuisance that a canal across the island was opened in 1809 with tree-lined roadways on each side and numerous bridges for north and south traffic. However, the canal became Canal Street a few years later when the waterway was bricked over and its function changed to that of a sewer.

From a depth of 100 feet at Chambers Street the rock profile rises slowly toward the south to offer a convenient solid foundation for the towering structures of the financial district.

At City Hall the rock is 90 feet below ground level. At "Broad and Wall" it is about 50 feet down. At Trinity Church it is 36 feet from the curb level to the rock below. But the builders of the Hudson Terminal, just a few hundred yards away, had to reach down from 85 to 110 feet for bedrock footing. At the Battery the Manhattan Schist dips under the waters of the bay and does not appear within striking distance of the surface again, though it holds its place as an underlying stratum of the islands in the bay as well as the Boroughs of Queens, Brooklyn, and Richmond. The hills of Staten Island are carried on the back of a core of Serpentine, an intrusive metamorphic formation of a later date.

The Fordham Gneiss, Inwood Dolomite, and Manhattan Schist, topped off with the Serpentine ridge of Staten Island, are the most important rock formations within the city limits, but there are others that are the result of intrusion and erosion down the ages. Together they form what the geologists tell us is "a sunken, eroded, and glaciated mountain ridge" of ancient time that now impassively carries New York and all its hurly-burly on its shoulders. We accept the verdict of the geologists on the rock profile of New York City as a sunken and eroded mountain ridge of long ago, but the glaciation we can see for ourselves. The evidence is all over the place and easy to come upon in any of the five boroughs. Great masses of exposed rock made smooth by glacial action can be seen in many city parks. On these smooth surfaces you may trace scratches made by boulders that were pushed or dragged along by the advancing ice. Great boulders are found isolated in odd places where they sank to the ground as the ice melted under them in the retreat to the northward some 12,000 years ago. Most of the soil covering the rocky foundation of the city is of glacial distribution. It was pushed, carried, scraped, swept, or dropped into place by the glacial advance and subsequent retreat. It is called glacial till, or drift, and is composed of clay, sand, gravel, mud, and assorted debris.

Glacial scratches in Central Park

The line at which the last glacier halted in the New York area is plainly marked by a "terminal moraine." A glacier is a great slow-moving river of ice carrying an immense amount of surface scouring with it. Where the glacier halts, the melting edge becomes an unloading platform, and boulders, stones, and gravel are heaped in a long line that remains as a marker showing where the advance stopped and the retreat began. To be specific, it was not a glacier that "glaciated" the New York area but an "ice sheet." The difference is largely one of size. A glacier may fill a valley or more than one valley. An ice sheet will cover a continent or a great section of it. How many times ice sheets came below the Canadian border in North America is a matter of debate, but there is general agreement among scientists that within the past 1,500,000 years, called the Pleistocene Period, the ice advance from the north has reached down into the United States at least four times and that the last of such crushing invasions was by what is now known as the Wisconsin Ice Sheet.

The southward march began about 100,000 years ago and probably reached its peak some 50,000 years ago, at which time it is estimated that Manhattan and the Bronx were covered with a blanket of ice 1000 feet thick. The forward edge of this vast ice sheet pushed to the center of Long Island and curved gently southwestward toward Philadelphia. The ice covered about half of Brooklyn and Queens and practically all of Staten Island. The terminal moraine that marks the ice limit within the city limits runs from the Queens Village section through Prospect Park, across the Narrows, and down the south side of Staten Island to the water's edge just below Great Kills. Such sections as Flatbush, Garden City, and Hempstead are outwash plains formed by material carried there by the water from the melting face of the ice sheet.

The terminal moraine runs roughly northeast — southwest. This fact and the direction of the glacial scratches on exposed rock surfaces in Manhattan and the Bronx show that the ice mass was moving southeast as it crossed those boroughs. Another bit of evidence is that, coming across the Hudson River, the ice sheet carried bits of the Palisades with it into the Bronx. Incidentally, the Palisades, which are at least a scenic if not a legal part of New York, are of much later origin than the rocky foundation of the city. What we see when we look across the Hudson at the Palisades is the exposed edge of a thick intrusive sheet of igneous rock of diabase type. The spectacular rampart extends more than twenty-five miles along the west bank of the Hudson and reaches a maximum height of 540 feet.

One last note on the effect of the most recent glaciation of the area. Before the arrival of the Wisconsin Ice Sheet the Bronx River emptied into the Hudson, but, on the retreat of the ice, glacial till blocked up the old channel and the Bronx River, whose ordinary flow was much increased by water pouring from the melting face of the retreating ice sheet, had to dig itself a new channel in its rush toward salt water. It now empties into Long Island Sound, and if you visit the New York Botanical Garden in the Bronx you will see a beautiful little gorge it cut on its way there.

With rocks so close to the surface over most of the city area, it isn't strange that the borings for subway and aqueduct tunnels, for skyscraper foundations, for bridge piers and other structural purposes turned up a sparkling array of interesting minerals. Lest there be any confusion, it might be explained that — roughly speaking — rocks are minerals en masse, and usually a mixture of minerals, though this is not always the case. Sedimentary rocks like sandstone, limestone, and shale are mostly masses of one mineral, but the igneous and metamorphic rocks are often mixtures of several minerals and the rocks of the New York region are largely of this kind.

So it is that more than a hundred different kinds of minerals have been found in the rock formations of the city and the intrusive veins therein. Many beautiful specimens may be seen under glass in special cases in the Hall of Gems at the American

Museum of Natural History on Central Park West. Most of the glittering crystals on display in the three cases containing the New York City collection were gathered on Manhattan Island alone, but this is mainly because the borings and excavations in that section of the city were earlier and still are more extensive than those in any of the other boroughs. Most of the minerals on exhibition were found in the intrusive veins of the basic rock formations of the city and some of them are what are commonly known as semiprecious stones in the jewelry trade.

During the excavating for the Broadway subway at 65th Street, for instance, the workmen blasted out a vein of Microcline — one of the feldspar group — so studded with darker garnets that they look like raisins in a raisin cake. One of the Battery-to-Brooklyn tunnels uncovered an Almandine garnet as large as an egg. Seven dainty little Aquamarines were rescued from the subway excavation at 157th Street and Broadway and, just a block to the north in the same cut, two Golden Beryls were gathered for the museum collection. From a rock cut made at 122nd Street and Park Avenue the museum display was enriched by a big chunk of lovely Rose Quartz and a fine set of Smoky Quartz crystals came from shearing the face of the Fordham Gneiss in the construction of the Harlem River

Ship Canal at Spuyten Duyvil. A handsome Brown Tourmaline was found in the Inwood Dolomite at 218th Street near Broadway and a striking Black Tourmaline was picked from a surface exposed by blasting the railroad tunnel through the Manhattan Schist at 96th Street and Park Avenue.

These are just a few of the colorful minerals on display in the cases devoted to the New York City region in the Hall of Gems at the American Museum of Natural History. Go there and you will see many others of local origin. Walking through the halls of the museum recently, I encountered Dr. Frederick H. Pough, author of *A Field Guide to Rocks and Minerals* and former Curator of Minerals at the museum. When I mentioned that I had been looking at the minerals found within the city limits, he reached into his pocket and pulled out two fine little Amethysts chipped that very morning from rock blasted out of a cellar excavation for a new house near his own home in the Riverdale section of the city. In short, the hunt is still on and you may join it if you wish.

A considerable amount of the excavated native rock was used for building purposes in the swift growth of the city during the nineteenth century but this ceased almost completely when reinforced concrete, hollow tile, aluminum, and large areas of glass became the style in modern construction. But local sand and gravel pits furnished some of the "aggregate" that went into the concrete. William T. Davis, in his delightful *Days Afield on Staten Island*, tells of the men who came in schooners, presumably from Manhattan, to get sand from South Beach: "Great brawny fellows are many of these, that absorb nearly as much fresh oxygen and sunlight through their skins as a Hottentot, for they wear in summer hardly more clothes than the African. A flannel shirt and drawers, that are often sievelike in character, complete their apparel and, barefooted and bareheaded, they wheel the sand aboard the schooners, and for each voyage they receive five dollars."

Traprock of good quality in the form of a vein of Dolerite

forced up through the central Serpentine formation of Staten Island was another local product of commercial value and L. P. Gratacap, in his *Geology of the City of New York*, wrote of the beds of Limonite — the metal content of which is iron — found at Little Clove and Ocean Terrace on Staten Island: "The ore beds (a surface mine) in the Borough of Richmond have yielded something like 300,000 tons partly for blast furnaces and partly to reduce red ochre paint."

Good clay for the making of bricks was found on Staten Island and in other boroughs of the city. One of my childhood memories is of a brickyard along the "back road" above Kingsbridge between Bailey Avenue and the Putnam Railroad tracks near 235th Street. I remember the baked bricks in long narrow stacks about three feet high over which ran ridged "hutches" to keep off the rain. But what particularly attracted me at that early age was the plodding horse that walked in a circle and pulled along the outer end of a radial beam that turned the grinding machinery of the old-fashioned "pugmill" in the center. That must have been about 1896 or 1897. How such an antiquated method of making brick survived to that late date I do not know, nor do I recall the name of the owner or operator. But I well remember the owner and operator of an equally old-fashioned sawmill that stood just to the north and outlived the brickyard by some years. He was a Captain Hebble, a bearded Civil War veteran and a kindly old gentleman who was most obliging to small boys in the matter of sawing to size the wooden parts needed for the making of bobsleds.

The topic of minerals in New York City must include at least some mention of a very valuable and — luckily for all living things — abundant mineral, to wit: water. Ordinarily we do not think of water as a mineral. We look on it as a liquid, as distinguished from a solid or a gas. But that's merely a matter of form, and, if we give it a moment's thought, we realize that water is common in solid form as ice and in gaseous form as steam. Temperature determines the form in which it is found.

If we think of all matter as animal, vegetable, or mineral, it's clear that water must be among the minerals in that grouping.

Salt water, of course, has not been a problem in New York City "since time when the memory of man runneth not to the contrary." Nor was fresh water a problem to the native Indians of five centuries ago or the colonists of the Dutch and early English periods. There were cool springs, good brooks, and many clear streams on Manhattan Island. Fresh-water ponds were common enough, the largest one being the famous Collect Pond, whose south side ran close to what is now Worth Street in the "downtown" section. Those colonists who lived in the Bronx, on Staten Island, or on nearby Long Island were equally well supplied with good water. When they were needed, wells were dug without much difficulty at central points.

But by 1725 the colony at the lower end of Manhattan Island was outgrowing its local supply of good fresh water and was starting to pollute what supply it had. In 1748, at which time the population had grown to about 10,000 persons, Peter Kalm reported the well water in such bad odor that even the horses objected to drinking it. Collect Pond, once a fine pond and a favorite fishing resort, was denounced by the city fathers of 1796 as a "stagnant and mephitic" body of water and was ordered filled in as a measure of public health. All sorts of measures were tried as the city grew in size and the need of water increased. The run-off from the house roofs during rainstorms was collected in "rain barrels" or cisterns and used for washing. Water was brought from the suburbs in casks and hawked about the city streets. Deeper wells were dug in the city itself. The *Evening Post* of July 27, 1832 — William Cullen Bryant was the editor — reported that L. Disbrow had bored to a depth of 448 feet, 400 of it through solid rock, in Bleecker Street near Broadway to find "rock water" and, with the aid of a six-horsepower steam engine, produced 44,000 gallons from this "perforation" in twenty-four hours.

Such measures were not enough to solve the problem. The

great forward step came with the building of the Croton Aqueduct and its completion in 1842.   That, of course, was only the
beginning of a water-supply system that now taps an immense
distant area and delivers more than 1,100,000,000 gallons of
water daily within the city limits.   Some of this, to be sure, is
for industrial use and some for such public service as street
cleaning, fire control, and the upkeep of municipal parks and
recreational centers, but most of it goes to householders.   The
percentages vary from year to year but, roughly, the distribution is nearly 60 per cent for domestic use, a little over 20
per cent for industrial use, about 7½ per cent for municipal
purposes and tax-exempt institutions, another 7½ per cent for
leakage and breaks in the line, and 5 per cent for miscellaneous
affairs, including the supplying of great ocean liners with fresh

water at their Hudson River piers. The household consumption is approximately eighty gallons per person per day.

Keeping this water pure and clean at the delivery point is the task of the Department of Water Supply, Gas, and Electricity. In addition to other methods of purification and chemical treatment, the Laboratory Division of the department has forty-eight chlorine plants — perhaps more by the time this appears in print — in operation and more than 400 sampling stations, of which about 100 are within the city limits. From these sampling stations there are 30,000 collections that are put through 300,000 tests each year. The results of the tests determine what treatment the water is to have all the way from the original collecting point — probably in the Catskills, because more than 75 per cent of the water now delivered in the city comes from that area — to the user in New York City.

There is a considerable amount of surface scouring of mineral, vegetable, and even animal matter swept into the artificial lakes that are the original collecting areas. This pollution is at its highest after hard rains, but much of it settles out in storage there. Turbidity usually settles through storage but, where it occurs along the distributional system, alum is added to clear it up. Copper sulphate and chlorine are used to maintain control of the growth of microscopic organisms in the water. The copper sulphate dosage is one and one-half pounds per million gallons. The chlorine dosage, depending on local or seasonal conditions, varies from one to eight pounds per million gallons. The heavier dosages occur in summer when microbiological activity is at its height. Sometimes the "chlorine taste" of the water in hot weather draws a complaint from the householders but ordinarily the city water is clear, odorless, and tasteless. The "major mineral impurities" are salts of calcium and magnesium in such minute quantities as to be completely negligible as public health factors and the water is exceedingly "soft," which means it is excellent for washing purposes.

There are storage and distributing reservoirs in all five boroughs and some dust and soot settles on the surface of the
waters there, but tests have shown this to be of little consequence. Ducks, gulls and a few other birds and occasional
quadrupeds contribute some pollutional material to the reservoir waters but natural as well as departmental purifying
processes remove any real danger from that source. There are
always some diatoms (a form of algae) of one genus or another
in the water and a lesser amount of microscopic crustaceans,
but they are kept down to harmless proportions and most of
the time those who drink the water have no suspicion that it
has any animal or vegetable content.

However, such matters occasionally get out of hand when
there is an accumulation of solid material (twigs, leaves, insects, feathers, soot, or silt) in the screens at the inlets or outlets
of storage or distribution reservoirs. When such collected
material becomes a mass of decomposing substances, it may
add a bad taste to the water. In such cases it is detected
almost immediately by the official samplers, but before they
can remedy the situation it may be detected by the householders, too. Aside from such occasional and unimportant
deviations, New Yorkers may well boast of the good, clear,
fresh water they get by turning on the tap in the kitchen or
the bathroom. The quality is high, even if the quantity continues to be a growing problem with the seemingly endless
growth of the city.

Chapter 3

Geography and Climate

NEW YORK CITY contains within its municipal boundaries approximately 320 square miles of land and 65 square miles of
inland waters. As of this writing (1958), the population is
listed at 7,795,471 but undoubtedly some extra inhabitants
have been added since the most recent census-takers closed their
books. The city area is irregular in outline and much longer
than it is broad. It has a "long axis" that runs NNE/SSW
from the Westchester County line on the north to the southerly
tip of Staten Island, a distance of about thirty-six miles as the
crow flies. The widest part of the city from east to west is the
sixteen-mile stretch from the Nassau County line at Lakeville
Road on Long Island to the Hudson River waterfront at 23rd
Street. To place the city land limits more accurately for world
travelers, the extreme eastern point is at 73° 44′ West Longitude in the New Hyde Park section on Long Island, the extreme northerly point is on the east bank of the Hudson River

at Mount St. Vincent at 40° 55′ North Latitude, and the southerly and westerly limits practically coincide at the lower tip of Staten Island, the Tottenville section, at 40° 30′ North Latitude and 74° 15′ West Longitude. The historic and handsome City Hall in downtown Manhattan, the hub of municipal authority and activity, though often rocked by major political and minor seismic tremors, remains firmly fixed at 40° 42′ 23″ North Latitude and 74° 0′ 29″ West Longitude. Although in the United States we look on New York as a "northern city," it is more than 700 miles south of London, more than 500 miles south of Paris — and some 70 miles south of Rome!

Geographically and politically, New York City is divided into five boroughs, each one of which is also a county of the state of New York. The five boroughs are Manhattan, Brooklyn, Queens, Richmond, and the Bronx. The definite article is required in the last instance. No other borough rates that distinction, nor does the Bronx rate it as a county. We say "Bronx County" as we say "Queens County" and "Richmond County." But we do not say "Manhattan County" or "Brooklyn County," because as divisions of New York State the Borough of Manhattan is New York County and the Borough of Brooklyn is Kings County. As a matter of fact, the Borough of Richmond, which is also Richmond County, is better known and more often referred to by New Yorkers as Staten Island.

Apropos of Staten Island, it might be pointed out that only about one-eighth of the city territory is on the mainland of North America. New York is a city of many islands. In addition to the great sections on Manhattan Island, Staten Island, and Long Island, the inland waters of the city are dotted with such local landmarks as: Liberty (formerly Bedloe's) Island on which stands the famous Bartholdi statue with uplifted torch; Ellis Island that formerly served as a port of entry for millions of immigrants; Governors Island that is an Army post and headquarters under the name of Fort Jay; Welfare (formerly Blackwell's) Island that, with its municipal hospital and jail, serves as a midstream support for the Queensboro Bridge; Ward's and Randall's Islands that do duty as steppingstones for the Triborough Bridge; Riker's Island and the small but picturesquely named North Brother and South Brother Islands in the East River; City Island that grew up as a community of boatbuilders and sailmakers on Long Island Sound; Hart's Island nearby — and if you count the little islands in the Lower Bay and the numerous nameless patches of dry ground sticking up above the waters of Jamaica Bay, you might say truthfully that the Mayor of New York City, geographically, is the Chief Magistrate of an archipelago.

Indeed, the city's waterways were the reason for its founding and have been its chief asset in its extraordinary growth. The great harbor is one of the finest in the world. The Hudson is truly a lordly river, a full mile wide where it washes the west side of the city and provides convenient berths for the largest passenger liners afloat. The Harlem River and the East River, though they have fresh-water tributaries, are essentially tidal straits, and so are the Arthur Kill and Kill Van Kull that separate Staten Island from the New Jersey mainland. All these inland waterways, plus the ocean frontage, give the city a total of 578 miles of shoreline with 320 miles of piers and bulkheads alongside which ships may tie up.

This makes New York the greatest ocean port in the world and it is not uncommon for a hundred ocean-going vessels to arrive or depart in a single day. Add the local traffic — the ferries, the lighters, the tugs, the long strings of scows and barges of all kinds — and it is plain that the inland waters are incessantly stirred by, moving keels and churning propellers. Where there is shipping on such a gigantic scale, there is naturally a considerable amount of casual flotsam and jetsam to soil the waters, but far worse than that is the pollution the city for many years has been pouring into its own rivers and bays from countless sewer outlets in the various boroughs. Such fouling of waters has had a considerable effect on the marine plant and

animal life of the area. It has, for instance, killed off some
valuable food plants, reduced the supply of edible fish in city
waters, and made the local shellfish unfit for human consumption. However, a program is under way to abate and finally
cease such pollution. Already some progress has been made
but it will take some years — 1964 was mentioned as a goal in a
recent official conference — and many millions of dollars to
clear these troubled waters.

There is still another form of pollution that affects life in
New York City: air pollution. New York is not only a great

ocean port, a great business mart and a great financial center, it is also a major manufacturing community. Its mills, factories, foundries, laboratories and power plants pour smoke and acid fumes into the atmosphere as well as industrial waste into the already soiled city waters. To this must be added the exhaust fumes of the hundreds of thousands of motor vehicles on the crowded streets. This is a problem with which large cities in many lands are faced. New York is facing it with a Department of Air Pollution Control, set up in 1944 when the annual fall of solid matter — mostly soot — over the city amounted to 162 tons per square mile per year. Within ten years, with the aid of spotters in tall office buildings and even helicopters on patrol, the department succeeded in reducing the fall of solid matter to about sixty-two tons per square mile per year. Part of the reduction, however, was due to a decrease in the use of coal and an increase in the use of oil as fuel for boilers, engines and furnaces of the area. This cut down on the amount of soot going skyward but increased the amount of irritant gases poured into the atmosphere. Thus air pollution remains a problem in the city and probably always will.

One thing about New York that hasn't changed much in the last five hundred years is the climate. It is more or less generally agreed that we are in a retreating Ice Age in North America and that the temperature has been gradually rising since the last glacial climax that covered Manhattan Island and vicinity with a great blanket of ice. But that was thousands of years ago. By the time Henry Hudson and his crew dropped anchor in the offing, the climate of the region was not noticeably different from what it is today, except perhaps in one respect. The "perhaps" is inserted because the change is recent, not well established as a regular meteorological feature, and, as some experts allege, may be only a casual disturbance of the old order. However, some scientists who have studied the matter insist that there has been a slight shift in the hurricane path whereby the city is now subjected to occasional, and sometimes repeated, havoc by heavy rains and high winds in late August or September, whereas formerly such storms passed to the eastward over the open ocean. A shift in the polar air current — or some other malign influence beyond the reach of municipal authority — has been blamed for the intermittent hurricane damage to the city in the last twenty years.

To the meteorologist the climate of New York is temperate, though its inhabitants on occasion would call it most intemperate with its sudden shifts of weather without notice. The area covered by the city is so large (approximately 400 square miles of land and water) that there may be a great difference in conditions in different sections of the city at the same moment, but official statistics gathered over the years bear out the statement that the climate is, indeed, temperate. The normal annual precipitation (including melted snow) is 40.38 inches; the average relative humidity is 70 per cent; the average annual temperature is 53.4° F.; and the area is favored with sunshine 59 per cent of the time when the sun is above the horizon. That's not bad at all.

The highest temperature ever recorded by the United States Weather Bureau office at 17 Battery Place was (in the shade, of course) on July 9, 1936, when the mercury in the thermometer rose to 102.3° F. The lowest was on February 9, 1934, when the same mercury dropped to 14.3° below zero Fahrenheit. The greatest continuous snowfall occurred on December 26 and 27, 1947, when 25.8 inches of snow came down to halt practically all vehicular traffic in the city for more than twenty-four hours. Neighborhood grocery stores and butcher shops ran out of supplies and groups of men, women, and children gathered at strategic points where they hoped milk trucks eventually would appear. When the milk trucks did push through the snow, the milkmen were besieged by parents who clamored for priority because of infants at home. It was a full week before New York was back in stride again.

But let us not go to extremes. The average temperature for

August in the city is 73.2° F., and for February it is 32.7° F. A common swing of the mercury through a normal year would be through a range of about 90° F., running from 5° above zero on a bitter winter day to the 95° heat of a summer day that brings the newspaper headlines, CITY SWELTERS: BEACHES JAMMED.

That's about as close as we can come to an accurate description of the city so far as geography and climate are concerned. Absolute accuracy is impossible in either category. The weather, of course, never can be guaranteed. It changes with appalling swiftness and devastating results on occasions. Nor, strange to say, can the geography be guaranteed, either. Inlets are filled in to make solid ground where there was water a few years ago. Islands are built up from mud and sand is dredged from the bottom of a bay. As recently as March 30, 1957, the morning newspapers carried the story that the city had purchased two small islands in the Lower Bay from the Federal Government — Hoffman Island of 11 acres extent and Swinburne Island of 2½ acres — and planned, by filling the watery region between, to make one island of 250 acres extent. There is much "made ground" along the city's waterfront and the process goes on to this day in a small way.

It's true that some ground has been lost, too, as in the cutting of the Harlem River Ship Canal through the Marble Hill ridge in 1895, but that was a small loss and part of it was made up years later when the loop of the river to the northward was filled in. I was a toddler when the canal was cut and thrown open to shipping but I was a schoolboy before the old riverbed was filled in and many a summer day I went swimming in it, diving from the abutment of what we called "the Iron Bridge" over the river at what is now solid ground at 230th Street and Broadway.

The cutting of the canal and the filling of the old riverbed to the northward involved items of historical and political import. One was the disappearance of Farmer's Bridge, over which travelers went eastward toward the Boston Post Road. Farmer's Bridge stood at what is now Exterior Street and 225th Street. Another was the disappearance of King's Bridge, the ancient structure that gave its name to the whole area and spanned the river at what is now Kingsbridge Avenue just below 230th Street. These ancient crossings were colonial landmarks. The political result of cutting a canal through the northern tip of Manhattan Island and then filling in the old loop of the river to the northward was to join a portion of Manhattan Island solidly to the Bronx and cut it off by water from its "motherland." Thus the residents of Marble Hill, bound by solid ground to the Bronx, legally are Manhattan Islanders and vote and pay taxes as residents of the Borough of Manhattan and New York County. However, nobody bothers about the distinction except the tax assessors and the captains of the election districts.

As the great metropolis stands, and as the old maps prove, it is an agglomeration of scores of towns and villages — even hamlets — whose names now survive as designations for different sections of the city. You will see them on the signboards of the railroad stations for city commuters who use the New York Central or the Long Island Railroad in their daily travels to work and back: Woodside, Jamaica, Queens Village, Flushing, Mott Haven, Tremont, Fordham, Woodlawn, Spuyten Duyvil, Riverdale, and Mount St. Vincent. Murray Hill, once an actual elevation and a favored residential district, survives as a telephone exchange. Great are the changes on the face of the earth within the city limits in the past few hundred years, but the sun and the stars look down on it now as they did a million years ago, the seasons march across it according to ancient and unhurried schedule, and if we look in the right places, we can find things that have not changed since the only human inhabitants of Manhattan Island were Indians in an encampment on a slope running down to the bank of a great river.

Chapter 4

Beginning in a Small Way

Now THAT we have our city located and charted, let us take some visitor who is interested in natural history and show him as much as we can of the myriad forms of plant and animal life to be found within the territorial limits of New York City. We could begin in a small way by going out to a park pond or down to any one of the many salt-water beaches of the city and dipping up a cupful of water. It is impossible to gather as much as a drop of salt, brackish, or fresh water in its natural state without finding some form of life existing in it. Plant and animal life abound in all open waters and vary in size from the microscopic single-celled diatoms and Protozoa of the plankton of the sea to the largest living creature the world ever saw, the 100-foot, 150-ton Blue Whale (*Sibbaldus musculus*) that feeds largely on its microscopic neighbors in the ocean in the shape of the aforementioned plankton.

No members of the whale family are listed as permanent

residents of the city waters, though some of the smaller ones do drop in occasionally and are received as distinguished visitors. But within the city limits there are springs, brooks, streams, ponds, and lakes, fresh- and salt-water marshes and, from the Sea Gate to Far Rockaway, more than seventeen miles of wonderful sea beach. A great portion of Staten Island faces the open ocean. In short, you will find fresh, brackish, and salt water in large quantities in our city; and the forms of life flourishing therein are so numerous and so varied that only a brief account of some of the more noteworthy species can be offered in this book.

Whether we dip our cupful of water from the ocean at Coney Island or from a park lake in any of the five boroughs, microscopic examination will disclose that it is teeming with life in miniature forms, all of it interesting and much of it dazzling in design. But that is the concern of the laboratory technician peering through a microscope. We are for the open air, armed only with field glasses and a small magnifying glass, and we shall take note of single-celled animal and plant life — Protozoa and Thallophyta — only when they occur in colonies large enough to be visible to the naked eye, which frequently many of them do. The phosphorescence in the sea at night, for instance, is caused by the presence near the surface of incredible numbers of tiny luminous one-celled creatures (about 4,000,000,000 to a quart of sea water) called Noctiluca by the scientists, and most of what we call "seaweed" in salt water and "green scum" on the surface of fresh-water ponds is an accumulation of billions of microscopic and often single-celled plants of the Algae group. In the case of most seaweeds they occur in colonies recognizable by size, shape, color, and particular pattern.

Let us go down to the sea by subway and then on foot along the beach at Coney Island or the Rockaways to have a look at some of the seaweeds torn loose from their watery moorings and left high and dry with the wrack strewn along the upper

Kelp and Sanderlings

part of the beach by the last high tide. In an examination of living things in any area it is logical to begin with plants rather than animals because all animal life on the face of the earth — and in the waters thereof — ultimately depends for survival on plant life. It is true that many animals are completely carnivorous, living entirely on the flesh of other animals, but the line of food supply inevitably must trace back to vegetable matter, for the simple reason that animal life needs what we call vitamins to support it, and the manufacturing of vitamins, with one or two minor exceptions, is the basic property of the plant world. On some other planets it is possible that there are other vital arrangements but on this third planet outward from the center of our solar system the significant situation is that plants can get along without animal life but animal life as we know it could not exist without plant life.

Seaweeds flourish in greater abundance and variety along a rocky coast. The ocean front of the New York area is largely sandy, but many species that grow in deep water offshore or along distant rocky regions are torn loose and eventually carried by wind and wave to the city beaches and here we find red, yellow, brown, green, and purple seaweeds of different kinds and shapes either floating in the water or cast up on the sand. We find the brown Bladder Wrack (*Fucus vesiculosis*) with little egg-shaped swellings along its many flat branches. Here and there will be bright green masses of Sea Lettuce (*Ulva lactuca*), some of it roundish in shape and a foot in diameter, some of it in the form of a 2-foot blade with a curly or frizzled edge. Somewhere along the beach we are sure to come on the long narrow blades of Henware (*Alaria esculenta*), looking amazingly like 7-foot or 8-foot strips of some brown plastic material rather than a massive colony of microscopic plants.

One of the red algae group of seaweeds found in the area is the Chenille Weed (*Dasya pedicillata*) that has graceful plume-like branches where it grows in the water but turns into a purplish jellied mass when it is cast up on the beach. However, if placed back in the water it will regain its graceful appearance and, by slipping a sheet of good quality white bond paper underneath as it floats in the water, you can take it up and preserve it on the paper in its natural color and feathery design. Biology teachers often use such trophies as decorations for classroom walls.

On some occasions the wrack along the beach will be thickened by what look like chopped-up bits of sponges or rubbery remainders of some kind of smashed-up seagoing cauliflower crop. This is the Irish Moss or Carrageen (*Chondrus crispus*) that, pink to purple in its growing days in the tide pools, lies in pale masses that bleach as they dry along the beach. I never have seen anybody collecting it along the city beaches but gathering and processing Irish Moss was a profitable industry at one time in New England and it is still sold in small quantities in cardboard containers garnished with printed matter to the effect that the contents are good for men, women, and children, being "rich in chemical phosphates and iodine." To cure a cough or a cold, the reader is advised to "simmer a handful in a pint of water; strain and add juice of 1 lemon and sugar to suit. This makes a soothing cough mixture and can be taken freely." What it actually amounts to is a mass of gelatine that added flavoring may make quite palatable but otherwise is insipid. However, it is ignored on the city beaches by strollers who perhaps have no ideas of its virtues, such as that it is 65 per cent gelatine and, if you don't care to eat it, you can use it to make soap or stiffen white cloth. Whatever the attitude in New York, the natives of Gloucester, Massachusetts, still gather it by hand when the gales pile it up in rows on the little beaches in the rocky coves of the great headland that is Cape Ann.

Just a step above the Protozoa in the animal world are the Porifera, or what we call sponges; colonies of tiny creatures that cluster together and live attached to the ocean floor or other submarine anchorage in fresh and salt water. There are many kinds of sponges in our city waters but none is commercially valuable and some are more or less harmful. There are salt-water species that bore holes through the shells of shellfish and feed on the contents and there are fresh-water sponges that unless kept in subjection would increase and multiply in the city aqueducts and reservoirs to the point of clogging pipes and adding an unwanted flavor to the water. It's easy to find sponge fragments along the beaches or, indeed, living colonies attached to the submerged timbers under piers, but not many persons pry into such places and only the scientists take note of the sponge population of New York City waters.

Just to be orderly in this brief survey of animal life in the water, we move along to the coelenterates, those queer creatures of so many different and almost incredible forms, some of which look so much like submarine plants that we call them "sea anemones" and others that, widely different in appear-

Sea Anemone and anchovies

ance, we know as "jellyfish." Some grow singly and some join together in large colonies. Some spend most of their lives in what is called the hydroid stage, during which they cling, plant-like, to some kind of support. Others, like the jellyfish, occur mostly in the free-swimming or medusa stage. Coelenterates are essentially living tubes with one end open and that end fringed with tentacles tipped with stinging cells to aid in the capture of prey. This holds true no matter what the size of the coelenterate, whether it is single or part of a colony, or whether it is in the hydroid or free-swimming stage.

According to the specialists in the field, more than fifty species of coelenterates occur as either fresh- or salt-water residents of our area and a few extra oceanic kinds occasionally are washed ashore. Since they live in water, the marine hy-droids of the sea-anemone type are fixed to rocks, submerged plants, or the submerged parts of piers and bulkheads and thus seldom are seen except by those who deliberately search for them. But all too often in late summer the salt waters of the bathing areas — particularly those on Long Island Sound — are swarming with the other type, the free-swimmers, in the shape of an obnoxious, transparent, and abundant jellyfish, *Aurelia aurita*, that may be as much as 10 inches in diameter. This creature can be lifted without discomfort on the calloused palm of the hand, but the effect of the stinging cells on the arms or legs of a swimmer is decidedly detectable and quite irritating.

There are numerous other kinds of hydroids and jellyfish to be found in the area. Many of them are so small that the effect of their stinging cells on the human skin is negligible. There are also a few species of those creatures known as "comb jellies," or Ctenophora, that look like jellyfish but have no stinging cells and perhaps for that reason few persons notice them at all.

The gruesome report of Hamlet concerning the last banquet at which Polonius was an attendant — "Not where he eats, but where he is eaten; a certain body of politic worms are e'en at him" — is apropos at this point. Worms are the subject of our

story. They come after the comb jellies in the scientific catalogue of animal life. The worms of salt and fresh water are a
study in themselves, a study pursued by remarkably few persons.
Those who have applied themselves to the subject, however,
separate these largely longitudinal creatures into three great
divisions: the flatworms (Platyhelmia), the ribbon worms
(Nemertea), and the segmented or annelid worms (Annelida),
this last group including the earthworms and leeches.

Most of the worms are visible to the naked eye if you have
good sight and look in the right places. Since many of them
are parasitic, it would be ordinarily impossible to see them unless you dissected their hosts. Some are mere specks less than 1
mm. (1/25 inch) in length and best seen under magnification
and others may be measured by inches or feet, including the
largest of the group found in New York City waters, the almost
incredible *Cerebratulus lacteus*, one of the ribbon worms, that
feeds near the low-water mark on tidal flats and though only an
inch in width may reach a length of 20 feet! This is, in fact,
the longest worm found in North America, but the story goes
that a European relative has been known to reach a length of
90 feet!

The tube-builders of the annelid group are wonderful to behold. The Sabella Worm (*Sabellaria vulgaris*), which may be
captured at low tide along the city waterfront, is a good example of these curious creatures that, with the aid of what look
like tiny tentacles or plumes or fernlike fronds at the front ends
of their bodies, pick up or sweep in particles of sand or lime
and gradually encase themselves in tubes that they lengthen
as needed to house themselves in comfort. The tentacles, of
course, sweep in food as well as building material. The Sabella
Worm at full growth is only an inch or so in length but its tube,
which often bulks much larger than the tenant, is a help in
locating the creature in the water.

There are other species of tube-builders in fresh as well as
salt water and the actions of these little construction engineers

are well worth watching when the occasion offers. Worms as a group are rather generally neglected in the field of nature study. Perhaps one reason for the neglect is that so many of them are tiny creatures from 1 mm. to 10 mm. in length, are transparent or only slightly colored, and live under stones in water or among the leaves and branches of aquatic plants, where they are difficult to find even by one who goes in search of them. But they are there to be found in great numbers and baffling variety. Before leaving the subject of salt-water worms it should be noted that fish and other aquatic creatures taken in salt water within the city limits often are brought to boat with marine leeches of one kind or another attached. Leeches are a kind of annelid worm but the marine species in our area are few in number and unimportant compared to the fresh-water species to be encountered later in this book.

We now move on to the Arthropoda, a vast grouping of invertebrate creatures with jointed legs, a group further divided into such familiar classes as crustaceans, arachnids (spiders and their relatives), myriapods (meaning millipedes and centipedes), and insects, the last being in number of species named and described by far the largest class in the Animal Kingdom. There was mention earlier of a cupful of water in which we could find microscopic forms of plant and animal life. We are dealing with bigger things now, and had better use a pail.

Dip up half a pailful of fresh or salt water anywhere in the area except in one of the city reservoirs and you will have hundreds of water fleas (Cladocera) and copepods (Copepoda) therein. These are tiny crustaceans, midget members of the great class that includes such restaurant items as shrimp, crab, and lobster. Water fleas and copepods are important ingredients of the plankton of the sea and are food for plant and animal life in lakes, streams, ponds, and brooks. Young fish are nourished on them. In return, some copepods nourish themselves on fish, being parasitic on many species. These tiny crustaceans vary in size from 1/100 inch to several inches

or more in the case of some parasitic species that attach themselves to Menhaden and Broadbill Swordfish, but most species
of copepods and water fleas that you might find in a pail of
water dipped at random in the area would be less than ¼ inch
in length and a magnifying glass would come in handy in looking them over.   In fact, a low-power microscope would be
better, because many species are curiously and wondrously
fashioned and the details are enchanting.   Or even amazing.
We shall look into the matter further when we go into the
fresh-water reaches of the city.   We are still, so to speak, on
the beach.

   The late Roy Waldo Miner, for many years Curator of Living Invertebrates at the American Museum of Natural History,
in his magnum opus, *Field Book of Seashore Life*, quotes the great
Agassiz as stating that "the barnacle is nothing more than a
little shrimp-like creature standing on its head inside a limestone house and kicking its food into its mouth with its feet."   In
the *Encyclopaedia Britannica* it is Huxley who is credited with the
"graphic phrase" to the effect that "a barnacle may be said to
be a crustacean fixed by its head and kicking the food into its
mouth with its legs."   By either authority, it's a good short
description of a barnacle.   These creatures are crustaceans that
swim about freely in salt water in their salad days but as they
grow up fasten themselves to almost any kind of solid object
they find in the water or between tidemarks such as rocks,
seaweed, pier piling, bulkheads, driftwood, channel markers,
bell buoys, bathing-beach floats, and even the bodies of sea
turtles and whales.   In the days of "wooden ships and iron
men" they were a particular pest because the ships had to be
careened frequently to scrape the bottoms clean of the barnacles
that completely covered the exterior planking and cut down the
sailing speed of the vessels.

   The most common of the group in New York salt waters is
the Rock Barnacle (*Balanus balanoides*), a rough-coated object
about ½ inch in extent measured in any direction and shaped

somewhat like a truncated little pyramid or sagging "mob cap." It clings in enormous numbers to rocks and timbers exposed at low tide. If you look for this abundant barnacle you will find other species, including some brought in from far places by ocean traffic, but be careful when walking in such slippery places: a fall among barnacle-covered rocks or timbers may leave the clothing or epidermis much the worse for wear and tear.

In the chapter on the storming of Torquilstone Castle in *Ivanhoe* there is a dramatic moment when Wamba the Jester is asked how many the attackers of the castle might be. "Gallant sir," replied Wamba, "*Nomen illis legio;* their name is legion." So it is with the Crustacea of our region. They are overwhelming in number. They abound in salt and fresh water. They feed on plant and animal life and, in turn, are food themselves in vast quantities for other living organisms. They come in many shapes and they range in size from barely visible specks in the water to, alas, no longer the regal American Lobster (*Homarus americanus*) that has quit local waters, but at least to the good-sized and delightfully edible Blue Crab (*Callinectes sapidus*) that is still sought and caught by men and boys on the beaches, in the salt marshes, and even along the stringpieces of the piers and wharves of the harbor, the rivers, and Long Island Sound. I myself — *moi qui vous parle* — often as a boy went crabbing along the northerly loop of the Harlem River with a long-handled net and a piece of meat on the end of a string. The technique was to hurl the piece of meat out into the river and then drag it slowly shoreward. If a Blue Crab was beguiled by the bait and followed it shoreward, the net was put into operation. When the operation was successful, the crab went into a potato sack hopefully provided for the occasion and the hunt continued. We often caught a dozen or more fair-sized crabs and cooked and ate them right there on the riverbank. I doubt, however, that the crabbing in the Harlem River is as good now as it was when I was a boy.

Blue Crab

There are other species of crab to be found in New York waters. One is the familiar Little Hermit Crab (*Pagurus longicarpus*) so often found inhabiting the dark little shells of the Common Periwinkle (*Littorina litorea*). In deeper water or in larger shells you will find the Large Hermit Crab (*Pagurus pollicarus*) that also is common in the area. Probably the prettiest of the "true crab" group in city waters is the Lady Crab (*Ovalipes ocellatus*) that runs a bit smaller than the Blue Crab and sometimes is called the Calico Crab because of the pinkish-mauve top shell or carapace that is thickly sprinkled with dark dots. It really has an attractive appearance when first taken from the water.

The marshes and mud flats, of course, abound with little Fiddler Crabs (*Uca* sp.) of two or three species. This is the group in which the males have one claw much larger than the other and go about with this oversize claw either folded across the front of the body or waved aloft threateningly like a battle-axe. You can see these odd little creatures by the hundreds on the mud flats when the tide is out and, if you are close enough, you can hear the creaking of their joints as the little armored battalions march in zigzag fashion over the mud. The little Grass Shrimp, or Common Prawn (*Palaemonetes vulgaris*), is a resident of Jamaica Bay and other such salt-water sections of the city and so is the Sand Shrimp (*Crago septemspinosus*), though it is harder to find because it is the color of the sandy bottoms it prefers and also because it buries itself in the sand if it is between tidemarks when the tide is out.

Everyone who has walked an ocean beach has seen sand-pipers of one kind or another feeding along the water's edge, retreating and advancing with the wash of the waves as they break on the sand. Such shore birds probably are feeding on sand fleas or sand hoppers that look like hunched-over minia-ture shrimp and are, even when stretched out straight, less than ½ inch in length. Did you ever notice bubbles of air on the surface of the wet sand from which a wave has just re-treated? Such bubbles betray the presence of sand fleas in their burrows just below the surface of the sand. One of the common species along the water's edge on the ocean beaches is *Talorchestia longicornis*. If you kick up the damp seaweed lying in the wrack at the high-water mark, you may set pale flealike creatures popping about in all directions. These might be *Orchestia agilis*, an abundant sand flea of the area that prefers the upper part of the beach provided it can find food and shelter there in soggy masses of seaweed, Irish Moss, and as-sorted debris. However, there are other species along the beaches and quite different ones in the marshes and, all in all, a student could make a career of observing, collecting, dissect-ing, and describing the life cycles of these tiny Crustacea.

It may come as a surprise to some readers that the familiar Horseshoe Crab (*Limulus polyphemus*) is not a crab or even a crustacean but is a member of the class Arachnoides along with scorpions and spiders and some other creatures. Small or large — and our Horseshoe Crabs reach a length of 20 inches — they often are abundant along the seashore and the edges of the salt marshes of the region throughout the warmer months. They are fearsome in appearance but quite harmless in reality. They are a link with the long ago, and their prototypes are found as fossils as far back as Paleozoic time. Despite their ancient lineage, these Horseshoe Crabs are not always treated with dignity when they are found dead or dying on the beaches or in the marshes. In some areas where they become stranded in large numbers they are rudely gathered up and ground into fertilizer.

Now we turn to the largest class of Arthropoda or jointed-leg creatures, the insects and immediately we are in for a shock. Apparently salt water is not good for insects. Though world-wide in distribution and far outstripping all other nonmicroscopic forms of animal life in known species and total numbers, they are almost complete abstainers from salt water. We find them in countless numbers in fresh water in our area, but the only one worth mentioning in the salt-water reaches of the city is a dark wingless creature about 1/8 inch in length, fuzzy and "crawly" in appearance, that goes under the name of *Anurida maritima* and is valuable as a scavenger where it runs about the rocks, the vegetation, or the surface of the pools between tide-marks. Like all insects, it breathes air, of course, but it can carry air bubbles down with it and make use of them for an extended stay under the surface of the water. You will need a magnifying glass if you want to have a good look at this insect adventurer in tidal territory.

Moving along to the Mollusca, we find that most of the living creatures included in this great group much prefer salt water to fresh water. The main divisions of the great group are the Amphineura (the chitons that look like tiny seagoing armadillos), the Gastropoda (mostly what we call snails), the Scaphopoda (tusk shells, of which only one species is found in the area), the Cephalopoda (the squids, cuttlefish, and octopuses), and, most important of all, the Pelecypoda (clams, oysters, mussels, and their relatives).

The common chiton of the seashore and tidal waterways of the city is the *Chaetopleura apiculata* that looks like a miniature gray or light-brown ¾-inch turtle with its head, tail, and feet pulled in, and is found in shallow water, usually clinging to some solid object. In other words, all that you see of it at first — and this is the case with many other and more notable members of the mollusk group — is the shell. To see the animal underneath, you have to pry it loose and turn it over. Even then, practically all you see is the elongated fleshy foot of the little creature.

You probably will have some difficulty in finding a living individual of the one species of Scaphopoda that occurs in the area because it is almost lineal in shape, is only about 2 inches long at maturity, and feeds standing upright all the way from shallow water to the depths of the sea. However, you will find abundant positive evidence of its presence in the vicinity if you walk the beaches and scan the sand between tidemarks. It is called the Common Tooth Shell (*Dentalium entale*) and somewhere along the sand you will see the empty limestone dwellings of such former tenants in the shape of narrowly conical and slightly curved 2-inch shells that much resemble the hollow white fangs of a venomous serpent. There are plenty of such shells along our beaches and you can't miss them if you make even a casual search.

But who looks for such trifling objects when there are so many other and more beautiful shells to be gathered on the beaches? The "sea shells" most often sought and carried home — sometimes preserved in beautiful and valuable collections — are the former and usually spiral homes of the gastropods, the snails, that inhabit the salt waters of the earth. There are fresh-water and land-going gastropods, too, but they are fewer in number and their abandoned homes, rather drab on the whole, go unnoticed and uncollected. At the seashore it is another story. Shining shells of different shapes, colors, and sizes are eagerly collected and often long treasured. In our area they range in size from about ¼ inch in some of the smaller species to the great whorled shells of the Knobbed Whelk (*Busycon caricum*) or the Channeled Whelk (*Busycon canaliculatum*) that are often 6 inches in extent and sometimes longer.

These huge whelks are the creatures that in life shed their eggs in long strings of what look like flattened, circular little straw-colored oiled-paper bags about ½ inch in diameter, all fastened by the rim to binding streamers that may be 2 or 3 feet long. These strings of egg cases often are thrown up on the beach and doubtless puzzle many who find them. The Channeled Whelk, with the smoother shell, is the more common species in the area; its strings of egg cases may be distinguished by the fact that each individual egg case has a single encircling rim, whereas those of the Knobbed Whelk have two sharp encircling rims to each egg case.

Certain gastropods leave curious mementoes along the beaches. These are the snails that produce the "sand collars" that are washed ashore in late summer and often puzzle those who find them at the water's edge. They are easily as large as the palm of your hand and look something like soggy circlets of grayish-brown cardboard washed up by the waves, but actually they consist of sand particles glued together in the general shape of a miniature cape, open at the front, with a recurved collar running around the top. When first cast ashore they have about the consistency of wet cardboard, but as they dry out on the sand they come apart more easily and eventually crumble away. The large sand collars are the result of the egg-laying activities of the Moon Shell Snail (*Lunatia heros*) and a near relative that lives in a much similar shell and is favored with the name of Sand-collar Snail (*Lunatia duplicata*) despite

Moon Shell

the fact that the production of sand collars is not a specific distinction but a family trait.

How all this comes about is that these snails, and smaller members of the family whose sand collars attract little or no attention, lay their eggs on the underside of a glutinous casing they exude around the circular bases of their shells and then shed the whole mass on a sandy bottom, where the glutinous casing soon acquires a coating of sand particles that stick together long enough to be the sand collar of the beach. The original glutinous casing doesn't extend all the way around the shell of the egg layer, which is why the sand collar always is "open in front." The Moon Shell, cream to white in color, almost globular in shape and 2 to 3 inches in extent measured in any direction, is common along the ocean front of the city. The shell of the Sand-collar Snail, less common in the area, is much similar in appearance but easily distinguished by the fact that in the Moon Shell there is a little hole — the "umbilicus," the opening of the central hollow around which the shell is spiraled — beside the white entrance, whereas in the Sand-collar Shell this hole usually is hidden by a flange extending from the main entrance.

Probably the most abundant of all snails in our region is the Common Periwinkle (*Littorina litorea*), whose small and usually dark shell with a sharp tip is a familiar sight in countless numbers along the shore and on the rocks, piling, bulkheads, and old timbers of the tidal zone. This is the little snail that, roasted, is a staple article of diet in Europe and the "hot winkle" hawked about the dock regions of London, but our citizens never have developed a taste for it. The snail and its shell on this side of the Atlantic are — as Henry the Fourth, on the authority of Shakespeare, said of Richard the Second — "seen but not regarded."

There are, of course, innumerable other marine gastropods in our area. A collector would not have to go beyond the city limits to gather a handsome assortment of the limestone architecture of these creatures whose homes, to most persons, are far more attractive empty than tenanted. We have to stretch a bit, however, to claim any of the Cephalopoda (the squids, cuttlefish, and octopuses) for our home waters. For the most part, they are offshore or deep-sea denizens, but frequently some of the smaller kind are hauled up by our offshore fishermen and occasionally one, or its corpse, is washed up on a city beach. It is evident that a New Yorker has little chance to learn much about Cephalopoda by direct observation, but there is plenty of reading matter on the subject in the city libraries and from it there has been extracted the following information on the group:

1. Almost all these creatures have ink sacs enabling them to send out a cloud of darkness to obscure the waters around them as a means of defense.

2. It's the Common Cuttlefish of Europe (*Sepia officinalis*) that produces the sepia ink for the artist as well as the cuttlebone you so often see placed in the wire of canary cages for the benefit of the health of the captive songsters.

3. The Giant Squid (*Architeuthis princeps*) of the North Atlantic has been found with a 10-foot body length and tentacles that stretched out 42 feet farther, making it the largest invertebrate known.

4. It was the beautiful segmented shell of an inkless cephalopod of oriental seas, the Pearly or Chambered Nautilus (*Argonauta argo*), that stirred Oliver Wendell Holmes to sing:

> *Its webs of living gauze no more unfurl;*
> *Wrecked is the ship of pearl!*
> *And every chambered cell,*
> *Where its dim dreaming life was wont to dwell*
> *As the frail tenant shaped its growing shell,*
> *Before thee lies revealed, —*
> *Its irised ceiling rent, its sunless crypt unsealed!*

From that poetic flight we descend to a sad subject, a truly melancholy matter concerning certain mollusks of our region, the Class Pelecypoda, which means the bivalves — the oysters, clams, scallops, mussels, and their relatives. There still are some forty to fifty species to be found in the salt-, brackish-, and fresh-water stretches of the city but, where once the edible salt-water species were dug, picked, raked, or dredged up in large quantities for the home table or the public market, the searcher for the succulent bivalves, because of the pollution of city waters, now finds himself faced with signs reading (and this is copied directly from such a sign in the Pelham Bay section):

CONDEMNED SHELLFISH AREA
NO CLAMS, MUSSELS, OR OYSTERS
PERMITTED TO BE TAKEN IN
THESE WATERS.

BY ORDER OF
THE BOARD OF HEALTH

As everybody knows, the American Oyster (*Crassostrea virginica*) — one of medium size and in top condition, served cold on the flat half shell and ingested with a dash of lemon — is food for the gods. Long ago it was happily harvested by the Indians and colonists in this region, and early travelers who had it served to them spoke and wrote of it enthusiastically.

Prince's Bay on Staten Island was once one of the busiest oyster harbors along the North Atlantic coast. As the city population increased and the oyster beds of local waters were raked bare, the Staten Island oystermen brought in seed oysters from Chesapeake Bay and planted them for cultivation. But they fought a losing battle to water pollution. There were numerous reports of cases of typhoid traceable to the eating of local oysters. The Department of Health finally banned the taking of shellfish in the area in 1916 and that was the end of the home-grown oyster industry in city waters.

Antiquarians still go poking about park lands and the few surviving open stretches of the city in search of masses of shells that are "kitchen middens" or refuse piles of Indian encampments of long ago. Most of the shells in such heaps are those of the bivalve *Venus mercenaria* that on the New York menu is listed under three different names according to age and size. In its younger and smaller days it goes by the name of Cherry-stone Clam. A little later and a little larger, it appears on the table as a Little-Neck Clam. If left long enough undisturbed in the water, it grows up to be the bigger and tougher Quahog, or Hardshell Clam. Quahog shells, of course, are common along the beaches. If you look at the inside of the shell you will see that it usually has a dark blue, violet, or purple border. It was from this portion of the shell that the Indians of New York and New England fashioned the more valuable beads of "wampum" that served them as money and also for personal decoration. The less valuable white "wampum" was made from the shells of some of the whelks.

But the Indian diet, as the uncovered kitchen middens proved, included the American Oyster, the Common Scallop (*Pecten irradians*), the Common Edible Mussel (*Mytilus edulis*), and other species of shellfish, some of which the white settlers and their successors never could bring themselves to swallow. The American Oyster is a finicky creature that doesn't like polluted water and, to the best of deponent's knowledge and be-

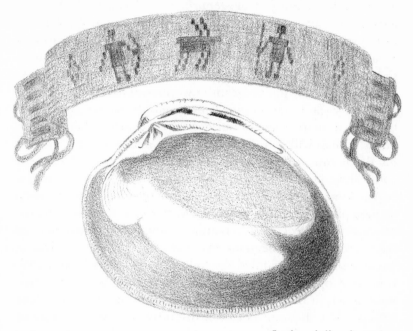

Quahog shell and wampum

lief, has now abandoned most if not all of its former submarine haunts within the city limits; but the clams, mussels, and scallops are a hardy lot. Despite the pollution of the water, they still cling to the tidal rocks, the piling, and the bulkheads of our area. They still flourish on sandy bottoms in shallow water and bury themselves in the mud flats of the salt marshes.

Large or small, they are found in great quantities and of many species. Along the ocean beaches you will come upon hundreds of shells of the Surf Clam (*Spisula solidissima*), the largest clam of the region and a favorite for clambakes. There, too, you will find either the Razor Clam (*Ensis directus*) or, more often, its empty shell that is 6 or 7 inches long and somewhat the shape of an old-fashioned razor handle. It is not quite as sharp as a razor along the edge but sharp enough to cut if carelessly grasped or stepped on. If you walk the mud flats of the city bays and inlets at low tide you will see many little jets of water spurt up around you, each jet indicating a Steamer or Softshell Clam (*Mya arenaria*) that has pulled in its siphon at your approach and is digging downward for safety. It is possible that the program now afoot to abate and eventually abolish pollution of city waters may bring the shellfish of the area to market again, but even if that doesn't happen, the hardy species will still flourish in city waters and serve as food for the herons, the gulls, the ducks, and the shore birds that come and go with the change of seasons.

Any kind of wood that remains submerged in salt water, such as pier pilings or the hulls of wooden ships, is subject to the attentions of the curious creatures called shipworms for the simple reason that they look like worms and in the old days of wooden ships often riddled the hulls of sailing vessels with their tunneling operations in the planking. They go about their work much in the manner of the wood-boring larvae of many insects. But they are not even distantly related to worms or insect larvae. They are, incredible as it may seem at first glance, bivalves! However, though the narrow cylindrical soft-bodied creatures may be a foot or more in length, the hard parts are reduced to a pair of "valves" not more than ½ inch long at the head end to act as augers in boring through the wood and two tiny anchorages where the "tail end" is held fast to the surface of the timber in the open water, from which all their food is obtained. Apparently they tunnel into the wood merely to lead protected lives. The two species that do the submarine boring of timber along the city waterfront are *Teredo navalis* and *Xylotrya fimbriata*, according to those who are acquainted with these undermining agents.

We have not yet finished with the seashore or the harbors and rivers with their docks and piers. We have the echinoderms to consider, and this includes the starfish, sea urchins, and sea cucumbers. It is true that many starfish are deep-water residents in life, but in death their stiffened corpses are strewn along the beaches for all to see. The dead bodies of the dwellers in shallow water are, of course, more common on the beaches and sometimes occur in such numbers as to be a nuisance despite their beautiful design and remarkable structure. The most abundant species found in death on the shore is the Common Starfish (*Asterias forbesi*) that usually has five "arms," ranges from 6 to 10 inches or so in diameter at full extent, and varies in "topside" color from orange through brown to purplish and is always lighter and brighter on the lower surface.

There are more than a dozen species to be found along the shore or in the water off the ocean beaches of the city. Although all of them are radial in structure and most of them have "five spokes to the wheel," not all are as completely star-shaped as the Common Starfish with its separated "arms." Some look like five-sided flat cakes and others have the shape of a miniature bearskin spread to dry — a central mass with five rounded projections at widespread angles. As a matter of fact, all echinoderms are radial in structure. It's a mark of the great clan. The sea urchins that look like little round balls covered with spines — some are flattened to look like animated pincushions — are radial in design beneath that rough exterior.

Either along the beach or in shallow water you may find the Purple Sea Urchin (*Arbacia punctulata*), from 1 to 2 inches in diameter, or the somewhat larger Green Sea Urchin (*Strongylocentrotus droehbachiensis*) — there's a name for you — that really is green, whereas the Purple Sea Urchin usually looks muddy brown in color in the water.

Children who eagerly collect "sand dollars" along the beaches probably have no idea that they are dealing in echinoderms or what is left of them after death. These curious and fragile little objects that derive their name from the fact that they are about the size and shape of a silver dollar and look as though they were made of sand are the empty body-coverings of departed echinoderms of the thinnest kind. The common species of our area — at least the one I found most easily along the beaches — is *Echinarachnius parma*. The topside plainly shows the radial design in what looks much like a five-bladed, feather-edged propeller in the center of the "dollar." On the underside there is a central hole that served as a mouth for the living creature, of which no visible sign remains when the delicate covering is found on the sand.

The sea cucumbers, which look like big slugs or snails without horns or shells, are represented in the city's salt waters principally by the darkish Common Thyone (*Thyone briareus*) that has a rough outer covering, grows to a length of 4 or 5 inches, has a cluster of threadlike tentacles at the forward end to sweep food into its mouth, and is difficult to find because it usually lies with its body buried in the sand or mud and only its head exposed, for feeding purposes. Experts who know where to look and what to expect find it easily, however, and also a few related species, for which they go digging beyond our depth. There are more queer creatures in the city salt waters than we can grapple with. They are too many and too much for us and we must leave them to the experts who specialize in that field.

There are, for instance, the tiny creatures of the Bryozoa

group called moss animals because, living in colonies, they look like moss on submerged rocks or shells or pier piling. There are creatures of the ascidian group called sea squirts because they contract themselves if disturbed and, being full of water, they discharge some in the process. To the scientists they are important because millions of years ago it seemed that they were destined for higher things like true vertebrate life, but somehow they became backsliders in the evolutionary line. For the most part, the ascidians of our area are little oval animals with rough coats and one end open for the purpose of engulfing food and discharging waste, all of which is accomplished by passing food-laden water in and out of the stomach and intestines of the creatures. One of the larger species — and the most common in the area — occurs in clusters called Sea Grapes. The individuals are pale, ovate creatures about an inch in diameter with two tiny hollow tubes projecting at the "head end," one being the intake and the other the outlet of the feeding system. You may find these clusters on timber, rocks, or even vegetation in shallow water. The scientific name of the species, *Molgula manhattensis*, justifies its selection as an appropriate representative of the ascidians of this area.

We will now turn our backs on the sea, head for the city center, and pause there to consider further excursions.

Chapter 5

Fresh-Water Wonders

OUT WE GO, now, to search for what treasures we may find in the fresh-water streams, ponds, and park lakes within the city limits. Under the placid surface of an ordinary pond we are sure to find an extraordinary assortment of plant and animal life, a miniature world in itself. If we did not go below the surface, many of us — whether we live in the city or in the country — would scarcely suspect its existence. To the city explorer it offers boundless opportunity for exciting discoveries, with the added advantage that some of the trophies of the expeditions can be brought home for further examination and closer study.

From the city center we could start in almost any direction and eventually reach a body of fresh water containing an entrancing variety of invertebrate life. Staten Island, though now threatened with a belated rush of settlers by the building of a bridge over The Narrows, still has some farmlands watered

by springs and brooks that the Indians and colonists knew three
centuries ago. The same may be said for the outlying sections
of Queens and the Bronx. There are ponds and park lakes in
all five boroughs. Each has much to offer, but the Bronx is my
"home ground" and I suggest a trip to Van Cortlandt Park in
the northwestern part of that borough. There you will find a
lovely little lake and an adjacent swamp that has proved a
happy hunting ground for city naturalists of all ages and degrees of ignorance or learning.

Tibbetts Brook is a little stream that dawdles down from
Yonkers to water the swamp and then fill the park lake before
it goes underground to empty eventually into the Harlem River
Ship Canal near the Spuyten Duyvil cut. Originally, of course,
it ran above ground through cattail marshes and wet meadows
all the way from the lake outlet to the old northern loop of the
Harlem River, crossing Broadway at about 240th Street en
route and providing several good swimming holes to which I
gave my patronage as a schoolboy. However, it was tucked
underground some forty-odd years ago and the marshes and
low meadows were gradually filled in and built upon. As a
matter of fact, I had a hand in tucking it under, because it
reaches its destination (the ship canal) through the Spuyten
Duyvil Outlet Sewer, in the construction of which I played an
integral part — timekeeper and young man in charge of steel
reinforcement — for the sum of $12 per week.

One of the good points about the Van Cortlandt Park swamp
as a lure for naturalists is that it is readily accessible from midtown Manhattan. If you take a Seventh Avenue subway train
marked "Van Cortlandt Park" from Times Square to 242nd
Street, a short walk diagonally across the broad playing field
known as the Parade Ground will bring you to the swamp that,
though it has been cut down in size sadly in recent years, still
has many things of interest to offer including a limited area of
cattail marsh at the lower end. If you go there in any of the
warm months of the year and dip up a cup of water anywhere

in the swamp, you will have hours of fascinating study within your grasp.

Fresh-water algae are there in abundance either as floating masses or as soft coatings of various green or brown hues on submerged stones or other solid objects. There are Protozoa that can be seen with the naked eye only where they are massed in colonies. These and the sponges and other microscopic forms of life are too many and too much for us. We can only note them in bulk in passing and leave the matter of identification of the various species to the expert with laboratory equipment and special training. Here we can deal only with those forms of aquatic animal life in which the individual creatures are visible to the naked eye or at least clearly seen under an ordinary hand lens or magnifying glass.

Better than a cup of water for this purpose is a glass of water, and it should be a thin, clear, light, and completely unadorned drinking glass for best results. When you dip up the water there probably will be some mud or silt in it. Let this settle and then hold the glass up to the light. Now if you look carefully you will see that some of the particles that appeared to be tiny specks of dirt in the water are little creatures moving about under their own steam. Up with the magnifying glass to have a better look at them! This will require a little practice because the tiny creatures move in and out of focus rapidly. Also, the better the light, the better the view of the creatures in the water. One way to improve the view is to gather the swamp water in a bottle, take it home, pour it into a clear glass and use an electric light bulb placed behind the glass as a source of illumination. But, either way, there is much to be seen.

There are hydras (coelenterates) in abundance and some may stretch out to a half inch in length, but they are not easy to spot immediately because all of them are small, many of them are transparent, and the tinted ones often are found clinging to objects of similar color in the water. The common Green Hydra (*Hydra viridissima*), for instance, is easily mistaken

for a tiny tendril growing out of the plant stem to which it may be clinging, but a close scrutiny through a magnifying glass will disclose the half-dozen or so threadlike tentacles "at the outer end" as they wave slowly about in the water in search of food. These and other hydras cling to all sorts of submerged objects such as stones, mosses, plant stems, and the lower surfaces of the floating leaves of aquatic plants. These hydras flourish most abundantly in still open water in warm weather, which means that the best time and place to look for them is in a pond or pool of a summer day.

The innumerable worms that occur in fresh water will baffle all but the experts. The flatworms, ribbon worms, thread-worms, hairworms, and annelid worms come in many sizes and shapes but only a few of the larger and, to the ordinary observer, more interesting kinds can be mentioned here. As a child were you ever shown such a curious object as "a horse-hair that turned into a worm"? If so, the magic "horsehair" probably was one of the gordian worms (genus *Gordius*) that look almost exactly like a horsehair twisting and turning slowly in the water. Though they may grow to be more than a foot in length, they still keep their hairlike appearance.

The most notable as well as the most pestiferous of the worm group in fresh water are the leeches encountered by waders or swimmers in lakes, ponds, or streams. Or even suburban swimming pools! Of these undesirables we may find the Common Leech (*Macrobdella decora*) and the European Medicinal Leech (*Hirudo medicinalis*) that was brought from Europe for medicinal purposes and has become established in the New York City region. These leeches will attack horses, cows, or other wading animals as well as humans. The Common Leech is a rather attractive creature aside from its annoying method of making a living by sucking blood. It has a flattish shape, grows to a length of 3 to 6 inches, is reddish orange on the underside, and its greenish topside shows a row of red dots down the middle and a row of smaller black dots along each side. A colorful combination, you might say. The European Medicinal Leech is less colorful in appearance. It grows to a length of about 4 inches and has a series of brown stripes running the length of its greenish upper surface.

There are other local leeches that specialize in attacking fish, amphibians, and reptiles. Turtles and frogs are common victims and in the Van Cortlandt swamp you frequently will find small green-and-yellow Turtle Leeches (*Placobdella parasitica*) around the tail areas of the handsome Eastern Painted Turtles and the ugly Snapping Turtles so numerous there. But it would be sheer luck if we found any one of these leeches in our glass of water dipped from the swamp stream. Leeches are the clinging type. They cling to their victims while feeding and they cling to stones, plants, or submerged timber while resting. However, they swim about while foraging and sometimes they occur in regular swarms in pools, ponds, and slow streams, so it's just possible that we might scoop one up by dipping a cup or a glass in the swamp stream at the right time and place. You never know what you are going to come up with when you dip in such waters.

Of one thing you may be sure: you will have a plentiful supply of tiny active crustaceans to view through your magnifying glass. There will be seemingly fierce little carrot-shaped copepods — probably *Cyclops viridis* about 2 mm. in length, one of the most abundant species — darting about jerkily as they seek and swallow invisible food. If you focus carefully you will be able to see their antennae curling back from the mouth region to give them a bewhiskered appearance. And if you think you see one with a wide dark tail split into two sections, take another look. The true hairlike "tail assembly" extends beyond the darker objects that identify the individual as a female with egg masses glued to either side of the body just forward of the tail.

Of the water fleas (Cladocera) you may have the *Daphnia longispina*, which is about the same size as the *Cyclops viridis* but of quite a different shape. At first glance it may look like a tiny bean moving about rapidly in the water but soon you will note the waving antennae on the hunched-over head and a stiff projecting tail, from which it derives its specific name of *longispina*. It is almost certain that you will have dozens of ostracods of the genus *Cypris* in your glass of water, too. About the same size as the water fleas and copepods just mentioned, they look like tiny clams whose hinged half shells open and close rapidly in the act of engulfing food. Ordinarily they are fairly quiet and often feed on the bottom in shallow water, but if you shake your glass gently you will stir the *Cypris* captives to a brisk exhibition of free swimming.

You may have to dip your glass several times to come up with any of the fresh-water relatives of the sand fleas of the ocean beaches. The scientists call them Amphipoda but fishermen along the streams call them "scuds" or "fresh-water shrimp" because they look like small shrimp. The best way to collect them is to run a dipping net through the mosses, algae colonies, or other plant growths in the water. One species that is common in the area bears the colorful name of *Hyalella knickerbockeri*, but is a colorless creature about a half inch long with a "face" like a tiny hippopotamus. Another common species is *Gammerius fasciatus*, which may be an inch in length. If you drag the net lightly along the bottom you are bound to trap fresh-water sow bugs of the common kind named *Asellus militaris*. These are oval creatures about a half inch long with seven pairs of legs and a formidable-looking pair of widespread antennae out front. Most of its relatives are salt-water addicts but if you climb the bank above the swamp and turn over a good-sized flat stone or move a log or old plank that has been lying on the ground for a year or so you may find some land-going sow bugs — *Oniscus asellus* or some other common species — of somewhat similar appearance but broader across the back. These solid-ground sow bugs look even less like Crustacea than the ones in the nearby water and it's hard to believe, on sight, that they are in the same class with the large and luscious lobster.

However, our swamp and adjacent lake can produce Crustacea that do look the part in a small way in the form of cray-fish (colloquially spelled and pronounced "crawfish"). These

creatures do look like lobsters in miniature. These are the largest of our fresh-water crustaceans, but a good-sized specimen would be only 3 or 4 inches in length. You may find them under stones in brooks or streams or in tunnels along the banks of ponds and lakes. The most common species of our region is *Cambarus bartoni* that grows to a length of about 3 inches and has a smooth carapace, or upper shell, at the forward end. A slightly larger species said to be in the vicinity — I have only a hearsay acquaintance with it — is the Spiny Crayfish (*Cambarus limosus*), the common name deriving from sharp little projections on its carapace. In a few places along the streams and lakes you may find little mud cylinders an inch or so in height that have been erected by the Chimney Crayfish (*Cambarus diogenes*) living below in flooded chambers. At one time there was quite a colony of them at the northeast corner of Van Cortlandt Lake; some of them had the temerity to tunnel up into the fairway of the municipal golf course that fringes the lake at that point.

In, on, and around the city ponds and streams you will find water mites of one kind or another. These are tiny aquatic members of the Class Arachnoidea, which means spiders for the most part. Water mites look like mere red specks drifting about in the water or moving slowly over the leaves of aquatic plants. The largest local species, *Hydrachna geographica*, is only ⅓ inch in length. However, all these tiny creatures have the eight legs of the spider class and though they spend most of their lives in the water in search of animal food of all kinds they are air-breathing like all the Arachnoidea and have to come up for a fresh supply from time to time.

Insects require a full chapter by themselves but at this point they must be mentioned in passing because there are so many kinds that live in or on fresh water all their lives and so many others that are fresh-water inhabitants in the larval or nymphal stage. The first group — those living in or on the water all their lives — would include the water beetles, water striders, water boatmen, back swimmers, whirligig beetles, and many others. The second group — those spending their younger days in the water — would include such notable flying insects as dragonflies, mayflies, damselflies, and "true flies," or Diptera, such as gnats, midges, mosquitoes, and flies of innumerable kinds.

We can start with some insects that spend practically all of their lives actually in or on the water. Of these the two kinds most common and most easily observed in our region are the whirligig beetles (Gyrinidae) and the water striders (Gerridae). They are abundant on the placid surface of Van Cortlandt Lake and all the other lakes, ponds, and slow streams in the area. You will even find them on the quiet pools and the back-water patches of rocky brooks. They are well and truly named. Whirligig beetles are small, dark, oval-shaped creatures usually seen rushing around apparently aimlessly in more or less compact groups like milling citizens in a Shakespearean mob scene. It almost seems as though some miniature Mark Antony had stirred them to riot over the assassination of a six-legged, armor-plated little Caesar and the instructions were: "About, — seek, — burn, — fire, — kill, — slay, — let not a traitor live!"

Even so, if you attempt to scoop up a few with your hand or with a dipper, you will discover that their movements are by no means as aimless as they seem to be. They dodge most expertly. They feed in their own style of hunting in packs for tiny animal life in the water and, if you watch closely, you will notice that there is a considerable amount of diving in the process. When diving, they carry a bubble of air down with them under their wing covers. It takes an entomologist to sort out the different species but you may see with the naked eye that they come in two sizes. The larger ones, up to a half inch or so in length, probably belong to the genus *Dineutes*. The smaller ones, little more than half the size of the larger kind, probably belong to the genus *Gyrinus*. All of the adults have wings and can fly, but they rarely do.

The water striders in action look more like water skaters in the way they glide over the surface so smoothly. In fact, they are called "water skaters" in some sections of the country. In general appearance a water strider looks something like a small, seagoing "daddy longlegs." The resemblance, to be sure, is strictly superficial and even there it fails if you count the legs. Like all spiders, the Harvestman Spider (*Liobunum vittata*), the one we commonly call a "daddy longlegs," has eight legs whereas the water striders, as insects, are restricted to six. In both cases, however, the creatures seem to be "all legs." The narrow bodies of the water striders of our area are a half inch or less in length but four of their six legs are about twice that length. The feet at the ends of the widespread legs make dimples on the surface of the water as the insects dart hither and yon rapidly in search of food. If the sun is shining and the water is clear and shallow, these dimples cast comparatively large round shadows on the bottom and quite often the moving shadows catch the eye before the water striders themselves are noticed.

Below the surface in the same lakes, ponds, streams, and brooks of our region you may see back swimmers (Notonectidae) and water boatmen (Corixidae), dark, roundish insects of a half inch or less in length. There are many and, to all except the experts, confusing species, but it's a simple matter to distinguish the back swimmers from the water boatmen. Both groups use their hind legs as oars in propelling themselves through the water, but in the back swimmers these legs so predominate over the others that a back swimmer resembles a "single sculls" oarsman, whereas the middle legs of the water boatmen, though used for grasping and not for swimming, are about the same size as the hind legs and thus a water boatman looks like a tiny "double sculls" racing shell in submarine operation. The back swimmers came by that name through the fact that they swim with their backs downward. They also hang head downward from the surface of the water when at rest or when replenishing their supply of air, which they do with their tails sticking up through the surface, though they do not actually breathe through their tails.

Larger insect inhabitants of these same waters are the giant water bugs (Belostomatidae), which, like the water boatmen and the water striders, are "true bugs" of the Order Hemiptera, and the diving beetles (Dytiscidae) and water-scavenger

Diving beetle (Dytiscus) *attacking immature frog*

beetles (Hydrophilidae) that belong in the "hard shell" Order Coleoptera. The adult water-scavenger beetles are said to be vegetarian but the adult giant water bugs and diving beetles feed on worms, tadpoles, mosquito larvae, small fish, and almost anything else they can catch. The larvae of all three will eat anything they can capture, including one another. In fact, the larvae of the diving beetles are called "water tigers" because of their seeming ferocity in attacking other creatures in the water with them. There are species in which the larvae grow to be more than 2 inches in length but the more common kind are only a half inch to an inch in length. Even so, they are fearsome little creatures that look like spindly-legged dragons and the sudden way they rush at their prey makes a capture seem like an assassination.

The adult giant water bugs, diving beetles, and water-scavenger beetles do all their feeding in the water. All of them can fly but the giant water bugs are the only ones that commonly take to the air and, in that different medium, most persons who see them hovering around bright lights at night call them "electric-light bugs." Some are 1½ inches or more in length. The diving beetles and water-scavenger beetles come in different sizes, depending upon the species, but only a few, comparatively, are over an inch in length.

These are just a scattering of the more common kinds of insects that are aquatic in habit and easy to find in fresh water in the New York City area. Beyond that, we have to face the fact that these same waters contain untold numbers of larvae or nymphs of other insects that we ordinarily think of as airborne creatures such as dragonflies and damselflies (Odonata), mayflies (Ephemeroptera), stoneflies (Plecoptera), alder-flies, fishflies, and dobson-flies (Megaloptera), and others of smaller size and less importance. Lest the reader be confused as to the difference between insect larvae and insect nymphs, it should be stated that nymphs are insect young whose eventual wings develop externally and whose youthful shape usually bears some resemblance, though wingless, to that of the adult. In the life cycle of insects this method of development is called "incomplete metamorphosis." Where the young bear no resemblance in shape or form to the adult, do not develop wings externally, and go through a comatose pupal state — like a caterpillar that wraps itself in a cocoon — to become an adult, they are designated "larvae" and the method of development is called "complete metamorphosis."

But whether they are larvae or nymphs, there abound in the fresh waters of the five boroughs of the city countless millions of insect young of hundreds of species. In one species the young in the water are better known than the flying adults. These are the "hellgrammites," so popular with fishermen as bait for bass. They look something like multilegged caterpillars 2 to 3 inches long, but they are the larvae of the Dobson-fly (*Corydalis cornuta*) that hatch out of round white egg masses stuck on the side of rocks, drop into the water, and spend almost three years there before they emerge to "pupate" on the streambank for a month or so before they take to the air as adult Dobson-flies. You can find them in the hellgrammite stage under stones in running water.

Those hyphenated or compound "flies" such as the dobson-flies, alder-flies, fish-flies, stoneflies, damselflies, and dragonflies — these last being the "darning needles" of the children — are not "true flies." They have four wings. A "true fly" has only two wings and belongs to the Order Diptera. Many of the families of the Order Diptera have aquatic larvae that swarm in fresh-water streams and ponds. Mosquitoes (Culicidae), midges (Chironomidae), and horseflies (Tabanidae) are in that group. Thanks to "mosquito control" measures, the mosquito population of the city has decreased notably in recent years. So has the horsefly population, with the gradual disappearance of horses and cows inside the city limits. But there remain more mosquitoes than are wanted and midges are found in swarms in the swamps and wet woods of the outlying sections of the city on sultry summer evenings, which means that there will be no shortage of their larvae in nearby fresh water for some time to come.

We have merely skimmed the surface of the subject of pond life and the like in our territory but we have been under water for some pages past and, like the insect larvae and nymphs that live long enough, we have to come up for air, sooner or later. This seems a proper time and place.

Chapter 6

An Ample Supply of Insects

To THE OBSERVANT, the world is full of everyday miracles and marvels, few of which are more baffling than the vast numbers, curious shapes, strange habits, and extraordinary life cycles of the insects that inhabit it. More than 650,000 species of insect already have been catalogued by the entomologists and new species are being brought in from week to week to be named and described. They are everywhere — in the air, in the water, in the ground. They are on the outside and the inside of plants and animals — and other insects. They flourish mightily in the woods and fields, but they also swarm in all our cities. New York is inclined to boast of its human population of almost eight million but only occasionally is there any mention of the insect population, to which, in numerical comparison, the human population is just a handful. But before investigating the insects of the area we have to take up another matter too often overlooked, even by many persons interested in the general field of natural history. That's the question of spiders.

Like the crustaceans mentioned in previous chapters, insects, spiders, and certain other invertebrate creatures are included in the great group or Phylum designated Arthropoda, all the inmates of which are distinguished by the possession of sets of jointed legs. There are numerous divisions of the Phylum Arthropoda but only three are important enough to most of us to require attention here. They are the Crustacea, small and great, which have ten legs each; the Arachnoidea or spider-like creatures, which have eight legs each; and the Insecta, all of which have six legs, no more and no less. Just in passing we must cast a glance at the centipedes (Chilopoda) and milli-pedes (Diplopoda), because we often find one particular centipede — the House Centipede (*Scutigera forceps*) — whisking in and out of cracks, crevices, drains, and dark corners of our dwellings and for the further reason that anybody who does any digging, weeding, gardening, or turning over of flat stones with-in the city limit is bound to come upon some such millipede as the wiry *Spirobolus marginatus* that is common throughout our region. These, too, belong among the Arthropoda. They are creatures with jointed legs and segmented bodies and the main difference to the eye (there are other and more important differences to the scientist) is that the centipede never has more

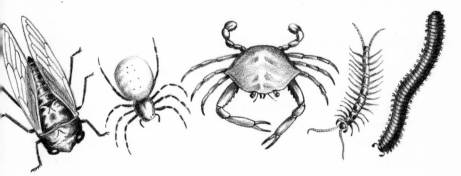

Arthropoda

than one pair of legs to a body segment, whereas a millipede, over all but its terminal sections, has two pairs of legs to a segment. With this brief acknowledgment of the presence of these multilegged creatures as regular residents of our city, we can move with a clear conscience to a more attractive field.

When you come to think of it, spiders are simply wonderful. In the first place, they are remarkable spinners and weavers and in the strength, symmetry, utility, and pure beauty of many of their woven structures they show their worth as architects and engineers. They can spin a silk thread so fine and yet so durable that for ·more than a century it was the standard material for use as cross-hairs in optical instruments. From ancient times cobwebs were used in the art of healing to stop the flow of blood from open wounds. Most spiders are relentless hunters and some are ingenious trappers. Many kinds are balloonists and, without wings, travel long distances by air. Darwin, in his account of his five-year trip on the *Beagle*, tells of ballooning spiders landing on the deck when the ship was sixty miles off the coast of South America, the nearest land, and there are records of much longer flights of these airborne adventurers. Many persons pull back at the sudden sight of a nearby spider and yet, except in self-protection or because its hunting instinct has been triggered by disturbing its web, no spider ordinarily will bite or otherwise harm any man, woman, or child. Spiders are not parasitic on mammals and, so far as is known, no spider is a disease carrier. Their favorite food is insects and they are in the main a help to agriculturalists.

That should be enough to give spiders in general a certificate of good character that too often goes unrecognized. As for the local supply of these talented creatures, it is far greater than we can cope with in these pages. It has been set down by those who know that there are some 600 species of spider in New York State, from which one must conclude that there must be several hundred species, at least, to be found within the city limits. It is even possible that the notorious Black Widow

Spider (*Latrodectus mactans*), which really is not as black as it is painted, might be encountered in the area, since it has been recorded in every one of the forty-eight states, but it is by no means common in the Northeast and the discovery of one in New York City certainly would cause talk and probably some mention of the incident in the *New York Times*.

However, all of us are familiar with spiders of one kind or another. The housewife who takes broom in hand to brush down a spider web in the corner of the ceiling is most likely destroying the home and hunting ground of the most common of house spiders of the temperate regions of the world, an unimpressive creature with the impressive name of *Theridion tepidariorum*. Everywhere we walk in the woods and fields of the outlying sections of the city there will be spiders of different kinds, mostly little ones that are easily overlooked. But everyone must have noticed the silken networks of the group aptly designated "the funnel-web spiders" scattered about on lawns and hedges when, silvered by droplets of dew or mist, they stand out in ghostly contrast to their backgrounds of greenery. The familiar daddy longlegs, by the way, is not a spider but a near relative of the Order Opiliones, in which the body structure appears to the eye to be one solid little mass, whereas in the Araneae, or spider category, there is a visible "narrow waist" between the abdomen and the foreparts. The mites (Acari) and scorpions (Scorpiones) are other relatives of spiders, but they prefer the warmer sections of the United States and New Yorkers on their home ground ordinarily have no truck or traffic with them.

That clears the way for a survey of the insect situation within the city limits and the best way to present the subject, at least by inference or implication, is to give the reader an account of how a book with the title *A Lot of Insects*, written by Frank E. Lutz, came into existence. Dr. Lutz, small, thin, bearded, and bespectacled, was a world authority on insects and for many years the head of the Department of Entomology at the American Museum of Natural History. One day half a century ago, he walked into the office of Dr. Frederick Augustus Lucas, then the director of the museum, and requested an expansion of the entomological staff and quarters, stressing the importance of the subject and mentioning, among other things, that insects far outnumbered all other forms of animal life on earth and should be treated accordingly. Dr. Lutz held forth with spirit but Dr. Lucas did not take offense. In kindly rebuttal to the Lutz oration on the number of insects in the world and their importance to mankind, the director remarked tolerantly that "exaggeration due to enthusiasm is excusable."

At that time Dr. Lutz was living in Ramsey, New Jersey, a residential town within easy commuting distance for those who worked in New York City. When he was at his home in Ramsey, Dr. Lutz was about twenty miles, airline, from his office in the American Museum of Natural History. His house was close to the center of the town, one block from the railroad station and one block off the main street. Behind the house he had a plot of ground 75 by 100 feet that included a few trees, some shrubs, some flowers, some grass, and a small kitchen garden.

To bolster his argument about the importance of insects and the need for larger quarters and more men for the entomological department, Dr. Lutz said boldly to Dr. Lucas, "I'll bet that I can find more than five hundred species of insect in my own backyard in New Jersey."

"Now I know you're exaggerating," said Dr. Lucas with a smile.

"I'll tell you what I'll do," said the persistent entomologist. "If the museum will agree to raise my salary by ten dollars a year for every species above five hundred that I honestly find on my back lot, I'll agree to have my salary reduced by ten dollars a year for every species short of five hundred that I fail to find there."

Dr. Lucas did not accept the offer, thereby saving a considerable amount of money for the museum. To be brief about
it, Dr. Lutz found 1402 species of insect on his 75 by 100 lot
and eventually wrote most entertainingly of the argument and
its result in his book, *A Lot of Insects*. It took time, however,
to produce all those insects and an even longer time to write
the book about them. The author had to do all the field work
and the editorial work on the project on his free time at home.
He had no trouble running up a long list of insects in a few
weeks, but these were common resident species that he knew
were sure to be found on the premises. Collecting the seasonal
or occasional visitors was a longer and more difficult task.
More than nine out of ten species found were native residents
or regular visitors in the area. The rare species were thrilling
to the captor but unimportant in the quest.

The first prize capture in the New Jersey backyard was a
large bee of the Euglossidae family, the first of its kind recorded
north of Mexico or the West Indies. Another good catch was a
large dark moth (*Erebus odora*) with a 4-inch wingspread and a
scalloped light band running through the middle of its wings.
Moths of this species are common in the Gulf States but the
adults can reach the New York–New Jersey latitude only with
the aid of favoring winds. Dr. Lutz had other distinguished
visitors but the importance of his collection lay in the length
of the list of common residents and regular visitors. The importance of the list to anyone interested in the natural history
of New York City is that Dr. Lutz made his collection only
fifteen miles west of New York City territory and that most of
the insects he found on his New Jersey lot might well be found
on a similar plot of ground of the same size in the Bronx, the
Borough of Queens, or on Staten Island.

There is no room for the long list of species that Dr. Lutz collected in his backyard plot in New Jersey but here is a summary
of the number of species of each order that fell into his adept
hands:

Thysanura (Silver-fish)	2
Collembola (Springtails)	1
Plectoptera (Mayflies)	3
Plecoptera (Stoneflies)	6
Odonata (Damselflies and Dragonflies)	10
Orthoptera (Grasshoppers, Crickets)	29
Phasmatodea (Walking-sticks)	1
Dermaptera (Earwigs)	1
Thysanoptera (Thrips)	2
Mantodea (Mantids)	1
Isoptera (Termites)	1
Corrodentia (Bark-lice or Book-lice)	1
Mallophaga (Bird-lice)	7
Anoplura (True Lice)	1
Homoptera (Cicadas, Tree-hoppers, Frog-hoppers, Aphids, etc.)	75
Heteroptera (True Bugs, including Water Boatmen, etc.)	62
Megaloptera (Alder-flies, Fish-flies, Dobson-flies)	2
Neuroptera (Ant-lions, Aphis-lions)	9
Mecoptera (Scorpion-flies)	3
Trichoptera (Caddis-flies)	32
Lepidoptera (Butterflies and Moths)	467
Diptera (True Flies, Gnats, Mosquitoes)	258
Siphonaptera (Fleas)	1
Coleoptera (Beetles)	259
Strepsiptera (Parasitic Beetles)	1
Hymenoptera (Sawflies, Ants, Bees, Wasps, etc.)	<u>167</u>
Total species	1402

Many of the insects captured by Dr. Lutz in his New Jersey backyard were mounted and grouped in special glass cases for exhibition in the American Museum of Natural History, where they still may be seen by those who are interested in local collections. It will be noted that three Orders, the Lepidoptera, Coleoptera, and Diptera, accounted for more than two-thirds of the total species. Most of us would expect that there would be moths, butterflies, and beetles in abundance, but that the Diptera ran to such numbers — 258 species — was a surprise to me as it probably will be to many readers. What the revelation did was to make me take a closer look at the flies I encountered on my walks through the Riverdale and Van Cortlandt fields and woods; I quickly realized what an astonishing assortment there was on hand. Furthermore, I was amazed at what shining little gems of burnished colors some of them turned out to be.

As to the prize captures of Dr. Lutz on New Jersey soil, I had one small triumph myself in my home in Riverdale. I was reading one summer night and was distracted by a small moth fluttering around the light bulb of my lamp. I brought the creature down with a fly swatter and then noticed that its forewings were of a striking pattern. I decided to try to track it down with the aid of the text and plates in W. J. Holland's hefty tome, *The Moth Book*. My victim looked exactly like the colored plate of the moth called *Atteva aurea* but the text had it that this moth was "distributed from the Gulf States southward and westward into Mexico and lands still further south." That seemed to eliminate New York City as a possible place of capture of any individual of that species, so I took the body of the deceased down to the American Museum of Natural History and left it for Dr. Lutz to identify. In due time I received word that it was a genuine *Atteva aurea* and that several others had been reported in the area. Dr. Lutz said that he didn't know how they had reached New York but suggested that they might have come by water or rail in fruit shipments from the tropics, possibly in banana boats from Central America.

Moths, to be sure, are overwhelmingly numerous in most temperate and tropical regions of the world. Dr. Lutz captured 432 species on his home ground in New Jersey and in his *Field Book of Insects* he stated of the Noctuidae alone: "We have about 2500 of this family in the United States." Apropos of this night-flying family, Dr. Holland, in *The Moth Book*, has a short and lively chapter on "Sugaring for Moths" in the dark of night with a bait of four pounds of sugar wetted down with beer and rum, the odd mixture being smeared on convenient tree trunks and stumps. He recounts the capture of some thirty species of moth that came to this odorous lure before a thunderstorm arrived to shatter the warm silence of a moonless night. But presumably that was in Pennsylvania, which was Dr. Holland's home territory. However, with similar bait and skill in hunting, the public parks and the outlying sections of New York City can still provide a notable assortment of moths that go about their business under cover of darkness. There are, for example, some thirty-odd species of the genus *Catocala*, the underwings, whose name is due to the fact that the hind wings, which are covered by the mottled gray-brown front wings when at rest, are spectacularly banded with black and either crimson, pink, orange, yellow, or white, truly a striking pattern when exposed.

Once again in our survey of the resources of New York City we have come upon an embarrassment of riches. The moths are too many for us. We have to take them as a pawn sometimes takes another pawn at chess, *en passant*. But the area has a bewildering supply of them, including the huge Cecropia Moth (*Samia cecropia*), the great pale Luna Moth (*Actias luna*), the numerous hawkmoths that many persons mistake for humming-birds around their dooryard flowers in the dusk, and many other moths, large and small, beautiful and plain, that only an entomologist could know and name.

We can, however, give more attention to the Lutz list of butterfly visitors on his lot for the simple reason that almost everybody takes note of the butterflies fluttering about the fields and gardens in the warmer months and can recognize at least a few common species. Another point is that Dr. Lutz found only 35 species on his premises and any or all of them, and other species to boot, might be found of a summer day in the public parks or the lawns, gardens, woods, or swamps of the more open residential sections

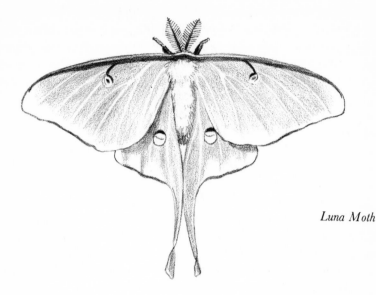

Luna Moth

of New York City. Here is the Lutz list with, where needed, some of the older names changed to conform with Klots (*A Field Guide to the Butterflies*):

1. Monarch (*Danaus plexippus* Linnaeus)
2. Regal Fritillary (*Speyeria idalia* Drury)
3. Great Spangled Fritillary (*Speyeria cybele* Fabricius)
4. Aphrodite Fritillary (*Speyeria aphrodite* Fabricius)
5. Silvery Checkerspot (*Melitaea nycteis* Doubleday)
6. Pearl Crescent (*Phyciodes tharos* Drury)
7. Baltimore (*Euphydryas phaeton* Drury)
8. Question Mark (*Polygonia interrogationis* Fabricius)
9. Hop Merchant or Comma (*Polygonia comma* Harris)
10. Mourning Cloak (*Nymphalis antiopa* Linnaeus)
11. Red Admiral (*Vanessa atalanta* Linnaeus)
12. American Painted Lady (*Vanessa virginiensis* Drury)
13. Buckeye (*Precis lavinia* Cramer)

14. Red-spotted Purple (*Limenitis arthemis astyanax* Fabricius)
15. Viceroy (*Limenitis archippus* Cramer)
16. Eyed Brown (*Lethe eurydice* Johannson)
17. Little Wood Satyr (*Euptychia cymela* Cramer)
18. Gray Hairstreak (*Strymon melinus* Huebner)
19. American Copper (*Lycaena phlaeas americana* Harris)
20. Spring Azure (*Lycaenopsis argiolus* Linnaeus)
21. Eastern Tailed Blue (*Everes comyntas* Godart)
22. European Cabbage Butterfly (*Pieris rapae* Linnaeus)
23. Common Sulphur (*Colias philodice* Latreille)
24. Black Swallowtail (*Papilio polyxenes asterius* Stoll)
25. Spicebush Swallowtail (*Papilio troilus* Linnaeus)
26. Tiger Swallowtail (*Papilio glaucus* Linnaeus)
27. Least Skipper (*Ancyloxipha numitor* Fabricius)
28. Indian Skipper (*Hesperia sassacus* Harris)
29. Leonardus Skipper (*Hesperia leonardus* Harris)
30. Hobomok Skipper (*Poanes hobomok* Harris)
31. Peck's Skipper (*Polites peckius* Kirby)
32. Tawny-edged Skipper (*Polites themistocles* Latreille)
33. Dun Skipper (*Atrytone ruricola* Boisduval)
34. Common Sooty Wing (*Pholisora catullus* Fabricius)
35. Silver-spotted Skipper (*Epargyreus clarus* Cramer)

There isn't a really rare butterfly on this Lutz list and the eminent entomologist missed some ordinary ones like the Painted Lady (*Vanessa cardui* Linnaeus) and the Little Sulphur (*Eurema lisa* Boisduval) found regularly on Staten Island and in the Bronx. Also, the Lutz list includes only nine skippers, whereas, away back in the Gay Nineties, another collector and earlier Curator of Insects at the American Museum of Natural History, William Beutenmueller, found nineteen species of skipper within fifty miles of New York City and, more recently, Dr. Alexander B. Klots, in his *Field Guide to the Butterflies*, included some thirty-odd skippers that might be encountered in the New York City area.

Though Dr. Lutz did not find it on his New Jersey premises,

the lovely Luna Moth is now and then a victim of the bright lights of Broadway, but more often it is discovered fluttering around less dazzling lights in the outlying residential sections of the city. In an American Museum of Natural History leaflet of long ago,* Beutenmueller listed 45 species of hawkmoths and 2 subspecies for the New York City region. Of these he wrote that 16 species were common, 11 uncommon, and 20 rare. Dr. Lutz noted only 10 species of hawkmoths on his property. Atop some of the tall structures of Manhattan — hotels, apartment houses, and even office buildings — there are penthouses boasting flower boxes or even little flower gardens and somehow, over the encircling expanse of steel, concrete and asphalt, there are hawkmoths that find the way to such lures on summer evenings. For the tenants of these swanky residences, this is probably the only special feature that comes free of charge.

As for all those other kinds of insects that Dr. Lutz came upon in his New Jersey lot, the majority may be found just as easily in one section or another of New York City. For instance, the Chinese Praying Mantis (*Tenodera sinensis*) that invaded Dr. Lutz's garden is common in the open areas of the city and its gray-coated, hive-shaped egg masses attached to twigs often are found by strollers when autumn has stripped the shrubbery of its leaves. A few years ago the owner of a delicatessen store on Riverdale Avenue near 238th Street found an egg mass in the vicinity and, not knowing what it was, brought it into his warm kitchen and put it on a shelf. Some time later he was startled to find his shelf crawling with young mantids. One late afternoon in summer, seated in a commuter train in Grand Central Station, I heard a commotion and looked up from the newspaper I was reading. The woman in the seat ahead of me was much upset by the sudden discovery that there was a Praying Mantis on the shoulder of her jacket. To her great relief, I removed it from its perch and wrapped

*Vol. 3, No. 2 (1903).

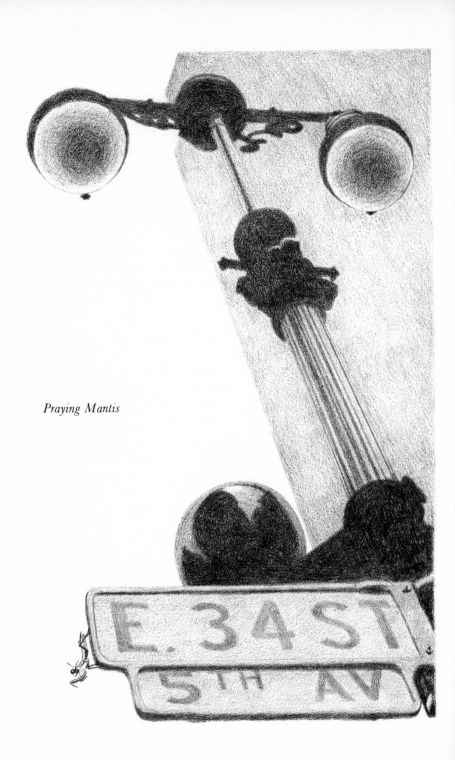

Praying Mantis

it loosely in a handkerchief for transportation to a more appropriate feeding ground.

These fierce-looking insects are really harmless to everything except the other insects on which they feed. Incidentally, the Eastern Walking-stick (*Diapheromera femorata*), of equally curious appearance, is also a more or less common resident of the city but is rarely noticed by the human residents of the region, whereas the Praying Mantis often "breaks into the newspapers." One reason why the Mantis draws more attention is that it has wings and often may be seen in somewhat labored flight like an overloaded miniature helicopter. The Walking-stick has no wings, looks almost exactly like a twig, and moves very slowly along twigs and small branches of shrubbery in search of food. Still another point is that the egg masses of the mantids betray their presence in any area whereas the Walking-stick leaves no telltale egg masses as evidence of its residence in any region. It drops its eggs one by one to the ground as it moves about. A Walking-stick starts out in life alone.

The Hymenoptera — sawflies, ants, bees, and wasps — are well represented in all the boroughs of the city. The Honey Bees (*Apis mellifera*) build their hives and hang their combs in the hollows of trees or other available quarters and occasionally have group pictures taken for newspaper publication when they swarm in public places. One such swarming group was photographed clinging to a NO PARKING sign on Dyckman Street and broke into print in the *Daily News*. Another swarming group gathered just above the sidewalk on the front of an apartment house on Washington Heights. One June day a man parked his car at 31st Street and Thomson Avenue, Long Island City, and when he came back to his car he found a swarm of bees draped from the handle of the right front door. A similar gathering on a low branch of a Carolina Poplar at 238th Street just off Broadway brought the police and a feature story on the front page of the second section of the *New York*

Times of Saturday, May 29, 1954. The big bundle of buzzing bees alarmed the housewives of the neighborhood, who feared for themselves and their children. One of the policemen called to quell the disturbance retained presence of mind enough to summon an old friend, a former policeman who lived in nearby Riverdale and kept a few hives of bees. He arrived quickly and cheerfully made off with the swarm that he lodged temporarily in a large cardboard box, for this was May and he had made a good haul according to the ancient doggerel:

> *A swarm of bees in May is worth a load of hay.*
> *A swarm of bees in June is worth a silver spoon.*
> *A swarm of bees in July isn't worth a fly.*

Other kinds of bees are numerous in the area, and so are hornets and wasps and their relatives, among them the comparatively huge Cicada-killer (*Sphecius speciosus*) that stings its prey into a coma-like state and carries it into an underground burial plot to serve as food for the larval wasp later emerging from an egg laid on a leg of the paralyzed victim. I found a whole colony of burrows of these big wasps along the right of way, and even between the ties, of the Putnam Division railroad tracks beside the Van Cortlandt swamp. Where there are Cicada-killers there must be cicadas, or "Othello's occupation's gone" and the play is ended. This is a continuous performance that goes on from year to year. There are always cicadas in and around the city but we have fallen into the error of calling them "locusts," a term more properly applied to short-horned grasshoppers. The common "locust" of our territory is *Tibicen sayi* whose shrill, wiry, buzzy drone — the "song" of the male produced by vibrating membranes on each side of the abdomen of the insect — is a characteristic sound of a warm and windless summer day. Another notable resident of the area is the famous Seventeen-year Locust (*Magicicada septemdecim*), the cicada that spends from thirteen to seventeen years in a wingless condition underground and then emerges to shed its nymph casing and spread new-found wings in a brief life, a week or two, as a flying adult.

Here we must include honorable mention of a delightful gentleman whose name and fame have been perpetuated in the establishment of the William T. Davis Wildlife Refuge on his native Staten Island. Dr. Davis was the self-appointed biographer of all the broods of the Seventeen-year Locust (there are different broods with different periodic cycles) in the New York area. He had their breeding locations charted and tried to be on hand at the time and place when the particular brood known to be in that location was due to emerge from the ground and take wing. When I came to know him and was invited to go on one of these expeditions with him and Edwin Way Teale, Dr. Davis was a small, thin, and jaunty octogenarian still filled with endless enthusiasm for his subject, which was natural history in general and entomology in particular. On this occasion it was Brood No. 1 we were after. When we arrived on the breeding ground on Long Island we found that the insects had the start of us. All we heard was the high, thin, trilling song of one lone Seventeen-year Locust, apparently the last singer of a departed choir, for the cicadas had come out of the ground and gone their separate ways. We found the evidence in some sixty-odd empty and transparent brown nymph casings left clinging to the trunks and branches of old apple trees in a neglected orchard nearby.

It was too bad that we were tardy and missed the main performance by Brood No. 1, because it was near the end of the trail for "the Cicada Man," as Dr. Davis was called. He died the following January (1945) in his eighty-third year. He left many notebooks filled with keen observations on natural history and one little gem of a book, *Days Afield on Staten Island*. In one notebook he had set down the following: "There is no need of a faraway fairyland, for earth is a mystery before us. The cow paths lead to mysterious fields."

A sound observation. On every hand, in the city as well as in the country, we see things in nature that baffle us. On a morning walk along a shady road in Riverdale one summer day I happened to see a long-legged, thin-bodied, clear-winged insect seemingly at rest on a dead log. I paused for a closer look and found it to be one of the ichneumon wasps — this one later identified as *Megarhyssa lunator* — in the act of depositing eggs, a truly remarkable operation and well worth watching if you ever have the chance to see it. These wasps are parasitic, chiefly on the wood-boring larvae of other insects, and though they are large and look dangerous, they are harmless to humans and helpful to trees. With their long needle-shaped ovipositors they drill into a log or the trunk of a tree and deposit their eggs in the tunnels made by wood-boring larvae. When the eggs hatch, the larvae of the ichneumon wasps track down the tunnel-builders and literally make themselves at home in the bodies of their victims that eventually die as a result of the intrusion.

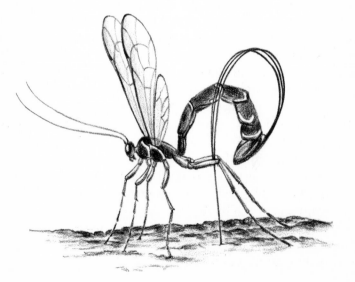

The adult female I saw this summer day had curled its abdomen into an upraised loop with the hind end pointing directly downward and apparently operating the long thin ovipositor that somehow was finding its way into the log. The drilling must have reached the right spot while I was watching because suddenly, where the abdomen and ovipositor were joined, there appeared a blue-gray patch that swelled rearward and upward until it was about the size and shape of a dime. To the entomologist who named the species it must have resembled a tiny silver moon and thus he ticketed the wasp with the specific designation of *lunator.* I took it that the phenomenon was related to the problem of forcing the eggs down the ovipositor and into the tunnel below in the log. I have forgotten how long I stood watching, but eventually the blue-gray circlet went back where it came from in the dark brown abdomen of the insect, the ovipositor was drawn out of the log; the wasp flew off slowly with legs and ovipositor dangling, and I went my way wondering how such things could be.

Less distinguished but more abundant insects in the open spaces of the city are the Common Cricket (*Gryllus assimilis*) and the familiar Katydid (*Pterophylla camellifolia*), which begin to tune up in August and then orchestrate the cooler September nights at a more leisurely pace as their tempo drops with the temperature. To the entomologist the Katydid is one of the long-horned grasshoppers and, as such, has several dozen quite common relatives throughout the area.

Dr. Lutz listed only ten species of damselflies and dragonflies as visitors to his garden. He had no pool of any size to attract a wider assortment. The quiet ponds of Staten Island and the Bronx offer a better display of these insistent hunters and remarkable aerial acrobats. Often I sat for hours on the railroad embankment along the Van Cortlandt swamp and watched the swoops and dazzling dashes of dragonflies and damselflies of many different kinds. They came in a bewildering variety of body coloring and wing pattern and some were jewel-like in their iridescence when the sunlight struck their body segments as they rested on plant stems or leaves above the water. The dragonflies are perhaps the strongest fliers of the insect world. On the average they run larger than the damselflies but apart from size there is another easy way to distinguish one group from the other. Dragonflies cannot fold their wings. When at rest their wings are held out stiffly in the same plane as that used in their vibratory flights but damselflies when resting fold their long thin wings back along their bodies. In some cases the abdomens of dragonflies are so thin that, in flight at least, the middle segments are visible only at very close range and to the onlooker at any distance the impression is that of an insect somehow flying in two separate sections like an airplane with a target in tow.

Dragonflies and damselflies are beneficial as well as beautiful and feed largely on the Diptera group, insects that most of us look upon with disapproval under the common names of gnats, midges, flies, and mosquitoes. There are more than 10,000 species of Diptera, or two-winged insects, in North America, and although Dr. Lutz found 258 species in his garden only about a dozen species come to the attention of the ordinary citizen or have any serious effect on the comfort, health, or household economy of the city residents of today. It was not always so.

All we have to do to realize the change in conditions is to look back to the post-Revolutionary period, when the rapid increase in population outran the possibility of ordinary, sensible sanitary regulations. In many sections of the city of those days the housing was wretched, the water supply inadequate and contaminated, the sewage system rudimentary, and the problem of garbage disposal left to the householder, who often merely tossed it out the front door or emptied it into the backyard, where further disposal or dispersal was attended to by roaming pigs, dogs, cats, rats, mice, various birds, many insects, and the ravages of time. The result was a ghastly series of deadly epidemics of yellow fever, cholera, typhoid, and other ills the flesh is heir to, with a death toll that was appalling.

You can well understand the part played by common household insects under such conditions. Adults and larvae, by one method or another, were carriers of disease. Of such insects the most abundant and pestiferous probably was the common Housefly (*Musca domestica*), but other important contributors undoubtedly were — not necessarily in order of effectiveness — the assortment of fleas that afflicted dogs, cats, rats, mice, and men. Other offenders were the Common Cockroach (*Blatta orientalis*), the Croton Bug (*Blattella germanica*), the notorious Bedbug (*Cimex lectularius*), and that evasive little insect hunted over the heads of children by mothers armed with fine-toothed combs, the Head Louse (*Pediculus capitis*).

This doesn't take into account some of the insects more readily encountered outdoors, such as the midges and mosquitoes, which must have played at least a minor part in the disease-spreading program of those old days; but we shall come back to one of the mosquitoes in a villainous role later on. As for those indicated in the previous paragraph, their relative importance as domestic afflictions and spreaders of disease has decreased greatly in the past century thanks to the installation of an admirable water-supply system and better sanitary arrangements in every way. There is also the matter of the erection of brick, stone, and reinforced-concrete buildings fronting on paved streets over a vast area. The metal and plastic house furnishings and kitchen equipment of the modern home offer no such comfortable breeding grounds for insects as did the old-style wooden furnishings. The bed with a metal frame supporting a mattress with a plastic cover affords little hiding place for *Cimex lectularius*. For the most part, and certainly as disease carriers, the insects so abundant and so deadly in old New York are now relatively scarce and harmless.

However, they do persist and should be recognized as legal

Mosquito, Croton Bug, Head Louse, Cockroach, Bedbug, and House Fly

and regular residents of the area. They must be mentioned in this book even if they are omitted from the *Social Register*. There even are some authorities who have an occasional good word for one or more of them. Writing of the cockroach in the *Encyclopaedia Britannica*,* the British entomologist A. D. Imms, M.A., D.Sc., ended his article with these words: "Although these insects are usually viewed with disgust they are not devoid of interest. They rank as the most primitive of all winged insects and are among the oldest of all the fossil forms of those animals. Their generalized structure and large size render them convenient objects for laboratory dissection and they are universally adopted as the most suitable type for commencing the scientific study of insects."

That definitely gives the cockroach scientific standing and
*Fourteenth Edition, Vol. V, p. 945.

perhaps Dr. Lutz intended to give the bedbug some social standing when he wrote in his *Field Book of Insects* (page 97): "Before the days of fumigation the bedbug was much given to going down to the sea in ships and almost certainly it came to America with our best families in the *Mayflower*." As for the lowly louse, it was Shakespeare who put these words in the mouth of Sir Hugh Evans in *The Merry Wives of Windsor* (Act I, Scene 1): "The dozen white louses do become an old coat well. It agrees well passant. It is a familiar beast to man and signifies love." There is, of course, the immortal verse of Robert Burns on the same subject, though the lines are not entirely laudatory.

The nearest thing to a kind word for mosquitoes that I could find in literature was a propitiatory plea in rhyme by William Cullen Bryant — then editor of the New York *Evening Post* — who begged one of the buzzing insects to let a gaunt poet alone and go bite somebody else, preferably a plump alderman. Bryant saluted his mosquito as a stranger in town — "Thou com'st from Jersey meadows, broad and green" — but there are some half-dozen species of mosquito breeding within our city limits. Probably the most abundant species is the *Aedes solicitens* of the salt marshes that sometimes swarms in almost incredible numbers around anyone who invades the marshes in August; but for many years the most pestiferous of the mosquito group in the region was the *Anopheles quadrimaculatus*, whose specific name is due to the four small black blotches on each wing.

In almost all of the 1500 or more known species of mosquito only the females try to draw blood, the males being content to live on plant juices. The *Anopheles* female is noted as a carrier of malaria, a disease that was a real scourge in New York City until comparatively recent times, when the United States Government, with local approval and some local aid, undertook an extensive program of mosquito control. One of the procedures was ditching or draining natural breeding areas and putting an oil film on the water. The eggs are laid in water and the young in the larval or pupal stage come to the surface for air. The oil film prevents them from getting air, and that's the end of them.

But adults and young flourished unchecked for the better part of a century. In my childhood days we were dosed daily with quinine. Every morning, before we had a bite of breakfast, a big jug of brown and bitter-tasting liquid called "Warburg's Tincture of Quinine" was brought out from the dining room closet. Each had to swallow about an ounce of the stuff from a small glass as a preventive. Despite this daily dosage, we all suffered considerably from recurrent malaria, and so did most of our neighbors. The Jerome Reservoir nearby was under construction at the time and the extensive excavation was dotted with little pools of stagnant water that were wonderful breeding places for *Anopheles quadrimaculatus*, for which reason the species increased and multiplied at an appalling rate and the ravages of "chills and fever" on alternating days made life miserable for men, women, and children — particularly the children — through all the warm months of the year. Happily, those days are over and malaria is no longer a health problem in the city.

Within the memory of middle-aged residents of the city there was an insect invasion in force. The intruder was the Green Japanese Beetle (*Popillia japonica*), which was first noted in the area in 1916. It was suspected that it had arrived in this country in a shipment of oriental plants for gardens and had slipped through Customs unnoticed. Within five years it became a positive pest and remained so for almost twenty years, with the adults in vast numbers munching on all sorts of leaves, flowers, and fruits and the larvae fattening on plant life at the grassroot level. Just as certain diseases sometimes lead to the production of protective "antibodies" in the human bloodstream, insect pests by their abundance sometimes open a road to their own destruction or, at least, abatement. In this case the untold thousands of Japanese Beetle larvae in the soil drew the

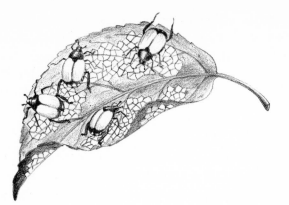

attention of ground-feeding birds to this new source of food and soon some species were gobbling up the larvae with relish and looking for more.   One species of bird credited with a major share in this attack on the Japanese Beetle battalions is the Starling that, until this sign of a useful life, was regarded as something of an imported nuisance itself.   The work of the birds — and possibly some insect parasites, too — stemmed the tide; the little beetles that had carried all before them began to lose ground.   Gradually the glass or metal Japanese Beetle traps installed on every little lawn and in every little garden within the city limits were taken up and put away as no longer needed.   The little beetle persists in the region but it no longer runs riot through the greenery.

The most important limiting factors in any kind of life cycle are twofold: food supply and rate of reproduction.   It was the reproduction rate that was checked in the case of the Green Japanese Beetle.   But in the case of the horseflies and many other Diptera that swarmed around stables and manure piles in the horse-and-buggy days of New York City, it was the food supply that dwindled away to practically nothing when the horses, retreating before the onrushing autos, vanished from the city streets.   Except for the few that draw the ancient barouches, landaus, and victorias — museum pieces in themselves — and stand in line at the 59th Street Plaza or carry the tourist trade cloppity-clop through Central Park and a smattering of smart cobs exposed to view under riders on the bridle path in the park, a horse is a rare sight in Manhattan today. A few honest and hard-working horses still may be seen on Staten Island or on the outskirts of Queens and the Bronx.

However, if the horseflies have dropped almost to the vanishing point along with the horse, there are other insects that have increased with the growth of the human population of the city. The greater the population of a given area, the more food, clothing, and other necessities must be kept in the immediate vicinity for ready delivery. Whether stored in warehouses, grocery stores, hotels, or private houses, such supplies are subject to attacks of insects willing to eat almost any kind of animal or vegetable matter and known to have attacked rubber bath mats, the insulation around electric wiring, and other such dainties. The books in all the libraries in the city must be protected against real and not metaphorical "bookworms." In his *Field Book of Insects* (page 326) Dr. Lutz tells of a particular bookworm named the Spider Beetle (*Ptinus fur*) that, only 1/5 inch in length itself, was charged with eating its way through a row of "twenty-seven large quarto volumes in so straight a line that a string could be passed through the opening and the whole series of volumes suspended."

The ironical part of insect life in a big city is that when the different species, large and small, are gathered and preserved for display or study in some such place as the American Museum of Natural History, they are there subject to attack by the aptly named Museum Beetle (*Anthrenus museorum*), though it must be confessed that the Museum Beetle is also found in less scholarly surroundings and will eat dried insects wherever it comes upon them. This little pest is a member of the Dermestidae family, a group not at all welcome in the home or business office. Four members of the family are known as

"carpet beetles," but the destruction of carpets is only one of
the many accomplishments of which they are capable during
their life cycles. The adults are comparatively harmless; the
larvae, on fairly good evidence, will eat almost anything and
everything.

The species that has given the most trouble because of its
widespread activities in city houses and offices in recent years
is the Black Carpet Beetle (*Attagenus piceus*). Like the others, it
is small (1/8 to 1/5 inch in length) and easily overlooked until
it has set up housekeeping and produced larvae whose destructive work catches the eye. Then the young may be captured
in flagrante delicto where they are munching on carpets, clothing,
upholstery, or whatever else they find to their taste; but the
adults tuck themselves away in cracks or chinks in the floor,
the walls, the framework of furniture, and such places and are
in a position to lay more eggs, which means further trouble
later. It is quite a difficult and often expensive matter to eject
these beetles from an apartment house or an office building in
which they have gained a foothold.

To the housewife, whether in the city or in the country, one
of the worst of insect pests is the familiar "clothes moth."
There are three species of clothes moths in the area, all of them
brought over from the Old World. Ordinarily they attack
woolens, though one is quite fond of furs. Cotton, nylon, silk,
and other fabrics usually are safe from molestation by this
group. The most abundant species is *Tineola bisseliella*, if a
name is required for the crime blotter. The adults are brownish moths of less than an inch in wingspread and at that stage
the only damaging thing they do is to lay eggs on woolen clothing or upholstery. They do not eat or drink. They rarely fly
more than one hundred yards and they die in a month or less
as a rule. But the females deposit an average of eighty eggs
that hatch in seven to ten days, depending on the surrounding
temperature, and the 1-mm. larvae go right to work on the
woolen background of the nursery. They remain in the de-

structive larval state for at least four weeks; the period may be extended to as much as two years if the temperature is low, wherefore it behooves the housewife to be vigilant at all seasons.

Despite all the paved streets, office buildings, manufacturing plants, apartment houses, and private houses in the crowded area, there is still much greenery to be found in the parks and the outlying sections of the city. Where there is greenery, there will be insects of multitudinous species. There will be inchworms or geometrids, the most common of which are the Spring Cankerworm (*Paleacrita vernata*) and the Fall Cankerworm (*Alsophila pometaria*). The larvae appear in such numbers at times that they fairly strip most of the shade trees of their foliage. When you walk in a grove under attack you can hear a pattering sound caused by the innumerable droppings of the munching caterpillars as they feed steadily along the lower surfaces of the leaves. I once found fifteen of these caterpillars on the lower surface of a single Linden leaf. Happily the attack is over in a few weeks and the insect-eating birds help to keep the damage down. The spring drive of the geometrids is at its height during the last week in May; the rear guards or laggards in the wood warbler northward migration feast on the "loopers" as they drift through the region.

About the time that the inchworms are working aloft, you will find the immature "frog-hoppers" or "spittle bugs" in their frothy surroundings on the stems and branches of grasses, flowers, and low shoots of all kinds. These curious and, for the most part, harmless insects of the Cercopidae family abound on plant growths at about knee-high level. Brush the froth or "spittle" aside and in the center you will find the youthful cercopid, a pale greenish-white little oval creature about 2 mm. in length with eyes like tiny inkspots. Later in the season you may find "tree-hoppers," also called "brownie bugs," of the Membracidae family lined up in rows along the slender branches of shrubs and small trees. There are many species of this family of queer-shaped insects that live on plant juices.

The one I encountered most frequently on my walks was *Enchenopa binotata*, a species that dotes on the sap of the Hoptree or Wafer-ash (*Ptelea trifoliata*), a shrub or small tree fairly common in the Riverdale–Van Cortlandt section of the city. On its branches in warm weather I was sure to find the egg masses, easily detected by a white covering, or the larva, or, most amusing of all, the triangular-shaped adults that measure less than half an inch in any direction and, facing one way like silent miniature soldiers in a line, somehow manage to look both solemn and ridiculous at the same time.

In September in our area you will find the birds on southward migration striking at the tips of the leafy branches of trees and shrubs and driving out "plant-hoppers" or "lantern-flies" (Fulgoridae) of the species named *Ormenis septentrionalis* that look like small pale green moths as they flutter about with the birds in pursuit. But these insects fly only in spurts and if you pick one up from the ground, which is easily done, you will find its wings and body covered with a fine white powder that comes off on your fingers. There are, of course, other species of this group in the area — and other species of many other groups. We have not even mentioned the ubiquitous Tent Caterpillar (*Malacosoma americana*), recognized by everybody when it is in the caterpillar stage and by few in the adult stage as a dull yellowish-brown moth with a wingspread of about an inch. But their half-inch belts of black-beaded egg masses easily can be found encircling the smaller branches of shrubs and trees — preferably the Black or Rum Cherry (*Prunus serotina*) — in the leafless months and the tents of the malefactors in the larval or caterpillar stage are all too common in the region.

Little mention has been made of the remarkable and as yet not completely understood relation between plant galls and the insects that either cause them or collaborate somehow in the making of them. Half a century ago Dr. Beutenmueller collected eighty-four species of gall insects in the vicinity of New York City, descriptions and illustrations of which were published in the *Journal** and later reprinted as *Guide Leaflet No. 16* of the American Museum of Natural History. That was pioneer work and much remains to be done in the field. A great deal could be done within the city limits. The ordinary person, of course, has little interest in most insects and a decided aversion to many of them, but to an entomologist it is a fascinating field and New York City, over its five boroughs, offers a terrain in which there are myriad kinds and endless numbers of insects to be observed and studied.

*Vol. 4, No. 4 (1904).

Chapter 7

About the Fish in Troubled Waters

NEW YORK IS one of the great ocean ports of the world and the riches of the sea come to Father Knickerbocker's doorstep. For our purposes in this chapter the riches of the sea are the salt-water fish inhabiting or visiting the city waters, with the much fewer fresh-water species of the area thrown in for good measure. The distinction between salt-water and fresh-water fish is only general in character and is not based on structural details or family traits. There are fish of many species that move regularly from one medium to the other — mostly from salt to fresh water — on spawning journeys. In our area the Sea Lamprey (*Petromyson marinus*) and the Brook Lamprey (*Lenthenteron appendix*), which the icthyologists place below the True Fish class, are in the group that move from salt water into coastwise fresh-water streams to spawn. Two of the True Fishes with the same habit are the Shad (*Alosa sapidissima*), netted commercially in the Hudson River each spring, and the

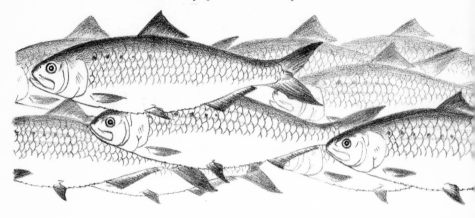

Smelt (*Osmerus mordax*) that finds its way into the smaller streams and brooks of the region.

These fish that journey from salt to fresh water for spawning purposes are referred to as "anadromous," a compound word from the Greek meaning that they "run up"; whereas the Common American Eel (*Anguilla rostrata*) is a "catadromous," or down-running, species because the female, after growing to maturity in fresh water, goes down to salt water and the depths of the Sargasso Sea to lay her eggs—and her bones, too, for that matter, since there is never any return from these anguillian spawning journeys.

The Indians who inhabited the region before the white man arrived made fish and other sea food a large part of their diet and had no trouble gathering all they needed in local waters. The colonists, as Daniel Denton noted in 1670, found the same waters "well furnished with Fish, as Bosse, Sheepsheads, Place, Perch, Trouts, Eels, Turtles and divers others." There grew in time a fishing industry of considerable size but in the last fifty years it has dwindled almost to the point of disappearance. Overfishing contributed to the decline and so did pollution of local waters by sewage and industrial waste products. As the population increased and city streets reached out to cover what

had once been field and forest, brooks and streams once the spawning ground of smaller anadromous species in coastal waters were blocked off or covered over in the building process. Such small fish in any area are a lure for larger fish that feed on them. When "bait fish" grow scarce, the bigger fish move elsewhere in search of food.

But these were minor matters in comparison with two major disasters that brought New York's commercial fishing fleet to the verge of extinction. One was the small but important rise in temperature of the sea water of the area, due to the glacial retreat mentioned earlier, and the consequent movement of great numbers of fish northward to cooler waters. Incidentally, this movement continues, of course, and the commercial fishing industry has been moving northward slowly and steadily to keep pace with it. The final crushing blow for the city fishing fleet was the development of refrigeration processes and transportation facilities to the point where fish and other sea food could be delivered in prime condition on the New York market by ship or rail from distant waters where the fishing was better and operational costs were lower.

What little is left of the local fishing industry consists mostly of the spring netting of Shad in the Hudson River and the marketing of leftover fish brought in by "party boats" catering to amateur fishing enthusiasts who pay a flat rate for a trip on such craft, with rod and bait usually included in the price. As a youngster I was taken along on one of the larger of such party boats and I have a dim recollection of a nauseating day because I was seasick throughout the trip, as were more than a few other adventurers on the boat. I remember the rail crowded with fishermen whose lines often became entangled and I recall noisy debates as to whether the ship, then at anchor, should move to another location or remain where it was. Those who were catching fish or at least getting bites were all for staying where we were. Those who were catching nothing were all for weighing anchor and trying another fishing ground. The captain was besieged with cries of "Move the boat!" and "Don't move the boat!" but I cared little whether he moved the boat or not unless it was back toward dry ground. There were a number of other children aboard and women, too, presumably their mothers in most cases. Men predominated, however. If a few of us were miserable, most of those on the boat seemed to be having a good time, and, indeed, I saw some fish of goodly size flopping about the deck after being hauled in over the side.

There are, of course, thousands of individuals who put out in their own boats and fish the local waters, and other thousands who fish from the shore or waterfront points of vantage of one kind or another. All a Manhattanite needs to go surf-casting is proper tackle and subway fare to Coney Island or the Rockaways. This adds up to considerable fishing activity throughout the year in local waters. As a matter of fact, hunting is forbidden within the city limits, whereas fishing is not only permitted but encouraged by the authorities as a recreational activity for the citizens. One of the points urged in favor of the costly program now under way to end the pollution of New York waters by sewage and industrial waste products is that it will improve the fishing in the area and possibly bring back some species driven out by the fouling of the rivers and harbor.

As to what kind of fish are sought or caught in city waters, I put that question to one of the local "Rod and Gun" editors and received an extended answer that included at least one surprise, which was that the most frequent haul of the anglers who fished from piers, wharfs, rocks, and riverbanks within the city limits was the Common American Eel — truly a fish though to most persons it looks more like a seagoing snake. Many of the edible fish of New York waters are seasonal visitors but eels are resident and active throughout the year except for the coldest weeks, when they usually bury themselves in the mud. They are fished for with rod and line. They are speared in shallow water. Traps are set for them. They are caught in the city reservoirs, park lakes, ponds, rivers, and bays. They are holiday fare at Christmastide over much of Europe, and some of the December fishermen on Hudson River piers or the shores of Pelham Bay are elderly foreign-born residents of the city who are keeping to an Old World custom in trying to provide eels for the skillet at that time of year.

With its great harbor, numerous estuaries, and more than thirty miles of ocean frontage, the city's salt-water reaches offer a great assortment of fish that are either regular residents, seasonal visitors, or occasional strays in the area. To list all the species a searcher might find within the city's salt-water limits would be a major project for a licensed ichthyologist — possibly the labor of a lifetime. All that can be offered here is a comparatively superficial survey of some species that may be of interest to the general reader. Sharks, for instance.

Everybody is interested in sharks, which are frequent intruders in New York City waters and often cause excitement among bathers at Coney Island or along the Rockaway beaches. The Brown Shark (*Carcharias milberti*) is a common visitor in the shallow waters of the bay in hot weather. Like the Smooth Dogfish (*Cynais canis*), also a warm-weather visitor in the area, the Brown Shark hunts by smell and amateur fishermen in small boats occasionally are much disturbed at the sight of the dorsal fin of this marauder cutting the water in which they both are seeking prey. The Piked or Spined Dogfish (*Squalus acanthia*), so named because of a stout spine on the forward edge of each dorsal fin, is a cold weather visitor and sometimes appears in schools. Other kinds of sharks are casual visitors along the beaches, in the bay, or in Long Island Sound; and on one occasion (October, 1911) a Great Blue Shark (*Prionace glauca*)

Brown Shark

was captured off City Island and the corpse was delivered at the American Museum of Natural History as proof positive of its occurrence in the area.

At one time there were numbers of sizable Sturgeon (*Acipenser oxyrhynchus*) taken in the Hudson River on their upstream spawning trips, but overfishing or the pollution of the water evidently discouraged them from coming into the river and of recent years they have been only a memory in the region. They were not particularly good eating and were chiefly valued for their eggs or roe, the sale of which as "domestic caviar" on the New York market rose one season as high as $6,000,000 and then dwindled to practically nothing. Now that the city has entered upon a program to end the pollution of the river, the federal Fish and Wildlife Service hopes to restore the Sturgeon as a seasonal visitor along Riverside Drive in Manhattan.

The Sting Ray (*Pastinachus centrourus*), an annoying flat-bodied creature with a long tail armed with a venomous spine, was once a regular visitor in the bay and along the ocean front but, happily for bathers, it has become a rarity. Four harmless family relations, however, occur in city waters. These are the skates — the Common Skate (*Raja erinacea*), the Big Skate (*Raja diaphenes*), the Clear-nosed Skate (*Raja eglanteria*), and the Barn-door Skate (*Raja laevis*) — whose empty egg cases are the little black leathery four-pronged capsules so often washed ashore and picked up by strollers on the beaches. Most of such egg cases found on the sand in our area are those of the Common Skate, which is resident in local waters. The others are seasonal visitors. The Barn-door Skate is common from October until June but its egg cases seldom are found along the shore, possibly because they are deposited far out in deep water.

New York natives or visitors who wish to see commercial fishermen at work have merely to watch in March for the long rows of nets that are set up on poles in the Hudson River from the Dyckman Street area to a point well above Yonkers. These are to trap the succulent Shad on their spawning run up the river. Though the Hudson is a mile wide at Riverdale and the nets are strung along the shallows west of the ship channel in the center of the river, I often watched the hauling of the nets through my field glasses as I walked the river road above the east bank and I could tell when luck was good by the silver glint of fish as they tumbled into the collecting dory in a steady stream.

The little Alewife (*Pomolobus pseudoharengus*), which looks like a small Shad and is a close relative, is another anadromous or "up-running" visitor for spawning purposes in our general area; another relative, the Atlantic Herring (*Clupea harengus*), is not anadromous. It deposits its eggs in salt water. It was once common in the vicinity and much appreciated as an addition to the food supply in many households but it is now only an irregular visitor. Still another member of the same group is the Menhaden or Mossbunker (*Brevoortia tyrannus*) that appears along the coast in immense schools in summer and thousands of which often sicken and drift ashore to die on the beaches, where they create a malodorous sanitation problem of some magnitude. The traveling Labadist preachers Jasper Danckaerts and Peter Sluyter wrote that in the early autumn of 1679 they saw the rotting remains of thousands of fish called "marsbancken" on a beach on Staten Island and other thousands were still drifting ashore. Nearly three centuries later, the *New York Times* of July 30, 1954, carried the following item under the heading ROCKAWAY IS RELIEVED:

> Forty tons of menhaden, which had eluded fishermen's nets only to die and be cast ashore along five miles of Rockaway Beach, were quickly scooped up and carted away Thursday morning by extra details from the Department of Sanitation. The versatile fish, which anglers call mossbunkers when they use them for bait, are caught commercially at a rate of 800,000,000 pounds a year in Atlantic and Gulf coastal waters. They are used for oil, fertilizer, poultry feed and other products. A combination of spawning season and the heat, varying salinity and

high nitrogen content of water near shore, causing embolism in the menhaden's brain, kills thousands of them at this time of year.

These fish, which grow to a length of 18 inches, feed on diatoms that they strain out of sea water by means of the very fine mesh of their gillrakers. The excess of oil in their flesh makes them unpalatable and the anglers who catch them usually chop them up for "chum" or bait for more tasty quarry. When netted commercially — as they are in New England waters under the name of "pogies" — they are processed for various purposes, principally for the "pogie oil" pressed out of them and the dried residue packaged for fertilizer or used as an added element in mixed poultry food.

Curving "whiskers" or drooping "mustachios" are the mark of the catfish clan, represented by two species in the area. The White Catfish or Channel Mudcat (*Haustor catus*) is caught occasionally in some of the larger bodies of water within the city limits. It grows to a length of 2 feet and owes its name of White Catfish to the fact that it is slate-gray above and white below. The darker and much more familiar Common Catfish, Bullhead, or Horned Pout (*Ameiurus nebulosus*) is common from the tidal region to the smallest ponds in the five boroughs. It is a resident in most of the park lakes and frequently is yanked out of the water by junior fishermen who are a bit fearful of its spines and take some time in getting it off the hook. This species reaches a length of 18 inches but a twelve-incher is considered a good catch in municipal waters. I once saw an Osprey take one of about that size out of the lake in Van Cortlandt Park.

Probably the most abundant fish of any size in the city ponds, lakes, and reservoirs is the introduced European Carp (*Cyprinus carpio*) that grows to a length of 18 inches or more. It is a bulky bottom-feeder that likes slow streams or still water. It spawns in the shallows and often its back sticks out of water when it is swishing around in search of a favorable spot in which to de-

posit its eggs. It is a prolific, hardy, and fast-growing fish and is raised commercially on fish farms in many parts of Europe, where it is a staple article of diet, but it has not yet found general favor as a table dish in this country.

Another notable introduced species that has "gone wild" in the area is the familiar Goldfish (*Carassius auratus*) of oriental origin that has spread around the world through shipment for sales in pet stores. Although it is most often seen in glass bowls, it is hardy in pools, ponds, and slow streams in temperate regions and apparently does good work as a scavenger as well as a destroyer of insect pests in the larval or nymph stage in the water. It grows to a length of a foot or so and rivals the European Carp and the Common Catfish in its ability to survive in muddy water. It does not rival the Common Catfish as a tasty dish, however. It is considered even less toothsome than its larger relative, the Carp.

Pet Goldfish that are turned out of their glass bowls into neighborhood pools retain their bright color but their descendants grow gradually darker in hue and in a few generations the offspring revert to the dull brownish or olive-drab color of the species as it originally was found in the wild. Those suburbanites who think to add a decorative touch to their estates by putting Goldfish in their garden pools often are surprised at the consequence, which is that the Belted Kingfisher comes regularly to poach and occasionally one of the heron tribe is found stalking solemnly about the pool in the process of stuffing itself with a fish dinner in glittering installments.

If the stolid Goldfish has been added to our aquatic fauna, a finer fish has been withdrawn. The valiant, beautiful, and delicious Brook Trout (*Salvelinus fontinalis*) was a resident of these parts when the boroughs that are now New York City had clear cool streams running over stony beds to empty into tidal water, but with the almost total elimination of such streams the lovely Brook Trout has retreated to Westchester and the further reaches of Long Island. If there are any to be seen within the city limits these days, they must be fingerling strays from outer parts or bold adventurers like the eight-incher that was found swimming in the gutter on 58th Street between Fifth and Madison Avenue when a break in a water main flooded that street in the spring of 1956. The arrival of this unexpected and distinguished visitor was reported on the front pages of the city newspapers.

However, there are still a few ponds and streams within the city limits that conceal in their depths — or occasionally yield — such prizes as the Chain Pickerel (*Esox niger*) or the Banded Pickerel (*Esox americanus*), which is also called the Brook Pickerel. As a matter of fact, the capture of a Brook Pickerel in the area would be more of a curiosity than a good haul because it rarely reaches a foot in length and, being narrow in shape like other members of its fighting family, it has little to offer as a dinner dish. But the Chain Pickerel grows to a length of 2 feet or so, affords some fun when hooked on a light line, and makes a good meal if you don't mind a little labor in sorting out the numerous small bones found in its flesh.

In those same ponds and streams you will find the Horned Dace (*Semotilus atromaculatus*), a petty annoyance to trout fishermen. It is abundant in the streams in which they cast their lures and eagerly takes the bait they destine for nobler quarry. It is called "Horned" because of little rough spots or tubercles on its head. It grows to a length of 10 inches and is a favorite with small boys fishing in park lakes and neighborhood ponds. The Horned Dace bites readily and isn't bad eating. Other occupants of such waters, but lower in the social scale, are the Common Sucker (*Catostomus commersonii*), which grows to a length of about 18 inches, and the Chub Sucker (*Erimyzon sucetta*), which grows to about half that size. They are found mostly in ponds or lakes or the pools of streams. Where they lie lazily in clear water — looking somewhat foolish with their round mouths open all the time — they are often speared or snared with loops of wire dangled from the tips of long poles.

Occasionally they will take bait, too. The flesh of these fish is soft but many persons eat it and like it.

Most of us pay little attention to small fish and pass them over as "minnows" or "killifish" whether or not they actually belong in such groups or are the young of much larger fish. There are many species of these little fish — few more than 6 inches in maximum length — in our region and only the expert can sort them out. Some of the more common or more interesting kinds deserve at least passing notice here. One is the freshwater Mud Minnow (*Umbra pygmaea*). It grows to a length of about 4 inches, is rather mottled·and darkish in hue, prefers shallow water with a mud bottom, comes up now and then to gulp air, and buries itself in the mud to escape enemies. It is said of the Mud Minnow that it can turn its head without moving its body, which certainly is a rare accomplishment among fish as it is among insects. Eugene Smith, in describing some fish of the region in a paper he prepared for the Linnaean Society of New York more than half a century ago, wrote of the Mud Minnow that it is "as voracious as a pike and as durable as a catfish . . . and can live in a moist ditch." A little fish of that reputation cannot be ignored.

Another small fish deserving of notice is the Common Killifish (*Fundulus heteroclitus*), only 2 to 4 inches in length, found in schools in shallows along the shores of salt and brackish waters (it does enter fresh water at times) and valuable as a destroyer of mosquito larvae in the "wriggler" stage. A close relative slightly larger in size is the Striped or Bass Killifish (*Fundulus majalis*) that sticks mostly to salt-water shallows along sandy shores. Another species, slightly smaller, is the Broad Killifish (*Cyprinodon variegatis*) that deserves mention because, although the females are always dull in color, in the spawning season the males are bright blue and flaunt orange fins. All these killifish, incidentally, belong to a large group — the Order Cyprinodontes — that includes such well-known "tropical fish" as the Guppy, the Platy, and the Swordtail.

The little sticklebacks, whose name stems from their sharp dorsal spines, are an interesting group because of their odd nesting habits. The males build nests in most cases like flimsy tunnels fashioned of plant fibers and fastened to some aquatic plant growth. Then the females are herded into these nests to deposit their eggs. They go in one end and out the other. Except for depositing the eggs, the female plays no part in the family life. The male not only builds the nest but guards it until the eggs hatch and then guards the young for a brief period. The Four-spined Stickleback (*Apeltes quadracus*) is common in the salt or brackish weedy shallows of our area but there are two other species — the Ten-spined Stickleback (*Pungitius pungitius*) and the Two-spined Stickleback (*Gasterosteus bispinosus*) — that are found occasionally in mildly brackish or fresh water reaches within the city limits.

A perennial favorite for display in any aquarium is the delightful little Sea-horse (*Hippocampus hudsonius*) that, with its curled tail and its wondrously horse-like head, swims about in an upright position through most of its life. One of its relatives is the odd-shaped and well-named Pipefish (*Syngnathus fuscus*), thinner than an eel and with a bony exterior arranged in rings that give it the appearance of a creature put together in short sections. It has a tiny mouth at the end of a long snout and is altogether a curious little object. Pipefish and Sea-horses move about in the welter of plant growth in sections of the tidal regions and, in particular, they like to roam through submerged acres of Eelgrass. When a blight struck the Eelgrass along the Atlantic Coast some years ago, one of the consequences was a scarcity of Sea-horses and Pipefish along the same coast. Now that the Eelgrass is returning to its former haunts, it is expected that these curious little fish will once again be resident in round numbers amid the long waving ribbons of this lush marine growth. An added feature in the life of the Sea-horse is that the female deposits her eggs in a pouch on the "front" of the male's lower section and there they remain until they hatch. When the young Sea-horses emerge from the egg, they swim horizontally for some time and then gradually raise their long-snouted heads to swim in the vertical position for which they are noted. They reach maturity and a length of about 6 inches in a year.

Coney Island is famous in song and story as a seaside resort filled with Ferris wheels, roller coasters, shooting galleries, merry-go-rounds, and a hundred other attractions for old and young, some with a rowdy or raffish tone to them. With the coming of the automobile, the heyday of Coney Island was over. Pleasure seekers of moderate or limited means could go farther afield on their holidays. It is still jammed, of course, on hot summer days, but some of the old flamboyance has gone and even a touch of dignity was brought to the area recently when the new aquarium, truly an institution of learning, was erected there and opened to the public. One thing, however, remains unchanged at Coney Island. You can find fishermen there every day in the year. From the beach or the piers in late fall, for instance, you will see them fishing for the Silver Hake or Whiting (*Merluccius bilineatus*), called "Frostfish" by some anglers because it arrives in cold weather, though not the coldest of the year as a rule. The Silver Hake may reach a length of two feet but the adults caught in New York waters average only a foot or so in length. There is a spring run as well as a fall run of these fish along the ocean beaches and sometimes, when a strong northwest breeze makes the surf break short on the sand, the Silver Hake pursuing little "bait-fish" are so eager in the hunt that some of them are partially stranded in the wash of retreating waves and they can be caught in a dip net before they can get off the beach.

The famous Cod (*Gadus morrhua*) of New England fishing history is a late fall and early spring visitor in the region but it prefers to stay offshore in deep water and is only occasionally caught by pier fishermen or surf-casters. The Tomcod (*Microgadus tomcod*), which is a dwarf replica of its great relative and grows only a foot or so in length, formerly arrived in great numbers on late fall and early spring migrations and fine catches were made not only along the ocean shore but in Long Island Sound and even from Hudson River piers. But the sad report is that the visiting ranks have thinned out and there hasn't been a good run of Tomcod in the area in a dozen years. Another relative of the Cod that sometimes puts in an appearance in early spring is the Pollack (*Pollachius virens*) that, running from one to four pounds in weight in local waters, although much larger ones are caught elsewhere, swims in schools near the surface, takes the baited hook with real dash, and provides good sport for fishermen using light tackle.

Common names often lead to much confusion. To one pier fisherman a "Frostfish" is a Silver Hake or Whiting. To a man on the next pier, a "Frostfish" is a Tomcod. If a Coney Island angler hauls in a fish that he calls a "Ling," it may be either the Common Hake (*Urophycis tenuis*) or the Squirrel Hake (*Urophycis chuss*). These are bottom-feeding fish with threadlike ventral fins far forward, used for tactile purposes in finding food. They, too, have a threadlike tip to the first dorsal fin. The Spotted Hake (*Urophycis regius*), also found in the area, doesn't have this dorsal fin but has white marks along the lateral line as a distinguishing mark. The hakes or "lings" are cold weather visitors in our waters.

The Summer Flounder or Fluke (*Paralichthys dentatus*) is a common warm weather resident of the region and averages about two pounds or more. The Winter Flounder or Flatfish (*Pseudopleuronectes americanus*) is, despite its common name, a permanent resident of local salt waters. These flatfish are interesting to the scientist as well as the housewife who serves them up as "filet of sole." When they emerge from the egg they swim in the normal position of the ordinary fish, with the tail in a vertical plane and the eyes on opposite sides of the head. But as they grow they gradually turn so that eventually they go through life swimming on one side or the other. In this process the eyes retain their "front and center" position and relative distance from one another, with the result that both eyes of the adult are on one side of the fish — the uppermost in swimming. Some flatfish turn over and swim with the left side down and others turn the other way and swim with the right side down. The Summer Flounder turns clockwise to its right and swims with its left side up. The misnamed Winter Flounder

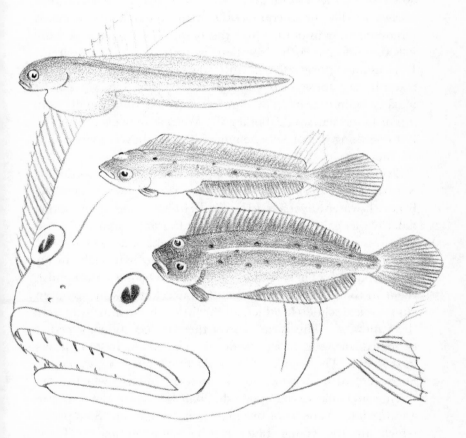

turns the other way and goes about with its right side up. You can tell the way any flatfish has turned by the position of the fins. Look at one on ice in a fish store that has the swimming side down. Looking forward from the tail to the head: if the full-length dorsal fin fringes the left side of the fish, it turned over on that side and both eyes are on the upper or original right side of the fish.

Two smaller flatfish of local waters are the Sundial or Windowpane (*Lophopsetta maculata*) and the American Sole (*Achirus fasciatus*). The first acquired the name Sundial because it is almost circular in outline and the name Windowpane because it is thin and has such clear flesh as to be almost transparent. It is usually thrown back with contempt by fishermen who catch it, but those who have kept and cooked it say that it makes a dainty dish. The American Sole is quite small; only junior fishermen would bother to take one home and cook it. For one thing, it has very rough scales that have earned for it the nickname of "Hogchoker."

Two important little bait-fish of the area are the Silverside or Spearing (*Menidia notata*) that sticks to salt water and the Brackish-water Silverside (*Menidia beryllina*) whose given name describes its habitat. These two little fish are so much alike in appearance that even experts have to take a second look to make sure which is which when a specimen is brought in for identification. Their haunts and habits help to distinguish them in the water. The brackish-water kind swim about in close-ranked schools in which all the little fish are approximately the same size. This is the reason they are occasionally netted or seined and put on the menu as "whitebait" in restaurants in the city. The schools of the kind that prefer salt water are not so crowded in ranks nor as uniform in size, which saves them from being served up as whitebait but leaves them to face another fate. They are the main food supply of "Snappers," which are the young Bluefish (*Pomatomus saltatrix*). These appear in late summer and are caught in considerable numbers by waterfront fishermen using the Silverside as bait. The adult Bluefish, running at about the same time, is a prize that surfcasters and offshore fishermen seek along the ocean front, but the catches are relatively few. By most anglers the "Blues" are considered the finest of the edible fish of the region. That they also are good fighters only adds to the zeal with which they are pursued.

Before we drift entirely out to sea we must pay our last respects to some species found in fresh water within the city limits. There are three different kinds of sunfish in the area. The Common Sunfish or "Punkinseed" (*Eupomotis gibbosus*), to the delight of small boys, is abundant in slow streams, ponds, park lakes, and city reservoirs. Less common but duly registered residents of the area are the Long-eared Sunfish (*Lepomis auritus*) and the Black-banded Sunfish (*Mesogonistius chaetodon*), if the names are needed for the record. At one time the introduced Calico Bass or Crappie (*Pomoxis annularis*), which grows to 10 inches or more in length, was found in fair numbers in the Hudson River. Apparently the pollution of the water drove it out because there have been no catches of this species in recent years.

The Golden Shiner (*Notemigonus crysoleucas*), which is also called Roach or Bream and grows to a length of a foot or so, is a resident of ponds and park lakes; and so is the Yellow Perch (*Perca flavescens*); but the White Perch (*Morone americana*) likes a taste of salt and is found in the brackish-water regions. In the lakes of Westchester County the Large-mouth Black Bass (*Micropterus salmoides*) is tolerably common and doubtless some find their watery way down to the Bronx but it could be regarded only as a distinguished visitor and a rare sight for any angler within the city limits.

The Striped Bass (*Roccus saxatilis*), however, is a regular visitor and during the spring runs of this species into fresh water for spawning purposes there are "stripers" of ten pounds or more in weight caught from rowboats or by shore fishermen along the Hudson River, and even larger ones have been hauled in at Coney Island. The slant-headed Sea Bass (*Centropristes striatus*) is an offshore bottom-feeder that is caught in abundance from boats. They are not nearly so handsome as the "stripers," nor do they run as large, but they are good eating and occasionally come close enough to shore to be listed as of regular occurrence in city waters.

The lowly Porgy or Scup (*Stenotomus versicolor*), short, narrow and deep-bodied, is another bottom-feeder often caught by rowboat anglers in the summer and early autumn. It isn't a prize catch by any means but it is a good pan fish and, to amateur fishermen, much better than no fish at all. Where the Porgies go, the Weakfish (*Cynoscion regalis*) follow in chase. Even so, Weakfish are not narrow-minded in the matter of diet. They also feed on Menhaden and almost any other fish they can catch and swallow. Most fish feed on smaller fish but some species lend an appearance of ferocity to the procedure, and the Weakfish is one of them. As the Porgy is pursued by the Weakfish, the Weakfish is pursued by the Bluefish. The line of pursuit by no means ends there. A similar series in another great biological division stirred no less a person than the great Jonathan Swift to write:

> *So, naturalists observe, the flea*
> *Hath smaller fleas that on him prey;*
> *And these have smaller still to bite 'em;*
> *And so proceed* ad infinitum.

It is not any mildness of disposition that earned the Weakfish its name but a structural weakness around the mouth that makes it difficult to bring this fish to boat when hooked. Unless it is played carefully, the hook will be torn out of the mouth. Some anglers favor "hellgrammites," the larvae of the Dobson-fly, as a bait for Weakfish; others prefer shrimp as a lure. Still others toss chum overboard and rely on a shining metal jig to snare any Weakfish that come to investigate the chum. The jig, of course, has to be kept in motion to make it flash like a bait-fish, so it is customary to carry a file along to brighten up the metal lure when it becomes dull. I have tried all three methods without conspicuous success but the jig, at least, was simpler, because no small fish ate away the metal as they did the luscious shrimp or hellgrammites of the baited hooks. By the time some of my rivals afloat had caught a Weakfish, they had more than paid for it with its weight in shrimp. No matter what the bait or lure, a three-pound Weakfish will give a fisherman a good fight on light tackle — and a good dinner if the hook doesn't pull out.

Once when I was a youngster I asked an angler on the bank of the Hudson at Spuyten Duyvil what kind of fish he was catching. I understood him to answer, "Lay-fee-yets," and interpreted this as the Bronx version of Lafayette. The Lafayette, Spot, or Goody (*Leiostomus xanthurus*) is a small fish up to about a foot in length that is common in the brackish waters of the city. The name Spot is in deference to a dark spot behind the gill covers on each side. Whoever named it Goody was a man easily pleased. The Butterfish (*Poronotus triacanthus*) is another candidate for the frying pan that is common in the tidal waters of the city from May to October.

The familiar Mackerel (*Scomber scombrus*) of the North Atlantic is an irregular visitor in our waters. Its wanderings are unpredictable, but it frequently comes northward along the coast in spring and spawns in deep water from Long Island to Nova Scotia. On these runs they are not in the best of condition and after spawning they go well offshore. However, they are occasionally hooked in municipal waters; a two-pounder is considered a good catch by local fishermen. The so-called "Tinker Mackerel" is merely a young Mackerel. The related Chub Mackerel (*Pneumatophorus grex*) is an irregular summer visitor and so is the Spanish Mackerel (*Scomberomorus maculatus*).

Most city anglers know them only by report or reputation. The men on the bay or in small boats offshore must have other fish to fry or they will go hungry.

Since the lordly Bluefin Tuna (*Thunnus secundo dorsalis*), which grows to a length of 14 feet and a weight of 1500 pounds or more, is caught regularly off the south shore of Long Island, it seems probable that it trespasses on municipal waters occasionally but nobody yet has hauled one into a rowboat on the Upper Bay or in the East River. Other salt-water notables in the same category are the Little Tunny (*Euthynnus alleteratus*), the Albacore (*Germo alalunga*), the Oceanic Bonita (*Katsuwonus pelamis*), the Common Bonita (*Sarda sarda*), and that great game fish and mighty roamer of the deep, the Broadbill Swordfish (*Xiphias gladius*). Occasionally there are good runs of Blackfish or Tautog (*Tautoga onitis*) in the bay and in Long Island Sound, and those two dainties of southern waters, the Common Pompano (*Trachinotus carolinus*) and the Round Pompano (*Trachinotus falcatus*), now and then venture into the city's coastal waters in late summer and early autumn when the water temperature is at its mildest.

The heavy-bodied Drum (*Pogonias cromis*), which really does make a low booming or grunting sound when traveling in schools, is a rare warm weather visitor in the bay or along the ocean front. The smaller Bergall, Nibbler, or Cunner (*Tautogolabrus adspersus*) is a resident species not to be despised as an article of diet. The White Mullet (*Querimana curema*) and the Striped Mullet (*Mugil cephalus*) are small fish up to a foot in length that can be scooped up in hand nets from shallow water in the warmer months of the year. They are edible but not invitingly so; since they seem to taste better to other fish than they do to fishermen, they are mostly used as bait when they are caught.

In our waters, as in all the waters of the world, there are certain kinds of fish more often caught than sought. In this region the list would include such squareheaded, spiny-finned, ugly-looking creatures as the Sculpin or Hackle-head (*Acan-thocottus octodecimspinosus*), the Carolina Sea-robin (*Merulinus carolinus*), the Striped Sea-robin (*Prionotus strigatus*), the Blow-fish, Puffer, or Swellfish (*Sphoeroides maculatus*), the well-named Toadfish (*Opsanus tau*), the Rough-coated Orange Filefish (*Ceratacanthus schoepfii*), and the really awesome Angler-fish (*Lophius piscatorius*) that deserves special mention for several reasons.

One cold December day a fishing party in a small boat on Long Island Sound saw a Coot (*Fulica americana*) that appeared to be in difficulty. It was flapping its wings desperately as if

Angler-fish

endeavoring to fly, but instead of rising it was gradually sinking lower in the water. The fishermen moved over to investigate and found the rear half of the body of the bird to be firmly held in the maw of an Angler-fish that was slowly pulling its victim under water. One of the fishermen, a bird enthusiast, speared this particular *Lophius piscatorius* and the Coot, greatly relieved but somewhat the worse for wear and tear, paddled off slowly toward shore.

Although this Angler-fish, which derives its name from the antennae that dangle as lures around its wide froglike mouth, rarely reaches a length of more than 2 or 3 feet in our region, it has a huge head for its size and widespread jawbones (the gape is often more than a foot in width) armed with three or four rows of strong, sharp, firmly rooted teeth! Occasionally the joined jawbones of a defunct Angler-fish are washed up on the sand and carried off as a strange souvenir of the sea. Most persons who find such skeletal trophies take them to be relics of sharks of some kind because of the frightful array of teeth; but a shark's teeth, efficient as they may be in life, fall away in death and decomposition because they are set in cartilage and not imbedded in the jawbones as are the teeth of the Angler-fish. I was shown a pair of Angler-fish jawbones brought into the American Museum of Natural History for identification. The array of teeth was horrendous.

Halt! We must get back to solid ground even though the fish mentioned by name in this chapter are only a small minority of the number of species occurring in New York City waters. This was proved long ago by the late John Treadwell Nichols, who joined the staff of the American Museum of Natural History not long after being graduated from Harvard and rose to become head of the Department of Fishes, a position from which he retired in 1952, bearing "his blushing honors thick upon him." At the museum he was fondly referred to as "Big Nichols" to distinguish him from several smaller members of the staff of the same name.

Nearly half a century ago this same J. T. Nichols, Esq., compiled a list of the fish to be found within fifty miles of the center of New York City.   Since water is an open highway for anything that swims, any member of the fish class found within fifty miles of the city might easily wander into municipal waters and be legally listed as a visitor within the area.   The young Mr. Nichols, as appears by his printed report in the *Abstracts of the Proceedings of the Linnaean Society of New York** found no fewer than 237 species of fish that fitted into such a category.   Perhaps Tokyo, Buenos Aires, or Rio de Janeiro could rival that, but not London, Paris, Berlin, or Moscow.

*Nos. 20–23 (1907–1911).

Chapter 8

Amphibians and Reptiles

AMPHIBIANS AND REPTILES are a decidedly interesting group, whether you consider them attractive or not. The term amphibian is of Greek derivation — *amphi* (double) + *bios* (life) — and refers to the fact that most, though not all, amphibians have two stages in their life cycles: an early one in which they live in water and breathe through gills, and a later one in which they develop lungs and can live on land if they please, as many of them do. The term reptile traces back to the Latin *repo*, *repere*, *repsi*, *reptus*, a Third Conjugation verb meaning to creep or crawl, words we usually associate with slow movements, and there again the general designation has exceptions. What most of us call lizards are reptiles, and some of them dart about so quickly that they are known as "swifts."

If ancient lineage is a social distinction, the amphibians are the aristocrats of animal life on land. The ancestors or prototypes of the amphibians of today ventured ashore in the

Devonian Period of the Paleozoic Era some 300,000,000 years ago to try life on land on at least a part-time basis. Amphibians are plentiful in all the temperate and tropical regions of the world. They are found in the uplands and lowlands, in streams, ponds and lakes, in swamps and in forests, but never in the ocean. There are no salt-water amphibians. It must be remembered that at the time of the original emergence of this group from the Devonian seas, the oceans of the world were fresh water. Since that time the rains and rivers of 300,000,000 years have been carrying salt — as well as other solid or soluble matter — to the sea and leaving it there, as a result of which we can now extract about two pounds of almost pure salt from a cubic foot of sea water. For that reason the amphibians will have none of it in their lives.

The amphibians you may expect to find in New York City are of two kinds: salamanders, or "tailed amphibians," and frogs and toads that have no noticeable tails after they pass the tadpole stage in their lives. When salamanders are measured it is usually found that the tail is almost half the length of the creature, and in some cases the tail is longer than the body. William L. Sherwood, an authority on New York's amphibians, wrote long ago that salamanders receive little study because most persons consider them repulsive in appearance. Well, some are repulsive in appearance according to ordinary human standards, but others are quite attractive.

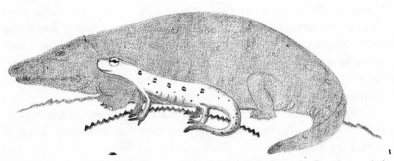

Red-spotted Newt alongside Eryops *largest amphibian from the Permian period*

Many persons confuse salamanders with what they call "lizards," another group designation that in our area includes skinks, swifts, and chameleons. The distinction, however, is basic. Salamanders are amphibians; lizards are reptiles. Reptiles may — and many do — spend a great part of their lives in water, but they have to come up for air at intervals. They never have gills; they always have lungs. Aside from that, salamanders have smooth skins, while lizards, like all reptiles, have scaly skins. Most lizards love the sun and bask in it, whereas salamanders avoid the sun and hide in cool, dark, and damp places. Most of them like to keep their skins moist. For those who wish to look into the matter more closely, there is the point that lizards have five toes, usually clawed, on their front feet and salamanders never have more than four and may have fewer.

James A. Fowler, in a *Bulletin* of the University of the State of New York* listed 31 species of amphibians that have been recorded in New York State, of which 17 were "tailed amphibians," or salamanders, and 14 "untailed amphibians," or frogs and toads. At least a dozen kinds of amphibians are easily found within the city limits by those who know how and where to look for them; their way of life is such that most of them go unnoticed by ordinary citizens. Even some that are often heard are rarely seen. Think for a moment of the one amphibian that millions of men, women, and children of the metropolitan area know — not by sight but by ear! That's the Spring Peeper (*Hyla crucifer*), whose voice joins with others of its kind to sprinkle the dusk and fill the dark with a sustained treble chorus in late March and early April of each year. We all hear it, but who sees it? To all of us it is a sound in the night. How many who heard it a thousand times ever have seen and recognized the little singer by day?

Frogs and toads we can hear, at least in season. They croak, peep, or trill. In that way they attract our attention, even if

*Vol. 41, No. 7 (1955).

they are hard to track down individually. But salamanders, to the human ear at least, are voiceless creatures that give no audible hint of their presence in the community. Furthermore, most of them spend the greater part of their lives either in the water or under stones or logs and thereby escape public notice. They lead obscure lives in hidden places. But for all that they are not hard to find, even in New York City. There are still some streams, brooks, swamps, and ponds in the more open areas of the city. Go there and search. Turn over flat stones along the edges of such waters. Look under old planks and logs mired in damp ground. Scan the moist ledges in wet woods. Sooner or later you will find yourself face to face with a salamander of some kind, and probably the surprise will be mutual.

One of the "tailed amphibians" you might uncover in such a search is the Spotted Salamander (*Ambystoma maculatum*) with a black body decorated with a row of round yellow spots along each side and down the top of its tail. Though only 6 inches or so in length, it has all the fearsome appearance of a miniature dragon, but it is quite harmless. In fact, it is the Spotted Salamander that will be harmed if you pick it up. Handling it has a tendency to remove the slimy covering serving as a protection in keeping its skin moist. The related Jefferson Salamander (*Ambystoma jeffersonianum*) produces less commotion when discovered because it is much slimmer than the Spotted and duller in color. A smaller member of the same blunt-nosed group is the Marbled Salamander (*Ambystoma opacum*) that rarely grows more than 4 inches in length but catches the eye with its black and white or "marbled" pattern.

Probably the most common salamander within the city limits is the Northern Dusky Salamander (*Desmognathus fuscus*), whose name fits it well. It is dusky in color and from 3 to 5 inches or so in size, the males running larger than the females. It prefers moist ground to water as a habitat and the noteworthy feature of the species is that the female coils around the egg mass deposited under logs or stones to protect the eggs until they hatch and the larvae can make their way downhill to nearby water. Most female amphibians are not so solicitous about the next generation. They lay the eggs and display no further interest in the matter.

The Dusky Salamander is one of the lungless group in which the adults breathe through the linings of their mouths and throats. Two water-loving members of the same family are the Northern Red Salamander (*Pseudotriton ruber*), plentifully sprinkled with black spots, and the Northern Two-lined Salamander (*Eurycea bislineata*), small and dainty and so thin as to be practically transparent. These salamanders like clear running water, of which only a limited amount remains above ground within the city limits. In contrast to these water-dwelling species is another member of the lungless group, the Red-backed Salamander (*Plethodon cinereus*), quite small and thin and noteworthy among the "tailed amphibians" of our area in that it never enters the water at any stage of its career. Moist ground is all that it needs to feed, breed, and survive. It is fairly common in what woodlands remain on Staten Island, in Queens, and in the Bronx.

Just to show how complicated salamander life may be, there is the common little Red-spotted Newt (*Diemictylus viridescens*) of 3 to 4 inches in length that is equipped with gills when it hatches from the egg in water, develops lungs for a later land career that may last as long as two or three years, and then returns to the water to spend the remainder of its life with a broadened tail that helps it to swim about like a fish. In ordinary salamander life the land stage is the adult phase but in this case the Red Eft, the name under which it lives on land, is still immature and doesn't come of age until it goes back into the water to become the adult Red-spotted Newt. They vary in body color in the water stage but usually are greenish in hue and liberally sprinkled with spots, two rows of which along the back are red. In the land stage they are orange-red with two rows of dark red spots along their backs. Red Efts are fairly common on the woodland floors in some sections of the city. One more odd thing about this species is that on Staten Island and probably in some other regions it skips the land stage entirely and sticks to water all its life. I know that is not true in the Bronx for I often found the lively little Red Eft lurking under flat stones or foraging over the dead leaves on the ground in wet woodlands.

It should be added that all the "tailed amphibians" listed here as residents of the area are not evenly distributed over the five boroughs. Only a few species are found in Brooklyn and Manhattan and some that survive in Queens and in the Bronx will be sought in vain on Staten Island. If a salamander species becomes extinct on Staten Island, that's the end of it unless it is reintroduced by human agency. But if a resident species dies out in the Bronx, it may be restocked naturally by infiltration from Westchester just to the northward. County lines are no barriers to creatures that travel by land or fresh water, but an expanse of salt water is a barrier to an influx of amphibians. That is why any loss on Staten Island will not be made up by invasion from neighboring territory.

As to the "untailed amphibians" within the city limits, meaning the frogs and toads, the most abundant is the familiar Spring Peeper already mentioned, which is a frog. Toads are more terrestrial and have warty skins as a rule and a glandular swelling behind each eye. Otherwise there is no important distinction between frogs and toads, and indeed one common resident of the region goes by either name. That is the little tree climber with the scientific name of *Hyla versicolor* and the choice of Treefrog or "Tree Toad" as a common name. Not only does it have two names but it comes in different colors: brown, green, gray, and almost white. But in any color they are equipped with toe pads or disks that exude a sticky substance enabling them to cling to smooth surfaces, even at a vertical angle. This is the explanation of their climbing exploits

Treefrog

These really attractive little creatures grow to a length of 2 inches or so but more often the ones you may find will be smaller. They have a delicate trilling call or song almost bird-like in quality that they tune up in the dusk and continue inter-mittently through the warm nights of late spring and early summer. The best way to find one is to track it down as closely as possible by ear in the dusk or dark and then turn on a flash-light for the final search on a tree trunk or branch. If caught in the beam of a flashlight, a Treefrog usually remains motion-less and, if approached slowly, may be picked off the tree by hand for closer inspection.   If you capture one, be sure to look at its toe pads.

As a matter of fact — and as its scientific name *Hyla crucifer* indicates — the Spring Peeper is a close relative and a member of this family of climbing frogs.   The Peepers, too, have toe pads, but they do not climb as high nor stray as far from water as do the Treefrogs.   They more often utter their piping calls from the branch of a shrub or a plant stem sticking up out of the water.   The Spring Peeper is only about an inch in length but its vocal equipment is so efficient that its shrill calls can be heard nearly a mile off on a quiet night.   It is not as soft on the ear as the purring trill of the Treefrog but, when first lifted each year in the twilight "among the sallows and the windy gleams of March," it is cherished as the herald of spring and the promise of fresh greenery over a landscape drab and drear from the ravages of a retreating winter.

Another member of the same family and the smallest frog occurring in the area has toe pads so small and ineffective that it doesn't climb at all.   It's the Southern Cricket Frog (*Acris gryllus*) that lives along the grassy edges of ponds and slow streams and gains its name from the notes the male gives off in the courting season, a series of *chirks* somewhat insect-like in quality.   It is just over an inch in length at most, brownish of hue with a sprinkling of small dark spots, and it has a light green or yellowish line running down the middle of its back.   It is by no means common in our area, which is close to the north-east limit of the range of the species, so if you come upon one within the city limits you may consider it something of a batra-chian prize.   For that matter, a searcher may have to comb the far reaches and lonelier sectors of Queens and the Bronx to find Treefrogs or even hear their thin trilling voices calling eerily in the twilight of a warm day in May.

It is not so with the Green Frog (*Rana clamitans*), however.

While not nearly as abundant as the Spring Peeper, it is common in the ponds and park lakes of all five boroughs and plentiful along the borders of the swamps and streams in the outlying sections of the city. This is the frog, about 4 inches in length and green or greenish brown in color, that sits along the edge of a pond, lake, or stream and gives a squeaky croak as it jumps — plop! — into the water at your approach. Despite its small size it has a reputation for ferocity and voracity and even has been charged with "cannibalism" in the form of feeding on tadpoles of its own species. It rarely wanders on dry ground beyond reach of water in one jump, and often sits in the water with only its head exposed, from which point of vantage it occasionally gives off a resounding *tchung!*

Less plentiful but more majestic is the famous Bullfrog (*Rana catesbeiana*). Under cultivation this species is reputed to reach a length of 8 inches but in the park lakes and some of the larger ponds on the outskirts of the city a six-incher still would be exceptional. In fact, a five-incher at the northern end of the Van Cortlandt Park Lake will cause me to stop, look, and listen. To some listeners its deep voice grumpily calls for a *jug o' rum! jug o' rum!;* to my ears it never utters anything but a hoarse and meaningless *ker-r-rumppp!* Either way, its voice has an air of solidity and authority and its presence lends dignity to the scene where it lords it over lesser forms of batrachian life in our region.

The Bullfrog is truly aquatic and spends all its life in the water. A really adventurous little amphibian is the slim and graceful Wood Frog (*Rana sylvatica*) that often wanders far from its watery cradle. This is a handsome frog about 2 to 3 inches in length — the male is the smaller — and quite smooth of skin. It is marked to match the dead leaves of the forest floor along which it forages, a pattern of light and dark brown with a narrow black patch running backward from the eye. The eggs are deposited in some woodland pool in early spring and, after a tadpole stage varying from six weeks to about twice as long, de-

Wood Frog and Indian Pipes

pending on the weather and local conditions, the young emerge as tiny frogs that immediately start hunting for food in the undergrowth of the woods. It takes these frogs four years to reach full growth, such as it is. They are lively creatures and extraordinary jumpers for their size. It is easy to see one in motion when it leaps from under your foot but it's hard to find when it lands at the end of the jump, so well does it blend into the background of the woodland carpet. In the adult stage they have so little affinity with water (they go to it only to answer the mating call in spring) that their hind feet are only partially webbed and their front feet not at all. Since the woods within the city limits are now confined to scattered patches on Staten Island and in the outlying sections of Queens and the Bronx, the Wood Frogs of the area must be sought in such local refuges. Even there they are comparatively scarce and hard to find.

Some frog fanciers hold that the Northern Leopard Frog (*Rana pipiens*) is even more handsome than the Wood Frog. It's a matter of taste. The Leopard Frog is another wanderer from the water but it doesn't go as far as the Wood Frog. It is so frequently found in open grassy places that some persons prefer to call it the Meadow Frog. It has a bronze or green body studded with rows of roundish white-edged dark spots and though rarely exceeding 4 inches in length, it is so abundant in many parts of its wide range in North America and so easily caught that it is the main source of supply for the frogs' legs served up in restaurants. The slightly smaller Pickerel Frog (*Rana palustris*), rarely more than 3 inches in length, is somewhat similar in color and pattern, but the two rows of spots on its back are roughly rectangular and lack the conspicuous light edging of the Leopard Frog spots. Perhaps the easiest distinguishing mark is the brilliant orange color of the underside of the hind legs of the Pickerel Frog, which, incidentally, is not as abundant or as widespread as the Leopard Frog, nor does it travel as far from water.

Moving over to the toad department, there are two kinds of toad — and just possibly a third — that are still resident in the region. The well-known, dust-colored, warty-skinned, slow-moving American Toad (*Bufo americanus*) still thrives, though in decreasing numbers, in the public parks of the city and in outlying open ground. It doesn't attract much attention for several reasons, one being that it moves about and feeds mostly at night. Another is that it disappears at the first sign of cold weather, digging itself in for a long period of hibernation in a favorable spot. At full growth a female may be up to 4 inches in length. The males are smaller. Both sexes ordinarily are silent but the males give off low sweet trills when the sexes gather at the ponds wherein the females deposit their strings of eggs in May. The eggs hatch in about ten days and the tadpole stage takes up seven to nine weeks of the career of the American Toad. Once it develops legs and takes to dry ground, it never returns to the water except for the annual spring reunion of the sexes at the ponds. Fowler's Toad (*Bufo woodhousei fowleri*), a trifle smaller but much similar to the American Toad in appearance except that it has a median light line down its dark-spotted warty back and generally has three warts instead of one or two in each dark spot on its back, is the more common species in some sections of the city. It has approximately the same habits and life cycle as the American Toad but it does not lift as melodic a note at the meeting of the sexes at the ponds in spring. The sound that Fowler's Toad gives off on such amorous occasions can only be described as a husky and ghostly *ur-r-r-r-r*.

Although the Eastern Spadefoot (*Scaphiopus holbrookii*) is fairly common over most of the eastern part of the United States, it is definitely a rarity on city territory. There has been only one report of its occurrence within the city limits in recent years and that came from Staten Island, where, strangely enough, the familiar American Toad doesn't occur at all. At least no report of its appearance has been filed. Fowler's Toad is the resident species. The Eastern Spadefoot owes its name to horny projections along the inside of the soles of its hind feet that help it to dig in soft ground the tunnels and burrows in which it lives and feeds. Since it is less than 3 inches long and rarely is seen above ground, doing most of its foraging under stones and logs, it often escapes notice even where it occurs in fair numbers; this can't be the case in our territory, or else expert searchers would be reporting it with regularity. It must be that the Spadefoot has been discouraged by the spread of reinforced concrete and other such hard surfaces within the city limits and has left permanently for unpaved ground.

It's our loss. Toads are useful creatures and helpful to Man, being active guardians of field crops and protectors of trees, flowers, fruits, and garden vegetables from the ravages of insects. The word toad applied as an epithet or a term of disapprobation is a libel on these gentle amphibians. Familiarity with them will not breed contempt — nor warts, as the ancient fable has it — rather, a deep respect and perhaps even a little affection for these possibly unhandsome but certainly quiet, friendly, and helpful creatures.

All this adds up to ten species of "untailed amphibians" that you might expect or at least hope to find resident on city territory and active in the warmer months of the year. Of these the Spring Peepers are by far the most numerous and widespread, and also the most insistently vociferous in season. Our Green Frogs and Bullfrogs also announce themselves in good strong tones where they are locally common in and around ponds and lakes. To come upon the wider ranging Pickerel Frogs, Northern Leopard Frogs, and Wood Frogs will be a harder task, and getting a good view of the little Southern Cricket Frog will be a real task. As for the Treefrog and the two resident species that are legally entitled to the name of "toad," the American and the Fowler's Toad, they are best sought after dark. All you need for a successful search is a good place, a good ear, a good flashlight — and a good deal of patience.

After the Amphibians on the geological calendar and the biological family tree came the Reptiles, whose ancestral lines can be traced back to a vague beginning somewhere in the Triassic Period of the Mesozoic Era, or something more than 150,000,000 years ago. They were an evolutionary step beyond the amphibians in that they didn't need to go through a tadpole, gill-breathing aquatic stage early in their life cycles. They did not have to undergo a change of form or metamorphosis to reach the adult stage. When they hatched from the egg they were miniature adults in general shape and vital construction. They had lungs when they came out of the shell. Though many of them were aquatic in habit, spending most of their lives in water, they still had to lift their heads above the surface to breathe. The surviving aquatic reptiles follow the same procedure today.

Back in the Triassic Period some of the forerunners of the reptiles of modern times increased in size and strength as they roamed the vast fens, morasses, and swamps of that ancient day. They developed the scaly skin that further distinguishes the group from the amphibians. They became, in some cases, great armored animals such as the dinosaurs and phytosaurs, ghastly in appearance in our belated view but rather harmless in fact because they were vegetarian in taste. Some of them, like the pterodactyl, developed wings and became flying reptiles. Some of the smaller kinds developed teeth and carnivorous habits. Later there came that sharp-toothed, great-jawed species known as *Tyrannosaurus rex*, fiercely armed for attack, heavily armored for defense, a type seemingly invincible, impregnable, and eternal. But it is long extinct. The whole race of dinosaurs disappeared some 100,000,000 years ago. They could not cope with changing conditions in a changing world.

However, some of their smaller relatives managed to survive the many changes on the face of the earth through the lapse of ages since the Mesozoic Era, and in New York City their descendants or offshoots of their descendants are represented by a number of native turtles, lizards, and snakes. The armor of the turtles is evidence of their ancient lineage. Actually, they antedate the vanished dinosaurs. Lizards and snakes, as such, are of much later development and there is no trace of them before the Cenozoic Era. Since the turtles are the older type and age, by honored custom, takes precedence over beauty, these slow-moving creatures armored above with carapace and below with plastron will be considered first among the city's resident reptiles.

The most abundant turtle of the area is the harmless and handsome little Eastern Painted Turtle (*Chrysemys picta*) that is only 4 to 6 inches in length and quite timid of disposition. The dark carapace has red markings around the edge above and below and the plastron is bright yellow. Where these turtles are lined up in a row on a half-submerged log they are easily recognized by the bright yellow and red striping along the sides of the exposed heads and necks. Their timidity generally pre-

Eastern Painted Turtles in Van Cortlandt Lake

vents any close inspection. When anybody approaches, they slide, scramble, or plop into the water and disappear. You can see dozens of them — from a reasonable distance — any summer day along the edge of the Van Cortlandt lake or the slow stream that winds through the adjacent swamp.

A somewhat smaller, much less attractive, and far less common species in the area is the Stinkpot or Musk Turtle (*Sternothaerus odoratus*) that looks and acts much like a small high-backed, foul-smelling Snapping Turtle. Its dark, well-arched carapace often is garnished with greenish plant growth (algae) and the plastron is narrow, thus giving the creature plenty of "leg room." If any further aids to identification are needed, it has two yellow stripes along the side of its head and if you find one and pick it up the odor it gives off will not only clinch the identity but justify the name by which it officially is known — Stinkpot! Still smaller and less common — in fact, seldom found — in the region is the mild and not particularly malodorous Eastern Mud Turtle (*Kinosternon subrubrum*) of somewhat the same general appearance as the Stinkpot but with a wider plastron and not so high a carapace.

From a social standpoint, the aristocrat of the armored group is the Northern Diamondback Terrapin (*Malaclemys terrapin*). It dwells in brackish waters and in our territory is found mostly along the shores of Staten Island. Terrapin stew, properly prepared, is considered a choice dish and is served in the best restaurants at a fancy price. The Diamondback is not a large turtle. A seven-inch specimen would be a prize catch in our area but they do grow a bit larger elsewhere and usually bring about a dollar an inch in the market. They have thick carapaces with segments so scored with concentric lines as to give them the "diamondback" appearance that accounts for their common name. There are enough of them along the Maryland shores to make them important commercially, but within the limits of New York City they are more often found on the menu than in the marshes.

The Wood Turtle (*Clemmys insculpta*) that grows to about the same size as the Northern Diamondback Terrapin also has a heavy carapace with bizarre "sculpture." The main segments or individual shields are shaped like little pyramids with radial lines as well as concentric grooves. These quiet and harmless creatures, largely vegetarian in diet, are as much at home in the woods as the Eastern Painted Turtles are in ponds and lakes. They prefer moist or wet woods but, except for the breeding season when the sexes meet in water and the eggs are laid in moist ground, they may wander far in dry woods or even open fields. They are not particularly numerous in any part of a wide range over the northeastern portion of the United States, and with the decrease of wooded areas within the city limits the Wood Turtle has become almost a rarity as a resident in the region.

The Spotted Turtle (*Clemmys guttata*) is a rather shy little creature with a dark — almost black — carapace dotted with yellow spots. It is found in the swamps and ponds where the Eastern Painted Turtle abounds but it is much less common and also a bit smaller, being rarely over 5 inches in length. Though they never eat except when they are in the water, they have a tendency to go on excursions over dry ground now and then, a risky procedure for such creatures in crowded territory. Perhaps that explains why the species seems to be getting scarcer year by year in the area.

Apropos of that, in the horse-and-buggy days of my childhood the Eastern Box Turtle or Box Tortoise (*Terrapene carolina*) was a familiar creature in all five boroughs of the city and often a pet in gardens for the good it did in destroying adult and larval forms of annoying insects. But the automobile has played sad havoc with these slow-moving, land-loving members of the turtle tribe and, although still fairly common on Staten Island, only the remnants of a once populous clan remain in other parts of the city. This is the most terrestrial of the turtles of the region. It is also the only one that can "button up" completely and present an armored exterior at all points. About 5 inches long at maturity, it has a high-arched carapace of dark brown covered with light brown or yellowish dots and streaks and a hinged plastron that can be fitted tightly against the carapace when the creature pulls in its head and legs. Here is a turtle that really can go into its shell. It has no need of and little taste for the still waters that delight so many of its relatives in armor. It even hibernates in dry ground, whereas the other turtles that take to the fields or the woods in summer seek a moist terrain in which to bury themselves in the winter.

It's just possible that Blanding's Turtle (*Emydoidea blandingi*) and the Bog Turtle, formerly called Muhlenberg's Turtle (*Clemmys muhlenbergi*), may be rare residents or occasional wanderers in our area. Blanding's Turtle grows to a length of 5 to 8 inches and is easily recognized by its bright yellow throat. The Bog Turtle is only about 4 inches in length at maturity and is marked with a brilliant patch of orange on each side of its head to the rear of the eye. These turtles, if found within the city limits, would rate some attention not only in scientific circles but in the news columns of the daily papers.

As for the famous or infamous Snapping Turtle (*Chelydra serpentina*), it flourishes mightily in all the ponds, lakes, and slow streams of the region despite many efforts to abate its numbers. The Snapper has a long neck, a long tail, and a short temper. Or at least it seems that way. It may carry a carapace up to 18 inches or so in length but most of the adults I have encountered in the Van Cortlandt swamp and lake sector have been little more than half that size. The carapace is ample, rough, and thick, with three prominent longitudinal ridges, but the plastron is small and allows the legs great freedom of movement. Its comparatively long legs enable it to lift its body well off the ground and it can move much faster on land than any of the other turtles resident in the region. It is voracious and fearless and has a terrific bite. It will attack, kill, and eat almost any aquatic creature it can catch and is espe-

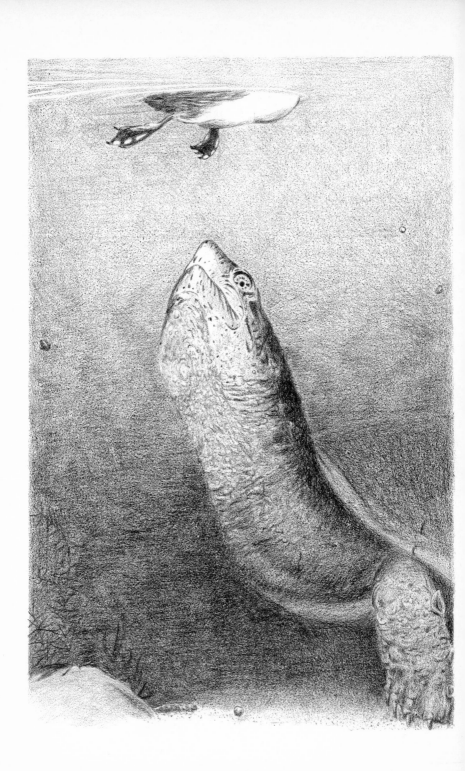

cially destructive to ducklings. In one of the ponds of the Bronx Zoo a huge Snapping Turtle killed a Mute Swan by crushing the bird's skull with its jaws when the Swan was feeding with its head under water.

On warm June days I have seen Snapping Turtle females digging holes and laying eggs therein along the golf course causeway and the railroad embankment bordering the Van Cortlandt swamp. This is a curious performance and well worth watching. The female scrapes away with her feet in soft ground until she has a depression about as wide as herself and some six inches or so in depth. When ready to lay she hoists herself up a bit with head half extended, and an egg drops from her vent to roll to the low point of the depression. She relaxes for perhaps a minute, then raises herself again and another egg drops down. This may go on until she has laid as many as two dozen or more round white eggs about three-quarters of an inch in diameter with tough but pliable shells. Even with a group of persons gathered around and small boys poking at her with sticks, she goes ahead imperturbably with her task. When she has finished laying, she scrapes the ejected earth over the eggs and packs it down as best she can before moving down the embankment to return to the water. So steady and impassive is the female turtle in the process of producing the eggs that the operation seems automatic. Sometimes I think that the egg-laying would go on even if the turtle's head were cut off.

Undoubtedly the abundance of Snapping Turtles in the swamp and lake in Van Cortlandt Park has caused many casualties among the ducklings hatched in the area. I once saw a female Wood Duck leading a flotilla of fifteen newly hatched ducklings along one of the inner canals of the swamp and I rightly feared for their safety. Only five of the ducklings survived to reach the flying stage. Other enemies, of course, may have accounted for some of the losses, but I'm convinced that Snapping Turtles played an effective part in the gradual decrease of the number of ducklings in that brood. I realize that

Snapping Turtles are just as much an integral part of the wildlife of the region as the Wood Duck and the fact that I prefer
the Wood Duck is a matter of no importance in the general
scheme of things. Also, I know that nature usually maintains
a balance if Man doesn't interfere, so I don't worry too much.
Let the impassive female Snapping Turtles lay ever so many
eggs, comparatively few will yield young turtles. Most of the
clutches are discovered and the eggs therein devoured by such
animals as the raccoon, the mink, and the skunk. The skunk in
particular is skilled in the detection, excavation and consumption of turtle eggs.

Three of the sea turtles of the North Atlantic are the great
Atlantic Leatherback (*Dermochelys coriacea*) that sometimes grows
to a length of 7 feet or more and may weigh as much as a ton,
the Atlantic Loggerhead (*Caretta caretta*), usually not more than
3 feet in length and 300 pounds in weight, and the Atlantic
Green Turtle (*Chelonia mydas*), the chef's favorite for the con-
cocting of turtle soup. In warm waters the Atlantic Green
Turtle grows to a great size — sometimes as much as half a ton
in weight — but those that venture into cold water are much
smaller and in the New York area one weighing 100 pounds
would be a good catch. These seagoing species are summer
visitors offshore and now and then are taken by local fishermen
or sighted by passengers on ships. At odd times, however,
they wander into New York Harbor and thus must be enrolled
as part of the fauna of the region.

That about covers the turtles by land and sea within the
legal limits of Father Knickerbocker's realm. Now for the
lizards, and perhaps it should be singular — lizard — since only
one species, the Five-lined Skink (*Eumeces fasciatus*) actually re-
sides in the area by choice. This is a slender lizard some 5 or
6 inches in length. The young have very fancy bright blue tails
but this fades into gray in the adults. The body color is variable but in most cases it is black or olive-brown marked with
five longitudinal light stripes that grow duller as the creature

ages. This little lizard forages around stones and logs in search of insects on which to dine and it is one of the most northerly in range of its tribe. Since lizards prefer a warm climate and plenty of sunlight, most of the species that occur in the United States are found in the Southwest. Few if any venture as far north as the Canadian border.

Aside from the Five-lined Skink, the only other resident lizard in any of the five boroughs is the Northern Fence Lizard or Pine Swift (*Sceloporus undulatus hyacinthinus*), found in considerable numbers on Staten Island, where it was deliberately introduced by Carl F. Kauffeld of the Staten Island Zoological Society. In 1942 he caught twenty-nine of these lizards in the Pine Barrens of New Jersey, where they occur naturally, and transported them to Staten Island for release in the Rossville sector. As stated in one of the publications of the Staten Island Zoological Society, "the reason for releasing these lizards in Staten Island, where no lizards occur naturally, was the hope of developing a ready source of food near at hand for lizard-eating snakes in the Zoo's collection." The introduction was successful. The Fence Lizards increased and multiplied and now the species is well established in this extension of its natural range.

It is named the Fence Lizard because it is seen so often scampering along fence rails in its hunt for insects, but it also scurries about the stumps of trees and around fallen logs for the same purpose. It is about the same length as the Five-lined Skink, although broader of body and larger and with quite spiny scales. It is brownish in color with dark wavy crossbands and the males have blue patches on the underside.

As for snakes, the third division of the Reptile Class of the region, the most common resident species is the familiar Eastern Garter Snake (*Thamnophis sirtalis*) that may reach a length of 3 feet but ordinarily is less than that. It comes in various body colors such as red, brown, green, and black but usually has dorsal and lateral stripes of greenish yellow by which it may be known. It is abundant and harmless and some persons insist that it is beneficial, though this is a debatable point. Much like it in general appearance but smaller, thinner, more graceful and much less common is the Eastern Ribbon Snake (*Thamnophis sauritus*), on which the dark body color and the yellow striping are in greater contrast. Also, the Eastern Ribbon Snake is much more aquatic than the Eastern Garter Snake and does much of its foraging in the ponds, brooks, and lakes of the area. It is a fast traveler either on the ground or in the water.

An occasional cause of local disturbance in the outlying sections of the city is the discovery of an Eastern Milk Snake (*Lampropeltis doliata*), whose pattern of red or brown blotches on a buff or tan background usually frightens the beholder into a belief that it is the venomous Northern Copperhead (*Agkistrodon contortrix mokeson*) and a dangerous creature. The truth is that the handsome Milk Snake, which runs to a length of 3 feet or more, is quite harmless, generally good-tempered, and definitely beneficial in that it feeds mostly on mice. Since mice are common in and around barns, Milk Snakes often are seen in barnyards, a circumstance that perhaps gave rise long ago to the legend that accounts for their common name — that they suck milk from the cows in the barns at night, a feat to stagger the imagination. In the first place, it's an impossible performance for a snake, and in the second place, no sensible cow would stand for it for a moment.

Still another cause of false alarm within the city limits is the Eastern Hognose Snake or Puff Adder (*Heterodon platyrhinos*) that runs to 2 feet or more in length and has a rather stout body variable in color but usually reddish brown or gray, with dark patches along its back and sides. This snake puts on a great show of ferocity when disturbed, flattening its head like a Hooded Cobra and hissing and striking at the same time, but a child could pick it up with safety because it never bites anything except the frogs and toads it feeds upon. If its show of ferocity doesn't work, it has another trick it tries in order to be left alone: it turns over on its back and pretends to be dead. The Eastern Hognose Snake was formerly fairly common over much of our territory but the growth of the city has driven it out of all but a few sections. It likes open ground and sandy regions, and the best place to look for it within the city limits would be southern Staten Island or on open ground to the rear of the ocean beaches in Brooklyn and Queens.

Even Central Park in the heart of Manhattan has a supply of resident snakes and one of them is the tiny Northern Brown Snake, formerly called DeKay's Snake (*Storeria dekayi*), brown above and pinkish below and usually only a foot in length, though they do come longer. It lives under flat rocks and feeds mostly on worms. Another still smaller reptile of much the same general color and feeding habits is the Eastern Worm Snake (*Carphophis amoenus*) that also is brown above but is salmon-red below. This one prefers to live in moist ground under planks, logs, or fallen timber of any kind and is more often found in the wet woods of the Bronx than in Central Park where the Northern Brown Snake is quite at home.

Many of the park lakes and ponds of the area have an abundant supply of the species most easily seen within the city limits, the Northern Water Snake (*Natrix sipedon*). Mostly they appear as little round dark objects on the placid surface of the water, the little round dark objects being the protruding heads of the snakes whose bodies lie below the surface. I have seen as many as a dozen at a time in Van Cortlandt Lake. In the water, and when they first emerge, they seem to be quite dark brown in color but they often drape themselves over the branches of shrubs or on dead limbs along the shore line and, when they dry, they take on a lighter hue and you can see that they have reddish-brown transverse bands along their bodies. As they grow older, however, the pattern grows duller. They feed in the water or along the shore on small fish, frogs, tadpoles, and other aquatic creatures and, if on shore when disturbed, they immediately take to the water. The Northern

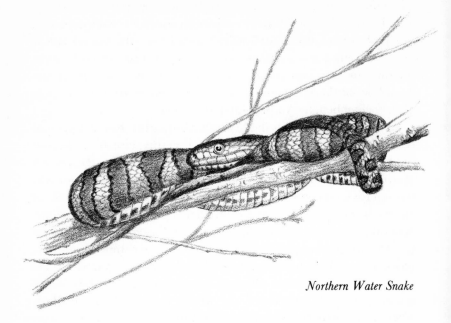

Northern Water Snake

Water Snake undoubtedly is next to the Eastern Garter Snake in abundance in the region.

The largest snake that remains a resident of the city, though in small and gradually decreasing numbers, is the Northern Black Racer or Black Snake (*Coluber constrictor*) that is fairly heavy of body and may grow to a length of 6 feet. However, few of that length are encountered and a five-footer on the premises would command my deep respect. Some authorities write the second common name as one word, Blacksnake. The official name now is Black Racer, for the speed with which it can travel over the ground. Under any name it is bluish-black above, gray below, and has a white throat and chin. On bright cool days in spring or autumn it may be found sunning itself in some warm exposed position such as the flat surface of a smooth boulder that has been warmed by sunlight. You may still find it in some of the wilder sections of Staten Island,

Queens, and the Bronx. It hunts around old outbuildings, along stone walls, and in thickets and woods. It often climbs small trees or shrubs to rob birds' nests of eggs or young and it also devours nestling rabbits; but it should stand in high favor with farmers, gardeners and even ordinary householders of the suburbs for the number of rats and mice it destroys in a year.

If disturbed when hunting in a thicket or on a woodland floor, it has an alarming habit of vibrating its tail among the dead leaves in a way to convince innocent bystanders that they have a deadly "rattler" to deal with, but the Northern Black Racer is not venomous. In fact, New York City has no resident venomous snakes. The Northern Copperhead infests some of the little islands in the Westchester lakes that are part of the New York City water supply system, but there is no record of any one of them visiting the city in recent times. Black Racers, of course, will bite vigorously if irritated. They are harmless if left alone, and often become semi-tame around hospitable dooryards.

The dainty little Northern Ringneck Snake (*Diadophis punctatus*) is another reptilian resident of the city but in quite limited numbers and even these rarely are seen because of their small size (they are very slim and rarely more than a foot or so in length) and the fact that they spend most of their lives under flat stones or logs feeding on worms, salamanders, insect larvae, and other such tidbits. The Ringneck is gray or blue-gray above and bright orange-yellow below, with a collar of that same bright color running across the back of its neck. It is completely harmless but gives off an unpleasant odor when frightened. It is said that they tame easily and make good pets to keep in a terrarium.

Another slim, graceful and truly beautiful little reptile that occasionally is encountered within the city limits — the chances of seeing it are better in the Bronx than anywhere else — is the Smooth Green Snake (*Opheodrys vernalis*) that usually is not more than a foot or so in length. It hunts in grassy places and along the branches of shrubs and low trees for the insects on which it feeds and, being a glowing pale green in color, it is not easily detected against the background of green foliage. My best view of a Smooth Green Snake occurred when I was poking through some shrubbery in search of a warbler's nest and found myself staring the lovely little reptile in the eye where it was looped along a Black Locust branchlet. It stared back at me for some seconds with apparent unconcern and then moved off smoothly with unhurried grace.

This makes a total of ten species of snakes that might fairly be considered residents of the region, but only two species, the Garter Snake and the Water Snake, are abundant enough to be encountered frequently by those who walk in what woods and open fields remain within the city limits. Milk Snakes and Black Racers are few and far between in the outlying sections of the city. Ribbon Snakes are not common and probably the few that are seen are mistaken for Garter Snakes by ordinary observers. The Hognose Snake or Puff Adder is found in only a few seaward sections of the city and the four dainty little snakes of the area, Northern Brown, Worm, Smooth Green, and Ringneck, are found only by those who know how, when and where to look for them.

Here it must be admitted that not many persons deliberately go looking for snakes. Among humans a fear of snakes is so general that it often is called instinctive, a term indignantly rejected by ophiologists, which is the group name for snake experts and admirers. Certainly there is little reason to be afraid of most snakes and particularly those of the northeastern section of the United States where venomous snakes are few and these few have to be sought in special locations to be found at all. There are other beliefs and prejudices concerning snakes that have no logic or truth about them. Snakes do not "charm" birds with hypnotic stares, nor do snakes have slimy skins. Their skins are composed of dry scales that in most cases are shiny and smooth but in some species are ridged or "keeled" in a way to make the skin rough to the touch.

Snakes are not "charmed" by snake charmers armed with flutes, flageolets, or musical instruments of any kind. From our point of view snakes are deaf. They have no ears or other specialized organs of hearing, but they can feel vibrations in the ground or water and perhaps even in the air. The long forked tongue that a moving snake keeps darting in and out of its mouth has no venom on it in any species and is used as a tester, taster, or feeler in search of food. All snakes produce eggs but in some species the eggs hatch within the body of the female and live young are born, sometimes of surprising length. In our area, for instance, the young of the viviparous Water Snake may be 6 inches or more in length at birth. The Garter Snake, Ribbon Snake, and Northern Brown Snake also produce live young. But the Milk Snake, Smooth Green Snake, and the Black Racer lay eggs whose hatching period varies greatly according to the species and the weather.

Since snakes are not warm-blooded like mammals but take the temperature of the surrounding atmosphere, they cannot endure freezing weather and are forced to hibernate in regions where the winters are cold, as they are in the northeastern section of the United States. Which means that all snakes in our region hibernate. The individuals of some species go into the ground alone in sheltered places, and individuals of other species gather together at the rear of caves or deep crevices in rocky regions. Some travel miles to reach such snake dens in the autumn. Some snakes eat other snakes. Eagles and hawks and some other birds eat snakes. Skunks and raccoons not only eat adult snakes but dig up snake eggs and devour them with gusto. But in thickly populated areas, such as our city, the worst enemies of the resident snakes are the human inhabitants. Why almost every man's hand is against them is an age-old question to which I never have heard a good and sufficient answer. Please, if you see a snake, do not be the first to cast a stone.

Chapter 9

Lowly Forms of Plant Life

YOU MUST HUMBLE yourself to scrape any real acquaintance with such lowly forms of plant life as liverworts, lichens, and mosses. You have to get down on your hands and knees and pore over them through a magnifying glass. Liverworts, the first plants to emerge from the ancient oceans to root themselves on rocks and soil at the water's edge, we now have with us in the shape of greenish masses of clustered cells on the moist surfaces of stones, stumps, logs, tree trunks, and just plain wet ground, including the banks of streams and the shores of ponds and lakes. Related to them are the mosses, of which we have many kinds on the premises. Most of the mosses are soft to the touch and attractive to the eye and many of them hold up neat little cases of spores for inspection in late spring or summer, but we can give them only a passing glance of admiration as we hurry along to larger things such as fungi and ferns. Even so, we have to make one intermediate stop — a short one — to peer at the lichens that we find growing on stone walls, gravestones, boulders in shady places, tree trunks and branches, and other fixed objects.

Probably the oldest existing partnership in the world is that shared by certain algae and fungi in the joint and continued production of those forms of plant life that we call lichens. This partnership has been operating successfully in a wholesale way over the greater part of the land surface of this planet for hundreds of millions of years and is still going strong. A lichen is an alga surrounded by a fungus. The alga, which contains chlorophyll, manufactures the food for the combination. The fungus provides the thready anchorage to the surface on which the lichen is growing and also is a great help in gathering and retaining the moisture needed for growth. Scientists have a name for a "mutual benefit association" of this kind. They call it symbiosis. It occurs here and there in different walks of plant and animal life and is the object of continual study.

There are lichens of many kinds in our area. Individually, of course, they are tiny plants and we take note of them only in masses or communities. Even then we too often give them the wrong name. At some time or other you must have been told that you would never get lost in the woods if you remembered that the moss grows on the north side of trees. Such a statement is subject to challenge on two counts. One is that the "moss" mentioned doesn't grow on the north side of trees all over the world, for a number of reasons, including differences in north and south latitudes and the direction from which come the prevailing moisture-laden winds. A second point is that the green growth referred to as "moss" probably on examination will turn out to be a mass of lichens.

This error is compounded in the literary field. Longfellow's evergreens in the land of Evangeline — "the murmuring pines and the hemlocks, bearded with moss" — actually were draped with threads of green-gray lichens miscalled Usnea Moss, and probably they were *Usnea barbata.* John Masefield's tramp whose idea of Death was "jest a quiet stone, all over-gray wi' moss" probably was mistaken in more ways than one. Almost certainly he had lichens in his mind's eye, though he had moss on his lips. And it would be a closer approximation of the truth if a certain time-honored adage ran: A rolling stone gathers no lichens.

You can't help seeing lichens if you wander anywhere in the woods or fields of any region. The rocks and ledges in Manhattan Island's green pastures, Central Park, are embossed with lichens and so are the gravestones in downtown Trinity graveyard. If you look at some of the great boulders standing in the open in Bronx Park you will find them decorated plentifully with the thin, delicate blue-green or blue-gray tracery of *Parmelia* lichens, the most abundant of which in our area is *Parmelia conspersa*. You will notice that the fringes of the rounded patches usually are lighter than the interior portions. In the woods of Staten Island or Queens you will find rocks and boulders covered with the thicker, coarser and often curling clusters of parchment-like lichens of the *Umbilicaria* group, dull brownish gray in dry weather, rich green after a rain, and always coffee-colored on the underside. These are sometimes called "rock tripe," and if you use a magnifying glass you will see the little holes on the underside and the little protuberances on the upper surface that account for the nickname. It is alleged that some persons make a tasty soup of these lichens.

On a moist bank you may notice a wrinkled, gray "mossy patch" sprinkled with bright crimson dots that on closer inspection you will see are raised up on tiny gray shafts. If this sight meets your eyes, you probably will be looking at a mass of *Cladonia cristatella*, lichens called British Soldiers because of the "red coats" of the fruiting nobs atop the spore-bearing branchlets. Incidentally, a hardier relative of thicker growth than our British Soldiers is *Cladonia rangiferina*, better known as the "reindeer moss" of the arctic tundra and a staple article of diet in the lives of the nomadic Barren Ground Caribou of that

Pixie Cups and British Soldiers

cheerless region. But here we have to leave the lichens, that odd partnership of algae and fungi, and turn to fungi that lead lives of their own.

Put a loaf of bread in a dark, damp place for a few days and it will be moldy. If you open a jar of jelly in the kitchen and let it stand unused, the top of the jelly soon will be covered with a moldy growth. Molds are fungi. So are yeasts, mildews, plant rusts, smuts and blights, and other agencies that cause excrescences or disfigurements in ordinary plant life. But these are matters for microscopic examination and we will have no traffic with them. They are for the experts and laboratory study. We merely mention for the record that they live and flourish in many forms in New York City as they do in every city around the world, and we move along to other forms of fungi easier to examine by hand or with the naked eye.

All of us have seen fungus growths of different shapes, sizes, colors, and kinds on tree trunks, fallen logs, and dead wood wherever it stands or lies. Old stumps usually are covered with them. Some of them are edible, but most of them are tough and tasteless. We can leave them to wild animals with sharper teeth. Some of them are really attractive in color and design, however, and if you examine them you will find in most cases the underside is a flat surface punctured with innumerable tiny holes. These holes eventually serve as outlets for the countless spores each growth produces. The round "puffballs" often found on lawns or in open grassy fields are edible fungi and a real delicacy when gathered at the right time and dished up in the right way. The right time to pick them is when the interior is still white and firm. A recommended way to prepare them — *crede experto* — is to cut them into fairly thick slices, fry them in butter, season them with pepper and salt, and serve them on toast. In the face of such a dainty dish it is hard to realize that, left to an uncooked fate in the field, it would soon have changed to a sooty mass of millions of spores ready to shoot out into the air like brown smoke at the slightest touch on the crinkly container.

Puffballs of baseball size or larger are fairly common in our region. Much less common and much smaller members of the same fungus group are the earthstars or geasters (pronounced *Je-as'ters*) that have a somewhat star-shaped, parchment-like supporting base for the puffball center. This basal structure lies flat on the ground when moist and curls up toward the puffball center in dry periods. Geasters frequently are found in the woods — they seem to like pine groves in sandy regions — but, being neutral in tint and only a few inches in diameter, they are easily overlooked amid the litter on a woodland floor. However, if you happen to see one, search the nearby ground carefully and probably you will find others. Like many fungi, they tend to colonize.

There are many kinds of edible fungi to be found in the woods, thickets, and fields — mostly in the wet woods — of New York City. Often in my excursions I encountered elderly men whose accents bespoke foreign birth, with a stick in one hand and a basket or perhaps a large paper bag in the other. The stick was for poking around among the dead leaves to uncover any edible fungi that might be lurking there and the basket or bag was for carrying home the swag. I entered into conversation with many such collectors and looked over their trophies with considerable interest.

When the average raised-on-the premises resident of New

York speaks or hears of "mushrooms" it is taken for granted that there is only one kind, that it is often served with a good steak, and that there will be serious or perhaps even fatal results if, instead of a "mushroom," you swallow a "toadstool" by mistake. The luscious dainty referred to is the common Meadow Mushroom (*Agaricus campestris*), found not only in the wild but domesticated for the restaurant trade and for canning purposes. It is common on fertilized lawns and pasture lands, sometimes springing up in abundance after a rainy spell. It is a fine mushroom, to be sure, but by no means the only edible species of the area. When I looked into the bags or baskets of the elderly collectors I met in the field, I found that more than a dozen species of the region were considered good enough to eat and abundant enough to make the search for them profitable. As for the allegedly deadly toadstools that might be garnered or eaten in error, the truth is that the term toadstool has no official standing at all. It means nothing to a botanist. Both "mushrooms" and "toadstools" are gilled fungi that come in many shapes, sizes, colors — and various degrees of edibility. Many are harmless but tough or tasteless. Some are delicious. Some are deadly poison and no fooling about it. "Gathering mushrooms" is dangerous work unless you are well acquainted with the many different species that occur in any area.

One of the edible species of lawn and pasture that the ordinary observer might shrink from in horror is the Shaggy-mane or Horsetail Mushroom (*Coprinus comatus*). Despite its lethal appearance, it is good eating if gathered before it begins to turn black and drip an inky fluid, a mark of the *Coprinus* clan. But growing in the same woods, thickets, or meadows with the many edible species of our region are the Fly Amanita (*Amanita muscaria*) and the Deadly Amanita (*Amanita phalloides*) that are definitely and dangerously poisonous. There are other toxic species of the area not so violent in effect and there are odd-shaped and strangely colored edible kinds not nearly so attractive to the eye. By and large, it is difficult for the inexpert

Fly Amanita

to distinguish the harmless from the harmful species. In fact, it is dangerous to try. Better get a handbook or field guide and study up on the subject before going out with a basket and a stick for a mushroom hunt in the woods and fields.

Now for the ferns that spread their fronds in beauty to the delight of many walkers in the woods and fields, some of them through all the months of the year. Long ago I purchased for the sum of one dollar a small oblong paperbound booklet with an orange-colored cover bearing the title *Ferns* heavily printed over a frond that served as a background. It was a pocket manual of the ferns of New England and the Middle Atlantic States with line cuts and text as an aid to the identification of the ferns of that region. There were illustrations of the particular ways in which the different species fruited and in many cases there were cross sections of the fern stems (or stipes) shown because the pattern of the "vascular bundles" is another aid to the identification of a puzzling fern. This booklet, the work of Farida A. Wiley of the American Museum of Natural History, was a revelation to me. And a delight. Within a year, by diligent search and ardent scrutiny, plus much thumbing of the booklet, I had all the native ferns of the neighboring woods and fields at my mercy, and I enjoyed every moment of it.

I did better than that. I corresponded with Miss Wiley for the purpose of finding out how many different kinds of fern she had located within the city limits. In reply there came a list of some eighteen species varying in size from the neat little Ebony Spleenwort (*Asplenium platyneuron*) that grows almost secretly out of moist shady banks or the crevices of stone walls to that towering quartet of the Pteridophyta of the region, the Royal Fern (*Osmunda regalis*), the Interrupted Fern (*Osmunda claytoniana*), the Cinnamon Fern (*Osmunda cinnamomea*), and the Ostrich Fern (*Matteuccia struthiopteris*). Nor was that all. There was the further information that sixteen of the eighteen listed species flourished in the wilder parts of Riverdale and Van Cortlandt Park, my own bailiwick. The lovely Maidenhair Fern (*Adiantum pedatum*) was reported only from Staten Island and even there it was losing its fight for survival within the city limits. That might have been expected. If beauty is its own excuse for being, as Emerson implied, it may also be the cause of its own disappearance from the scene. The Maidenhair Fern, with its lifted and rounded fronds of feathery foliage, is a trophy too beautiful for the thoughtless to leave untouched in the wildwood.

The other listed species not reported from my home grounds was the familiar Christmas Fern (*Polystichum acrostichoides*) and the curious thing is that I never had noticed its strange absence in the area. It is common to abundant on the rocky slopes of moist woodlands around New York City and, seeing it so frequently in such places, I had taken it for granted that it also grew in the rocky woodland slopes of Riverdale and Van Cortlandt Park. I was a trifle shocked to learn that it was unreported where I believed it to have been flourishing bravely. It was a challenge that could not be ignored. For days I scoured the woodlands of Riverdale and Van Cortlandt Park, scanning all the rocky slopes, peering in every likely nook and dell, but all in vain. Not a frond of this sturdy species did I find. Once again I suspected that the fern's good qualities were the reasons for its scarcity or even extinction in our neighborhood. Its name is justified. It is green at Christmas and practically throughout the winter. There are other evergreen ferns in the region but they are frailer in character and often are buried among dead leaves or covered by snow. The Christmas Fern stands out bravely at such times and its fronds of deep green would be natural trophies for random strollers in the woods. Overpicking is the only explanation I have to offer for its absence in the neighborhood.

However, Riverdale has one distinction in the field of native ferns. In a low swampy stretch of unfrequented park land it nourishes a fine colony of Ostrich Fern. Here in the summer shade the stiff and deeply grooved stipes reach upward in long curves with the fronds spreading out like ostrich plumes. It is the only stand of these ferns that I know within the city limits. There may be other stands of it in our territory, just as there may be patches of Rattlesnake Fern (*Botrychium virginianum*) in shady spots in the Bronx or on Staten Island, but Miss Wiley found it only in the Douglaston section of the Borough of Queens.

The most common fern in the swamps and moist woodlands of the region is the Sensitive Fern (*Onoclea sensibilis*), with its broad blades that turn wan and pale at the first touch of frost and linger in a ghostly way over the woodland floor. Appropriately enough, the little feathery New York Fern (*Thelypteris noveboracensis*) grows everywhere in the wet woods and the

Marsh Fern (*Thelypteris palustris*) fringes the Van Cortlandt swamp with its feathery foliage. The Hayscented Fern (*Dennstaedtia punctilobula*) springs up like a light green ruff around boulders in the meadows and the lovely Lady Fern (*Athyrium filix-femina*) pushes up modestly in shady nooks in many sections of the city. In the more moist parts of the wooded regions you may find the Crested Fern (*Dryopteris cristata*) and, in the undergrowth protected by towering oaks and maples on rocky hillsides, there will be the Spinulose Woodfern (*Dryopteris spinulosa*), or some close relative in the *Dryopteris* group. Along the woodland paths, standing knee high as you walk past it, grows the stiff Brake Fern or Bracken (*Pteridium aquilinum*) that is not as sturdy as it looks; slenderer and daintier ferns still will be green when the tall Bracken has been killed by early frosts.

The Broad Beech Fern (*Thelypteris hexagonoptera*), mentioned as a resident by Miss Wiley, I found of a spring morning when looking for migrating warblers in a patch of wet woods in the eastern section of Van Cortlandt Park; and along an ancient stone wall through which water was seeping in the Riverdale sector, with tall trees arched over the roadway, I found the Rusty Woodsia (*Woodsia ilvensis*). Often when we are looking for one thing we find another. I had found some Ebony Spleenwort higher up along the wall and was scanning the crumbling stonework, a retaining wall that was being breached by time and steady pressure from a steep wooded slope above it, in the hope of finding more Ebony Spleenwort when I chanced upon the Rusty Woodsia. Going back the next year to look for the Rusty Woodsia, I made a real discovery a rod or two still farther down along the same wall. At first I thought it was my Woodsia but when I inspected it closely I noticed some differences: the stipe (stem) and leaves of the Rusty Woodsia were hairy or scaly and in this foundling they were smooth. I didn't dare pick any as a specimen to take home and examine critically. There were just a few sparse tender fronds growing in one moist niche in the old wall.

I went home, thumbed my Wiley booklet on ferns, searched through the fern section of Volume I of Britton and Brown, pored over what other books I had on the same subject, and all evidence pointed in one direction: I had come upon the Fragile Fern or Brittle Fern (*Cystopteris fragilis*). All authorities, including Miss Wiley, listed it as common in New York State, New England, and the Middle Atlantic States, but it was new to me and it was not included in Miss Wiley's list of ferns found in New York City. I did not trust my identification of the fern. I penned a plea to Miss Wiley to journey out to Riverdale to see for herself. I met her at the end of the subway at 242nd Street and Broadway and drove her to the wood road and stone wall in the Riverdale sector. I pointed out the spot and the little green fronds. She looked, turned, and spoke. It was Fragile Fern, Brittle Fern, or Common Bladder Fern. Under any English name it was still *Cystopteris fragilis*. I couldn't have felt better if I had been knighted, yet somehow I resented the name Common Bladder Fern. Common by all accounts east, south, west, and north of New York City, it was a distinct addition to Miss Wiley's list of resident species within the city limits. On my own list I set it down as the Fragile Fern. That name seems much more appropriate, and lingers more fondly in memory.

One more group of spore-bearers of the region must be mentioned. These are the horsetails of various kinds, the most abundant of which is the Field Horsetail (*Equisetum arvense*) that springs up everywhere in waste ground but seems to have a special fondness for railway embankments, moist roadsides, and ditches. The stiff, hollow, conspicuously jointed, leafless, pinkish-brown fertile stems with cone-like spore-bearing tops are the first to appear in spring and where they stick up from the ground a foot or two in height in clumps and patches they might be likened to a crop of doll's drumsticks or perhaps some strange kind of extra-thin, inedible and incredible asparagus stalks. As children we used to pull the sections of the jointed stems apart and put them back together again, not necessarily in the order in which we found them growing. If you tap the oval top over your cupped hand in late April or early May, the ripe spores will fall out and settle on your palm in the form of a fine greenish-yellow powder. The infertile green stems with whorls of needle-like branches at the joints come up later and are not as stout or as stiff as the fertile stems. In fact, the difference in appearance between the fertile and infertile stems is such that it is hard to believe that they spring from the same underground root and are separate parts of the same plant.

Of all the plants mentioned in this chapter only the ferns — and not all of them — catch the eye or win the admiration of the ordinary walker in the woods and fields, but all the spore-bearers are of ancient and honorable lineage. They belong among the "first families" in plant life. Some ancestor or prototype of the Field Horsetail was a towering calamite standing perhaps a hundred feet tall in the fens of the Mississippian Period some 250,000 years ago. And even before that — 50,000 years earlier — the giant ferns of the Devonian Period were the plant wonders of an awakening world.

Chapter 10

An Endless Array of Flowers

THERE ARE some technical points to be cleared up before we can take to the primrose path and go wandering among the city's flowers. If we were following the accepted botanical line we would, on emerging from the region of the ferns and fungi, find ourselves in a grove of evergreens and it would be many pages before we would be permitted to meet even the first flowers of the year such as Shakespeare's

> *Daffodils*
> *That come before the swallow dares and take*
> *The winds of March with beauty.*

We may enjoy ourselves and at the same time be duly respectful of authority. The botanists have good and sufficient reasons for linking and listing the families of "seed-bearing plants" in a definite order from the pines to the composites — asters, daisies, goldenrods, and such — without regard to the size, shape, or outward appearance of the species involved. A tiny flower, a creeping vine, a luxuriant shrub, and a tall tree can be grouped as fellow members of the Rose Family by a botanist, but the ordinary person does not think in such terms or see flowering plants in that light. To most of us the green world is divided into such apparently natural groups as grasses, vines, flowers, shrubs, and trees. A little investigation will reveal that the differences among many members of such groups are greater than the similarities and that our usual groupings, if an attack is pressed, are indefensible.

Even so, an unsuspecting reader should not be bludgeoned with botanical procedure or, still worse, bored by it. He should have information presented to him in a manner that seems logical to him and in terms that he can best understand. At the same time, and in the hope that some bit of botany will stick to the reader as a bur often fastens itself to the clothing of a wanderer in the woods or fields, the systematic arrangement of the botanists will be followed as closely as possible within the broad groupings that seem plain and logical to the average intelligent citizen.

We shall put off, then, the presentation of the pines and their cone-bearing relatives until we come to the chapter on trees and take up the next order of business according to the botanists, which is the Cattail Family. Both the Broad-leaved Cattail (*Typha latifolia*) and the Narrow-leaved Cattail (*Typha angustifolia*) are common in the fresh-water marshes of the city and it is no trick at all to distinguish one from the other without going to the bother of measuring the width of the leaves. In the heavier flowering spike of the Broad-leaved Cattail there is no visible dividing line between the upper staminate flowers and the lower pistillate section, whereas in the Narrow-leaved species there is almost always a definite gap and a portion of the stem visible between the two sections.

It may seem strange to refer to cattail spikes as clusters of flowers but they have all the essential requirements to fill the

bill: stamens that produce pollen and pistils that, when fertilized by the pollen, produce seeds. In both species the staminate tops of the flower spikes fall away first and leave the dark
brown cylinders of ripening seeds to withstand the frosts of
autumn and the ravages of the winter winds. Some of the
ragged cottony remnants still clinging to the dry dead stalks
in spring will serve to line the nests of half a dozen kinds of
marsh birds. At the lower end of the Van Cortlandt swamp I
found the Broad-leaved Cattail to be the dominant species but
there are patches of the Narrow-leaved species here and there,
mostly along the edges where you will also find the American
Bur-reed (*Sparganium americanum*) with its prickly-looking globular clusters of flowers spaced at intervals along the upraised
fruiting stalks.

There are, of course, many other kinds of water plants in the
area, whether we call them weeds, grasses, or flowers. One of
the most abundant is the Broad-leaved Arrowhead (*Sagittaria
latifolia*) that also goes by the names of Duck Potato, Swamp
Potato, Wapato, and a few other things. The name Arrowhead is derived from the angular shape of the large green leaves.
The edible tubers on its submerged roots — good food for ducks
and other residents or transients — account for some of the
other common names. The three-petaled white flowers with
centers of golden stamens are quite attractive in summer.

As far as the calendar is concerned, the earliest flower of the
area is the sturdy — and malodorous if crushed — Skunk Cabbage (*Symplocarpus foetidus*) whose pointed and protective "hood"
or spathe striped with purple and green pushes up through the
frozen floor of the swamp while February snows are still falling.
If you clear away the snow and brush aside the dead leaves and
grasses that may be encumbering the crest of the pointed hood,
you will be able to peer into the protected hollow and see the
fleshy oval spike, or spadix, sprinkled with the "excrescences"
that are the true flowers of this curious plant. Not so bold is that
close relative with the clerical name, the Jack-in-the-Pulpit (*Ar-*

isaema triphyllum) that waits until "April melts in Maytime" before it takes its stand above the lesser growths at ground level in wet woods and damp thickets. The common but often overlooked Arrow Arum (*Peltandra virginica*) with leaves of somewhat the same size and general shape as those of the Broad-leaved Arrowhead is another member of the same group and shares the family trait of providing a protective covering for the flower-

Broad-leaved Arrowhead

ing spike or spadix. The Arrow Arum abounds in and along the banks of the little stream meandering down through the Van Cortlandt swamp but to most persons who take any notice of it at all it is merely, in bulk, a mass of large green leaves stirring gently to the tug of a sluggish current in a slow stream. The explanation is that the green flowering spike is only partially exposed through a side opening in a long conical spathe, or hood. As a matter of fact, only the staminate section of the flowering spike is exposed to view at all. The pistillate flowers are obscured in a hollow below the opening. In due time the protective wrapping around the fertilized pistillate flowers becomes a tough egg-shaped covering for the 2-inch cluster of marble-sized berries that are the fruit of this plant. In late summer or early autumn you can find such clusters trailing in the water in a downstream direction at the end of long rubbery stalks. The enclosed berries are green in the early stage of development but turn quite dark as they age in the stream.

While we are still knee deep in the swamp, so to speak, it should be mentioned that there and elsewhere in the confines of New York City are many kinds of grasses, sedges, and rushes, some of which are very useful and others of which are highly colorful in season, but most of which we shall leave for the experts to unravel. A student could spend a lifetime collecting and describing the innumerable species of these great groups that are to be found in the fields, woods, swamps, and marshes within the city limits. One grass, however, must be mentioned because it is a growing pest. That's the Common Reed or Phragmites (*Phragmites communis*) that, in great masses, raises itself to a height of as much as 12 feet in fresh water and brackish marshes and produces at the pinnacle a foot-long feathery fruiting plume that frequently is dyed a gaudy color and hawked on street corners as a curiosity. The marching battalions of this plant have gained a tremendous amount of wet ground in and around New York City in the past fifty years and it is taking over territory formerly held by much more valuable vegetation.

It affords some shelter to mammals and birds but it provides no food for such creatures and it chokes out many succulent aquatic plants on which they formerly fed. When I was a boy there was no sign of Phragmites in the Van Cortlandt swamp and now a towering growth covers half the little marsh at the lower end of the swamp at the expense of cattails and other former tenants of the conquered territory. Once a rare sight in the New York region, today it meets the eye in all directions. It springs up quickly wherever there is "casual water" in ditches or vacant lots and it stretches for miles along the motor parkways where they fringe the rivers, bays, inlets, and brackish marshes of the area.

Let us turn to the duckweeds of our territory, a much more pleasant topic. Around the railroad bridge at the lower end of the Van Cortlandt swamp the water on either side, in warm weather, always is covered with a mass of floating greenery made up of duckweeds of various kinds. If you scoop up a handful and go over it with a magnifying glass, you will find that most of it consists of two kinds, Greater Duckweed (*Spirodela polyrhiza*) and Lesser Duckweed (*Lemna minor*). However, it's just possible that you may be lucky enough to come up with some tiny individual plants — mere green grains — of the species named *Wolffia columbiana* and distinguished in botany as the smallest flowering plant known to science. All the duckweeds are tiny floating or submerged flakes of greenery but in this case the whole plant is about 1 mm. (1/25 inch) in diameter and the flower consists of one stamen and one pistil of microscopic size.

Climbing to higher ground for the moment, along the banks of the swamp and lake and, indeed, in many moist situations in the region, you may find the Spider-lily or Spiderwort (*Tradescantia virginiana*) with the golden tips of its six stamens standing out brightly against the background of the three deep blue to purplish petals. The buds are produced in a cluster and, though the individual flowers may last only a day, the buds open in succession and the blooming period runs from early May well into July. This flower is so attractive that you will often find it cultivated in gardens. A close relative and one of the most abundant flowers throughout the five boroughs is the little Asiatic Dayflower (*Commelina communis*) with its pale blue petals pushing their way out of an enfolding leaflike bract. These persistent flowers spring up almost everywhere in moist ground but they prefer some protection from the sun and flourish at their brightest in the shady dooryards of suburban homes.

If you have never looked closely at this common flower, do so, and you will note some curious details. Two light blue petals catch the eye but there is a third small and inconspicuous petal almost white in hue. The story is that this floral arrangement of two handsome petals and a third insignificant one, a generic trait, was the reason Linnaeus named the genus after the three brothers Commelin, early Dutch botanists, two of whom were ornaments of their profession, while the third never amounted to much. Complete belief in this flowery tale is not binding on botanists or innocent bystanders. What fascinates me about the flower is the color, shape, and arrangement of the six stamens. Every so often I pick one of the flowers for the pure pleasure of looking at the stamens through a magnifying glass. As can be seen at once, they are of two different kinds. Usually there are three fertile ones (never more than that) tipped with golden pollen-bearing anthers and three or sometimes four sterile ones that are shorter and tipped with little dark crosses. This is a small matter over which to rejoice but "a thing of beauty is a joy for ever" and I find the stamen array of this common little flower a source of recurring delight.

Now we go back again to the bogs, marshes, and swamps to pay homage to a few more plant residents of moist territory. One is the handsome Pickerel-weed (*Pontederia cordata*) that occurs in colonies in water where you might expect to find the fish after which it is named. The large, shining, and usually heart-shaped leaves are spread for weeks in spring before the stiff flowering spikes encircled by many slashed purple flowers come into bloom and serve notice that summer has arrived. In the leaf department, however, the most impressive plant of our swamps and wet woods is the White Hellebore (*Veratrum viride*) that the French-Canadians call "Tabac du Diable" because of a fancied resemblance to the tobacco plant in height and size of leaf. It's quite common to find plants 2 or 3 feet high — they do grow much higher — and the sharp-pointed oval leaves, which may be a foot in length, are in effect pleated by the prominent and stiff parallel ribs. The flowering panicle that the plant holds aloft in late spring or early summer is generally overlooked because the little flowers are green or greenish yellow and quite unimpressive compared to the flaring leaves that are bound to catch the eye of any wanderer in moist shady places.

The White Hellebore is a member of the Lily Family though the plant is not what most of us would call lily-like in leaf or flower. There are, as a matter of fact, many plants of the Lily Family growing wild within the city limits but, for the most part, only the experts know the intricate ties that bind them into a family group for the botanists. The Wild Leek (*Allium tricoccum*) and the Field Garlic (*Allium vineale*), for instance, and other pungent plants of the same genus that flourish mightily in our wet woods, fresh meadows, and neglected lawns — as they do over most of temperate North America — are members of this famous family. Indeed, the humble and odorous Field Garlic probably is the most abundant and certainly is the hardiest representative of the family in the five boroughs of the city. When almost everything else has faded in autumn and before most other plants dare to spread their finery in early spring, little clumps of dark green in the wet meadows will mark where the indomitable Field Garlic defies death and destruction by bleak winds and cruel frosts. Having paid this tribute to the fortitude of the Field Garlic, it must be added in all fairness that some persons have a greater admiration for the Wild Leek because its clusters of soft long-ovate leaves that thrust up through the woodland floor in March are the first greens of the season to go into the soup.

A flower more easily recognizable as a member of the family is the Common Day Lily (*Hemerocallis fulva*) that has escaped from the gardens into which it was introduced in this country and grows wild wherever it finds a foothold in good ground on moist banks and roadsides. Originally a native of Asia, it was long cultivated in Europe before it was set out in American gardens. The flower buds come in clusters but the buds open in succession and each handsome flower lasts only a day, which accounts for the name of Day Lily. Incidentally, the flowers rarely produce seed. It's the root system that sends up most of the new stems. The Tiger Lily (*Lilium tigrinum*), also Asiatic in origin, is an occasional fugitive from gardens in the outlying sections of the city but usually it becomes a trophy for the first passer-by who finds it in bloom.

Two other cultivated members of the Lily Family that have gone over the garden wall in our region are the Grape Hyacinth (*Muscari botryoides*) and the Star-of-Bethlehem (*Ornithogalum umbellatum*) that I often found in brave bloom along the river road before the last patches of snow had melted in the neighboring ravines. Mid-April is the time to watch for them. Watch you must, because they are smallish plants easily overlooked or trodden underfoot. Usually it is the Grape Hyacinth that catches the eye first with its stiff little stalks hung with tiny blue flowers almost globular in shape. When I see them, I know it's time to scan the roadside for the low clusters of Star-of-Bethlehem flowers, little waxy-white six-pointed stars crowning the clumps of green and grasslike leaves that surround them.

There must be more than a dozen members of the Lily Family native and still resident in our territory. Some are known and cherished, some are ignored, and one is a rampaging villain. Let us consider some of the more respectable members first. One of the loveliest is the misnamed Dogtooth Violet (*Erythronium americanum*) that shyly droops its yellow head over its purple-spotted leaves in wet ground in the woods from mid-April to early May. Some persons call it Adder's Tongue. Others follow John Burroughs, who gave it the name of Trout Lily for what he considered two good reasons: it is a member of the Lily Family and it comes into bloom about the time of the opening of the trout season on nearby streams.

The first book about nature written by John Burroughs was *Wake-Robin*, a title suggested to him by his friend Walt Whitman. The Wake-robins, of course, are the trilliums of wet woodlands and other moist and shady places. Wake-robin has a good ring to it and it's an appropriate name for flowers that come into bloom when Robins are gladdening our lawns again, but all of them are still trilliums to the botanists. A century ago there may have been three or four kinds of trilliums on

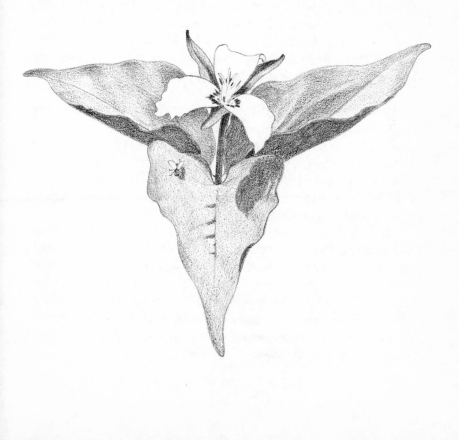

Manhattan Island alone of the city's current possessions but the best one can do now in all the five boroughs is to come across an occasional last stand of Red Trillium (*Trillium erectum*) in some remote and shaded spot far removed from Times Square. It is the only one I ever found within the city limits. Perhaps other searchers have been luckier.

A plant flourishing everywhere in our wet woods and along the shadier portions of moist roadside banks is the False Solomon's Seal (*Smilacina racemosa*). The slanting stems, amply furnished with fair-sized leaves, carry at the top a feathery plume of little white flowers, forerunners of the clusters of hard little red berries into which they eventually turn. In the same shady places but not nearly in such numbers we have what you might call the true Solomon's Seal (*Polygonatum biflorum*) — there are three species in New York and New England but this is the common one in our woods — that has smoother and softer leaves and is altogether a much more delicate plant in appearance. The little bell-shaped flowers of the Solomon's Seal are carried, mostly in pairs, under the slanting stem, dangling on thin stalks growing out of the leaf joints.

An unpretentious relative (we are still within the confines of the Lily Family) that covers the woodland floor in great patches in our region is the well-named Wild Lily of the Valley (*Maianthemum canadense*). In some places the stalks of little white flowers raised above the low growth of (usually two) dark green leaves are so numerous that they look like a web of white spread lightly over the ground under the trees.

The Wild Lily of the Valley is a flower that you can't miss in our woods in May, but finding bellworts — so named because the drooping pale yellow flowers are shaped like long narrow bells — is quite another matter. Long ago I came upon a goodly patch of Perfoliate Bellwort (*Uvularia perfoliata*) on a moist shaded slope above a roadside retaining wall in Riverdale, and year after year, "with ever-returning spring," I looked for and found this patch in bloom. Because of the way the narrow leaves are draped over the flowers, the colony always had for me the appearance of a miniature cornfield planted for Lilliputian reapers. This is the only species that I ever discovered in my city rambles but I am told that the Sessile-leaved Bellwort (*Uvularia sessilifolia*) also is a resident of the area.

Now for the blot on the 'scutcheon of the Lily Family, a real pest of the region and variously known as Bullbrier or Catbrier (*Smilax rotundifolia*), a plant that flourishes wickedly in neglected woods, along stone walls, in thickets, and almost everywhere in waste places. It climbs fences and low trees and frequently forms entangled clumps as difficult to penetrate as just so much barbed wire. Almost every wanderer in the woods and fields has scraped some acquaintance with the intertwined stems and the vicious thorns of this plant but few notice the roundish sprays of greenish-yellow flowers in late spring or the later clusters of rather attractive blue-black berries that are mostly concealed by the foliage until the leaves begin to fall in the autumn. There are other members of this *Smilax* genus in our fields and woods, not nearly so abundant or offensive; we can afford to leave them to the students of botany.

We could easily skip the Wild Yam (*Dioscorea villosa*), too, except for one bit of incriminating evidence that betrays its presence in our territory. It's a thin-stemmed climbing vine with ordinary heart-shaped leaves and drooping strings of small and inconspicuous greenish-yellow flowers. Nobody nowadays eats the lumpy little tubers that grow along its roots. In fact, another name for the plant is Colic-root, which sounds like a warning. But if you prowl through Van Cortlandt swamp or some similar wet ground in the leafless season, you may come face to face with little clusters of curiously three-angled seed capsules clinging at intervals along the thin stems of the plant that wind themselves about the shrubbery. These eye-catching clusters are proof that, though the leaves and flowers have come and gone unnoticed, the Wild Yam holds its ground within the city limits.

Many familiar garden flowers take to the wild, none more readily than the bright yellow Daffodil (*Narcissus pseudo-narcissus*), whose sword-shaped leaves begin to push up even before the frost is out of the ground in March. A native of Mediterranean countries, it is a favorite for planting in our parks and private gardens and is common as an escape in the moist meadows of our territory. I have even found scattered adventurers blooming alone or in small groups in our wet woods.

The Daffodil belongs to the Amaryllis Family that has furnished so many decorative members for cultivation here and abroad. A native and uncultivated species is the Yellow Stargrass (*Hypoxis hirsuta*) that is more or less common in open woods, along shaded roadsides or in moist meadows in our territory. It is well named. It does look like a grass that somehow has blossomed out with little six-pointed yellow stars as a floral display. It begins to bloom in May and you might find it still in flower in early autumn. In those same open woods and moist meadows you will find the Blue-eyed Grass (*Sisyrinchium angustifolium*) — or some similar species — and if you look closely you will see the little needle-point tips to the six segments of the flower face. This is the mark of the blue-eyed grasses and in the marshes and sandy areas of the city you may find other species of this group. They belong to the Iris Family, of which the two most prominent members in the region are the Common Blue Flag (*Iris versicolor*) and the Slender Blue Flag (*Iris prismatica*) that are found in the marshes, swamps, wet meadows, and even moist ditches throughout the area. The Slender Blue Flag is more tolerant of salt in the water and is the more abundant species in tidal marshes. The long leaves of this species are only 1/2 inch or less in width, whereas the leaves of the Common Blue Flag, which predominates in swamps and wet meadows, are about an inch in width.

The word "orchid" has an expensive ring to it. Most persons think that an orchid is a tropical flower grown in a greenhouse and sold at an exorbitant price in a florist shop. The fact is, of course, that the Orchid Family, though largely tropical in habitat, has hardy members that grow in the wild as far north as Canada. Several dozen species of orchid are native to the woods, fields, swamps, bogs, and marshes within fifty miles of the Empire State Building at 34th Street and Fifth Avenue and there is no doubt that most of these species formerly were found in what are now the five boroughs of the city. Today only one species, which few persons would suspect to be an orchid at all, is commonly encountered on moist roadsides or in wet meadows in late summer and early autumn. That's the small, pale and modest Nodding Ladies' Tresses (*Spiranthes cernua*), of which the flowering scape rarely reaches up more than a foot or two from the ground. You will have to peer at the spike of little cream-colored flowers through a magnifying glass to appreciate their beauty and note the details of construction that place them in the Orchid Family.

A few years ago the lovely Rose Pogonia (*Pogonia ophioglos-soides*) was found growing in a small swamp in an outlying section of the Bronx and not far away, in the remnant of a fine bog, a searcher found some Grass Pink or Calopogon (*Calopogon pulchellus*) in full flower, but "improvements" altered the terrain and the lovely little orchids disappeared. Ten or fifteen miles north of the city line, in the wet woods of Westchester, you can still find the Moccasin Flower or Pink Lady-slipper (*Cypripedium acaule*), the Yellow Lady-slipper (*Cypripedium calceolus*), the Showy Orchis (*Orchis spectabilis*), the Downy Rattlesnake Plantain (*Goodyera pubescens*), and other members of this fascinating family, but if they survive within the city limits they must be lurking in nooks unknown to me.

Do you know the Wild Ginger (*Asarum canadense*) with the large, soft, long-petioled, kidney-shaped leaves (usually just two of them) and its odd, cup-shaped, three-pronged, brownish-purple, stalked small flower that droops almost down to the ground? It is still to be found on moist slopes in rocky woods in the Bronx and doubtless in similar sites in other boroughs.

If you grub up a bit of the shallow root and taste it, you will know how the plant obtained its common name. The root has a flavor much like that of the commercial ginger that comes from an entirely different and unrelated plant of Asiatic origin, the *Zingiber officinalis*.

Only the botanists can cope with the numerous members of the Smartweed Family (*Polygonaceae*) in the area. As a boy I became well acquainted with the Common or Red Sorrel (*Rumex acetosella*) that we called "sour grass" when we plucked it and chewed it with relish for its tartness on the tongue. Much later I learned that a favorite singing perch for the Grasshopper Sparrow was the tiptop of some stalk of Sour Dock (*Rumex crispus*) in a hayfield. Farmers, to whom it is a pernicious weed, look upon it in another light — and under another name. They call it Curly Dock.

Of the group that gave its common name to the whole family, the Smartweeds, there are well over a dozen species flourishing in waste places, wet and dry, throughout the five boroughs. Most persons look down on them as weeds but for me they lend color to the landscape and they furnish food for birds and beasts. One of the common species is the kind called Lady's-thumb or Heartweed (*Polygonum persicaria*) that grows lushly in moist ground and bears cylindrical spikes of little pinkish flowers in profusion. A common species of the swamps and shallow parts of ponds is the Water Smartweed (*Polygonum punctatum*) whose greenish-white flowering spikes hang in multitudes over the water in late summer. One of the vine-like species plentiful in our territory is the Climbing False Buckwheat (*Polygonum scandens*) that is so named because, where it clambers up fences and along stone walls or hedgerows, its spikes of greenish flowers eventually become clusters of nutlets in three-angled wrappings that catch the eye as the leaves thin out in late summer.

The tallest and showiest member of the family in the area is the Japanese Knotweed (*Polygonum cuspidatum*) that is sometimes called Mexican Bamboo because of the tall jointed stems it so quickly shoots up into the air. It grows in clumps in moist ground and the thick stem rises with almost incredible speed as soon as the frost leaves the ground. By mid-June these astonishing plants are 6 feet or more in height. The generous leaves, almost as broad as they are long, are rather square-cut across the base and sharp-pointed at the outer end. The long, greenish-white, drooping spikes of little flowers are fairly attractive and the angled fruit capsules are interesting; but the plant's tendency to move in and take possession will have to be curbed or it may become a spreading pest like the Phragmites of the area.

We can dismiss the Goosefoot Family of the region as largely an aggregation of coarse and often offensive weeds with the exception of the succulent samphires of the salt marshes that knowing folk gather to put in pickle or use as a relish with other dishes. These odd low growths of the marshes, whose jointed stems and numerous branches look as though they were made of opaque glass but feel rubbery to the touch, are practically colorless in summer but turn red en masse at the coming on of autumn and add a rich tone to the tidal areas they occupy. There are three species occurring within the city limits but the most abundant one is the *Salicornia europaea* that has come to us from across the Atlantic.

At this point there must be registered a deep apology for dismissing all the other members of the Goosefoot Family as condemned weeds. This is botanical snobbery of the rankest kind. It also raises again an old question to which there never has been given a clear and decisive answer, to wit: What is a weed? Emerson's answer was: "A plant whose virtues have not yet been discovered." That won't do at all. Many "weeds" furnish much food for wild birds and mammals. These are positive virtues, long known to birds and many mammals, including naturalists. James Russell Lowell wrote: "A weed is no more than a flower in disguise." A diplomatic statement and just what might have been expected from a man who

served as United States Minister to both Spain and Great Britain. A better answer is the one handed down from some anonymous sage: A weed is a flower out of place. Let this cushion the fall of the Goosefoot group, the amaranths, and other common weeds as we drop them from consideration and concentrate on more colorful matters.

There is the Pokeweed or Pokeberry (*Phytolacca americana*), for instance. Everything about this plant is colorful. With a thick stem, sturdy branches, and large leaves, it may grow as much as 10 feet in height around dooryards, old walls, hedge-rows, and waste places generally. It bears long cylindrical spikes of white flowers that turn into dark purple berries be-loved by birds, thrushes in particular. And late in the season the thick stem, the branches, and even the tiny stalks that support the dark berries turn a wonderful rich wine color, the hue of a Burgundy of some good vintage year in the Dijon valley. The American Indians made a dye from the dark berries and boiled the young leaves and ate them as a kind of spinach. I have tried this dish and do not recommend it.

Hail to a childhood favorite! The youngsters who find it carpeting the wet woodlands of our area from mid-April to mid-May joyfully call it the Spring Beauty as they make treas-ure trove of it, but the botanists are more particular. They designate our happily abundant flower the Narrow-leaved Spring Beauty (*Claytonia virginica*). They look white against the woodland floor but if you bend down and inspect the little five-petaled flower faces you will see that many of them are tinged with pink and most of the petals are finely streaked with pink to purple lines. The flowers are quite sensitive to changes in temperature. On a warm sunny day in late April you may find all the Spring Beauties wide open. The following day, if the sky is gray and the temperature has dropped sharply, not a flower will be showing its face.

The lowly but lovely Spring Beauty is a close relative of the Common Purslane or Pusley (*Portulaca oleracea*) that also is abundant in the area but is not looked upon as lovely. In fact, it is viewed with alarm as a pernicious weed infesting lawns and gardens and one that should be dealt with severely. However, it had a defender in Thoreau, who wrote in *Walden:* "I have made a satisfactory dinner, satisfactory on several accounts, simply off a dish of purslane (*Portulaca oleracea*) which I gathered in my cornfield, boiled and salted." It may also be said for the persecuted Purslane that it produces innumerable seeds much appreciated as tidbits by many birds and small mammals. But say what we may, the gardener will not tolerate it.

Everybody looks down on chickweeds but, since they pop up everywhere in temperate climes around the world, they cannot be ignored. They abound in woods and fields. They grow in wet and dry ground. They intrude in gardens and on the finest lawns. They even push up through cracks in city pavements and side-walks. They occur in so many species and varieties that they sometimes baffle even the botanists. Two that you will encounter "all over the place" in our territory are the Common Chickweed (*Stellaria media*) and the Common Mouse-ear Chickweed (*Cerastium vulgatum*), but there are other species too numerous to mention and — for us, at least — too difficult to identify. The Common Chickweed may be found in bloom almost every month in the year. Surely it deserves a medal for bravery. Few persons bother to look at the little white flowers because they are so small. Under a magnifying glass they are quite attractive, and you will note that the five petals seem twice as numerous as they are because, in most species, they are so deeply lobed that each one looks like two.

Chickweeds are members of the Pink Family. So are the campions of many kinds that grow along our roadsides and in waste places. My choice as the daintiest one is the Starry Campion (*Silene stellata*) with finely fringed petals, but a great favorite with children is the Bladder Campion (*Silene cucubalus*) because they can pinch the top of the inflated calyx with the fingers of one hand and make it explode — pop! — by striking it smartly on the palm or the back of the other hand. Other members of the family are the familiar Soapwort or Bouncing Bet (*Saponaria officinalis*) that prefers railway embankments as a place of residence and the Deptford Pink (*Dianthus armeria*) of roadsides, meadows, and lawns whose little flowers, opening one at a time, have five notched pink petals liberally sprinkled with tiny white dots.

Of water lilies in general it may be said that they are as quietly beautiful as they are painted, even if the painter is Claude Monet, one of whose canvases on the subject — he did a whole series — hangs in the Metropolitan Museum of Art. The White Water Lily (*Nymphaea odorata*) of our placid pools, ponds, and park lakes opens its large, handsome, many-petaled flowers in June amid the floating greenery of the great round leaves that lie widespread on the water. The Yellow Pond Lily or Spatterdock (*Nuphar advena*) prefers shallower water. In Van Cortlandt Park, for instance, the White Water Lily grows in the lake and ventures out into deep water, whereas the Yellow Pond Lily is abundant along the edge of the slow stream that comes down through the swamp. Its large, thick, ovate leaves stand rather stiffly at an angle above the water and from May until well along through the summer it holds up bright yellow flowers of curious construction, something like a doorknob with a fancy fringe.

Before the Pond Lily comes into bloom in the stream, the whole floor of the swamp on either side is covered with the shining yellow flowers of the Marsh Marigold (*Caltha palustris*) that, coming in April when buds are just opening on shrubs and trees, stand out in glittering splendor against the light greenery around and above them. Some persons prefer to call them Cowslips but that name is better applied to one of the European primroses. In other words, the English have an earlier patent on the name. While it makes no difference to the average citizen, a botanist would like to have it pointed out that the shining yellow segments of the Marsh Marigold flower are not petals, but sepals so colorful they look like petals. In most plants that include sepals in their floral display, the sepals are green, but there are many species in which the sepals are the colorful part of the flower. It's a peculiarity that occasionally comes as a family trait in whole or in part; an example is the Crowfoot Family, to which the Marsh Marigold and many other common flowers belong.

The buttercups, for instance. They, however, are among the petal-bearing members of the Crowfoot Family. We have more than a dozen kinds of buttercup growing blithely within the city boundaries. Some prefer ponds and swamps, some take to the woods, some brighten the meadows, and some even invade lawns. We even have white buttercups! But except for such trickeries, practically everybody can recognize a buttercup on sight and there is no need to go into the matter of the dozen or more species of *Ranunculus* that occur in our territory. Another petal-bearing member of the family is the beautiful Wild Columbine (*Aquilegia canadensis*) — and what wonderful petals they are that this plant hangs out in rocky woodlands! They are deep red with yellow throats and they shoot backward in long spurs. But the Wild Columbine with the feathery foliage and delightful flowers is becoming more scarce every year within the city gates, and soon may vanish altogether.

Not so with the Black Snakeroot or Bugbane (*Cimicifuga racemosa*), the tallest member of the Crowfoot Family in our region. Here is a plant that is holding its own in our rich woods. In June or July you will see its long racemes of flowers raised aloft like great white candles above the undergrowth in the woods or along shaded roadsides. Like the Marsh Marigold, it has no petals, but in this case the color is supplied by the numerous little white stamens that jut out in all directions from each little flower along the stalk that may be 2 feet or more in length and often is raised 5 or 6 feet above the ground.

A few weeks after the Black Snakeroot has raised its white candles in the woodlands you will begin to find the Tall Meadow Rue (*Thalictrum polygamum*) coming into bloom in wet meadows and ditches. Like the Black Snakeroot, it is a tall plant and another member of the Crowfoot Family that produces flowers without petals, and once again the numerous white stamens are the parts that catch the eye. But the Tall Meadow Rue spreads its filmy blooms in wide panicles and usually the plants grow in clumps or patches in more or less open ground, whereas the Black Snakeroot sticks mostly to shady places and often stands apart like a lone sentinel in the woods. The Early Meadow Rue (*Thalictrum dioicum*) is a plant of our wet woodlands but it attracts little attention through the fact that its flowers of the same type are greenish yellow and blend easily with all the other fresh greenery of the woodland floor in late April.

In May in the same woods we find the lovely little Rue Anemone (*Anemonella thalictroides*) that derives its specific name — in Latin as well as English — from the fact that its thin and delicate leaves have approximately the same shape and scalloped outline as the foliage of the Meadow Rues. It never reaches a foot in height and usually carries its frail leaves and little round white flower only some 6 inches above the woodland floor. It grows with, and among, patches of the much more common and often abundant Wood Anemone or Windflower (*Anemone quinquefolia*) and is easily overlooked for that reason. The flowers are much alike in size, color, and general appearance and also in the fact that they have no petals. The flower faces consist of white sepals that look exactly like petals. This is the same old family trait breaking out again (we are still dealing with the Crowfoot Family) and we have a few more petal-lacking representatives to meet.

One is the Liverleaf or Hepatica (*Hepatica americana*), whose thick, rusty, three-lobed, last year's leaves and this year's hairy-stalked little purplish to pink flowers nestle so closely among the dead leaves that only a keen search in the April woods will uncover them. This year's leaves will come out fresh and green after the flowers have faded from the scene. Then there is the

Hepatica

Woodbine or Wild Clematis (*Clematis virginiana*), the last of this petal-lacking group to clamor for attention in our territory. It is a familiar and abundant vine, a climber of fences, stone walls, hedgerows, and assorted shrubbery with an almost endless purplish stem, trifoliate leaves, and, in summer, clusters of fragrant white flowers in which the sepals play the colorful part. Later the flowers turn into long woolly threads that curl back in a way to form filmy spheres that hang along the vine and stand out to catch the eye when the leaves drop off in September.

So much for the Crowfoot Family, though truth compels the confession that we have skipped about horribly and mentioned only the more prominent or more abundant members in our territory. There are many other representatives of the crowfoot clan hereabout for those who have the time and the desire to seek them out. We have to move on to other matters, such as a certain secret I share each spring with only a few close friends. That's the nook in which we find in April that lovely and delicate white flower with the most unlovely name, the Bloodroot (*Sanguinaria canadensis*). The ghastly name is due, of course, to the thick orange-crimson juice that oozes from a break in any part of the plant. It's wonderful how the single, large, fleshy leaf protectively encircles the flower stalk and bud until the time comes for the spreading of the numerous pure white petals. Bloodroot survives in only a few favored localities within the city limits. We who share the knowledge of this particular patch feel like fellow conspirators as we keep watch in early April for the first sign of Bloodroot on a certain tree-studded bank that we pass regularly on our morning walks.

Just to keep the record straight, Bloodroot is a member of the Poppy Family. Another member of the family that is fairly common in wet shady places is the Greater Celandine (*Chelidonium majus*) of European origin, a branching plant almost bushlike in shape that keeps producing rather fragile four-petaled yellow flowers all the way from mid-May well into late summer. Pluck one of the deeply segmented leaves and the orange juice oozing out at the breaking point will bear testimony to its membership in the Poppy Family.

Some flowers look as though they had been turned out by candy makers or toy manufacturers. One of them is that childhood favorite, Dutchman's Breeches (*Dicentra cucullaria*), whose little yellow-tipped ivory-colored flowers really are shaped somewhat like a tiny pair of upended Dutch breeches of the kind worn by Peter Stuyvesant and the busy burghers of New Amsterdam before the English came up the bay to take over the town. It is still locally common on sloping ground in wet woods. I find the feathery foliage quite as attractive as the quaint flowers that children love to gather in early spring. There is a ravine in the Riverdale region that, to my own knowledge, has nurtured Dutchman's Breeches April after April for half a hundred years. Perhaps the Indians found them on the same steep slopes a thousand years ago.

It may seem that family lines are too much stressed here, as though this were some sort of botanical social register. Actually they help to simplify the problem of presenting even a small part of the flora of any region. Take the Mustard Family, or Cruciferae, of our territory, for instance. They are far too many for us. They include not only innumerable wild species but many of our ordinary table vegetables and relishes such as cabbage, turnip, radish, water cress, Brussels sprouts, cauliflower, broccoli, and the common condiment that carries the family name. Most commercial mustard is manufactured from the seeds of cultivated Common Black Mustard (*Brassica nigra*) of Old World origin. The plant boasts a medical history going back as far as Hippocrates in the fifth century B.C. and perhaps earlier. In this country it has run wild along with many of its European and Asiatic relatives. There was no need to import mustards of any kind because we started with a plentiful supply of native species. The family is worldwide in distribution. The justification in stressing family groups leaps to the eye in this case. With a few exceptions not worth mentioning, all the plants of this family that you may encounter in our region will be displaying, when in bloom, the family medallion in the shape of a four-petaled flower. The Latin name for the family is Cruciferae, or "cross-bearing," a reference to the fact that the four petals usually are set in the form of a little Maltese Cross. There are, to be sure, other plants that produce four-petaled flowers but if you are walking in the wild in our territory and find a four-petaled flower that baffles you, look first among the Cruciferae or Mustard Family for the identity of the mysterious stranger. It's odds on that you will find it there.

It is no exaggeration to say that the Common Black Mustard will grow anywhere. I have found it coming up through the cracks in a "hot-topped" parking lot in midtown Manhattan.

It is not only persistent and widespread but almost incredibly hardy and I regularly find it in bloom as late as November. For that reason, though its little yellow flowers are nothing to boast of, I long ago put it on my Roll of Honor for the region. To farmers and gardeners, however, it is a confounded weed and so are many other members of the family, such as the familiar Shepherd's Purse (*Capsella bursa-pastoris*) with its fruiting stalks of triangular notched seed pods that are supposed to resemble in miniature a shepherd's purse of old days, the Penny Cress (*Thlaspi arvense*), and the Pepper-grass (*Lepidium virginicum*), plants that grow along our highways and byways and on the playing fields in our public parks.

There are, on the other hand, several respectable members of the Mustard Family in the region. One is the Water Cress (*Nasturtium officinale*) that trails its stems and segmented green leaves in brooks and clear streams and adds tang to the salads of those who know its worth and where to find it. Another is the local flower of the mustard flock, the Bulbous Cress (*Cardamine bulbosa*) that grows in wet ground and tops its stem with a cluster of quite nice little white flowers in early May. It is plentiful along the edge of the Van Cortlandt swamp; the white flowers, held a foot or so above the ground, stand out against the green background of the swamp floor. It is attractive enough to get its picture in most of the flower guides of the region. Near the ocean front, of course, the notable member of the family is the rubbery Sea Rocket (*Cakile edentula*) that grows in abundance in the sand and among the pebbles above the high-tide mark and bears little pinkish or purple flowers in the summertime. On the slopes in wet woods in the region you still may find the Two-leaved Toothwort or Crinkleroot (*Dentaria diphylla*), whose white petals are sometimes tinted with purple. It blooms early in May. If you grub up a bit of the crinkled root and chew it, the tang to it may surprise you. The flavor is really sharp, almost peppery.

The other mustards of the area — a great store of them — we

must leave to the botanists and move on to pay tribute to a few members of the Rose Family in our territory. Two that decorate our meadows and open hillsides from June well into the summer are the Broadleaf Spirea or Meadowsweet (*Spiraea latifolia*) with its conical clusters of little white or pink five-petaled flowers and the Steeplebush Spirea or Hardhack (*Spiraea tomentosa*) whose flowering spike is longer and thinner and whose little flowers are deeply tinted with pink or light purple. Steeplebush is the best name for this plant because the flowering cluster often shapes up in steeple form. If you never have done so, look at the lower surface of any leaf of the next up-standing Steeplebush you find in the fields. You will see that it is light chocolate in color and quite woolly in texture; hence the *tomentosa* — meaning that it is covered with a matting of hairs — of the scientific name.

Wild Strawberries! Who as a child didn't thrill to that cry from some companion in the fields on a June day of long ago? There was a time within the memory of some of the older residents of the region when a wanderer of the meadows and hillsides could gather enough wild strawberries to make a family dessert or a three-layer shortcake, but nowadays the decreased crop is gathered largely by birds and small mammals — children included. The common species of the area is *Fragaria virginiana* and you will still find the open-faced little white flowers here and there in the fields about the city in early June. The competition among man, bird, and beast for the fruit is keen and only the lucky collect enough for a feast. The berries, if you can find any, will be quite small but delicious in flavor.

The collective raspberries and blackberries of the region have stood up a little better under the increase of population be-cause they are not so choosy with regard to terrain and, being armed with sharp thorns, are not so easily handled or trodden underfoot. They persist in waste ground, in old fields, along the edges of wood roads, and other wild places within the city limits. Probably the most abundant of the group in the area

Blackberry

are the Prickly or Northern Dewberry or Low Running Blackberry (*Rubus flagellaris*) and the tall, stiff-stemmed and well-
armed common Blackberry (*Rubus allegheniensis*) that sometimes
occurs locally in sufficient numbers to form almost impenetrable
thickets. These and many other species offer tasty fruit in
season at the expense of an occasional deep scratch from sharp
thorns, but the most decorative of the whole group is the
Flowering or Purple-flowering Raspberry (*Rubus ordoratus*) that
displays rose-purple flowers almost 2 inches in diameter. This
plant is by no means abundant in the area, although found
regularly in small numbers among other brambles in shady
places; the showy blossoms are sure to catch the eye of those
who walk the woodland roads. Indeed, the rather heavy sweet
perfume of the flowers will attract attention at ten paces. The
pale red fruit that follows is rather tasteless.

For enchanting odor, of course, there is nothing in our
region to surpass the beautiful and fairly common Wild or
Pasture Rose (*Rosa virginiana*) of open fields and roadsides.

There are other species in the woods and swamps, some of them native and others that are fugitives from cultivation such as the Sweetbrier (*Rosa eglanteria*), the Eglantine of English poetry, a plant of twofold sweetness. The crushed leaves are even more strongly aromatic than the beautiful pink flowers. The Sweetbrier occasionally is found around old cellar holes in our parklands, a somewhat melancholy reminder of the loving hands that planted it long, long ago.

When I was a boy I was told that certain common little yellow flowers I saw growing close to the ground in pastures and other places were "yellow strawberry blossoms" and, being more interested in baseball than botany at the time, it never occurred to me to question the matter. Furthermore, I did note a general "strawberry look" in shape of leaf and flower, which made the misinformation easy to swallow and digest. It was years before I learned that I had been botanically bilked and that the little five-petaled yellow flowers were cinquefoils, or five-fingers, of some kind, probably the Common Cinquefoil (*Potentilla simplex*), which is the most abundant of the five or six kinds found in our region as the Rough-fruited Cinquefoil (*Potentilla recta*) probably is the tallest and bushiest of the group. The name cinquefoil or five-finger refers to the compound leaves that in most cases consist of five leaflets or "fingers" of different shapes and sizes in the various species. If I had known enough to look closer in my younger days, I would have noticed that the strawberry leaflets come in threes and not in the fives — or sometimes more — that mark the cinquefoil clan.

There are many other members of the Rose Family to be found in our territory, including some familiar shrubs and trees that we shall encounter later in another chapter, but we must not linger longer with the cinquefoils and their relatives. Other flowers demand our attention. One is the Sensitive Pea or Wild Sensitive Plant (*Cassia nictitans*) with little yellow flowers and long, narrow, compound leaves whose numerous leaflets fold together over the midrib if you cut the stem below or pluck the plant from the ground. This you will find in bloom in the summer along the roadsides or in waste ground. If you wish to test its sensitivity, just pluck a leaf and note how quickly the leaflets begin to close up.

Now we move into the Bean Family, or Fabaceae, a group represented in our territory by dozens of genera and hundreds of species. Only the comparative few that regularly attract public notice need be mentioned here. Most of the plants of this family bear flowers of the sweet pea or "butterfly" type and produce fruit pods of the garden pea or bean model except that in some species the pod may contain only one seed and in others a great many more than any cultivated bean or pea pod ever enclosed. The plants vary in height from the bare inch or two of the dainty, clover-like, yellow-flowered Black Medick (*Medicago lupulina*) that trails along the ground to the ninety-foot altitude of the towering tops of certain narrow trees long known and locally famous under the name of Shipmast Locusts (*Robinia pseudo-acacia* var. *rectissima* Raber) in the Flushing section of the city on Long Island.

Many of the floral displays of the members of this famous family are colorful and the individual flowers often appear in panicles, racemes, "heads," or other such clusters that are bound to attract the attention of even the most unobservant person who occasionally takes a walk in the woods or fields. There are the clovers, for instance. Everybody has seen a flowering head of clover of one kind or another, but few think of it as a cluster of flowers. To most of us it represents fodder for cattle or fine food for the rabbits of the region. For me the Red Clover (*Trifolium pratense*) has three great virtues: it is abundant in our fields, it produces colorful heads of sweet-smelling little flowers, and it is found in bloom from May to November. The pink and white heads of the Alsike Clover (*Trifolium hybridum*) are a delight to see in our fields, too. Then there is the Rabbit-foot or Old Field Clover (*Trifolium arvense*) that grows in poor ground or waste places and hangs out grayish-pink woolly heads of flowers that resemble miniature powder puffs.

There is much more to it than that. In the fields and along the roadsides in summer you will find the fragrant flowering spikes of the sweet clovers; or melilots, held shoulder high — the White Sweet Clover (*Melilotus albus*) and the Yellow Sweet Clover (*Melilotus officinalis*). Not only are the flowers pleasantly odorous but the leaves retain a fragrance when dried. The Wild Lupine (*Lupinus perennis*), with its spikes of lovely blue flowers, brightens some of the waste ground of Staten Island and the Long Island section of the city. On the other hand, the Rattlebox (*Crotalaria sagittalis*) is more abundant in the Bronx. It is a rather low plant and one might easily overlook the little yellow flowers that it holds a foot or so above the ground in June, but if you walk through a patch of Rattlebox in September, your shoes will brush against the black oval capsules and the hard little seeds therein will rattle audibly to prove that the plant is well named.

If you walk in the fields or woods at all you can't miss running into a wide assortment of tick trefoils (*Desmodium*) and bush clovers (*Lespedeza*) of many species. The tick trefoils prefer shaded ground but the bush clovers, though there are some trailing species, usually are found standing up tall and straight in open fields. They were favorite food plants of the Japanese Beetle when that insect pest was in its heyday in our territory. As for the tick trefoils, if you roam the autumn woods you will find evidence of their abundance in the vicinity by the innumerable seed pods that stick to your clothing by means of the little hooked hairs with which they are thickly covered. It's a chore to get rid of them because each pod or segment thereof seems to require individual attention.

The lowly but useful Cow Vetch (*Vicia cracca*) with its feathery foliage and racemes of little blue flowers is quite common as an escape along fences and roadsides, and so is the somewhat similar but taller and more loose-jointed Crown Vetch or Axwort (*Coronilla varia*) that bears roundish clusters of pinkish flowers. The Hog Peanut (*Amphicarpa bracteata*) climbs rather aimlessly along stone walls and fences of any kind and the Ground-nut or Wild Bean (*Apios americana*) with its roundish clusters of strong-scented brown and purplish flowers of curious shape (they always remind me of textbook drawings of the semi-circular canals of the ear) creeps in winding fashion over the ground or twines itself amid shrubbery in moist shady places. One more member of the Bean Family must be mentioned. That is the Beach Pea (*Lathyrus maritimus*) of the ocean front and sand dune areas of the city, an abundant and hardy plant that bears attractive clusters of pinkish-blue or light purple flowers during the summer.

That will do for the Bean Family for the moment, though there are some other members of the family to be presented when we take notice of the native trees of our territory. But at this point we can afford to ignore family relationships and do some exploring among unrelated flowers. One of them is an old favorite of mine, the humble little five-petaled Yellow Wood Sorrel (*Oxalis europaea*) that is common as an intruder on lawns and in gardens everywhere in the area. We have other species, to be sure, but this is the most abundant by far and it grows right out in the open for all to see. The wafer-thin, clover-like leaves are a fitting accompaniment to such a delicate and attractive little flower. If you chew the leaves you will detect the acid taste that has given the name to oxalic acid.

Ever since childhood I have known and loved the Wild Geranium or Spotted Crane's-bill (*Geranium maculatum*) that decorates the floors of our wet woods in May with its lacy foliage and light purple flowers, but it was many years before I discovered the reason for the optional name of Crane's-bill. If you do not know, look at one of the plants a few weeks after the petals have fallen and you will see that the elongated style projecting from the cupped calyx does somewhat resemble the long thin bill of a crane or heron, especially when it is pointed downward on a slant toward the ground. In the Bronx, at least, you will also find the Siberian Crane's-bill (*Geranium sibiricum*), a much taller plant with much smaller and generally paler flowers, growing along the roadside in Riverdale and some of the paths in Van Cortlandt Park. How this Eurasian plant arrived in the Bronx is a mystery, but from that start in the New World it has spread over considerable territory to the westward.

The milkworts are a modest group of flowers that easily remain unnoticed even though some species are abundant in open areas within the city limits. It's probable that the Yellow Milkwort (*Polygala lutea*), found sparingly in swamps on Staten Island and in the Long Island section of the city, is mistaken for a yellow clover by most of those who notice it at all. The flower cluster certainly does have the appearance of "a head of clover." Perhaps even the Purple or Field Milkwort (*Polygala sanguinea*) that grows straight up to a height of a foot or more in poor ground (even through cinder filling on roadways and embankments!) may suffer from the same mistake, but, if so, with less justification. The heads of pale purple little flowers that top the stems throughout the summer are cylindrical in shape rather than round. In both cases, as in all the milkworts of the area, the leaves are simple and entire and not at all like the compound leaves of the clovers. The dainty little Fringed Polygala or Flowering Wintergreen (*Polygala paucifolia*) I often found in rose-purple bloom in May in the Westchester woods, but I have not yet come upon it in my walks within the city limits.

There are many kinds of euphorbias that have been set out on private estates and in the city parks. The only attractive one that has become a common wayside wanderer throughout the area is the Cypress Spurge (*Euphorbia cyparissias*), a garden flower of Eurasian origin that went over the fence long ago. The plants grow in patches and the linear leaves radiating from the straight and stiff stems remind me of bottle brushes. The flowers are carried in an open spray, or umbel, at the top of the stem. They are small and have no petals at all but the petal-like appendages just below the flowers are greenish yellow and thus the whole spray seems to be a cluster of pale yellow flowers. The Spotted Spurge or Wartweed (*Euphorbia maculata*) is a common creeping pest in lawns and gardens and an abundant resident of waste places in our territory. There are other euphorbias, native and imported, in the region, all of them with one trait in common: a milky juice that exudes from any break in leaf or stem.

One of the most abundant and attractive plants of the water-courses, wet woods, and damp thickets in the region is the Spotted Touch-me-not or Jewel-weed (*Impatiens biflora*), whose spurred orange-yellow flowers are liberally spotted within by

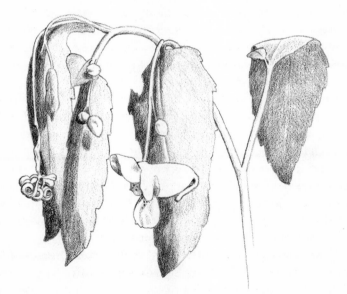

darker dots. The plant also is known as Silverleaf because the leaves, when held under water at proper angles, suddenly take on a silvery sheen. The same is true of the leaves of the Pale Touch-me-not (*Impatiens pallida*) that is quite similar but not so common in our territory. The flowers of the Pale Touch-me-not are pale yellow and their throats are not so darkly or so plentifully spotted. The interesting feature of these plants is the way the seed pods "explode" and shoot the seeds out to fall on the ground some distance away. Children are always amused by this botanical action and soon learn to trigger the explosion by lightly pinching the tip of the swollen seed pod in late summer or early autumn. Merely brushing against a plant with pods ready for action sometimes will set off a fusillade. Hence the name Touch-me-not in English and *Impatiens* in Latin.

Here and there in the outlying wooded areas of the city you will find the seemingly endless stems of the Fox Grape (*Vitis labrusca*) loftily entangled among the trees like a great snake or runaway cable with a curious brown and papery covering loosely attached to it in long strips. The vine also runs along stone walls and over fallen timber. The grapes vary in abundance from season to season and are rather sharp in taste. Birds and climbing mammals enjoy them in the raw but for human palates they are best served up in the form of wild-grape jelly. The related Virginia Creeper (*Parthenocissus quinquefolia*) is abundant not only in the woods but along stone walls and hedgerows in the open on Staten Island and in Queens and the Bronx. The greenish-yellow flower sprays are generally overlooked but the clusters of blue berries stand out amid the contrasting foliage when the five-fingered leaves turn a rich red in late August or September.

Toward the end of summer, just when surf-bathing is at its best along the ocean front, the salt marshes of the seaward sections of the city are brightened by the flowering of the wonderful pink Rose Mallow (*Hibiscus palustris*) and the smaller Marsh

Mallow (*Althaea officinalis*). Inland we have the Common Mallow (*Malva neglecta*) of no such stunning appearance or high social standing. It is a plant of weedy growth in waste places including the fringes of dump heaps, and its flowers are pale and small. In the same waste places as well as around dooryards we have the *Malva rotundifolia* that — chew the seeds and you will know the reason — is called "Cheeses" by countryfolk. At any rate, it is more trig and trim than *Malva neglecta*, though lower in stature. Its leaves have nice round blades instead of lumpy lobes and it puts more color in its petals. It is, furthermore, a sturdy flower and I have found it in bloom in November. Long live the friendly little Cheeses!

Our next acquaintance was best described by the great John Gerard of England in his famous *Herball* (London, 1597) as follows:

> Saint Johns wort hath brownish stalks beset with many small and narrow leaves, which if you behold betwixt your eies and the light, do appear as it were bored or thrust thorow in an infinite number of places with pinnes points. The branches divide themselves into sundry smal twigs at the top whereof grow many yellow floures, which with the leaves bruised do yeeld a reddish juice of the colour of bloud.

Thus did the famous herbalist describe the Common St. John's-wort (*Hypericum perforatum*) of Europe that, transplanted to these shores, has spread across most of the continent. All through the summer the roadsides, waste places, and fallow fields offer for inspection the rather raggedy sprays of open-faced, five-petaled bright yellow flowers produced by the narrow-leaved, much branched plant that grows to a height of 2 or 3 feet. If you look at the petals through a magnifying glass you will see that most of them seem to be "hemstitched" with black dots all around the edges. If you are familiar with this flower you will have no trouble in recognizing the other St. John's-worts of the area through the family resemblance. There are some half-dozen or more species growing within the city limits and they vary in size from the goodly height and spread of the Common St. John's-wort, the tallest of the lot, down to the profusely branched and almost leafless Orange-grass (*Hypericum gentianoides*) that stands stiffly to a height of a foot or so in sandy or gravelly ground. It springs up readily between the ties of little-used railroad tracks and along the center strips of seldom-traveled old dirt roads.

Except that they are by nature such modest flowers them-selves, we might well boast of our city violets. We have them in great quantity and good quality. There are probably two dozen species to be found in the woods, meadows, and marshes of our territory. For most of us it is enough if we merely separate them by colors and call them blue, yellow, or white violets, as the case may be. Possibly the most abundant of the blue kind in our moist meadows is the Woolly Blue Violet (*Viola sororia*), or perhaps it is the Meadow Violet (*Viola papilionacea*); it is difficult to know. There is the same problem, except to a lesser extent, in sorting out the white and yellow violets of the area. Unless you are an expert and can distinguish them at a glance, you will have to note the details of size, shape, color, branching, and veining of leaves and petals and then turn to a flower guide or botany book to track down the species in hand. It may be that some of our original species have been evicted by human intruders or crushed under the weight of added buildings. I once knew where there was a clump of Bird-foot Violets (*Viola pedata*) on a shaded bank in Riverdale, but now that spot is covered by a huge apartment house below whose battlements roars the incessant traffic of the West Side Highway.

The tale of native flowers that have been driven out or trod-den underfoot by the increase in population of the five boroughs is offset in part at least by the occasional appearance of added floral inhabitants from other lands. One of the most abundant of these is the Purple Loosestrife (*Lythrum salicaria*) that stands up straight and tall in our fresh-water marshes, around the edges of ponds and along the banks of slow streams. This plant of Eurasian origin has increased notably in the area — and all over New York and New England — in my lifetime and now dominates the marsh floral display in midsummer with its long flowering spikes of five-petaled pinkish-purple flowers.

The upland or dry-ground rival of the upstanding Purple Loosestrife is the Great Willow-herb or Fireweed (*Epilobium angustifolium*) that springs up quickly in burned areas (hence the name Fireweed) and sometimes holds its terminal spikes of four-petaled light purple flowers at eye level or higher. It often appears as a roadside plant and blooms throughout the summer with the buds opening in succession upward along the terminal flowering spike. A characteristic feature of this tall plant is a midsummer flowering spike with unopened buds at the top, widespread petals in the middle, and linear seed pods splitting and showing the long cottony filaments attached to the seeds at the bottom of the display. There are other epilobiums in our territory but the Great Willow-herb is not only the tallest but the most abundant and the one most commonly seen by persons who live in or visit the city.

Of the familiar evening primroses there is appropriate mention in a footnote on page 1064 of the Eighth (or Fernald) Edition of *Gray's Manual of Botany*, to wit: "A hopelessly confused and freely hybridizing group . . . " With that warning, all that needs to be stated here is that the stiff-stalked Common Evening Primrose (*Oenothera biennis*) that grows to a height of 5 feet or more stands in serried ranks along roadsides and in waste ground all over our territory. The odorous four-petaled yellow flowers, carried on long calyx tubes in terminal spikes, like the dark better than bright sunlight and open in the evening; hence the name for the group. I never made any attempt to sort out the other members of the group on my home ground in Riverdale but I did find the one called Day Primrose or Common Sundrop (*Oenothera fruticosa*) in bloom along Delafield Lane in Riverdale and also in Van Cortlandt Park. This is a much smaller and more delicate plant with golden-yellow flowers that do not fear the light of day.

Enchanter's Nightshade (*Circaea quadrisulcata*), despite its

intriguing name, is merely a weed of the woods or shaded roadsides that has tiny white flowers carried aloft in a thin terminal
spike. Nobody in his right mind, except a botanist, would
bend over to look at the insignificant two-petaled flowers; the
plant would not be mentioned here but for the fact that everybody who walks in the woods is bound to come into contact
with the little round bristly seed pods that cling in annoying
numbers to cotton or wool clothing. Since the plant grows
not much more than knee high, trousers, skirts, and stockings
are the accouterments usually cluttered with such unwanted
booty of the wildwood.

The rich woods in which aralias flourish have almost vanished from our territory but those who search diligently enough
will surely find three species and possibly a fourth member of
the family either in the wooded sections of our larger public
parks or whatever other rich or rocky woods remain within the
city limits. The Hercules-club (*Aralia spinosa*), which is really
a shrub or small tree fearfully and wonderfully covered with
needle-sharp spines, probably should be classed as an escape in
our woods since its real home is southward, but it has established itself in the wild within the city limits as a weedy shrub
with stiff spine-covered stems and striking doubly or triply compound foliage. The Spikenard (*Aralia racemosa*) generally goes
unnoticed in the woods until late in the summer when it hangs
out its long heavy clusters of little purple berries. The Wild
Sarsaparilla (*Aralia nudicaulis*), with its doubly compound leaf
held umbrella-fashion over the flower stalk that eventually
produces three roundish clusters of dark — almost black —
berries, is by far the most common of the group and is found in
abundance on our woodland floors. I am told by Joseph
Monachino of the New York Botanical Garden staff that our
smallest member of the Aralia Family, the Dwarf Ginseng
(*Panax trifolium*), still grows in our woods but I never encountered
it there.

The Parsley Family (Umbelliferae) has a wide representation

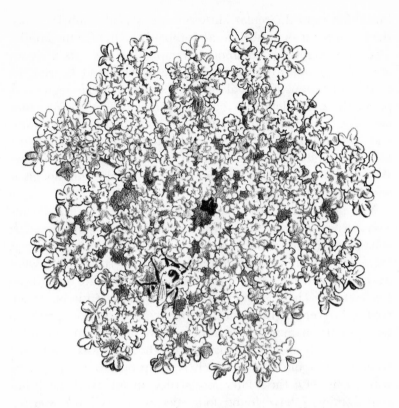

in the region, although comparatively few species are prominent enough or colorful enough to attract public attention. One, to be sure, is overwhelming. That's the Wild Carrot or Queen Anne's Lace (*Daucus carota*) that is found in abundance in open meadows, along roadsides, and in waste ground and blooms from May to October. This is the family that produces for the kitchen such vegetables, garnishes, aromatic herbs, and condiments as carrot, celery, parsley, parsnip, sweet cicely, coriander, lovage, dill, fennel, caraway, and anise. Most of the cultivated species and their uncultivated relatives that we look upon as weeds in the wild have alternate compound leaves, hollow stems, and little five-petaled flowers that are displayed in the flat-topped circular clusters botanists call umbels, hence the Latin name of Umbelliferae (umbel-bearing) for the family. The thick-stemmed Common Parsnip (*Pastinaca sativa*) is an abundant escape from gardens and often is found bearing its clusters of yellow flowers along the roadsides in our region.   I prefer the more delicate Golden Alexanders (*Zizia aurea*) that are native in our wet meadows and along the edges of swamps and watercourses.   In the same damp terrain and along the shores on ponds and streams you will find the tall white-flowering Water Hemlock (*Cicuta maculata*) chiefly notable for an alkaloid poison contained in its root.

Not many paragraphs back there was mention of the Purple Loosestrife (*Lythrum salicaria*), whose long purple flowering spikes are an attractive feature of our marshes in summer. Here we run into other flowers called loosestrifes and, what may seem a trifle strange, they are not related to the Purple Loosestrife.   They belong to a different family entirely.   Such confusion over English names is the reason botanists prefer to deal in Latin names, of which there is only one double-barreled name to each species; though, alas, the botanists sometimes come close to blows over which is the proper one.   Peace be with them!   Of these later loosestrifes, members of the Primrose Family, I have found four species, all yellow-flowering, in the Riverdale and Van Cortlandt area and I take it that they are found locally in other sections of the city.   The most abundant by far is the Whorled Loosestrife (*Lysimachia quadrifolia*) that grows knee high in open woods and bears little star-shaped, long-stalked yellow flowers in the axils of the whorled leaves on the upright stems.   Another upright member of the group is the Swamp Loosestrife (*Lysimachia terrestris*) that reaches a height of 2 or 3 feet in wet meadows or along the soggy borders of ponds and marshes.   Because the yellow flowers are clustered in a narrow cone at the top of the stem, they are sometimes called Swamp Candles.   The lowliest of the lot is Moneywort (*Lysimachia nummularia*), which might better be named Creeping Loosestrife since that is its method of growth around the edges of lawns, on moist roadsides, or in wet woods; but long ago somebody dubbed it Moneywort because of the roundish or coin-shaped little leaves growing opposite one another along the prostrate stem. The tallest of the group is the Fringed Loosestrife (*Steironema ciliatum*) that has branching stems and may attain a bushlike growth 4 feet in height. I always looked forward to finding it in bloom in June each year in Van Cortlandt swamp because its broad sharp-tipped yellow petals form a flower face about an inch in diameter, which makes it to my mind the handsomest of the quartet.

The dainty little star-shaped flowers of the Scarlet Pimpernel (*Anagallis arvensis*), an introduced Eurasian relative of the loose-strifes just mentioned, appear in similar fashion on long thin pedicels growing out of the axils of the opposite leaves, but this is a lowly plant of lawns and open spaces and it may take dili-gent search — or at least a close scrutiny of likely terrain — to find them in bloom. Although it is true that the flowers are brick-red, they are only ¼ inch in diameter at most and rarely are carried as much as a foot above the ground. Furthermore, they only open wide in fair weather, for which reason they are sometimes called the Poor-Man's-Weatherglass. Thus, though the plant blooms throughout the warmer months and grows in scattered places all over the area, few persons except deliberate searchers are sharp-eyed enough to find the dainty Scarlet Pimpernel in bloom.

As a matter of fact, I have tested the matter frequently when walking the woods and fields with acquaintances and I find that as a group city dwellers rarely notice small flowers unless they occur in overwhelming abundance on the ground or in massed and colorful clusters above it. Take the dogbanes, for instance. We have three species in the area and two of them are abun-dant along the roadsides or in the woods, fields, or waste places in three of the five boroughs — Richmond, Queens, and the Bronx. They grow 4 or 5 feet in height and hang out sprays of little bell-shaped flowers from late May or early June through July and August, pink-tinted in the case of the Spreading Dogbane (*Apocynum androsaemifolium*) and white or greenish white in the case of the one called Indian Hemp (*Apocynum cannabinum*). Yet few persons to whom I pointed them out could give them a name and most persons queried admitted they never had noticed the flowers before. The answer is that the little bells of modest hue dangling from the flowering sprays (cymes) are only about ¼ inch in length.

However, there are extenuating circumstances. It's just possible that many persons who do take notice of the plants either in flower or seed go their ways in the belief that these are milkweeds of some kind. Not only are the leaves somewhat milkweedish in shape and texture and the seed pods constructed on the milkweed design (except much thinner) but a milky juice oozes out if you pluck a leaf or flower or yank a seed pod loose from its mooring. These are the resemblances to the milkweeds. The main differences are that the dogbane flowers are little bells whereas the milkweed flowers are double-ended like old-fashioned egg cups or hourglasses and the fibrous bark of the dogbanes is so tough that the original residents of the area, the Indians, used it for lashings and bindings; hence the name of Indian Hemp for one of the common species. Just try to pull one of the stems or branches apart and you will appreciate the tensile strength of dogbane fibers.

Almost all the milkweeds, of course, justify their common name by the sticky white juice that flows from a break in any part of the plants. Some seven or eight species are found in the region but two are outstanding, one because of its abundance and the other because of its beauty. By far the most abundant species is the sturdy-stemmed, thick-leaved Common Milkweed (*Asclepias syriaca*) that furnishes board and lodging for Monarch butterflies. The adults feed on the flowers and the females attach their eggs to the underside of the large oval leaves. The handsomest of the group is the Butterfly-weed or Pleurisy Root (*Asclepias tuberosa*) with its goodly clusters of rich orange flowers. It is an exception among the milkweeds in that it has no milky juice and the narrow leaves are alternate, not opposite, on the hairy stem.

Everybody knows morning-glories as a group and there are at least a half-dozen species to be readily found in the region, all with the typical funnel-shaped flowers that help to identify the group. The colors of the flowers are no guide because in a single species the variations may run from white through pink and blue to purple, as in the case of the Common Morning-glory (*Ipomoea purpurea*) that twines its way along our roadsides and untrimmed fences. Another one of the more abundant species is the Hedge Bindweed (*Convolvulus sepium*), whose flowers of wider "funnels" vary from white to pink. Of the related and almost leafless dodders, those parasitic pests of farmers and truck gardeners, probably the most abundant local species is *Cuscuta gronovii*, whose orange-yellow stems are found clutching and winding about a perfect host of self-supporting and self-respecting plants in the open spaces of the city.

We shall never get on at this rate. We must move faster, even if we ignore families, genera, and species in a way to make a botanist shudder. We shall skip along to the mints, a marvelous family. You will recognize them by their family features, though not all the species have all the family marks. In general, these family traits are square stems and two-lipped flowers that often grow out of the leaf axils or surround the stems at such points. Only a few of the many species in the region may be mentioned here. The most abundant member of the family in the area undoubtedly is the Self-heal or Cure-all (*Prunella vulgaris*) that holds up its rather blocky head of little bluish or violet flowers almost everywhere on open ground in our territory except on well-weeded lawns and in well-kept gardens.

A more upstanding member of the family is the Motherwort (*Leonurus cardiaca*) that displays its cut leaves in waste places and in summer rings its upper leaf axils with somewhat bearded pinkish-purple flowers. If you walk over the eastern edge of the Van Cortlandt Park Parade Ground and dip down to what was once the right of way of the Getty Square branch of the Putnam Division Railroad you will be — in the flowering season — up to your ankles in Blue Curls or Bastard Pennyroyal (*Trichostema dichotomum*) with curiously long stamens sticking out and curling back beyond the little blue flower faces. The flowers are attractive in the summer but the little seed pods, or nutlets, that come later can be a nuisance in the way they cling to silk or cotton socks or stockings at ankle height.

The Germander or Wood Sage (*Teucrium canadense*) is common in the woods and along shady roadsides and often holds its spikes of purplish flowers knee high or more. Then there are the Skullcaps (*Scutellaria*) of perhaps half a dozen species and possibly you will also find the Horehound (*Marrubium vulgare*) with its clusters of white or faintly tinted little flowers encircling the stem at the leaf joints. On a roadside above the Hudson River in Spuyten Duyvil I encountered the Giant Hyssop (*Agastache nepetoides*) standing head high, a most imposing plant and not a common one in the area. The old-fashioned Catnip (*Nepeta cataria*) has disappeared from many places where it once flourished in the wild state but it is still found in some of the parks and on private estates.

One of the most pleasantly odorous members of the family is the American Wild Mint (*Mentha arvensis*) that grows lushly along the edges of streams and brooks. It pushes up in wet ground in meadows, and often a walker is first aware of it through the delightful aroma arising from the bruised plants that are being trodden underfoot. Then there is the lovely little Ground Ivy or Gill-over-the-Ground (*Glecoma hederacea*) with its creeping stems and little round leaves that give it the ivy look indicated by its specific Latin name (*hedera* being Latin for ivy). It is found in somewhat shaded and preferably moist waste places all through our territory and bears an abundance of little blue flowers throughout the spring.

The Bee Balm or Oswego Tea (*Monarda didyma*), though native to the region, is rare in the wild now but common in cultivation, one reason being that its bright scarlet or crimson tubular flowers are a great attraction to hummingbirds. The plant blooms in the summer, as does the Horse Mint or Purple Bergamot (*Monarda fistulosa*) that also is becoming scarcer within the city limits, though I have often found it in moist fields and along roadsides in Westchester. One of the yellow-flowering members of the family is the Horse Balm or Collinsonia (*Collinsonia canadense*) that grows to a height of 4 feet in the woods or along shaded roadsides and puts on exhibition in late summer a large terminal spray or panicle of ½-inch lemon-scented yellow flowers with stamens sticking out well beyond the corolla lip.

That is definitely short shrift for the Mint Family, or Labiatae, in our territory but we have no choice. Other common to abundant plants demand attention. Everywhere along fences and walls and roadsides in sun or shade you will find the Climbing Nightshade (*Solanum dulcamara*) and, if it is summertime, you will find clusters of red berries on the vine as well as sprays of little purple flowers with yellow stamens that form golden cones in their centers. The cultivated potato and tomato — yes, and the decorative petunias, too — are members of the Nightshade Family, and so is the Ground Cherry (*Physalis heterophylla*) often found on the fringe of cultivated ground with drooping bowl-shaped greenish-yellow flowers that turn into inflated seed pods later. Another member of the family common in our area is the Jimson-weed (*Datura stramonium*) with its long, white or tinted, funnel-shaped flowers and its later egg-shaped seed pods covered with sharp prickles. Because of these prickly seed pods, some persons prefer to call it Thorn-apple. Still another member of the family is the introduced European Matrimony-vine (*Lycium halimifolium*) that has run wild in our neighborhood and makes entangling alliances with brambles and shrubs in thickets in many sections of the city. In late

spring and early summer it bears long-stalked, ½-inch, somewhat bell-shaped purplish flowers that grow out of the leaf axils.

Byron, in his "English Bards and Scotch Reviewers," wrote
these stirring lines:

> *Oh! Amos Cottle! — Phoebus! what a name*
> *To fill the speaking trump of future fame! —*

The lines come in pat as an introduction to the Figwort Family,
or Scrophulariaceae (Phoebus! what a name!) with many
genera and innumerable species in our territory including one
introduced tree, the Paulownia, which will be encountered
later. Here we can mention only a few of the flowery members
of the family, beginning with one of the tallest, the Common
Mullein (*Verbascum thapsus*), whose spearlike stem rises 6 or 7
feet above the rosette of large flannel-like leaves on the ground
below. The terminal spike is a narrow cylinder of countless
buds that open a few at a time through the summer and the
five-lobed yellow flowers, up to an inch in width, are really
handsome even if the plant as a whole has a crude appearance.
But the really delicate and beautiful flowers of this genus are
those that the Moth Mullein (*Verbascum blattaria*) scatters along
its thinner stem instead of presenting them in a tight cylinder
at the top. The yellow flowers are held out from the stem on
little stalks, or pedicels, so that they have the advantage of
being presented singly. What is truly piquant about them is
that the upstanding five stamens are bearded with violet hairs
in such a way as to give the flowers the appearance of golden
butterflies much like the design that the short-tempered and
long-feuding James Abbott McNeill Whistler used as a signa-
ture — the famous "butterfly remarque" — on many of his
paintings, etchings, and lithographs.

Next in the family line we have the well-named Turtlehead
(*Chelone glabra*), whose white or pink-tinted flowers, really
shaped somewhat like a turtle's head with the mouth open,
come into bloom in July on moist banks or in roadside ditches.

Common Mullein

Much more abundant in the area and with a longer blooming season is the common Butter-and-Eggs or Toadflax (*Linaria vulgaris*), whose spikes of spurred two-lipped yellow and orange flowers show in shape how closely related it is to the fancy snapdragons of the florist shops and cultivated gardens. It blooms from late spring until well along in autumn and flourishes so abundantly in some regions that it is sometimes looked upon as a weed — but never by me.

There are half a dozen or more species of gerardia to be found from our seaward salt marshes to our inland roadsides, fields, and open woods, including a few with yellow or pink flowers, though most of them run to light shades of purple. The one I found most common in my pilgrimages over upland territory in Riverdale and Van Cortlandt Park was the Slender Gerardia (*Gerardia tenuifolia*) that has small and dark-spotted purple flowers, but occasionally in damp places I came upon the Purple Gerardia (*Gerardia purpurea*) with its large purple flowers on shorter stalks. The genus, of course, is named for John Gerard, the great old herbalist.

Most members of the Figwort Family have five-lobed flower faces but the little blue veronicas offer four-lobed faces for inspection. The most abundant of the group on dry ground in our area is the Common Speedwell (*Veronica officinalis*) with trailing or sloping stems rarely raised as much as a foot above ground and the little flowers displayed along the outer or upper end. In wet places, particularly around the shaded edges of ponds or along watercourses and often mingling with Forget-me-nots that have five-lobed faces, you may find the American Brooklime (*Veronica americana*).

With this brief glimpse at a few members of the Figwort Family resident in our region, we move along to the Madder Family (Rubiaceae), of which four species must be mentioned here and one later when we come to the shrubs. Probably the most abundant as well as the most familiar is the dainty little Bluet (*Houstonia caerula*) that is also called Innocence or Quaker Lady and sometimes appears in such numbers in spring as to give the appearance of a light blue mist hovering just above the ground in dry pastures or on open hillsides. Then there are the curling and twining and weakly reclining bedstraws of roadsides, fence borders, woods, and waste places, most of them of weedy growth with whorls of linear leaves at intervals along the curving stems and clusters of little four-parted white flowers growing out of the leaf axils on threadlike stalks. There must be a dozen species in the area but the one I most commonly encountered lolling along the roadsides was the White Bed-straw (*Galium mollugo*). Another common kind usually found in shadier ground is the one called Cleavers or Goosegrass (*Galium aparine*). It is quite similar in general appearance but the stems are so thickly covered with stiff hairs that they have a sand-papery touch if you run your fingers along them. Another member of the Madder Family is the lovely Partridgeberry (*Mitchella repens*) with its creeping stem, its roundish little evergreen leaves growing opposite each other, and its pairs of little white four-parted flowers that in each case form but a single berry with two black dots on it to show where the twin corollas withered and fell away. It's a plant of woodland floors, and since such terrain is limited within the city limits it is no longer as common here as it is on the wooded slopes of New Jersey to the west and Westchester to the north.

Here we leave the madders and tangle with the honeysuckles, of which there are a half-dozen or so species, native and in-troduced, in our territory. The familiar honeysuckles (*Lonicera*) have been enshrined in song and story. Some of them bear sweet-smelling flowers and edible berries for the support of birds and other forms of wildlife in cold weather. For this we are appreciative and grateful. There is, however, one im-ported species, *Lonicera japonica*, that has become a pest through its habit of climbing over and around every other form of plant life in the vicinity. At first it was in high favor as a quick-growing ground cover, which it is, and its black berries are eaten readily by birds and mammals; but probably nobody ex-pected it to spread as it has done in tangled masses over the ground nor to climb as high as it does in strangling shrubs and trees. Getting rid of it is becoming a major problem.

For a score of years I could find the blue spikes of the Great Lobelia (*Lobelia siphilitica*) in five minutes on any August day by walking from my home to the shady border of Dodge's Pond in Riverdale, but the pond has vanished and the flowers with it.

In my lifetime I have seen a continued filling-in of bogs and ponds and a covering-over of brooks and streams to make subterranean drains of ancient open watercourses. A similar process has been repeated in all boroughs and some of our finest native flowers have disappeared as a result. Time was when I could find the brilliant Cardinal-flower (*Lobelia cardinalis*) in scattered patches in moist ground in our neighborhood, but now I have to go farther afield. The hardier Indian Tobacco (*Lobelia inflata*) survives in abundance for two good reasons: it can grow on hard dry ground and its flowers, though of delicate blue color and true lobelian shape, are too small to attract general attention. Thus they escape the picking that probably was the final and decisive factor in the removal of the more attractive Great Lobelia and Cardinal-flower from the local scene.

Take a deep breath now, for we are about to plunge into the Composite Family (Compositae), the last and greatest of families of the flowering world, if we take "flowering" in the ordinary and not the botanical sense. These are the flowers that do not appear singly but in close clusters or "heads" of various shapes and dimensions such as are displayed by the asters, the goldenrods, the thistles, the fleabanes, the sunflowers, the thoroughworts, and the like. The individual flowers are of two kinds and I was amazed when this was revealed to me. Consider a flower that everybody knows and loves, the common White or Ox-eye Daisy (*Chrysanthemum lecucanthemum*) of our June fields and roadsides. If asked, most persons would say that a White Daisy is a flower circular in shape with numerous white petals radiating from a yellow center. Right? Apparently right but completely wrong. In fact, entrancingly wrong. A White Daisy is not a flower but a group, a gathering, a collection, a "head" of many individual flowers. Each white "petal" pulled off to settle the childhood problem of whether he or she loves me or loves me not is an individual flower and each separate segment of the crowded yellow center is also an individual flower, but of a different kind. The white "petals" are called

ray flowers and the yellow center is composed of crowded disk flowers. Not all members of the family are like the White Daisy in having both flat, strap-shaped ray flowers and tiny tubular disk flowers, but most of them do. Some, however, are all ray flowers and some all disk flowers, as we shall see.

The sunflowers, of course, are like the White Daisy in having both strap or ray flowers and central disk flowers, though in this group the rays are yellow and the disk flowers may be yellow, red, or purple. The Common Sunflower (*Helianthus annuus*) of the garden with its enormous heads and its seeds beloved of wild birds is an escape in waste places in the area but we have some quite handsome "wild sunflowers" that are native and still fairly common in outlying parts of the city. This includes the Giant Sunflower (*Helianthus giganteus*) of wet places — Van Cortlandt swamp, for instance — the Thin-leaved Sunflower (*Helianthus decapetalus*) of shaded ground, and the Jerusalem Artichoke (*Helianthus tuberosus*) of moist roadsides, a plant cultivated by the Indians for the edible tubers on its roots.

Here and there in the fields and waste places in summer there are patches of the familiar Black-eyed Susan (*Rudbeckia hirta*), a favorite for picking and a perennial reminder of the kindness of old Professor Rudbeck to the poor young student at Uppsala University in Sweden who was to become the great Linnaeus. Less familiar as flowers but better known as nuisances are the half-dozen or so species of beggar-ticks that thrive in the area, some looking deceptively like wild sunflowers but all of them producing hooked seeds that catch on the clothing of humans or cling to the hairy coats of many mammals, including dogs and cattle. Probably the prettiest of the group is the Bur-marigold (*Bidens laevis*) that blooms late in the summer and throughout early fall in wet ground. It has golden-yellow rays about an inch long and thus might easily be mistaken for some kind of low-growing sunflower. The worst of the lot, because it is so abundant along roadsides where its seeds can attach themselves to the clothing of walkers, is *Bidens frondosa*. It is so common in the area that if you merely say "beggar-ticks," it is taken for granted that you mean this species.

South and west of New York the quite handsome Lance-leaved Tickseed (*Coreopsis lanceolata*) is readily found in bloom in dry fields in late spring or early summer but in our territory it occurs only sparsely as a stray or an escape from cultivation. I had the luck to find a few in bloom in the Van Cortlandt region but where they grew is now the paved surface of a park playground and I have never since then found it anywhere in the vicinity. There are certain common little flowers, and two of a kind in this instance, that deserve recognition for their persistence in refusing to be driven out of the city under any circumstances. They flourish in the poorest kind of soil as well as the richest. They often sprout and bloom defiantly in the cracks in the pavement of city streets and sidewalks. They look much like miniature stubby White Daisies and, so far as I know, they have no common names and so they must be tagged with their scientific labels, which are *Galinsoga ciliata* and *Galin-*

soga parviflora — species distinguished by differences in detail
over which the ordinary citizen need not puzzle.   The first-
named is the more abundant of the two in our territory, and the
hairier, but to the eye they both present blunt white ray flowers
and bright yellow central disk flowers that combine to form a
flower head about ¼ inch in diameter.   If you look carefully
you can't miss them because they are among the hardiest and
the most abundant "weeds" within the city limits.

Mention of weeds brings up the fact that Great Ragweed
(*Ambrosia trifida*) and the more lowly Common Ragweed (*Ambrosia artemisiifolia*) flourish wickedly along roadsides and in
waste ground within the city limits.   Anybody walking through
a patch of such plants in August will get a good dusting of the
yellow pollen that the inconspicuous greenish flowers produce
in appalling quantities.   The Board of Health has been spray-
ing with a weed-killer and has somewhat abated the crop, but
not without the loss of many beneficial and ornamental plants
growing near or among the ragweeds.   These members of the
Composite Family are blamed for most of the sneezing and
wheezing among human residents of the area that goes under
the name of "hay fever."   With this in mind, look again at
the generic name: *Ambrosia!*   It almost leads to the suspicion
that certain birds officiated at the baptismal font.   Ambrosia
perhaps to the Goldfinches and White-throated Sparrows joyfully feeding on the seeds in autumn, but anathema to the
human race.

While in the mood, we may best tick off some other unpopular members of the family, the clotburs (*Xanthium*), a
group that will call attention to themselves if anybody attempts
to overlook them.   The mark of the clan is the seed pod that is
about the size and shape of a large olive pit and is covered
with stiff little hooked prickles.   The leaves are usually large
and floppy and the flowers and burs are produced in the upper
axils in goodly quantities.   Botanists differ as to the number
of species and varieties in our region but, taking Britton and

Brown as a guide, the most common species is *Xanthium strumarium*, a plant of waste places and particularly abundant in the sea-beach regions, where it goes by the name of Beach Clotbur.

The sneezeweeds are a more attractive topic. In late summer you will find them in bloom in wet ground. We have two kinds in our area, the more common being the native *Helenium autumnale* that, with yellow rays and disk flowers, looks like a small sunflower with an exaggerated central disk shaped like a little haystack. If this central "haystack" is brown or purple, you will be looking at the Purple-headed Sneezeweed (*Helenium nudiflorum*), a plant that has moved in from the South and West. Other attractive though weedy members of the family are the chamomiles of heavily scented feathery foliage and daisy-like heads of white and yellow flowers. We have two white-rayed species that are more or less common in waste places and around old outbuildings in the area. The taller one, whose leaves have an offensive odor when crushed, is the *Anthemis cotula* of Europe that, introduced long ago and now widespread in North America, goes by various names such as Mayweed, Dog-fennel, and Stinking or Pigsty Daisy. The species of lower growth, whose flower heads rarely are lifted more than a foot or so above the ground, is the Field or Corn Chamomile (*Anthemis arvensis*).

The Common Yarrow or Milfoil (*Achillea millefolium*) is abundant everywhere in waste places and along neglected roadsides and its wide flat sprays of little white flower heads are in evidence from June well into November. I often crush the fernlike leaves to enjoy the strong spicy odor. Our Yarrow is of Eurasian origin, as are so many of the common flowers of our fields. Some reached here more or less by accident but most of them were brought over as beloved garden flowers by early colonists. One of the most cherished of that group is the abundant White Daisy that everybody knows and loves and another is the closely related Feverfew (*Chrysanthemum parthenium*) that much resembles the White Daisy except that the leaves are broader and of a fancier cut and the smaller flower heads usually are presented in terminal clusters instead of singly. Then there is the dooryard Tansy (*Tanacetum vulgare*) that has escaped to our roadsides, the fernlike leaves of which are even more strongly scented than those of the Yarrow. So far as the eye can discover, the tight little yellow heads of Tansy flowers are all of the disk type. With no visible fringe of ray flowers, they really do look like yellow buttons and they do taste bitter; wherefore the secondary name of Bitter Buttons for Tansy is fitting and proper. Still another Old World native now a familiar and long-time resident of our region is the Dusty Miller (*Artemisia stelleriana*) of our sandy seaside stretches where few other plants will grow. There it displays in abundance its finely cut, woolly-white foliage and holds up its spikes of insignificant yellow flowers throughout all the heat of summer.

We have not yet finished with the botanical immigrants that are now completely at home in this country. There is the Coltsfoot (*Tussilago farfara*) to consider, a plant used for centuries as a homespun remedy for colds. Indeed, the generic name *Tussilago* is derived from the Latin word for cough, *tussis*. As to its curative properties, our oft quoted friend John Gerard wrote: "A decoction made of the greene leaves and roots, or else a syrrup thereof, is good for the cough. The fume of the dried leaves taken through a funnell or tunnell, burned upon coles, effectually helpeth those that are troubled with the shortnesse of breath, and fetch their winde thicke and often. Being taken in the manner as they take Tobaco, it mightily prevaileth against the diseases aforesaid."

The belief in its medical benefits came with it overseas and I remember cough drops and candy canes flavored with Coltsfoot that were sold in country stores. With a sugar coating, this was medicine that went down easily with children. Possibly it still is sold in marts beyond my ken but I have not seen any of it for years. The plant itself is much misunderstood. There is no doubt that many persons who see great patches of the low-growing yellow flower heads in early spring mistake them for dandelions of some kind. Of course, a close look at the smaller heads on woolly stems made up of over-lapping segments would dispel the idea that they were dande-lions, but most persons give only a casual glance at such flowers. The plant thrives on moist banks in sun or shade and blooms in profusion on the sloping sides of vacant lots in outlying sec-tions of the city. Then there are the leaves with a growing habit that adds to the confusion concerning the plant. The leaves are large and spongy and woolly underneath and are supposedly shaped like a colt's foot — hence the English name of the plant — but usually they do not appear until after the

flowers have gone to seed and thus, for the ordinary observer, there is no visible connection to link leaf and flower as parts of the same plant.

Since dandelions have been mentioned, we might as well go into the matter here and now. Everybody knows the Common Dandelion (*Taraxacum officinale*) and those who love lawns of spotless green are inclined to look upon this plant as a persistent pest. But if it were rare it would be highly prized, for the flower heads are truly beautiful. You can find them in bloom throughout the year in our territory and the young leaves make a tasty salad, which is an added point in favor of the plant. There is a much less common red-seeded species but the average person could not be expected to distinguish it in the field. However, anyone who keeps alert when walking outdoors must notice many flower heads of the dandelion type that obviously are not the Common Dandelion of our lawns, meadows, and roadsides. Among them is the Dwarf Dandelion (*Krigia virginica*) that lifts its ½-inch golden heads about a foot above its basal rosette of much toothed leaves and another is the well-named and much taller Fall Dandelion that blooms much later in the season and holds larger heads of yellow ray flowers as much as 2 feet above the ground. Then there is the Goat's Beard or Salsify (*Tragopogon pratensis*) of neglected lawns, roadsides, and waste places, a still taller plant with handsome golden flower heads that may be 2 inches or more in width. This one you will know by its fleshy appearance and the smooth, narrow, clasping leaves that are alternate along the shining stem. There are other and still taller plants such as the Sow Thistles (*Sonchus*) and Wild Lettuces (*Lactuca*) that belong to this group marked by heads of yellow ray flowers and the milky juice that runs through the clan but the best we can do for them here is to dismiss them as roadside weeds and move on to something more attractive.

The "something more attractive" is the goldenrod group of which it is stated on page 414 of Volume III of *The New Britton and Brown:* "Nearly a hundred species, native chiefly to North America . . . reaching its greatest complexity in eastern U.S. The species are often difficult to define, and numerous hybrids are known, frequently between species not very closely related. The basal and underground parts are often necessary for accurate identification." In the face of that solemn warning, no attempt will be made here to cope with the dozens of species that a botanist might turn up on a tramp through the woods, fields, swamps, and marshes of our territory of a September or October day. We must mention the Silverrod (*Solidago bicolor*) because, though a true goldenrod, in most cases the tiny ray flowers of this species are white like those of the White Daisy and thus we have a "white goldenrod." Sometimes the ray flowers of the Silverrod are yellow and thus we have the explanation of the specific label *bicolor* for the species. It is common enough among the other goldenrods of the city but not conspicuous because the plant usually consists of a single unbranched stem 1 to 3 feet tall with small clusters of flower heads along the upper part. Beyond that we have a truly gorgeous assortment of really golden goldenrods that lend glorious color to our autumn landscape.

Next we have the asters of different hues, a group even more beautiful than our goldenrods and definitely more difficult to unravel. A footnote on page 1419 of Gray (Eighth Edition) reads: "The most complicated and difficult section in our flora, the specific lines, especially in the narrow-leaved series, including Nos. 34–56, too often obscured by hybridization." Once again we have reached an impasse and once again we must retreat to safe ground by simply stating that there are dozens of species of aster in the area, that they vary in flower color from pure white through yellow and blue to rich purple-violet and that, of one species or another, they abound in our woods, meadows, and marshes and along our hillsides and our roadsides from midsummer to frosty November.

Despite the warning of the botanists, I venture just a trifle farther among our asters.   The finest of them all to my eye is the New England Aster (*Aster novae-angliae*) that sometimes grows 6 feet tall in lush patches in fairly rich open ground or wet meadows and flaunts magnificent sprays of deep purple-violet ray flowers surrounding golden circles of disk flowers. Sometimes these wild flower heads are 2 inches or more in width and can vie with the most colorful attractions of the Park Avenue florist shops.   Another species that finds particular favor with me is the low-growing Stiff or Savory-leaved Aster (*Aster linariifolius*), whose ray flowers are light blue as a rule and sometimes almost white.   This species is found over a wide range in the eastern half of the United States and often appears in thick patches on dry uplands.   I like it because it usually appears in abundance where it appears at all and, with sprays of flower heads bunched at the tops of the stiff stems, it takes little time to gather a bouquet presenting a solid floral surface.   For years I patronised a patch on a hillside above the Hudson where Spuyten Duyvil merges into Riverdale, but with the increase in population in that area I fear for its survival.

Before we leave the asters we must salute the Golden Aster (*Chrysopsis mariana*) of the sandy seaward sections of the city. It is an aster only in English.   The scientific name shows it to be in a different genus, but Golden Aster does very well as a label because it looks the part and holds its handsome aster-like heads of golden disk and ray flowers in clusters a foot or so above the ground.   And while on this same ground we are bound to take notice of the thick stems and leaves and the great sprays of thickly clustered flowering heads of the Seaside Goldenrod (*Solidago sempervirens*) that blooms from August into October within sight and sound of the sea.

Back we go to the uplands or at least higher ground within the city limits to find the fleabanes that to me look like soft silky daisies or asters with ray flowers as thin as threads.   In our territory all the disk or central flowers are yellow but the thin and delicate ray flowers run from white through pink to blue, purple and violet, depending on the species. The Common Fleabane (*Erigeron philadelphicus*) whose ray flowers are usually tinted with pink or light rose-purple, grows to a height of 2 or 3 feet along our roadsides and blooms early in the spring. The Robin's-plantain (*Erigeron pulchellus*), which favors moist shady ground, doesn't reach up quite as high but produces wider heads — sometimes 1½ inches in diameter — with lovely fringes of violet-blue or purple ray flowers. We have two species with white ray flowers in the area, *Erigeron annuus* and *Erigeron strigosus*. Both species look much alike and go by the same name, Daisy Fleabane. As a rule, the first species mentioned has taller stems and slightly longer ray flowers but both species have a tendency to vary in detail (including color of the ray flowers), and specific identification should be left to the experts. If you tramp the salt marshes of the tidal regions of the city you may come upon the purple-flowering Marsh Fleabane (*Pluchea purpurascens*) but, frankly, the flowers are hardly worth the trip.

Probably the children of today, as of yore, refer to a certain low woolly gray plant with a small, lumpy, whitish flower head as Ladies' Tobacco or perhaps Indian Tobacco. It grows abundantly to a height of 6 inches or more in pastures or in open woods. The botanical name of the plant is *Antennaria plantaginifolia* — an imposing name for such a humble plant — and it is a close relative of the fairly common and quite handsome Pearly Everlasting (*Anaphalis margaritacea*) that is also found, though more sparingly, in the same kind of terrain, but preferably in pastures. The name of Pearly Everlasting is well deserved. Flower clusters picked in August and placed in a dry vase will hold shape and color well into the winter season.

When the Joe-Pye Weed comes into pinkish-purple flower, autumn is in the offing. In late August and early September it is in full bloom in wet meadows and along the open borders of streams, swamps, and fresh-water marshes, where its cocoa-colored to light purple flowers appear in great masses that con-

Joe-Pye Weed

trast brilliantly with the glowing goldenrods that fringe it on slightly higher and drier ground. The botanists have made three or four species of our Joe-Pye Weeds but this need not concern us too much. To the best of my knowledge and belief, the Joe-Pye Weed most plentiful in open wet ground in our region is *Eupatorium maculatum* and the one I commonly find in moist shady places such as woodland roadsides is *Eupatorium purpureum*. Both are tall plants with stiff upright stems that carry whorls of long narrow leaves and terminal sprays of hundreds of tiny flowers that vary in hue from pale pink to a fairly good purple.

A close relative is the familiar Boneset or Thoroughwort (*Eupatorium perfoliatum*) of similar terrain with dull white flowers and dagger-shaped opposite leaves joined broadly at the base so that the stem appears to be growing through the middle of a long single leaf sharp-pointed at both ends. This is the plant that provided, through the steeping of its leaves, the "boneset tea" favored as a home remedy in years gone by. It was supposed to ward off colds and break up fevers and in general to be "good for what ails you." The hardiest of this group in our territory is the White Snakeroot (*Eupatorium rugosum*), white by name because of the color of its flowers and "snakeroot" because of an old belief that its juice or a decoction made from its leaves was a cure for the toxic effect of bites by poisonous snakes. Like the Boneset, this plant grows to a height of 3 or 4 feet but its sprays of dull white flowers are not as broad as those of the Boneset and its ovate or broadly heart-shaped leaves are held well out from the stem on long petioles. I often find the White Snakeroot still in bloom in woods and thickets and along shaded roadsides in late October and early November. A vine-like plant of much similar whitish or slightly tinted flower sprays is the Climbing Hempweed or Climbing Boneset (*Mikania scandens*) that is plentiful in Van Cortlandt swamp and other such shrub-covered, well-watered wild places in our territory. It comes into bloom in midsummer and flowers as late as

October. That's the time when it is most noticeable as a gray-green drapery over swamp shrubbery from which the leaves have fallen away.

Sometimes 6 feet or more in height, as tall as the tallest of our Joe-Pye Weeds and growing in wet ground like them though not nearly so abundantly, is the noble Ironwood (*Vernonia noveboracensis*) that in late summer is crowned with wide, loose clusters of rather "frizzly" heads of rich purple flowers, much deeper in hue as a rule than the neighboring Joe-Pye Weeds. Its long narrow leaves that are pointed at both ends grow alternately along the stem, a detail helping to distinguish it from the neighboring Joe-Pye Weeds with their whorls of leaves before the flowers come out to make recognition simple.

We could be accused — and convicted, too — of snobbery if we overlooked the Common Burdock (*Arctium minus*) with its great rhubarb-like leaves and its many globular little heads of purple flowers that, when summer wanes, become the burs that cling so annoyingly to the clothing of humans, the coats of long-haired dogs, and the tails of cows. Even in the flowering stage the little round heads are so armed that they can be stuck together in all sorts of shapes — a pastoral pastime for children. It grows everywhere around houses and outbuildings and reaches its greatest fullness in a kitchen garden that has been abandoned to weeds. There the Common Burdock will grow 5 feet in height and as wide as it is tall. If you see a plant with flower heads about twice the usual size, you will have found the Great Burdock (*Arctium lappa*), something of a prize catch in a weedy way.

Because of the sharp prickles that cover the plants, most persons steer clear of thistles in the field. However, anyone who cares to go looking for them will have no trouble finding five or six species in our territory. The most common one on dry open ground is the familiar stout-stemmed Bull Thistle (*Cirsium vulgare*), whose heads of rather handsome purple flowers are sometimes 2 inches in diameter. In wet ground the common species is the taller and more branching Swamp Thistle (*Cirsium muticum*) with smaller heads of purplish flowers. If you come upon a yellow-flowering thistle it probably will be *Cirsium horridulum*, a species that prefers the seaward sections of the city.

A common weed of dry ground with attractive heads of flowers — when the blue rays are first spread — is the Chicory (*Cichorium intybus*) that grows to a height of 2 or 3 feet in zigzag fashion. This is the plant whose roots are ground up to produce the filler and flavoring agent that some persons (more in the southern part of the United States than in the northern) like to have in their coffee. If the floral display had any durability the plant would be prized, but the heads open in the morning and the bright blue rays wilt fast in sunlight. By noon the rays are pale white and the flower heads are closing up. Even so, the plants occur in abundance, new heads of flowers with bright blue rays appear each fine morning throughout a long blooming period from July to mid-autumn and, from dawn until the sun is high in the sky, a blue mass of Chicory in a field is a delight to the eye. Goldfinches dote on the seeds, and often on a sunrise stroll in summer I have disturbed melodious flocks of the little "wild canaries" feeding in Chicory patches.

Finally we come to the hawkweeds and once again there is offered pertinent information in Gray (Eighth Edition): "The genus, especially in Europe, broken by technical experts, with eyesight stimulated beyond that of ancient hawks, into thousands of so-called species, subspecies, varieties and forms . . . " The name hawkweed, of course, traces back to some legend that hawks fed on these plants to sharpen their eyesight. To keep clear of specific difficulties, we will mention only a few of the common species in our territory and leave the others for the botanists to handle. The most brilliantly colored of the group in our summer fields is the orange and red Devil's Paintbrush (*Hieracium aurantiacum*) that grows to a height of 2 feet or so and often is so abundant in hayfields that farmers look upon it as a pest. Of the yellow-flowering species the most abundant in fields and along roadsides is the King Devil (*Hieracium floren-tinum*) that reaches a height of 3 feet and spreads a looser cluster of flower heads at the summit. In the woods you will find the kind called Rattlesnake Weed or Poor Robin's-plantain (*Hiera-cium venosum*) with a still looser cluster of yellow flowers aloft and a basal rosette of shiny oval leaves conspicuously marked with purplish veins.

Here we must come to a halt, even though we have com-pletely ignored countless flowers of the area. For instance, we did not even mention in passing the shoulder-high Blue Vervein (*Verbena hastata*) and the equally tall White Vervein (*Verbena urticifolia*) that are abundant along moist roadsides and in wet meadows and that are topped in summer with numerous flowering spikes along which the buds open a few at a time to display little five-lobed flowers of blue or white, as the case may be. We did not pause to admire the lovely little Sand Spurrey (*Spergularia rubra*) that barely lifts its tiny five-petaled pinkish-purple flowers above the hard ground along footpaths or neglected roadways in the seaward sections of the city. The omissions are myriad and in some cases grievous, but all will be well for the reader who makes the end of this chapter the begin-ning of a wider and deeper acquaintance with the amazing number of wild flowers that not only survive but flourish within the boundaries of a great city.

Chapter 11

Of Trees and Shrubs

JUST OFF the road that runs from gate to gate in the New York Botanical Garden in the Bronx Park, and at the side of a path leading toward the famous Hemlock Grove, there stood for years a wooden signboard on which, in black letters on a yellow background, the following information was provided:

> The area between this road and the
> Bronx River is the only part remaining
> of the original forest which once
> covered the land on which New York City
> is now built. It has been called
> New York City's most precious natural
> possession. Your cooperation in
> preserving this unique area will keep
> it for the pleasure of future generations.

The signboard fell away under the onslaught of vandals, who luckily were not strong enough to uproot and carry off the

trees to which it called attention. They still remain in place, the single surviving unit area of virgin forest within the city limits, a wooded section undisturbed by axe or saw since Indians were the only human occupants of any of the five boroughs that now make up the city. The feature of the designated wooded section in the park is the Hemlock Grove where the tall evergreens stand in silence and majesty, beautiful but awesome, reminding one vaguely of the darker Gustave Doré illustrations for Milton's *Paradise Lost*. The species is *Tsuga canadensis*, the only hemlock native to New York and New England.

The Hemlock Grove in the park borders the Bronx River and runs westward to the top of a rocky ridge, where it thins out and gives way to different species of oaks and other hardwoods that are typical of the wooded sections of the city. Evergreens, either singly or in groves, are merely local and occasional in and around the city. Many that meet the eye have been set out for ornament. The predominant trees of the region are deciduous and stand bare to the winter winds.

But since we started in the famous Hemlock Grove of the Botanical Garden — a favorite "owl country" for bird-watchers — we might as well wander a little farther among the evergreens or cone-bearers of the area. The noble, picturesque, and pleasantly odorous White Pine (*Pinus strobus*) is native and survives in the wild as well as under cultivation. The native Pitch Pine (*Pinus rigida*) is the only tree that will grow in some of the windswept seaside sections of the city. The Scotch Pine (*Pinus sylvestris*), extensively planted, has become more or less naturalized as an escape. The Shortleaf or Yellow Pine (*Pinus echinata*) is native to Staten Island and so is the Scrub or Jersey Pine (*Pinus virginiana*), also found sparingly on Long Island.

New York City lies below the altitude and latitude lines of our native spruces but the Norway Spruce (*Picea abies*), an introduced species, has long been under cultivation and occasionally turns up as an escape. For lawn decoration in outlying sections of the city the Blue Spruce *(Picea pungens)* from the Rocky Mountains is a familiar sight.

Whether or not any truly wild larches or tamaracks survive in the area is difficult to determine. Both the native American Larch or Tamarack *(Larix laricina)* and the European Larch *(Larix decidua)* have been planted on lawns, along streets and in the public parks and many of them — long rows in some cases — are fine tall trees probably one hundred years or more in age, but I have not found any such native tamaracks growing in the local swamps where you would expect to find them if they were of wild stock. The feature of these trees, of course, is that they are needle-leaved cone-bearers like the pines and spruces, and yet they shed their needles every autumn just as the oaks, birches, maples, and other deciduous trees shed their broader leaves. The European Larch has slightly longer needles and slightly larger cones; otherwise it is quite similar in appearance to our American Larch. They are fine-feathered trees in summer when they wear the short, silky light green needles in tufts along the branchlets, but if on a winter walk you come upon a tall pyramidal tree that looks somewhat like a dead spruce and has small round cones hanging from its drooping outer branchlets, you will be gazing at an American or a European Larch.

The Northern White Cedar or Arbor Vitae *(Thuja occidentalis)* and the much similar Atlantic or Southern White Cedar *(Chamaecyparis thyoides)* once were common in the swamps and bogs and on moist open hillsides in our area, but now they are common only in cultivation on lawns, in public parks, and (particularly Northern White Cedar) as evergreen adornments of cemetery plots. If you are puzzled as to which is which — the "knitted," or "beaded," foliage is common to both — you can distinguish them easily in the fruiting season: the rather narrowly oval ½-inch or so cones of the Northern split toward the base to allow the seeds to escape; the little globular cones of the Atlantic split toward the middle.

The Red Cedar (*Juniperus virginiana*) and its relative the Dwarf Juniper (*Juniperus communis*) are almost on the same footing as the white cedars of the area except that they are not as highly prized for decorative purposes. They like open slopes, old pastures, and rough ground in general and not much of such terrain remains within the city limits. However, both the Dwarf Juniper and the taller and handsomer Red Cedar that provides the odorous wood for cedar chests and many lead pencils are still to be found in the wild as well as in cultivation in our territory.

The Ginkgo or Maidenhair Tree (*Ginkgo biloba*) with its lovely little semicircular leaves is of Asiatic origin, but it must be included here because it is such a common sight as a street tree in New York, as well as in many other cities all over the world. It is a fine tree for city planting because it is easily propagated, grows to a good height, has attractive leaves, is disease-resistant beyond most other trees, and thrives in the contaminated city atmosphere. It has other distinctions. In ancestry it is the oldest tree known. Fossils show that it existed more than 100,000,000 years ago and has come down to us practically unchanged since that time. It was discovered in China and much cultivated there and in Japan as a park and temple tree. As it became more popular in cultivation, it disappeared in the wild for centuries and it was only recently that it was again found growing wild in eastern China.

The staminate and pistillate flowers of the Ginkgo grow on separate trees, and since the pistillate, or female, flowers produce the mottled purplish ½-inch globular plumlike fruit that has a disagreeable taste and a bad odor when crushed underfoot on sidewalks, the staminate trees are preferred for city planting. You will recognize the tree in foliage by the semicircular leaves narrowly lobed in the middle, and in the leafless season by the short stubby twigs that look like artificial pegs or miniature stumps set along the branches and branchlets.

The willows are a group that baffle most of us. A botanist

on a day's tramp probably could find at least a dozen species, native or introduced, on Staten Island or in the Bronx. They range in size from much branched shrubs to good tall trees. Most of them are found in moist ground and have long, narrow, alternate leaves with persistent "stipules," or tiny leaflike attachments, at the base of each petiole. Not only do different species look much alike to the inexpert eye but the group hybridizes freely, which adds to the difficulty of distinguishing them in the field. Individual willows bear either staminate or pistillate flowers in the form of catkins that, in the case of our native Pussy Willow *(Salix discolor)*, are eagerly sought as the first floral trophies of returning spring.

The odd thing is that few persons recognize the Pussy Willow except in the budding stage, although it is fairly common in wet ground in our region, has leaves that are broader than most of its relatives, and often grows tall enough to be considered a small gangling tree. One of our introduced willows, however, is easily recognized at any season of the year. That's the Weeping Willow *(Salix babylonica)* with its pendulous branchlets and drooping narrow leaves, a familiar sight on private estates and in public parks, and occasionally encountered as an escape in our territory. The common tall native species of our swamps, wet meadows, and moist roadsides is the Black Willow *(Salix nigra)* that reaches a good girth of trunk and a height of 60 feet or so. The Shining Willow *(Salix lucida)* is abundant as a much branched shrub in wet places throughout the region.

The poplars are "country cousins" of the willows and are included in the Willow Family. Three native species are common to abundant in our parks and on waste ground in the city outskirts, and two imported species have made themselves at home here. The most abundant of the group is the Common or Eastern Cottonwood or Carolina Poplar *(Populus deltoides)* that, in the early days of tree planting in the city, was chosen for its rapid rate of growth; but it soon fell into disfavor for several reasons. One was that the long catkins that give it the name of Necklace Poplar in some regions littered the sidewalks for several weeks in spring. But the more serious charge was that the fine fibrous roots, following every trace of moisture in the ground, penetrated underground water pipes at breaks or leaky joints and spread inside the pipes to the extent of impeding the flow of water or even cutting it off altogether. The result was that the tree finally came under official ban for street planting, but it is still common in parks in all five boroughs and in waste places all through the area.

The Quaking Aspen or Trembling Asp (*Populus tremuloides*), which rarely reaches any great size, is common along roadsides, fences, the borders of woods, and in waste places with its roundish leaves so delicately balanced on stiff flattened petioles that they quiver and whisper with every passing breath of wind. The Bigtooth Aspen (*Populus grandidentata*) grows to be a quite tall tree and is conspicuous in the woods or on open ground in early spring because its unfolding leaves are so covered with whitish down on the underside that they almost look like white flowers along the bare boughs. As the leaves mature they lose this "white flannel backing," but in the case of the White Poplar or Abele (*Populus alba*), an introduced dooryard tree that has wandered into the wild, the heavy white or grayish felting remains on the underside of the blunt-lobed leaves throughout the season.

The last of the group to claim our attention is the picturesque Lombardy Poplar (*Populus nigra* var. *italica*), with the strongly and narrowly upcurving branches that give it the appearance of a tall tapering column of greenery. Here's a tree with an odd history. It is said that all the Lombardy Poplars of the world — and they now practically girdle the globe in the temperate zones — trace their ancestry to a single freakish "sport" of the common Black Poplar (*Populus nigra*) of Europe and Asia. It is not a distinct species but, as its triple scientific name indicates, merely a variety. Where it originated, nobody knows

but it bears the name Lombardy Poplar because it first came
into public favor as an ornamental tree in Lombardy, the
northern section of Italy, and from there spread all over Europe.
All the trees are staminate and hence no seed ever is produced,
but they are easily propagated by cuttings or sprouts that often
come up from the roots in such numbers as to require constant
control.

There is no sharp dividing line between trees and shrubs; they grade into one another. It is largely a matter of size and the fact that what we call a tree has a single stem we usually refer to as a trunk. Shrubs are smaller, ordinarily branch much closer to the ground, and may have numerous stems. Such details are trifles to the botanists, who arrange plants in systematic order; in this chapter we may descend from a tall tree in one paragraph to meet some sturdy but stubby shrubs in the next, as we do now.

The Northern Bayberry (*Myrica pensylvanica*), whose waxy little fruits were melted down to make the pleasantly odorous "bayberry candles" of colonial days and even more recent times, is abundant in thick patches in the seaward section of the city on Long Island and it is also fairly common in smaller patches on higher ground on Staten Island and in the Bronx. The Sweetgale (*Myrica gale*) pushes up here and there in swamps and marshes but it does not compare in abundance with the Northern Bayberry, though it does in attractive aroma of the crushed leaves and fruit. The Sweetfern (*Comptonia peregrina*), which is called so because of its fernlike leaves, though it is a long way botanically from the Fern Family, once was abundant in patches in open woods and upland pastures in our territory; recent building operations have cut deeply into its ancient terrain. However, it still survives in the woods and fields of some of the less frequented sections of our city parks. And happily so, because I never stroll by a patch without crushing a few leaf blades to enjoy the delightful odor produced thereby.

I never saw an automobile until I was ten or eleven years old. In my childhood days in the northern section of the city, horsepower was applied through four legs instead of four wheels. We had a stable adjacent to our house and so did many of our neighbors. There were farms around us and each farm had a redolent barnyard. The great barnyard tree was the noble Black Walnut (*Juglans nigra*) that, though I did not know it at the time, was even then fast disappearing over its entire range in the eastern half of the United States. Its virtues were the cause of its decline and fall. The wood was wanted for gunstocks and fancy furniture. Barnyards have almost disappeared from city territory, and so have Black Walnut trees. Nevertheless, some survive on Staten Island and in outlying sections of Queens and the Bronx. Some have been set out in Van Cortlandt Park and a few fair-sized trees are producing goodly crops of the edible nuts well worth the hand-staining that goes with the removal of the round green husk.

The closely related Butternut (*Juglans cinerea*) of much the same range as the Black Walnut is frequently encountered in open territory within the city limits. Its oval-oblong nuts are just as tasty and its wrinkled fuzzy and sticky greenish-brown husks just as darkly stain the fingers, but it is no such noble and upstanding tree as the Black Walnut. The compound leaves of both trees are somewhat similar but the Butternut has lighter bark and never grows up straight, tall, and strong like the Black Walnut. Rather, it seems merely to "lean upward" vaguely and branch at odd angles in an anemic way. It is not highly prized for its timber and its branches are easily broken by high winds. The nuts are by far the best part of this tree that, through broken limbs, often leads an invalid life and fades away at an early age.

We have five species of hickory that are more or less common to abundant in our territory, two of them with characteristics that make them easily known on sight. The Shagbark Hickory (*Carya ovata*) in maturity at least can be recognized by the "shagginess" of the gray bark that seems to hang on the trunk in narrow, oblong plates fastened in the middle and loose at both ends. This tall stout tree produces the largest hickory nuts of our region. Another species easy to identify, at least in winter, is the Bitternut Hickory (*Carya cordiformis*) that prefers moist ground and displays bright yellow buds through the leafless season. It is sometimes known as the Swamp Hickory because it is often found along the edges of swamp. The best name for it would be Yellowbud Hickory, but Bitternut has priority and a logical explanation: the kernels of the nuts are so bitter that unless everything else fails even the squirrels turn up their noses at them. This is one reason why the Bitternut is so abundant in the area.

Three other hickories found in the upland deciduous woods in three of the five boroughs — Queens, Richmond, and the Bronx — are the Pignut *(Carya glabra)*, the Mockernut *(Carya tomentosa)* and the Sweet or Oval or Red Pignut *(Carya ovalis)*, the last name deriving from the color of its twigs. The Pignut is quite common on the slopes and ridges of the Riverdale region. Possibly the Mockernut and the Sweet Pignut are found in greater numbers in other sectors of the city. All three species, of course, have the typical nuts and compound leaves with leaflets growing larger toward the tip that help to mark the group, but they differ in detail of bark, leaf, and fruit.

Family relationships that sometimes seem strange on first acquaintance always turn out in the end to be perfectly natural. With no knowledge of botany, for instance, one might expect the Birch Family (Betulaceae) to include only the birches of our woods, fields, roadsides, and riverbanks, but there is much more to it than that according to the botanists. The birches are the more important constituents and thus they give their name to the family, but it is extended to include the familiar alders of swampy ground, the hazelnuts of hillside and roadside, the abundant small tree called the Ironwood *(Carpinus caroliniana)*, also known as the "Blue Beech," and the taller but less common and less familiar tree in our region, the Hornbeam *(Ostrya virginiana)*. Whether shrubs or trees, all the members of this group have two family traits in common: alternate simple leaves and drooping catkins of staminate flowers in spring.

The American Hazelnut *(Corylus americana)* and the Beaked Hazelnut *(Corylus cornuta)* are found in the wild on the outskirts

American Hazelnut

of the city and I presume they once were common within the city limits. However, I must confess I found only the American Hazelnut in the Riverdale–Van Cortlandt region and, furthermore, I never was able to garner any of the delicious nuts, because the local squirrels did away with them while they were still too green for human consumption. Incidentally, the lengthening and softening of hazelnut staminate catkins is one of the early and heartening signs of returning spring.

The Ironwood is common in our woodlands as a small tree of usually slanting trunk and widespread lateral branches. The smooth, tight, twisting, two-toned bark looks as though it were made of metal bands of blue and gray color running sinuously up the trunk and out along the branches. This is the feature that gives the name of Ironwood to the tree and makes it easy to recognize at any season of the year. More than that, it fruits heavily in our territory and, after the leaves have fallen, the hanging clusters of nutlets ensconced in the sunken pockets of the rough, brown, leafy "bracts" remain on the tree for weeks as a further aid to recognition if any were needed.

The Hornbeam, though common in woodlands at no great distance from the city, is by no means abundant in our territory, which is too bad because it is an interesting tree if never a large one. In general it is a somewhat slender woodland or roadside tree with a delicate gray-brown bark that flakes off in paper-thin longitudinal strips. The thin birchlike leaves are so finely toothed as to seem almost fringed. The fruits are clusters of overlapping inflated seed pods so similar in appearance to the hops grown and gathered for the brewing industry as to give the tree a colloquial name of Hop Hornbeam. One of the easiest ways to find the tree in the leafy woods is to look for the yellowish clusters of seed pods that stand out against the green foliage in June. Unfortunately, the trees I know on city soil fruit only sparsely and irregularly. Even so, the Hornbeam is easily detected in winter by its flaky bark, its particularly slender branchlets, and the two or three little staminate catkins hanging stiffly from the tips of the twigs.

As for the birches that give their name to the family, they are among the most delightful trees of North America, but it must be conceded that nowadays their value lies almost entirely in the field of aesthetics. Years ago the wood of several species was used in the manufacturing of furniture and household accessories of all sorts but, as synthetics came into fashion for such purposes, birch went out. Now the lumberman looks upon the birches with indifference; even as firewood they are held in low esteem. Birch logs piled outdoors should be burned within two years or they will soften into soggy sawdust. But birches are lovely trees with light, graceful limbs and soft, whispering foliage. They clothe a hillside or fill a landscape admirably. In some the bark is strikingly picturesque. In others the odor of the bruised bark or the crushed twigs fills the air with sweetness. All the birches produce little cones — strobiles, to the botanists — filled with tiny seeds on which Goldfinches, Pine Siskins, and Redpolls feed with delight.

For all that, only two native species of birch are abundant in our territory. One is the Gray Birch (*Betula populifolia*), springing up quickly on waste land or burnt ground and common along roadsides and the margins of woods. Because of the white bark it acquires after a few years of growth it is frequently mistaken for the American White or Canoe Birch (*Betula papyrifera*), a much larger tree and native to higher and more northerly ground. However, this species that lightens the gloom of northern forests frequently is planted for decorative purposes within the city limits and so is the European White Birch (*Betula alba*), as well as other imported species and varieties. But the little Gray Birch with the sharp-pointed triangular leaves needs no tender care or encouragement in growing. It is almost weedlike in the way it moves in to take over neglected fields and roadsides. It is quite handsome when it reaches the white-bark stage but it rarely grows more than 25 or 30 feet in height (more often than not on a slant), has a comparatively short life span, and often is badly crippled by the ice storms of New York winters.

The second native birch abundant in the area is the tall, graceful, and odorous Black, Sweet, or Cherry Birch (*Betula lenta*), a delight to the eye at all seasons and a winter dinner table for some of our smaller wild birds. Strike the trunk with an axe and the air around becomes fragrant with the pleasant aroma given off by the bruised wood. Chew on a branchlet and you will taste the flavor of "birch beer." As "Cherry Birch" the wood was prized for the making of cheap furniture in years gone by. It is an abundant resident of our deciduous woods and has been so for untold ages. The River or Red Birch (*Betula nigra*) is common as a planted tree along some of the motor parkways of the city where the "aprons" are low and moist but it definitely is not common in the wild in New York City. It prefers the warmer climate to the southward, just as the Yellow Birch (*Betula lutea*) prefers the cooler climate to the northward. However, New York is the overlapping zone for the two species and both kinds are to be found within the city limits. Whether the trees are "wild" or not may be a matter of doubt in some cases.

The alders, as their catkins and seed cones testify, are close relatives of the birches. Several European species have been introduced into the area and possibly more than one native species occurs. The abundant species in our swamps and marshes is the Speckled Alder *(Alnus rugosa)* that carries the empty seed cones of the late autumn through the winter, along with the catkins prepared for spring flowering. If of a January day you look just above or behind the starting points of the clusters of staminate catkins, you will see the much smaller but equally hardy elliptical pistillate catkins bared to the wintry weather.

Everybody knows the Beech *(Fagus grandifolia)* by its smooth light gray bark. Less often noted are the long, slender, sharp-pointed winter buds that Thoreau called "the spearheads of spring." Like the Black Birch, the Beech is one of the common trees of the deciduous woods of the region, especially along the slopes above the Hutchinson River and the Bronx River in the northeastern section of the city. The little triangular beech-nuts, produced in little burs, are relished by birds and small mammals. They are so small that few persons bother to pick out the meat in the nutlets, but if you sample them you will find that they have a pleasant flavor.

The tree tragedy of the region — and of the whole north-eastern section of the United States — is the case history of the native Chestnut *(Castanea dentata)* of glorious memory. Here was a tree that truly "had all the good gifts of Nature." It grew tall and strong. It held great branches widespread. It furnished wonderful boards and beams for the lumberman and carpenter. In June the outer branchlets of the great trees were draped with cream-colored clusters of long staminate catkins. In autumn, out of fearful and wonderful spined burs lined with rose-pink satin, the Chestnut provided food fit for the gods and little children. Sometimes the burs opened on the tree and spilled the nuts — usually three to a bur, the one in the middle flattened on both sides — on the ground below. More often the nuts or burs or both were brought to the ground by clubs thrown up at tempting targets.

The noble Chestnut has vanished from our woods and fields, but this is one loss that is not to be blamed on the growth of the city. It was a blight, believed to have been introduced from Asia, that killed off all the great Chestnut trees of the Northeast and almost exterminated the species on the North American Continent. But a ray of hope remains. No cure has yet been found for the disease that, sapping from the base but showing its effects first in the topmost branches, was slow downward death to the great trees. The vitality of the species is such that sprouts from old stumps and roots have persisted in appearing from year to year and sometimes they grow big enough to produce a few burs and nuts. In turn, they become victims of the blight before they attain more than sapling size but, when they die off, new sprouts arise from the same source and apparently the process is to continue indefinitely. This raises the hope that, in time, an immunity will be developed by the shoots and saplings and once again we may have the native Chestnut in all its ancient strength and glory.

Now we turn to the oaks of our region, and the story is more cheerful. We have some wonderful native oaks of perhaps a dozen species spread over the five boroughs, many of them more than 100 feet in height and 200 to 300 years of age. After the hurricane of 1938 I measured some of the fallen oaks in Van Cortlandt Park and two measured 109 and 115 feet in length, respectively. In Pelham Bay Park I counted the rings on a freshly cut stump of a Chestnut Oak (*Quercus prinus*) and the tally ran to 215, though this was a tree of only medium height and with a trunk diameter of 30 inches three feet above the ground. We have much larger and older trees than that on the premises.

Among the finest and most abundant oaks in city parks or on private ground in our territory are the Black Oak (*Quercus velutina*) and the Red Oak (*Quercus rubra* var. *borealis*) that pro-

duce acorns in great quantities to the delight of the local squirrels and Blue Jays. The Red Oak acorn, in particular, is large
and handsome and an easy guide to identification of the species.
The Scarlet Oak (*Quercus coccinea*), whose deeply cut leaves
turn a brilliant red in autumn, is encountered occasionally in
our territory but it does not compare in abundance with the
Black or Red Oak, nor the Pin Oak (*Quercus palustris*) that not
only is common in the wild but also is a favorite tree for planting along streets and parkways. Mention of street and parkway planting brings to mind the Shingle Oak (*Quercus imbri-
caria*), probably occurring wild in our territory — it very well
could in the natural order of things — but I have found it only
as a planted tree along some of the motor parkways, where it

White Oak

is easily recognized in autumn by the unlobed, smooth-edged, elliptical leaves that, brown and lifeless, cling to the tree long after the other deciduous trees nearby have lost their foliage to the cold winds and rains.

The Blackjack Oak (*Quercus marilandica*) with its blunt-headed leaves grows on Staten Island and Long Island. I have searched for it in vain on my home ground in the Riverdale and Van Cortlandt Park region. The Post Oak (*Quercus stellata*) has the same status in my view. It is fairly common on sandy soil, of which there is an abundance on Staten Island and Long Island and very little in the Bronx. A good-sized tree with a large acorn in a fringed receptacle is the Mossycup or Bur Oak (*Quercus macrocarpa*), native to the general area, though I have not been able to find a specimen growing wild within the city limits. But it can be found — with many other wonderful native and imported species — in the New York Botanical Garden in Bronx Park.

The White Oak (*Quercus alba*), often of imposing proportions and great age, is common in the area. Less common but found fairly often in moist or wet ground is the rather raggedy Swamp Oak (*Quercus bicolor*). The Chestnut Oak, mentioned earlier, is quite common on rocky slopes in wooded areas throughout the region. It's quite possible there are other species in the area that I have not found on my pilgrimages. I suspect that Staten Island may harbor one or two of the southerly oaks missing from the Riverdale ridges. Except for hybrids, the different oaks usually are easy to identify by the appearance of the bark, the size and shape of the leaf, and, in particular, the size and shape of the acorn and cup.

There are a few trees that almost anybody can recognize at first sight. One of them is the American Elm (*Ulmus americana*), which is not only familiar but famous, and rightfully so. What would New England be without its elms? Happily for New Yorkers, the American Elm is native and abundant in the area. It is found occasionally in the woods, more often in meadows, and most frequently as a street and dooryard tree. It is a shade tree of noble presence and graceful bearing, a living combination of strength and beauty. Read Oliver Wendell Holmes on the subject. It was the favorite tree of the genial Autocrat of the Breakfast Table. The Slippery Elm (*Ulmus rubra*), a smaller tree with hairy twigs and winter buds and very bristly hairs on the upper surfaces of the leaves, is fairly common in our territory but apparently the city youngsters do not know it when they see it or they would hack away at it with jack-knives as the country boys do to get chunks of the "slippery" inner bark for chewing purposes. The English Elm (*Ulmus procera*) of more rugged trunk and less graceful branches long ago was introduced in the area and the species is represented by some tall, stout, and venerable trees scattered through the five boroughs. There are three or four stalwart specimens standing on a strip of park land along the Hudson River below the Riverdale railroad station.

A relative of the elms that is fairly common in the region but usually goes unnoticed is the American Hackberry (*Celtis occidentalis*), a tree with gray bark, elm-shaped leaves, and little bluish-black berries as autumn fruit and an aid to identification. Because of the fruit, another name for the tree is Sugarberry, but to my taste it's a misnomer. I never could detect any particular sweetness in the berries. The American Hackberry often grows to considerable size in the South but in our region it is a smallish tree whose sharply toothed green leaves often are blotched with gray patches and whose gray trunk frequently has rows or ridges of raised excrescences that stand out to catch the eye as an oddity in bark decoration.

Next in the botanical line in our territory stands the Mulberry Family, a group of trees with milky sap and "aggregate" fruits formed by seeds with fleshy coverings clustered together in a more or less globular shape. The most common of the group in the area is the White Mulberry (*Morus alba*), originally imported from Asia with the idea of starting a silk industry in this country since the silkworm — or Silk Moth *(Bombyx mori)* in the larval stage — feeds on its leaves. The silk venture failed completely but the White Mulberry made itself very much at home in North America. A rather small tree, its yellowish-brown bark and its curving branches stand out along fences and roadsides in the leafless season and in full foliage the toothed leaves often are deeply lobed in a bewildering way. In fact, an old wives' tale has it that no two leaves of a White Mulberry ever are alike, but that's going much too far. The tree fruits plentifully and its branches are alive with feathered feeders on the pale white ½-inch or so "berries" or cylindrical clusters of tiny fruits in June. However, it has a short fruiting season. Often the fruit ripens and falls in a single week.

The native Red Mulberry *(Morus rubra)*, a sturdier and shaplier tree with a longer fruiting season, is much scarcer in the region. In fact, it is almost rare in and around New York and, curiously enough, frequently is cultivated where the White Mulberry has been allowed to run wild. It is one of the best trees to plant to attract birds to a lawn or garden because it keeps producing its dark red to blackish fruits through July and August, thus giving the birds a long go at the same old fruitstand. The Paper-mulberry *(Broussonetia papyrifera)*, introduced from Asia for decorative purposes (though I see nothing particularly decorative about it), occurs either in cultivation or as an escape in the area in the form of a small tree or large shrub with smooth bark, irregular-shaped leaves, and reddish globular fruit of no great interest to man, bird, or beast.

The spectacular member of the family in our territory is the thorn-studded Osage-orange *(Maclura pomifera)*, with shiny leaves and almost monstrous fruit, the same being a lumpy, globular, yellowish-green mass as large as a good-sized orange with a fleshy interior resembling closely packed cauliflower. This small tree has the yellowish bark and the curving branches of the White Mulberry but the thorns are an added feature.

As schoolboys we used to hurl the fruit about in sham battles and our hands soon were covered with the sticky milky juice common to the family. To us the trees and their fruits were "Mock Oranges" but Osage-orange is appropriate enough. The tree is native to Missouri, Oklahoma, Arkansas, and Texas, territory over much of which the Osage Indians roamed centuries ago. However, it has been planted widely over the country as a hedge because of its thick manner of growth and its annoying spines. It is common enough in the outlying sections of the city, where it either has run wild or has lingered as a memento of dooryards of other days. When I last looked there were some Osage-oranges on the southern fringe of the playing field at the Fieldston School in Riverdale and another patch of them on the east side of Fieldston Road just before it crosses over the Henry Hudson Parkway.

Since the Sweetbay Magnolia (*Magnolia virginiana*) grows wild as far north as Gloucester, Massachusetts, and the Cucumber Magnolia (*Magnolia acuminata*) reaches Ontario, Canada, it is reasonable to believe that they once flourished in our territory; but it is doubtful that any survive in the wild now unless it's on park property, where it would be difficult to know whether they grew naturally or were set out by hand. In either case, there are plenty of magnolias of different species and varieties in the parks, on the aprons of the motor parkways, and on private ground within the city limits. Magnolias in bloom are a spectacular feature of the outdoor flower show of the city in spring. The curious fruits that come later are worth inspecting, too.

As trees go, most of the magnolias are on the small side. It is not so with their close relative, the towering Tulip-tree (*Liriodendron tulipifera*). This is one of the great trees of the region, with a massive cylindrical trunk that reaches upward like a noble pillar in Greek architecture. Where it grows in the open, you have to lift your eyes to behold with awe and admiration the heavy crown of odd-shaped leaves held high against the sky. Often it reaches a height of 100 feet or more. In June it bears in profusion the cup-shaped greenish-yellow flowers cross-barred with orange that give it the name of Tulip-tree. One of the earliest signs of oncoming autumn is the dappling of the shining green foliage of the Tulip-tree with spots of gold in August. After the leaves fall there are clusters of narrow, upright, conical seed pods that remain on the tree as an easy mark of identification as well as a deeply appreciated food supply for some of our seed-eating birds. The winter buds have curious coverings that make them look like miniature mittens, and when they open in spring the folded leaves are slowly raised, for all the world like tiny flags in celebration of escape from winter captivity. Happily for New Yorkers, this massive and beautiful tree is native to the area and still plentiful in our parks and on private ground.

Although it doesn't vie with the Tulip-tree in majesty or floral display in spring, there is much to be said for the Sassafras (*Sassafras albidum*) that is abundant throughout the area. For one thing, it is pleasantly aromatic throughout its system — from the roots to the tips of twigs and leaves. The leaves, incidentally, are quite variable in design. Some are ovate, but most of them have one or more deeply cut lobes. The Sassafras grows to be a fair-sized tree with a heavily corrugated trunk and greenish branchlets and twigs but more often it is found in the form of clumps of 2-foot or 3-foot saplings springing from some widespread common root system originating in a large tree that once stood — or may still be standing — in the vicinity. Trees 10 feet or more in height usually flower heavily, but since the flowers are greenish yellow and appear along with the young foliage of the same general hue they are easily overlooked. Furthermore, nothing much comes of them because most of our Sassafras trees bear only staminate flowers (usually the staminate and pistillate flowers grow on different trees) and thus produce no fruit. This is a pity, because the fruits are beautiful little oval blue berries nestling in a tiny, long-stalked wine-red cup much in the manner of a breakfast egg in its egg cup.

There is a great library of folklore on the curative values of decoctions made from the root or branch or twig or leaf of the Sassafras, but modern medicine relies on other drugs or specific remedies. That it is no longer gathered for the compounding of nostrums may be one reason why it is so plentiful in hedgerows and along roadsides throughout the region. An equally aromatic but less famous relative of the Sassafras is the Common Spicebush *(Lindera benzoin)*, a prevalent shrub of moist shady ground throughout our territory. "When the hounds of spring are on winter's traces" one of the loveliest sights "in green underwood and cover" is the bursting of the Spicebush into yellow bloom in our wet woods. The flowers are tiny but they appear in countless profusion along the slanting branchlets of this abundant shrub and many of them later produce smooth

Common Witch-hazel

little green berries that eventually turn red. Like the Sassafras, the Common Spicebush contains an aromatic oil easily detected by crushing or bruising any part of the plant at any time of year — root, leaf, bark, or berry. The Sassafras has an odor all its own but the Spicebush fragrance is quite similar to that of the familiar citronella that is used as a mosquito repellent.

Another fairly common shrub or small tree of moist woodlands throughout our region is the Common Witch-hazel (*Hamamelis virginiana*) that holds the distinction of producing the last wild flowers of the year in this part of the world. As floral displays they are really nothing to boast of but often the bare branches tossing in the cold winds of early November are literally draped with the stringy yellow petals of the clustered blooms. The little seed capsules stick on the branchlets throughout the winter, grow in size through spring and summer, and, generally in September, burst and scatter the seeds some distance away on the ground. Witch-hazel lotion, produced by crushing and grinding the branches and diluting the extract with alcohol and other ingredients, is still in commercial use as a rubbing fluid for sprains and other bodily ailments.

A grown-up relative of the lowly Common Witch-hazel is the Sweetgum or Liquidambar (*Liquidambar styraciflua*), a quite tall tree at full growth and a common resident of the area. It is the only native tree of the region with star-shaped leaves and thus is easy to identify when in leaf. It is just as easy to identify in the leafless season because of the numerous globular clusters of horny seed pods that dangle from the branchlets through the winter or litter the ground below the tree. Here again we have an abundant supply of food for seed-eating birds in cold weather. The gray-barked trees often are found with corky ridges running along the branches, sometimes to an extent that looks almost grotesque. The Sweetgum is a brilliant sight in autumn when its star-shaped leaves turn from sober green to a mixture of flaring reds and yellows. Though New York is close to the northern limit of its range, it thrives lustily here and is a common sight in all five boroughs.

Sycamores abound in New York City for the same reason that they abound along the streets of many European cities. They are fine shade trees of good size, they are disease resistant to a greater degree than many other trees, and their piebald trunks are an added and colorful attraction. Both the native Sycamore (*Platanus occidentalis*) and the London Plane Tree (*Platanus acerifolia*) are abundant as street and park trees in the city and are quite similar in appearance. If you wish to distinguish one from the other, look at the trees after the leaves have fallen and the brown globular dry seed clusters are hanging from the branchlets. In most cases the native tree has only one seed cluster or "buttonball" (hence another name for the tree) on a stalk, whereas the London Plane Tree usually hangs two buttonballs on a stalk. Also, the native buttonballs are an inch or more in diameter, while those of the imported tree do not reach that size. If you look at the base of the petiole (leafstalk) of a Sycamore leaf, you will find that it is a little hollow cone. That's because it is a protective housing for the buds of next season. Buds that are protected in this manner are referred to as "sub-petiolar."

It often comes as a shock to those who never dabble in botany to learn that a tall tree and a tiny flower may be members of the same family. Unless somebody told us or we read it in a book, few of us would suspect that all our cultivated apple and pear trees are members of the Rose Family and thus "blood relatives" of the wild strawberries of our meadows and the little yellow cinquefoils of our roadsides. The fact is that the Rose Family has numerous representatives among the trees and shrubs of our region. This would include many native species of shadbush, haw, and wild cherry. The ordinary shadbush or "shadblow" of our swamps that hangs out its five narrow white petals before the leaves appear in spring is the Oblong June-berry (*Amelanchier canadensis*) of the botanist. The colloquial name, of course, comes from the fact that the shrubs — or small trees — of this group bloom at about the time that the shad run up the rivers to spawn. Here and there on roadsides or slopes, or perhaps in the woods, you may find the tallest of the group in our region in the shape of a medium-sized tree, *Amelanchier arborea*, in which form it is often called "Serviceberry," but more scientifically Downy Juneberry. Pigeonberry is another name for the group. The dark "berries," which really are little pomes, vary from ¼ inch to ½ inch in diameter and usually are produced in abundance. They are pleasantly palatable but, unfortunately, they are subject to fungus infection and other ills that spoil most of them for human consumption. Nevertheless, many birds dine eagerly on them.

As for the hawthorns or haws *(Crataegus)* of the region, even the botanists are baffled by them and have come to no complete agreement on the specific names or descriptive details of the one hundred or more species to be found in the northeastern section of the United States. For our purposes they are not worth quarreling about because there are so few of them left in the wild in New York City now. They flourish best around the edges of swamps, on moist or dry rocky hillsides, and in old pastures, and there isn't much terrain of that kind remaining within the city limits. Because they are hardy and decorative shrubs with numerous clusters of white flowers in late spring and colorful displays in autumn of red "berries" (small pomes, in reality) they are plentifully planted in our territory and you will find many different species set out on park property and private ground. The only one readily identifiable, even by a novice, is the introduced Cockspur Thorn *(Crataegus crusgalli)* that may be known at a glance by its rather leathery shining leaves and its equally shiny and really formidable thorns that may be as much as 6 inches in length!

We have four species of wild cherries in the area but only two species are abundant. The little Northern Dwarf or Sand Cherry *(Prunus pumila)*, a shrub, is found only in the sandy tracts of the seaward section of the city and the Fire or Pin or Bird Cherry *(Prunus pensylvanica)* is only occasionally en-

Choke Cherry

countered. But the shrubby Choke Cherry (*Prunus virginiana*) is common on roadsides and in thickets and the wild Black or Rum Cherry (*Prunus serotina*) is abundant not only on park land but along roadsides and old fences in the outlying sections of the city. There are many wild Black Cherry trees of good size in the area. Beyond the fine tasty fruit they produce in elongated clusters, much appreciated by man, bird, and beast, these trees are highly esteemed by lumbermen for the wood that still is used for furniture and other commercial purposes.

In old days, of course, the Beach Plum (*Prunus maritima*) was abundant along the shore and among the dunes of the Long Island section of the city. You might hunt a full day now before finding a clump that, of a September day or in early October, would yield blue fruit enough to make a quart of jelly. Before leaving the Rose Family we must mention the Chokeberries, not to be confused with the Choke Cherry of the *Prunus* group. The Black Chokeberry (*Pyrus melanocarpa*) is abundant along the edge of the Van Cortlandt swamp and in similar moist ground in other sections of the city, and possibly there are one or two other species the experts have ferreted out. I have found the Red Chokeberry (*Pyrus arbutifolia*) farther northward but have yet to encounter it on city property. Of course, the mountain-ashes (*Pyrus*) seen in city parks and along some boulevards and motor parkways are members of the Rose Family, too, but all that met my eye seemed to be of European origin and nursery stock. They are chiefly notable for the clusters of orange-red "berries" — again little pomes — that hang on the trees for weeks in the autumn. We have a native species, *Pyrus americana*, that has compound leaves and sprays of white flowers rather similar to the leaves and flowers of the imported kind, but the "berries" of the native trees are considerably smaller.

Since the native and imported species are very similar in leaf, flower, and fruit, and since there are horticultural varieties and hybrids that further confuse the issue, it is best to view any one of these small- to medium-sized trees simply as a mountain-ash and turn to some more simple matter in the botanical field, such as the handsome shrub called the Redbud (*Cercis canadensis*), concerning which the only puzzling thing is why it was specifically labeled *canadensis*, since it doesn't grow wild as far north as Canada. In fact, I never chanced on any that I thought was truly wild in our own territory, though it is common — almost abundant — as a cultivated shrub on park lands and private estates within the city limits. Perhaps on Staten Island there are some wild Redbuds but, in any event, New York is about the northeastern limit of its natural range. The rose-purple flowers that come out in clusters along the branches before the leaves unfold in spring are the decorative feature of the shrub. It certainly is well named. The bright red buds stand out in vivid contrast to the dark bark of the bare branchlets in winter.

Not so well named is the Coffee-tree or Kentucky Coffee-tree (*Gymnocladus dioica*) that, like the Redbud, occupies a dubious position as a native-born resident of our area. However, it has a much wider natural range than the boundaries of Kentucky and not even a magician could brew coffee from its beans. Native to much of the South and most of the Midwest, it is found sparingly in the wild in the western part of New York State, but I doubt it reached dry ground east of the Hudson River without the aid of helping hands. Even so, it thrives well here and is common in cultivation and attracts much attention because of its picturesque bark, its very large and doubly compound leaves, and its hard, brown, leathery, elliptical seed pods — sometimes 6 inches in length — that cling to the stark and stubby branchlets throughout the winter. The panicles of greenish-white flowers that produce these odd seed pods are barely noticed amid the fancy foliage in late May or June. At any distance, the gray bark of the trunk looks as though it had been daubed on with a palette knife in the hands of a painter of the Impressionist School.

A close relative of the Coffee-tree is the Honey Locust (*Gleditsia triacanthos*) that I came to know well and favorably in my childhood days through its long, dark, twisted, ribbon-shaped seed pods, whose interiors contained a sticky sweet filling along with the roundish seeds. The tree, which is by no means common in our territory except where it has been planted in parks, has several other notable features. For one thing, it has fearsome thorns that often are doubly or triply compound and they occur not only on the branches but quite often jut out from the dark gray sandpapery bark of the trunk of the tree. A second feature is that the compound or doubly compound leaves — both kinds are found on individual trees — have the smallest leaflets of any of the broad-leaved trees of the northeastern part of the United States, and this gives the foliage a quite distinctive appearance. What surprises me nowadays is that I see so many of the long, twisted seed pods lying unnoticed on park lawns in the autumn. I suspect the city children of this era are ignorant of the tasty flavor of the interior of these neglected seed coverings.

The Yellowwood or Virgilia (*Cladrastis lutea*) that grows to be a fair-sized tree and hangs out long drooping clusters of cream-white pea-type flowers in spring, is not native as far north as New York but it thrives well in the area and has been set out extensively for decorative purposes in parks and on private estates. If you cut into the smooth gray bark of the trunk you will see immediately how the tree came by its common name. The color of the wood under the bark is a really bright yellow. The small beanlike seed pods clinging to the branchlets throughout the autumn and sometimes through the winter are a help in identifying the tree. Other aids to identification are the smooth gray bark and the fact that the buds are sub-petiolar like those of the sycamores.

The Black Locust (*Robinia pseudo-acacia*) is a common tree throughout our territory — as, indeed, it is over most of the eastern part of temperate North America — but originally its range and that of our other locusts did not reach this far north. It has been set out widely here and abroad since colonial days and is much esteemed for its picturesque shape — tall and gaunt in some cases — its lovely and sweet-scented drooping clusters of cream-white flowers in spring, and its delicate compound leaves with oval leaflets. It has thorns, to be sure, but they are no great matter and are mostly confined to the smaller branches and twigs. The bad feature of the Black Locust is that it sends up an almost incredible number of fast-growing shoots from its root system, and if left unchecked a single tree will become a grove in ten years. Keeping the Black Locust in subjection is often a local problem.

Along an old wall and in an open field in the northeast corner of Van Cortlandt Park I found clumps and patches of the Bristly Locust or Rose-acacia (*Robinia hispida*), a shrub with pink-purple flowers that appeal to the eye but lack the lovely odor of the flowers of the Black Locust. In this species the branchlets are covered with fine bristly hairs that, on the stem and older branches, harden into thorns. The Clammy Locust (*Robinia viscosa*), which grows to the size of a small tree, also occurs in cultivation or as an escape in the area. It has handsome yellow-dotted pinkish flowers that are practically scentless. It has the typical locust foliage but the twigs and petioles are covered with a sticky substance that earns the species its common name.

By all odds the most interesting of the group in the area is a variety of the Black Locust known as Shipmast Locust (*Robinia pseudo-acacia* var. *rectissima* Raber) because of its tall, straight, and narrow trunk. It was brought from Virginia to Long Island in 1683 by the seafaring captain John Sands and later extensively cultivated over the western part of Long Island for fence posts as well as shipmasts. It certainly grows taller and straighter than the ordinary Black Locust and it is said that the timber is better in every way. Flushing boasted a number of these tall trees and probably a rigid search of what open spaces are left in Bayside, Douglaston, and other Long Island communities within the city limits would disclose the presence of surviving specimens of this distinguished variety of the ordinary Black Locust. Since it sprouts readily from the roots like all our locusts, just cutting down the tall trees to clear the land for development would not necessarily kill off the race of Shipmast Locusts in the vicinity. Any roots left in the ground certainly would send up sprouts. But unless they were allowed to grow into reasonably tall trees, nobody would know them to be Shipmast Locusts.

From the Shipmast Locust to the Hoptree or Wafer-ash (*Ptelea trifoliata*) is a sharp descent. This is a shrub or small tree scattered here and there in our territory and usually found in the shade of taller trees. I first found it on a roadside in Riverdale and later discovered it to be quite common in clumps along the golf course edges in Van Cortlandt Park. The name Wafer-ash, which I prefer, is derived from the fact that its alternate compound leaves with three leaflets are at least vaguely ashlike in appearance and the seeds are enclosed in round wafers about ¾ inch in diameter. The name Hoptree is due to the odor of hops given off by the clusters of seed wafers. When the foliage begins to die in early autumn, the leaflets fall first and the stalks, or petioles, remain fixed like so many matchsticks along the branchlets.

It's probably too late now to try to track down the culprit who gave the name of Tree-of-Heaven to the Ailanthus (*Ailanthus altissima*) that, imported long ago from China, grows in waste ground all over the city and springs up like a weed in vacant lots. If you use your hand to strip the leaflets from the long compound leaves (we used to do that as children to make switches of the leafstalks) you will understand why a common name for this Tree-of-Heaven is Stinkweed. The staminate flowers have an offensive odor, too, but the pistillate flowers turn into attractive clusters of little flattened and twisted yellow seed pods with an attractive crimson blush. Since the staminate and pistillate flowers more commonly occur on different trees, the trees bearing pistillate flowers are allowed to grow where the trees with staminate flowers are ruthlessly removed as soon as they are recognized. This is a tree of rapid growth and needs little encouragement to become a neighborhood nuisance.

Much worse than the Ailanthus in any neighborhood, however, is Poison-ivy (*Rhus radicans*). We have it in large quantities as a shrub and climbing vine in the woods, along stone walls and fences, and in waste places throughout our territory. It is an abundant and rampant weed; every man, woman, and child should learn to recognize the plant by the shiny leaflets that come in threes and the clusters of yellowish-green flowers that turn into stringy masses of grayish-white "berries" — drupes to the botanist — that cling to the stems or branches of the shrub or vine after the leaves have fallen. The advantage of knowing it is that you can avoid it when you see it. Possibly you are immune to the irritating effect of the volatile oil of this plant, but most persons are not and some persons are painfully and seriously crippled by contact with it. Therefore everyone should learn to recognize this noxious plant at first glance.

Though the common name gives no hint of it, Poison-ivy is one of the five sumacs (*Rhus*) resident in our territory. Two species are baneful whereas the three others are harmless and even decorative. Poison-ivy is particularly obnoxious because it is so plentiful and so regularly encountered by those who walk in the wild; but the more powerful agent in producing skin irritation and anguish is the Poison Sumac (*Rhus vernix*), a tall shrub whose sleek compound leaves have shiny and shapely leaflets with red midribs that might serve as a warning sign. To put a hand on this shrub is to invite real trouble. Luckily it grows only in moist ground and usually is found in wet thickets or open swamps, into which few persons wander except local botanists and bird-watchers. Years ago there was

Poison-ivy

quite a patch of it in the Van Cortlandt swamp but it was eradicated when that portion of the swamp was turned into a new fairway for the old golf course.

Probably the most abundant of the harmless species in the area is the Staghorn Sumac (*Rhus typhina*), whose blunt younger branches are covered with the matted brown hairs that give the plant its common name. The furry branches really do resemble deer antlers in the "velvet" stage. The Smooth Sumac (*Rhus glabra*) lacks the brown hairs on its branches but otherwise is quite similar to the Staghorn in leaf, flower, and fruit. Both species are common on hillsides and roadsides and often occur in widespread clumps. The Winged or Dwarf Sumac (*Rhus copallina*), easily distinguished by the "wings" or flattening of the axis of the compound leaf (rachis) between the leaflets, is not nearly so common as the Staghorn and the Smooth Sumac, but you will find it easily if you look for it. In autumn, all sumacs are colorful. The Staghorn and the Smooth Sumac in particular turn a brilliant red that lights up the landscape. They also produce dark red pyramidal seed clusters not only colorful and persistent but furnishing valuable food for wintering birds.

The next group long ago had a Shakespearean salute, to wit:

> *Heigh ho! sing, heigh ho! unto the green holly:*
> *Most friendship is feigning, most loving mere folly:*
> *Then, heigh ho, the holly!*
> *This life is most jolly.*

The evergreen American Holly (*Ilex opaca*), cherished for its shiny and spiny leaves and persistent red berries, is fairly common on the Atlantic coastal plain as far north as southern New Jersey but it thins out rapidly from that point northeastward and probably was scarce in our region even in colonial and Indian days. It grows best within sound and sight of salt water, and ocean breezes are its favorite atmosphere. Possibly some of the decorative red-berried hollies of the seaward sections of the city are this native species, but most of them probably are the imported and cultivated English Holly (*Ilex aquifolia*) that has much spinier leaves and an abundance of handsome red "berries" as we call them, though the holly fruits technically are drupes.

The Common Winterberry Holly or Black Alder (*Ilex verticillata*), a shrub whose leaves are neither evergreen nor spiny, is a true holly and native to our territory. In fact, it should be plentiful in our swamps and moist ground generally but its lovely little red berries stand out so attractively along the bare dark branchlets in the autumn and early winter that the shrub literally is torn to pieces by vandals when they find it. However, some scattered bushes of this species still persist in the wilder and wetter nooks within the city limits. The less they are noticed, the longer they will live. The Low Gallberry Holly or Inkberry (*Ilex glabra*) is common as a low shrub in the sandy open areas behind the city's sea beaches. The shining berries of about ¼ inch diameter are a blue-black color that justifies one of the common names of the plant.

If it were not for the motor parkways of the city there might be a dearth of bittersweet in the area and that would be a pity because the clusters of seed capsules clinging to the leafless branches in autumn and gradually opening in orange and red are a colorful addition to the local landscape. Probably few motorists know or notice the shrub when it is in leaf and certainly the greenish flowers would never attract attention, but bare of leaf and laden with fruit, the two-toned seed capsules are bound to catch the eye and identify the bittersweet in November. Our native American Bittersweet (*Celastrus scandens*), which is more of a woody vine than a rounded shrub, is found in the wild in woods and along old stone walls, but most of the bittersweet seen along our motor parkways or on private estates is the Asiatic Bittersweet (*Celastrus orbiculatus*) or some other imported species. The native plant climbs high and far and can become a nuisance unless it is kept in subjection.

Another botanical display along our parkways is the Bladder-nut *(Staphylea trifolia)*, a shrub or small tree noted for the in-flated three-cornered seed capsules that hang on the branches after the leaves have fallen. It is native to the region but scarce almost to the vanishing point in the wild. The parkway planters, however, have secured its place in the community and have given it a chance to make itself better known to the human residents of the area.

We come now to the great maples (and the small ones, too) of the city. A wonderful and colorful group they are. They include five native species and two imported species that have made themselves very much at home here as well as in other parts of the country. The more important of the imported trees is the well-known and abundant Norway Maple *(Acer platanoides)*, a favorite as a shade tree and a street tree because of its clean trunk, regular shape, handsome foliage, and disease-resistant qualities. It is a mass of green flowers just before the leaves open in spring; if the flowers were white or pink the display would rival that of an apple tree or a cherry tree in bloom. But the flowers are green or greenish yellow, as in all the maples, and most persons take them for young foliage, even when the pollen from them litters the street below and turns the pavement almost golden with its abundance.

The other imported member of the group is the Sycamore Maple *(Acer pseudo-platanus)*, so named because the trunk is cov-ered with a lumpy or blistery bark that tends to split and fall off in patches somewhat in the manner of the sycamores, though by no means so colorfully. The Sycamore Maple is locally common to abundant in some sections of the city and rare or missing in others. It is easily known not only by the blistery bark of the trunk but also by its large fleshy leaves, its clusters of flowers dangling like bunches of grapes — the "keys," or fruit, naturally dangle in the same fashion — and the green buds it wears throughout the winter. Both the Sycamore Maple and the Norway Maple have escaped to the wild in our territory. You may run upon them anywhere in the woods or in the open.

The noblest of our native species is the famous Sugar Maple (*Acer saccharum*) that often grows to a magnificent height along the rocky ridges that are the city's backbone. There are still plenty of Sugar Maples in the woods and open fields within the city limits and from them you could tap sap to boil down to delicious syrup or maple sugar if the law allowed and you had the implements of the trade at hand. Aside from the sweet sap, this tree has other notable virtues. It is a fine timber tree and a lofty shade tree whose leaves turn beautiful shades of yellow and red in autumn. When blown down by the wind or, in our territory a more likely fate, cut down to make way for streets or buildings, a two-handed saw, a ten-pound sledge, and three or four iron wedges will turn it into first-class fuel for an open fireplace.

The Red Maple (*Acer rubrum*), which is sometimes called the Swamp Maple because it is so often found in swamps and moist ground generally, is not quite up to the Sugar Maple in height and breadth, but it is a sturdy tree of fair size and twice a year it is a thing of beauty — in late March and early April, when its innumerable crimson-red flowers with golden stamens are hardy and lovely signs of spring across a still-bleak landscape, and again in early September, when its leaves gradually take on a brilliant red hue and serve as heralds of oncoming autumn.

The Silver Maple (*Acer saccharinum*) is the weak sister of the larger members of the family. It is common in the wild and in cultivation in the area but it lacks the strength of character of the Sugar and Red Maples. It grows quickly and reaches a fair height, although it does not stand up well or long. It often loses large branches in high winds and it has long, weak, drooping branchlets that curl up at the tips, as if making a last effort to be brave. The much slashed leaves that give the tree its common name by showing their silvery undersides when the wind blows, have little color and no courage at all in autumn. They turn a sickly yellow and flutter feebly to the ground at the first touch of frost.

The Striped Maple or Moosewood (*Acer pensylvanicum*) with the beautifully streaked bark reaches only sapling size or less in the undergrowth of the slopes and ridges of the rocky woods of our region. Since such terrain is limited and growing scarcer each year within the city boundaries, there is not much Moosewood on the premises for city residents or visitors to find. The Ashleaf Maple or Box Elder (*Acer negundo*) is found locally in clumps and patches, largely because of its weedy manner of growth and its habit of seeding itself. It never grows to any great size in this part of the country and differs from our other maples in having compound leaves with three to five leaflets. This is the feature that earned for it the common names of Ashleaf Maple and Box Elder. Box Elder is misleading because it is a true maple, not an elder, the proof of which is that it produces seeds enclosed in the winged samaras, or keys, that are the mark of the maple clan.

There is no doubt that a large Horsechestnut (*Aesculus hippocastanum*) is a stunning sight when its dark foliage serves as a background for its great pyramidal clusters of pink-flecked cream-white flowers in late May or early June, but when used as a street tree, as it frequently is in many parts of this and other cities, it litters the sidewalks and pavements later in the season in a disorderly way with its shiny and lumpily globular nuts and fragments of the prickly husks enclosing them. It is common as an escape as well as a cultivated tree in our territory, but its original native ground was southeastern Europe and Asia Minor. You can recognize the tree easily in winter by its large dark gummy buds and the rather blistery dark bark of the trunk. Although our native buckeyes of the same family do not grow wild in our territory, here and there you may see a few in cultivation.

Names cause endless confusion, especially when you are offered a choice as on a table d'hôte menu. Is our next tree a

Basswood? Or do you call it a Linden? In England it would be a Lime Tree — Tennyson referred in rhyme to the "ruby-budded Lime" — though it is far removed from the citrus group. Whether you call it a Basswood or a Linden, the native tree of the species in our area is *Tilia americana,* but probably it is outnumbered by the imported *Tilia europaea* that has been planted extensively in our parks and as a street tree in many sections of the city. Aside from a few details (the leaves of the European tree are smaller) the two species are quite similar in general appearance and both are redolent with the sweet odor of the clusters of little cream-colored flowers that hang half concealed under the broad leaves in late June or July. At such times you can actually recognize the trees by ear — you could be blindfolded and still know when you were walking under a Basswood or Linden in bloom by "the murmuring of innumerable bees" gathered for the feast of pollen and nectar provided by the myriad blossoms. If you have never done so, take a look at the curious way in which the flower clusters are displayed on a stalk jutting out from the middle of what could pass for a narrow leaf.

It must be confessed that the lovely Basswood — or Linden, if you prefer — doesn't add much to our colorful autumn scenery. The leaves merely turn rusty or dull brown. In contrast we have the Sour-gum (*Nyssa sylvatica*) that shows to best advantage in the early autumn when its shining oval leaves turn a brilliant red that makes the tree recognizable at a distance, even across a wide valley. The Sour-gum grows only to medium size in our territory; southward, where it more often goes under the name of Tupelo or Pepperidge, it reaches greater height. The inconspicuous greenish flowers eventually turn into little blue oval "berries" (drupes) much relished by Robins, Mourning Doves, and other birds. A distinctive feature of this tree, unusual in our deciduous trees and easily noted in the leafless season, is that its comparatively short gray-barked branches extend horizontally from the trunk or slant slightly downward.

In the Flowering Dogwood (*Cornus florida*), which still flourishes in shaded ground throughout the area, we have a common
shrub or small tree much admired and also much misunderstood. Most of those who enjoy its beauty in the spring woods
call it "the dogwood" as though there were no other dogwoods
in the region. Furthermore, most of them look upon the four
showy cream-white bracts that surround the flower clusters
as the "petals" of each flower, which is far from being the case.
Individual dogwood flowers are very small and of our native
group in New York and New England only two species, the
Flowering Dogwood and the Dwarf Cornel or Bunchberry
(*Cornus canadensis*), have showy cream-white bracts surrounding

their flower clusters. I have not found the Bunchberry growing wild within the city limits, but perhaps somebody else has been luckier. It is fairly common throughout New England, and sometimes occurs in goodly patches. Before we part company with the Flowering Dogwood, one of the prize exhibits of the city's floral offerings in spring, it must be mentioned that the fruits in the form of elliptical red "berries" are much enjoyed by Robins and other migrating birds in the autumn.

Our other native dogwoods, of which three species are more or less common in our territory, are shrubs and for the most part go unrecognized as dogwoods. Probably they are lumped with the shrubby viburnums and possibly with the elders of the area, all of which produce clusters of little cream-white flowers in flat or rounded cymes. Half an eye, judiciously applied, will immediately set these groups apart. The little dogwood flowers are four-petaled. The corollas of the viburnums and the elders are five-lobed. As between the viburnums and the elders, the viburnums have simple unlobed leaves, whereas the elders have compound leaves of five or more leaflets.

Two of the three dogwoods that remain in comparative obscurity in our area really should catch the eye of any observant walker in the wild because of the deep burgundy color of the younger stems and branches of these shrubs. This is a feature plainly visible for at least six months of the year: the leafless season. Because these shrubs occur in wet ground such as the borders of swamps and are willow-like in weedy growth, a common name for both species is Red-osier Dogwood. The two species are quite similar in leaf and cream-colored flower clusters but the fruit of one, *Cornus stolonifera*, is dull white or slate color, whereas the *Cornus amomum*, the Silky Dogwood, which in some sections is called the Silky Cornel or Kinnikinnik, produces clusters of blue or bluish-tinged typical dogwood elliptical "berries." For somebody who finds these shrubs in flower and can't wait around for the fruit to ripen to make clear which species it is, there is an instant solution possible. Slit a twig or a branchlet. If the pith is white, the species is *Cornus stolonifera;* if tawny or reddish brown, it's *Cornus amomum.*

The third member of this neglected company of dogwoods in our territory often appears on high and dry ground and occurs in wide patches in fields, along roadsides, and along the fringes of woods. Its flower clusters are not flat but rounded, and it has narrower leaves than most dogwoods. It is an attractive shrub so generally ignored, even where it grows by the hundreds within or without the city gates, that few persons give it a common name. To the botanists, however, it is Red-panicle Dogwood (*Cornus racemosa*), which saves it from complete anonymity.

While we are in the shrubbery we might as well go on to clear up the remaining shrubs that are common to abundant in our territory. First and foremost are the viburnums, two species of which reach the size of small trees. These are the Nannyberry or Sheepberry (*Viburnum lentago*) and the Smooth Blackhaw (*Viburnum prunifolium*), both of which are fairly common on shaded roadsides, along the edge of woods, and on the fringes of swamps and ponds throughout the area. They are much alike in general appearance as well as in flower and fruit clusters, but the Nannyberry grows slightly taller and has noticeably larger leaves and fruit. The Nannyberry is more northerly and the Smooth Blackhaw more southerly in general distribution; in the New York region their ranges overlap.

As a matter of fact, only a botanist could sort out all the viburnums of the city precincts. The floors of the upland woods are studded with the Mapleleaf Viburnum or Dog-mackie (*Viburnum acerifolium*), whose flat clusters of creamy-white flowers turn into purple or black fruit. The fringes of the swamps, the moist thickets, hedgerows, hillsides, and road-sides abound in the Southern Arrowwood (*Viburnum dentatum*), the *dentatum* referring to the sharply-toothed leaves of the shrub. This is without doubt the most abundant of the viburnums in the five boroughs. We shall part with the group on that note, though there may be other species lurking in the vicinity — and other dogwoods left unmentioned — that a botanist would have no trouble in finding.

As for the elderberries, the Common Elderberry (*Sambucus canadensis*) with its wide flat cymes of cream-white flowers and its later sprays of blue-black fruits is common in moist ground but the Red Elderberry (*Sambucus pubens*), easily distinguished not only by the red color of the fruit but by the fact that flowers and fruit are displayed in pyramidal instead of flat clusters, is by no means common in the area. I found only a few bushes in the Van Cortlandt swamp. If it were common it could hardly be overlooked because its pyramidal clusters of cream-white flowers appear quite early in the year and stand out against the background of budding greenery in late April or early May. This species often is in fruit before the Common Elder comes into bloom.

The beautiful Pink Azalea or Pinxster Flower (*Rhododendron nudiflorum*) occurs sparsely in the wild on shady ground, but it is fighting a losing battle against building operations and vandals and eventually will survive only on private estates and in public parks where it is cultivated and protected. The lovely Mountain Laurel (*Kalmia latifolia*) probably was common in our rocky woodlands a century ago but I never found any that I thought was wild stock even as an escape from the numerous clumps set out along the fringes of our motor parkways.

The Coast or Sweet Pepperbush or White Alder (*Clethra alnifolia*), however, still is common to abundant in swamps, wet thickets, and moist ground generally throughout the area. Its cylindrical clusters of white flowers fill the surrounding air with fragrance in August. Much the same can be said of the hardy Buttonbush (*Cephalanthus occidentalis*), whose spherical clusters of honey-colored and sweet-smelling flowers are a distinct addition to the local scenery where they hang above the lower-growing greenery in swamps or the shallows of lakes and ponds.

Now we move back into the trees again and among a group that, with two exceptions, might be looked upon as suspicious characters in our territory. The first is the Sourwood or Sorrel Tree (*Oxydendrum arboreum*), which has a natural range to the south and westward from New York but has been planted in the area and even to the northward. Where it takes root in the open it has a habit of sending up numerous shoots surrounding the parent tree and for that reason it may have a bright future as a city tree. It hangs out large loose sprays of little white flowers in early summer. The remnants of these flower sprays in the form of tiny empty seed capsules in long rows cling to the tree through the winter and make it easily recognizable in the leafless season. Even the saplings bear these identification marks.

The Persimmon (*Diospyros virginiana*), famous in folklore and a familiar sight to the south and the west of us, barely edges into our territory as a native tree. I found three Persimmons of fair size in the Spuyten Duyvil–Riverdale section. The one in Spuyten Duyvil was still standing when I last looked, but it was standing on a lawn and whether it grew there of its own accord or was set out by hand remains a mystery. If it was planted by hand, it must have been half a century ago, judging from the height of the tree and the diameter of the trunk. This tree never betrayed itself by producing fruit, because it bore only staminate flowers. Anyone who knows the Persimmon would have recognized it immediately by the rugged bark on the trunk that is more deeply corrugated than alligator hide. The two Persimmons I found in an open cluster of trees in Fieldston just west of the Horace Mann School seemed to me to be of wild growth. The larger tree was about 45 feet in height and produced a good crop of fruit each year. However, both trees were uprooted and destroyed by the hurricane of September, 1938. Since that time I have not gathered a single persimmon within the confines of New York City.

There is nothing suspicious about the ash trees of our region.

They are on their home ground. Even so, only the White Ash (*Fraxinus americana*), which grows to a goodly height and girth, is common in the wild in the area. The others, except where they have been set out in parks or along streets and parkways, are few and far between. I found two small specimens of the Black Ash (*Fraxinus nigra*) along the fence on the west side of the railroad track about 300 yards north of the parkway cross-over at the upper end of the Van Cortlandt swamp. I doubt very much that they were deliberately planted in such an out-of-the-way location. I believe they must have grown naturally at that site. If you go looking for them you will recognize them in foliage by the leaflets of the compound leaves that bear enough resemblance to those of the elders to explain a discarded scientific name for this species, *Fraxinus sambucifolia*, meaning the ash with leaves like an elder.

Along that same stretch of railroad track but on the eastern side and fringing the golf fairways both above and below the cross-over bridge are a number of large shrubs or small trees of the kind called Fringe-tree or Old-Man's-beard (*Chionanthus virginicus*) because the flowers that appear in clusters in late May or early June have long, thin, white petals hanging down like strings. From New Jersey southward this is common in the wild as a shrub or small tree but in our territory it is common only in cultivation and is comparatively scarce as an escape. Thus it remains a suspicious botanical character in our midst.

The next exhibit is an outright foreigner, but one that has spread widely and taken deep root in our territory. That's the purple-flowering Princess-tree or Paulownia (*Paulownia tomentosa*), a tree of Chinese origin much cultivated in Europe and North America. Some authorities have it that the tree was named for Anna Paulownia, a daughter of Czar Paul I of Russia. Others state that it was named for Anna Paulownia, a Netherlands princess. Both views are correct, though the spelling of the name has been altered a trifle. Anna Paulovna, Grand Duchess of Russia and daughter of Czar Paul I, married the Netherlands prince who became William II of that country on the abdication of his father, William I, in 1840.

Aside from its regal name, the tree has some striking botanical features that catch the eye immediately. At full growth it is a tree of medium size with brownish bark, a stout trunk, and a good spread of rather stubby branches. All through the winter the bare branchlets carry not only many of the empty, pear-shaped dark seed capsules of the previous flowering season but the prospective floral display of the coming season as well, in the form of pyramidal clusters of long-stalked nodding flower buds seemingly covered with brown velvet. These pyramids of flower buds produce purple or bluish-violet tubular flowers an inch or more in length before the leaves are well out of the bud and thus the tree is a colorful sight at this season of the year. When fully spread, the large leaves are another distinctive feature of this tree, being hairy, heart-shaped, and from 6 inches to nearly a foot in length. Princess-trees are fast growers and, producing an abundance of seed, are inclined to spread like a weed. As an escape in the area they are the closest rival of the Ailanthus.

A tree with leaves suggesting those of the Princess-tree but even larger in size is the Common Catalpa (*Catalpa bignonioides*), much cultivated in our territory and fairly frequently found as an escape. It is native to the southern half of the United States but is hardy as far north as New England. In size, general growth, and appearance, the Catalpa is much like the Princess-tree, and because of the large leaves many persons probably mistake one tree for the other if the foliage is their only guide. But the pyramidal clusters of two-lipped tubular flowers of the Common Catalpa are white instead of purple or bluish violet, have yellow lines and purple dots in their "throats," and do not come into bloom for some weeks after the leaves have spread to their full and almost awesome dimensions.

The seed pods that cling to the tree through the winter are a sure and easy mark of identification of catalpas of any kind.

They are as thin as pencils, brown or dark gray in color, and from 10 to 20 inches in length. They look much like very long thin beans and, in fact, Indian Bean-tree or even Indian Cigar-tree are other names applied to the catalpas. The Common Catalpa is well named, since it is the one most commonly encountered, but two other species also are cultivated in our area and possibly may be found as escapes. They are the Catawba-tree (*Catalpa speciosa*), with slightly larger leaves and flowers, and the Chinese Catalpa (*Catalpa ovata*), the smallest of the trio and one easily distinguished in bloom by its yellow flowers.

In the last few pages we have been wandering mostly in the open, glancing at trees of dubious standing as real residents of the city precincts. But wherever they came from and however they arrived, they are on the premises for all to see. Indeed, there are many other introduced species doing so well in our area that it's quite possible they may "go native" in the long run. This would include the Golden-rain Tree or Pride-of-India (*Koelreuteria paniculata*), the Silverbell-tree (*Halesia carolina*), the Pagoda Tree or Chinese Scholar Tree (*Sophora japonica*), and the Amur Corktree (*Phellodendron amurense*), all of which may be seen in the New York Botanical Garden in Bronx Park as well as on many private estates in the outlying sections of the city. In time they may become "naturalized," but, even if they do, our native-born oaks, maples, and other hardwoods will forever furnish the colorful glory of our autumn foliage.

Chapter 12

Mammals within the City Gates

JUST AS a matter of record, the resident citizens outnumber any other kind of mammal to be found within the confines of New York City. But our business is with the quadruped mammals, a group from which Man is separated by physical, mental, moral, and spiritual attributes best explained or expounded by poets, professors, philosophers, or theologians. In the field of anthropology it is enough to state that this city probably — yea, almost certainly — contains representatives or descendants of all the known races of Man under the sun. It also contains a great many more "wild animals" than most of the human inhabitants suspect. And a considerable number of tame or domestic animals, too.

It's curious how we have grown into the habit of using the term animal as though it applied exclusively to four-footed mammals. We forget or ignore the fact that fish, birds, insects, and oysters belong to the Animal Kingdom, too. This is thoroughly unscientific but quite clear to readers or listeners and thus no great harm is done. We also make another distinction based on civilization rather than the laws of nature. We have "domestic animals" and "wild animals." Although the wild kind are more interesting, we must take stock of the city supply of domestic animals such as farm animals and cats and dogs. Farm animals, of course, are a minor matter but cats and dogs often make the headlines in the city's newspapers.

Although some farms and truck gardens are still to be found within the city limits, with the steady increase of buildings for business and residential purposes, the comparatively few farm animals of the area — the horses, cows, sheep, pigs, and goats — are a vanishing group. Those that survive these days are kept under regulations and conditions set forth by the Department of Health. But dogs and cats are a problem and often a cause of personal or neighborhood warfare between those who own them or love them and those who, while they may or may not love them, wish to banish them from the pavements of the crowded sections of the city.

By arrangement with the city authorities, dogs are licensed ($2 for the first license, $1 per year for renewals) by the American Society for the Prevention of Cruelty to Animals, a humane society that has done long and faithful service in alleviating the hardships and cruelties that horses, dogs, cats or, for that matter, any other creatures may be subjected to by thoughtless, selfish, or brutal persons within the city limits. In one recent year the SPCA licensed 276,119 dogs in the city and doubtless there were some running around unlicensed, though the society and the police do their best to track down such tax dodgers. Since cats need no licenses, there is no accurate way of checking on their numbers in the city.

However, one of the functions of the SPCA is to destroy, humanely, unwanted animals or those suffering beyond hope of relief from accident or disease. In the same recent year that saw the licensing of 276,119 dogs, the SPCA humanely destroyed

— usually by gas — 59,413 dogs and 133,436 cats! From these figures we might arrive at an estimate of the number of cats residing in the city at any given time. Take the figures as normal for any year (there was no indication in the society report that they were unusual in any respect): the dog population runs to about four and one half times the number destroyed in a year. Cats breed faster than dogs and kittens are more often unwanted than puppies; thus the mortality rate in the painless gas chambers would run higher for cats than it does for dogs. Even if we double the death rate in the case of the felines it still would leave us with more cats than dogs — roughly 300,000 cats — in the city. It is a rare thing to find a dog without an owner or a legal place of residence, but hundreds of the city's cats are homeless prowlers.

As for "wild animals" within the city limits, New York has a far larger population of wild quadrupeds than most of the resident bipeds suspect. That's because so many of the wild mammals are small in size and nocturnal in habit, as a result of which they are rarely seen except by those who look for them. We do have, however, some fair-sized mammals that occasionally are seen by daylight. Probably the largest mammal definitely recorded within the city limits in the past century was a young Sperm Whale (*Physeter catodon*) that apparently had lost its mother, followed a steamer into New York Harbor, and suffered an untimely death when it became stranded in Brooklyn's famous Gowanus Canal. The Saddleback or Harp Seal (*Phoca groenlandica*) sometimes is seen offshore at Coney Island in winter and the Harbor Seal (*Phoca vitulina*) occasionally ventures into the Lower Bay in the winter months.

The most primitive mammal in North America is the opossum, a marsupial with the typical nursing pouch for the young and thus a relative of the wallabies, kangaroos, and other native mammals of Australia. Common in the South, the Virginia Opossum (*Didelphous virginiana*) until recently was a rare animal in our territory, but now it is a settled resident and, being a bounteous breeder, it is rapidly increasing in numbers in the vicinity. It is, in fact, extending its range northward and eastward into New England, as are some other forms of life in this retreating Ice Age on the North American Continent.

Our opossum would never take a prize for beauty. It looks too much like a large, blond, long-haired rat with a naked tail almost as long as its body. This tail is prehensile and the animal often hangs by it while feeding in fruit trees. Although

it enjoys fruit, the opossum is not a finicky feeder. If need be, it will eat almost anything animal or vegetable, and has a fondness for eggs that makes it unpopular with poultrymen. Despite its sharp teeth, it is a timid animal and rarely puts up a fight if attacked. It is more likely to curl up and pretend to be dead — or, at least, it gives the appearance of putting on such an act, whatever the facts may be.

There are, however, exceptions to customs and family traits. At 2:45 A.M. of April 10, 1955, the police of the Wadsworth Avenue station on Washington Heights in Manhattan were notified that a noisy battle of some kind was raging along Audubon Avenue nearby. Two patrolmen were sent to investigate and found a Virginia Opossum engaged in what the *New York Times* reported to be "a glorious battle with nine alley cats." The plucky opossum was holding its own when rescued and sent to the SPCA shelter. Other opossums visiting the city or living here have not been so fortunate. Doing much of their foraging by night and being leisurely of gait, they occasionally become confused by headlights of autos on the highways at night and are struck and killed by the passing cars. Sometimes a mother opossum will move about in the darkness with half a dozen or more small offspring clinging to the fur on her back.

The Virginia Opossum is the only mammalian newcomer in our area. Most of the others have been natives of the region for thousands of years and even the imported species have been resident for several centuries. Moles, for instance, have been on the ground — or just under the surface — for ages. On park and private lawns and on the fairways of the municipal golf courses there will be found the raised roofs of the tunnels of the Eastern Mole (*Scalopus aquaticus*) and also, in many cases, the upright traps set like guillotines along the tunnels to execute the underground travelers. Moles actually do more good than harm to humans in their way of life, because most of their diet consists of injurious insects in adult or larval form; but they do raise unsightly ridges on otherwise smooth lawns and for that crime they are beset with traps or tempted with poisoned bait put out by indignant gardeners. They may eat some plant roots, as charged. More often the damage done to shrub roots or flower bulbs along mole tunnels is the work of mice who take advantage of the runways dug by the moles.

There is a widespread belief that moles are blind, but such is not the case. They have very small eyes either covered with a thin skin or so effectively concealed in the fur in which they are buried that they easily escape notice even when the animal is in hand. The fur screen undoubtedly obscures the vision of the mole but it also protects the eyes from loose dirt in its digging operations, which is more important. Eyesight is a minor matter to a mole that finds practically all its food by its senses of smell and touch. The Eastern Mole has a chunky roundish body, up to 6 inches or so in length, covered with a coat of thick velvety gray hair that is wonderfully soft to the touch. It also has a short naked tail, barely an inch or so in length and, in typical mole fashion, its front feet are twisted outward and clawed in a way to make them serve as remarkably efficient digging tools in the excavations of their tunnels.

The Starnose Mole (*Condylura cristata*), named for the really astonishing rosette of tiny protuberances at the end of its pinkish nose, is another resident of our region but it is by no means as abundant as the Eastern Mole, nor is it ordinarily a disturber of manicured lawns or treasured flower beds. It prefers wet meadows and the edges of swamps, though occasionally it is caught in traps set for the Eastern Mole. Although the two species are of about the same size, the Starnose is darker in color, almost blackish above, and has a much longer tail. Still another member of the clan that turns up in the area now and then is the Hairytail or Brewer's Mole (*Parascalops breweri*), much like the Eastern Mole in size and color but easily distinguished by the hairy tail that accounts for one of the names applied to this species.

Moles are reputed to be voracious feeders and ferocious fighters for their size. Shrews, which look like short-legged mice but are more nearly allied to the moles, have even worse reputations for gluttonous gorging and vicious dispositions. Some species are said to eat twice their own weight daily, and there are reports of shrew battles in which one contestant killed and ate the other — conduct that we, as humans, are likely to look upon as carrying a family quarrel too far. Shrews are insectivorous mammals like moles. They differ, however, in that they do not live in tunnels nor are their front feet twisted outward for added efficiency in digging. They forage along the surface of the ground, often under dead leaves and other litter, and you will more often hear them than see them at such work. They do much scratching and no little digging in the pursuit of food, and their tiny but comparatively broad and sharp-clawed front feet are a big help to them in the pursuit of their prey.

Three or four species of shrew are regular inhabitants of our territory. They are seldom seen because they are quite small and generally are working under cover of one kind or another. Occasionally one will "break cover" to run across a path or even scurry across a paved road, but even then they probably are mistaken for mice by those who see them for no more than a few seconds. The Masked Shrew *(Sorex cinereus)* of moist ground in our territory is a tiny grayish-brown creature with a body length of about 2 to 2½ inches and a tail up to 2 inches in length. The larger and darker Shorttail Shrew *(Blarina brevicauda)*, which usually is found on higher and drier ground, has a body 3 to 4 inches in length with a fine, close-fitting coat of dark gray fur that looks black at first glance. The tail that accounts for its common name is only an inch or so in length. I often found shrews of this species lying dead on woodland paths in the Riverdale and Van Cortlandt regions. Presumably they were left there by cats who caught them in the underbrush, started to carry them home and then decided to have no more to do with such prey. The proffered explanation is that something about the shrews — the odor or the taste — is disagreeable to cats, so they drop the matter and leave quietly. It is even said that the bite of the little creatures is slightly toxic but perhaps these bad reports about shrews are not due so much to the little animals themselves as they are to the parasitic mites that infest them and perhaps infect them. A third species found in our territory is the Least Shrew *(Cryptotis parva)* that wears a cinnamon or reddish-brown coat by which it may be distinguished from the Masked Shrew of the same approximate size but with a grayish-brown coat. The Least Shrew is a settled resident of Staten Island and the Smoky Shrew *(Sorex fumeus)*, slightly larger and dull brown in color, is reported there, too, but I have encountered neither on my home ground at the north end of the city.

We turn swiftly to higher things. Nature anticipated Man in devising an effective sound-ranging system. The bats, our only mammals that can truly fly, are equipped with built-in sound-ranging systems that, by means of emitted high-pitched squeaks and the registering of their reflected echoes in remarkably efficient ears, enable them to avoid solid objects in space that might bring damage or death to them in their flights in the dark. Our species feed entirely on the wing and mostly on insects that are harmful. Bats are odd-looking creatures and possibly even a little frightening in appearance to females who view them as no better than flying mice. They are, however, not a bit dangerous but quite timid and actually beneficial. If by any chance one is discovered in the house, you may be sure it has no desire to entangle itself in a woman's hair, though folklore has charged it with this type of disorderly conduct.

The wings of these flying mammals are merely modified forelegs — or arms and hands, if you will — equipped with thin flexible membranes that, when outspread, serve the same purpose as the flight feathers of birds. At the outer joint of the wing one of the digits — the equivalent of the thumb on the human hand — has been developed into a sharp little hook by means of which the bats are enabled to cling in an upright position on a vertical surface of wood, stone, or brick if they wish, but they also can rest comfortably while clinging to an overhead support with their feet and hanging upside down. Many bats are gregarious and gather in great numbers, particularly for migration or hibernation, as the case may be according to the species.

Of this group of marvelous mammals four species are of common occurrence in New York City and one species at least has been so considerate as to hibernate in a wing of the American Museum of Natural History on Central Park West. That was the Big Brown Bat (*Eptesicus fuscus*), which is big only in comparison with the Little Brown Bat (*Myotis lucifugus*) that has a body about 3 inches or so in length and weighs little more than a five-cent piece. The Big Brown Bat has a body half again as large and a wingspread of a foot or more. Both these species hibernate in caves, barns, church steeples, or any such protected places in the area but the Red Bat (*Lasiurus borealis*), which is between them in size but readily distinguishable by its color, is migratory.

The one common bat of the area whose name gives no hint concerning the color of its fur coat is the Eastern Pipistrel (*Pipistrellus subflavus*). The color is yellowish brown though it looks black as this smallest of our local bats flutters overhead in the dusk. This is the one most often seen in the twilight or gathering dark flitting lightly and silently about the roofs and chimneys of old houses or outbuildings in the more open spaces on the fringe of the city. Often there are Chimney Swifts on the wing with them at twilight and then the noiseless zigzag fluttering of the bats stands out in contrast to the chattering flight of the birds in sweeping curves. A few other species may be encountered in our territory but the Big Brown Bat, the Little Brown Bat, the Red Bat, and the Eastern Pipistrel are the ones that justifiably may be counted as regular residents of the area and, as far as most New Yorkers are con-

cerned, unsuspected participants in the night life of the city.

If a-hunting he would go, actually it is still possible for a man to go "coon hunting" in the dark of night on the outskirts of the city with a fair chance of bagging some game. However, since it is illegal to hunt within the city limits, the Raccoons (*Procyon lotor*) of the region lead a protected and well-fed existence. They are still present in numbers in the outlying sections of Queens and the Bronx. A good-sized adult Raccoon may weigh thirty pounds or more. They are destructive around poultry yards and vegetable gardens but, aside from that, they are harmless, handsome, and quite amusing animals that tame easily if caught young. The "black domino" or mask across the eye region gives them a sinister appearance, as though they were wrinkling their brows for the plotting of some deep mischief, but it may be only a raid on a row of garbage pails in some sparsely populated section of the city.

They rarely venture out until dusk falls and for that reason they usually escape notice unless some chance encounter discloses their presence in the vicinity. Such was the case in Riverdale recently when, shortly before midnight, a resident turned his dog loose in the yard and a few minutes later heard it yelping excitedly. The householder investigated and found his dog making frantic leaps under an apple tree from which a large Raccoon was looking down, audibly and visibly expressing complete disapproval of the whole proceedings. Up to that moment the dog owner never had suspected the presence of a Raccoon in the vicinity, but for those who know the ways of the wild the long-toed tracks in the mud or the snow indicate that this ring-tailed night-prowler is still a permanent resident of the wilder reaches of the Bronx.

The same thing may be said of the Longtail Weasel (*Mustela frenata*) and the Mink (*Mustela vison*) except that they are not as numerous as the Raccoons and perhaps the Mink is only a visitor, though a regular one, in the region. Dr. William Beebe recounts how, during his years at the Bronx Zoo, he trapped

eleven Mink along the Bronx River where it runs through the park and had the skins fashioned into a fur piece for his wife. A few years ago a man was caught trapping Mink in a marshy section of the East Bronx and was fined for doing so without a license. The Longtail Weasel, being a bold animal like all of its tribe, is not a bit afraid of hunting in broad daylight and I have met several of these fearless little fellows poking about in the Van Cortlandt swamp where I also found the telltale tracks of Mink though I never met one of these expensive fur bearers face to face in the area.

As for the Striped Skunk (*Mephitis mephitis*), the fatal and odorous evidence of its presence is found in the flattened corpses of the animals on the motor parkways in the outlying sections of the city. These handsome and harmless — if unmolested — animals trot about at night in leisurely fashion in search of food and, in crossing roads, make little effort to avoid cars. The result often is a strong odor in the dark and a messy mass of black and white fur on the concrete roadway in the morning. Skunks are largely beneficial in their way of life. They feed mostly on insects and fruit but they also catch mice and they are expert in finding the buried egg clutches of the Snapping Turtle. Like the Raccoon, they may do some damage around the poultry yard or the kitchen garden, but on the whole they are amiable creatures that do not turn loose their "liquid fire" unless they are frightened or provoked.

Probably the largest resident wild animals in the city are the foxes that are comparatively few in number but persistent in the northerly section of the Bronx where both the Red Fox *(Vulpes fulva)* and the Gray Fox *(Urocyon cinereoargenteus)* are found to this day. Every so often a resident of Spuyten Duyvil or Riverdale or the East Bronx sees a fox and reports it to the newspapers as something extraordinary in a big city, but the neat straight-line tracks in new-fallen snow each winter prove that foxes are as regular on their nightly rounds in the region as the postman is by day. In recent years a Gray Fox made itself at home in a rocky culvert under the river road in the Spuyten Duyvil region, and for all I know it may still be there.

At different times I have seen Red Foxes trotting steadily about their affairs through different sections of Van Cortlandt Park and I knew a fox earth that was obliterated by the building of the Henry Hudson Parkway on the west border of the swamp near the city line. Even so, the foxes refused to leave the neighborhood, for I saw some later in the area and a friend saw a vixen playing with young on the hillside west of the swamp ten years after the old earth had been run over and crushed by the wheels of progress. As a matter of fact, every fall of snow produces new evidence that foxes are still residents of the region, *anno Domini* 1958.

One encounter with a fox was most amusing. At 7:30 A.M.
on the morning of April 7, 1955 (I keep a journal), I was walking up the railroad track on the east side of the Van Cortlandt
swamp with Fred Nagler, the artist. It was a bright warm
morning and we were looking for birds. About a hundred
yards north of the parkway bridge we saw a fine, large, and
well-groomed Red Fox standing motionless just inside the wire
fence that separates the golf course from the railroad track.
Master Reynard was almost under the protection of a clump
of Forsythia fringing the golf fairway and it was apparent that
he hoped we hadn't noticed him, though we were not fifty feet
apart. But when we stopped and stared, he knew he was detected. There was a gate in the fence on either side of the
track at that point so that Park Department workers could get
through. Evidently the animal had come down from the
wooded slope to the eastward and planned to slip through the
partly open gates to hunt in the swamp on the west side of
the track. It was reluctant to give up the expedition but it
didn't trust us. It started to retreat across the fairway —
stopped several times to look back at us and reconsider — then
finally gave it up as a bad job and loped across the links to disappear in the undergrowth of the woods beyond.

It should be remembered that there is good foraging for
foxes along the city's northern border and, even if all the
resident foxes were destroyed, newcomers would drift in from
Westchester to take up residence in a short time. It is not so
with all outlying sections of the city, of course, nor with animals less wary than the proverbial fox. It is not so, for instance, with the familiar Woodchuck (*Marmota monax*) that
retains a bare foothold in our territory but is losing ground
steadily as more buildings go up and more pavement is laid
down. It isn't as sly, as secretive, or as swift of foot as most
of the other wild creatures of the area. It feeds by daylight,
early and late, grows to an over-all length of 2 feet, stubby
furry tail included, and is bulky of shape. It finds little

nourishment and too much human traffic in our parks. It prefers cornfields, apple orchards, and kitchen gardens, items that are lessening year by year in the city. Small boys and large dogs are death to this short-legged, broad-beamed, daylight-foraging animal if it wanders far from any of the three or four entrances to its underground apartments. Though it has a threatening look and gives a defiant chattering whistle through gnashing teeth when cornered, it is timid at heart and not tenacious of life. And when the Woodchuck disappeared from Staten Island, the myriad Woodchucks of New York and New Jersey farmlands had no way of sending fresh individuals to represent the clan on an island girt by salt water. Thus Staten Island is missing most of these larger mammals that for many years to come will be found regularly and in fair numbers along the northern border of the Bronx which is, as has been mentioned previously, the only borough on the mainland of North America. A newcomer seeking the city from that direction doesn't have to swim for it.

Under another name — just in case some city dwellers do not know it — the Woodchuck is the "Ground Hog" that, according to folklore, comes out of hibernation on Candlemas (February 2) each year to take a weather observation. If the sun is shining and it sees its shadow — so runs the old wives' tale — it goes back into its den to sleep for another six weeks of hard weather. But if the sky is overcast or rain or snow is falling, the Ground Hog stays out, confident that fine spring weather is in the offing. However, modern farmers look to the Weather Bureau rather than the Ground Hog for meteorological information and, furthermore, I never knew a Woodchuck or Ground Hog that would so much as stick its nose out of its burrow that early in February. I never looked for it to appear above ground until

> *March made sweet the weather*
> *With daffodil and starling*
> *And hours of fruitful breath.*

Perhaps both Woodchuck and Ground Hog are misnomers — it doesn't chuck wood and it isn't a hog — and the animal should be called the Overstuffed Ground Squirrel. It looks well fed to the point of bulkiness, actually is a member of the Sciuridae or Squirrel Family, and generally feeds on the ground though on a few occasions I have seen Woodchucks among the lower branches of old apple trees with slanting trunks. Another member of the family that prefers to stay on the ground is the Eastern Chipmunk (*Tamias striatus*) that, in the words of a small nephew, "looks like a little squirrel with a strip of bacon on its back." It also hibernates like the Woodchuck, but there the resemblance ends. The lively little Eastern Chipmunk is common enough in the larger parks of all five boroughs along with the tree-loving, acrobatic Eastern Gray Squirrel (*Sciurus carolinensis*) that is altogether too common in many parts of the city.

We must admit that the Gray Squirrel is a handsome and graceful animal and an arboreal gymnast of daring artistry but it is notorious for robbing the nests of birds of both eggs and young in the breeding season and in winter it is a pest around feeding stations designed to attract and nourish small birds through the months of snow and ice. A century ago the Red Squirrel (*Tamiasciurus hudsonicus*) was common in the area but it has not taken kindly to the growth of the city. I have not seen one on city territory since boyhood days in Kingsbridge groves and orchards. It has been stated that the Red Squirrel is more than a match for the larger Gray Squirrel in single combat but it is apparent that the Gray Squirrel can not only survive but thrive where the Red Squirrel dies out in a crowded region. Incidentally, if you see a black squirrel anywhere in the city, it will not be a new species for you but the Eastern Gray Squirrel wearing a fur coat of another color. Melanism — the occurrence of black individuals in species ordinarily of another color — is occasional over most of the range of this squirrel and quite common in some restricted area such as the northern section of the Bronx, where I have had as many as six black-coated Eastern Gray Squirrels in sight at one time.

By far the most attractive member of the family resident in New York City is the lovely and friendly little Southern Flying Squirrel *(Glaucomys volans)*, whose presence is unsuspected by most of the human inhabitants of the area. Yet the large-eyed, gentle little creature — it is about the same size as the Eastern Chipmunk — is fairly common in the wooded outskirts of the northern and eastern sections of the city and perhaps in other sections. It is hard to be sure because it is so seldom seen, being almost completely nocturnal in its way of life. Dusk is the beginning of its working day, so to speak.

One summer evening when I was sitting on the verandah of our rambling old house in Riverdale — like the fox earth mentioned earlier, this dwelling was "run over" by the construc-

tion of the Henry Hudson Parkway — I saw a dark object sail downward through the dusk toward the base of a White Ash that stood about twenty feet away on the lawn. I heard a soft *plop* as the object landed. There was just light enough for me to see that it was a Flying Squirrel that had landed head-upward on the trunk of the tree just a few feet above the ground. Then it shot up the tree like a streak and disappeared.

Later I made closer acquaintance with other Flying Squirrels of our neighborhood. One of them — we named it "Chicot" — came nightly to a bedroom window sill that served as a feeding station for birds by day. How it discovered this table d'hôte spread free of charge I have no idea, but my wife woke up one night to find a small dark form in outline on the window sill. Having associated only birds with that window sill, she thought it was one of the small owls and roused me to investigate, which I did. But as I came close to the window, there was a swift scurrying sound and the creature was gone. I borrowed from Hamlet to the extent of "A rat! A rat!" and was sorry I couldn't add "Dead for a ducat." But I thought better of it when I went back to bed. No rat could scurry as swiftly as that. I suspected a Flying Squirrel and was ready for it the following night. When the little form suddenly appeared on the window sill, I waited until I could hear it cracking sunflower seeds and then, with my wife in the dark behind me, I turned on a flashlight. Thus we made acquaintance with Chicot and soon we became firm friends.

We put out a special diet of shelled walnuts for the distinguished visitor each evening and it would sit there in the dark and nibble away calmly when we turned on the flashlight and even when we tapped on the glass an inch or so from its nose. I'm sure we could have tamed it to the point of handling it — others have done it easily — but we were afraid it would come into the house if we left the window open. The lady of the house, though delighted to have it as a window sill visitor, had no desire to have it as a house guest. So we all kept our respective distances and, since Flying Squirrels do not hibernate, we had Chicot as a nocturnal boarder at our window sill buffet all through the winter. It disappeared in the spring, probably intent upon family matters. And we never saw it again.

Telling the tale to others, we found that our experience was by no means uncommon in the region and that Flying Squirrels had made themselves free of bird feeding stations in other sections of the city. These creatures are almost incredibly agile and their swift scurries are almost like the swooping of birds. The "flying," of course, is mere gliding or volplaning from a high launching point to a lower landing place by means of the extra fold of skin along each side of the body that can be flattened out by the action of the fore and hind legs to which it is attached. This, in effect, makes something like a "sail plane" of the body of the animal. It must "fly" downward, of course, but it lands facing upward by a quick turn of the body and tail at the end of the "flight."

The Flying Squirrels are the quietest members of the family in the area. At most, all you hear from them is a series of little squeaks in the night. The Gray Squirrels, by far the most abundant members of the family, are also the loudest. They give off sustained volleys of hoarse, rasping coughs or barks that usually end on a squalling note. Such discordant noises command attention. The long, whirring rattle of the Red Squirrel or Chickaree is now a rare call in the region and the stout Woodchuck, another species on the way out, gives breath to its quivering downward whistle only when it is frightened or enraged. The Chipmunk utters chattering notes when it is excited or angry but its song of contentment — or its advertisement of its presence in a particular spot — is a slowly repeated and hollow-sounding *chock-chock-chock* that can be heard several hundred yards away of a quiet day in the woods or fields.

Roundish masses or clumps of dead leaves seen high up among the bare branches of trees in winter usually turn out to be the "summer homes" of the Gray Squirrels. In hard weather and for breeding purposes they prefer the hollows of trees and other protected nooks, but in late spring you will notice them climbing up trunks of trees with their mouths stuffed with fresh leaves and twigs with which to build these warm weather retreats for themselves. Flying Squirrels have the same habit on a smaller and lower scale. If you come upon a rounded mass of dead leaves in a crotch of a small tree or a tall shrub, give it a poke and perhaps a Flying Squirrel will pop out and scurry off like a shot. You never can tell what will happen when you look into such matters.

There are many square miles on the face of the earth where there are resident rats and mice and no human beings, but it is doubtful that there is a single square mile that contains resident human beings and no rats or mice. The common House Mouse *(Mus musculus)*, the Norway Rat *(Rattus norvegicus)*, and the Black Rat *(Rattus rattus)*, originally immigrants from Europe, are now thoroughly at home on the North American Continent, particularly the House Mouse and the Norway Rat that have swept from the East Coast along which they were introduced all the way to the West Coast and up to Alaska. The Black Rat, so far, is largely coastal and there is a wide stretch from the Appalachians to the Rockies that is yet free of its depredations. As a matter of fact, it was thought to be comparatively scarce in our territory until recent collections by professional exterminators who gave infested sections a thorough going-over proved by irrefutable evidence — dead bodies — that it was on the premises in round numbers. Even so, it is far behind the House Mouse and the Norway Rat in abundance in all five boroughs.

Conditions are bad but they could be worse. Indeed, they were worse a century ago and even fifty years ago when most houses were made of wood and there were livery stables on almost every street in Manhattan. Livery stables meant board and lodging for any number of rats and the occupants of old-

fashioned frame houses fought unending campaigns against the
House Mouse. It isn't that bad in Manhattan and downtown
Brooklyn now. Office buildings, hotels, apartment houses, and
shops of all kinds now are constructed of steel, concrete, and
glass. The increased use of plastics in offices and homes has
been an important factor in reducing the number of rodents
formerly holed up in private homes or business houses. But
it must be admitted that rats still range the waterfronts and
also the city dumps and even the swanky residential districts
where the householders do not see to it that their garbage pails
and cans are tightly covered as required by law. The Department of Health and the Department of Sanitation wage spora-
dic campaigns against the careless householders and the foraging rodents but, to date, they have not been able to reform
one group or eradicate the other.

The more common of the smaller outdoor mice of the region
are the Meadow Mouse (*Microtus pennsylvanicus*), the White-
footed Mouse (*Peromyscus leucopus*), and the Meadow Jumping
Mouse (*Zapus hudsonius*), all harmless and even attractive little
creatures, though it is difficult to bring most women to view
them in any such light. The Meadow Mouse — or Meadow
Vole, as some prefer to call it — is one of the most abundant
small rodents of the northern half of North America. It is a
chunky, short-tailed, well-furred little animal that varies considerably in color over its wide range. In our territory it runs
to a dark brown color with a body length of about 4 inches and
a tail about 2 inches long.

The mild Muskrat (*Ondatra zibethica*), which looks something
like an aquatic Woodchuck, is really only an overgrown mouse
or vole that prefers life in the water to life on land. It is a
common resident of the slow streams, ponds, lakes, and fresh-
water marshes of the city and its heaped-up houses of piled
vegetation are easy to spot when the surrounding greenery
of summer falls away in the late autumn. The bulky body of
the Muskrat is about a foot long and is covered with two kinds

of hair: a short beautiful undercoat of soft and silky brown fur and a long coat of coarser hair. Its stout naked tail— almost as long as its body—is vertically flattened to aid in propulsion and steering when the animal is swimming. Its hind feet are partially webbed as another aid to progress in the water.

The lower end of the Van Cortlandt swamp often contains a dozen or more Muskrat houses. It was there, as a boy, that I had my first glimpse of a Muskrat when I was playing ice hockey or "shinny." As I was skating over the clear ice I saw this animal swimming directly ahead of me just under the ice and moving about as fast as I was. I pursued it to the edge of the "pond" or cleared zone, where it slipped among the cattail stalks below and disappeared. That was more than fifty years ago and it is pleasant to know that Muskrats still swim there under the ice in winter. They also swim there and in the nearby lake in summer, often with their noses and foreheads cutting the surface of the water. One day last June I was standing at the water's edge, looking for marsh birds, when a Muskrat quietly emerged from the water at my feet and, without looking up, began to nibble at some roots. This went on for about a minute while I stood perfectly still. Whether it was the sight of my shoes as it turned to graze in that direction or some other clue I do not know, but suddenly the animal realized that it was not alone. It threw up its head for a quick glance and turned and dived out of sight almost in one motion.

Muskrats are quite prolific and often raise two or more broods in a year. That's why they are able to survive within the city limits where their natural habitat is limited and their natural enemies are reinforced by stray dogs, local rowdies who think that all "wild animals" are fair game at any time of year, and, though it is strange to think of it going on in a big city, poachers who set trap lines in the winter months and make their rounds by stealth. I found and removed a number of such steel traps set by poachers in the Van Cortlandt swamp.

Rabbits are common in the fields and thickets of Staten Island and in the outlying sections of the Bronx and the Borough of Queens. The resident species is the Eastern Cottontail (*Sylvilagus floridanus*) that may grow to a length of 17 to 18 inches and a weight of 3 to 4 pounds. It is wonderful how they persist in the face of diminishing open ground and increasing hazards in the form of stray dogs, roaming cats, fast-moving cars, and illegal shooting. House cats on the loose probably are their worst enemies, at least in their younger days. The alert full-grown Cottontails usually are able to elude prowling cats but, since they do much moving around at night, they frequently are confused by the headlights of cars and many are killed on the parkways. Despite these casualties and the harrying and chivvying by their natural enemies in the woods and fields, the rapidity with which they breed keeps the Cottontail population fairly steady and there is no immediate threat of their extinction as residents of the region.

To the best of deponent's knowledge and belief, this completes the list of the common mammals that regularly occur in the area either as residents or migrants. There were others, of course, on the premises long ago. The Beaver (*Castor canadensis*), the Black Bear (*Ursus americanus*), the Gray Wolf (*Canis lupus*), the Mountain Lion or Catamount (*Felis concolor*), the Bobcat (*Lynx rufus*), and the Whitetail Deer (*Odocoileus virginianus*) were residents of the region in Indian times but, like the Indians, they were gradually driven out by the invading white men. The Gray Wolf retreated to Canada and the Mountain Lion fled far to the south and west, as far south as Florida on the Atlantic side of the continent. But the Black Bear still can be found within one hundred miles of the city and the Bobcat, the Beaver, and the Whitetail Deer hold the rank of next-door neighbors in Westchester County.

Occasionally one or two of the Westchester deer wander into the northern section of the Bronx. A few years ago two such visitors lingered among the lawns, gardens, and remaining groves of shade trees in the Riverdale region for about a week before they decided that life in the big city was not for them. They disappeared, presumably in the direction of the Westchester acres from which they came. On September 20, 1955, the New York *Herald Tribune* had a front page story about a six-point buck that was found the previous day in the Midland Beach section of Staten Island and was taken under the protection of the State Conservation Department. The supposition was that it reached Staten Island by swimming from the New Jersey shore across the Kill Van Kull. Despite these and other such occasional incursions, New York City no longer can be considered home territory for these animals. Any Whitetail Deer found within the city precincts may properly be charged with vagrancy.

Chapter 13

Sea Birds, Shore Birds, and Waterfowl

AT ABOUT 10 A.M. on the morning of November 17, 1943—a brisk, bright autumn day—I was on my home ground in Riverdale walking southward along the river road toward Spuyten Duyvil. A northwest wind was pushing a bit roughly over my shoulder and raising a considerable chop on the broad expanse of the Hudson River on my right. Above the rush of the wind I became vaguely aware of a confused sound like the barking of dogs at a distance and then I suddenly realized — wild geese! While the Canada Goose (*Branta canadensis*) is a common migrant through the skies over the city, it's always a thrill to look up and see a V-shaped company of geese sweeping majestically overhead with a slow beating of wings and a hoarse clamor of cr-r-ronking that swells as the flock approaches and then fades away into silence long before the great birds themselves dissolve into the distant sky. So I turned around and raised my field glasses to inspect the oncoming southbound choristers and, to my surprise and delight, I discovered that these were birds I never before had seen in the wild.

In the wild? I was standing on Palisade Avenue in the northwest corner of New York City. Even so, these travelers above me might have come from beyond the Arctic Circle. They were Snow Geese (*Chen hyperborea*), great white birds with black wing-tips. I had time to count them twice and arrived at a total of 120 each time. They didn't fly in a steady V-shaped formation as Canada Geese usually do. This was a wider and looser "V" with alternate bulging and sagging along the front, a habit of the species that has earned them the name of "Wavies" among gunners. I watched them as far as I could see them winging their way southward high above the river. Long, long ago they faded from sight, but not from memory.

That was a red-letter day, of course. But other observers have seen Snow Geese on or over city territory on numerous occasions, and sometimes in much larger flocks. Birds of the wilderness regularly are recorded as visitors to this teeming metropolis. The approximately 400 square miles of land and water that lie within the city boundaries provide food and shelter for a delightful assortment of transient or resident birds. There are thirty-odd miles of ocean front along which one may see shore birds, sea birds, and waterfowl of many kinds. There are tidal flats and salt and brackish marshes. There are park lakes, ponds, and brooks. There are open fields, hedgerows, and rocky woods for upland birds. But in addition to all this, there are two other factors that make New York City a particularly favorable region in which to pursue the avocation of bird-watching or the study of ornithology.

One of these factors is that the city lies in what the scientists call a Transition Zone, a region in which the Carolinian and the Canadian Zone flora and fauna overlap. In other words, there are predominantly southern or Carolinian plants and birds that reach their northern range limit in this general area

and there are predominantly northern or Canadian Zone species that come this far south but very little farther except on high ground along the Appalachian chain. The second and even more important factor is that the city lies in a key position on the Atlantic Coastal Flyway so that it not only gets a full flow of avian traffic northward in spring but an extra concentration of southbound traffic during the autumn migration.

A glance at the map will explain this situation so far as land birds are concerned. When the adult migrants and young of the year head southward from the Maritime Provinces of Canada and a great part of New England, they have to veer westward to follow the coastline or the offshore islands or they will be lost at sea. Such a course funnels them through our region from August through October. This geographical pattern also accounts for the occasional mass invasions of winter visitants from the same territory to the northeast. There have been winters in which great flocks of northern finches appeared in the New York area and many individuals settled down for weeks at city and suburban feeding stations.

Before we go boasting of distinguished visitors, however, we had best deal with four species of resident birds that are almost as much a part of city life as the human population of the five boroughs. The Common Pigeon or Rock Dove (*Columba livia*), a hardy bird and steady breeder through all months of the year, is present in numbers that some persons consider appalling. Estimates of the Pigeon population vary from 250,000 to 350,000 or more but these are mere guesses. Nobody has bothered to take a city-wide census of these birds that, strangely enough, are most abundant on the pavement of the crowded sections of the city and live almost entirely on handouts from humans. Fifty years ago the Pigeons were outnumbered by the House Sparrow (*Passer domesticus*), but the automobiles that drove the horses off the city streets took the food out of the mouths of the House Sparrows in the same operation. Gone are the stables and barnyards of old days, and gone are the noonday nosebags from which the feeding horses scattered oats all over the surrounding pavement. Nesting sites disappeared, too, as old wooden dwellings were torn down and steel and concrete apartment houses and office buildings replaced them. Thus the House Sparrow population has had a sharp drop over the past half-century.

On the other hand, the Starling (*Sturnus vulgaris*) has had a spectacular rise in numbers in the region over the same period. These birds shun the pavement beloved by the Pigeons but they swarm on park and private lawns in the region and they congregate by the thousands at city dumps, where they find the table d'hôte very much to their taste. They have driven some of our native and more attractive hole-nesting birds out of the area but we must give the Starling some good marks on its report card. It feeds on the larvae of many insect pests, including the Japanese Beetle, has an extraordinary supply of chortles, whistles, and squeaks, and is a master mimic of the calls of other birds. Possibly the Starlings outnumber the Pigeons in the city. One recent "Christmas Census" listed 95,000 Starlings for Manhattan Island and another similar checkup raised the estimate to 140,000 for the same territory. And there were reports of many thousands in the other boroughs at the same time. However, these birds often scatter from Manhattan roosting places in the morning to forage in the other boroughs — or even beyond the city limits — through the day and then return to their Manhattan roosts at night. This could easily confuse the counting of flocks or individual birds at different hours of a Christmas Census that extends from dawn to dark.

It's this habit of congregating by the thousands in favorite roosting places that gives the Starlings a bad name. They cluster in the cornices and under the eaves of skyscrapers, public buildings, libraries, and museums. They crowd into the niches of gothic towers and spires that top some of our finest churches. They gather among the girders and struts under the steel bridges and viaducts of Manhattan. Best of all from a bird's-eye view, of a cold winter night they compete for perches in the framework of the flashing electric signs of the city, including those of the Great White Way, because the warmth thrown off by the lighted bulbs makes such dormitories the best places in town to bed down for the night. In some of their various roosts they gather in such numbers that their presence becomes a nuisance and their ejection a civic problem.

The Common Pigeon or Rock Dove, the House Sparrow, and the Starling share a common heritage: they are of European extraction. The Common Pigeon came here with the early colonists. The first successful crossing of the Atlantic by House Sparrows occurred in 1852. Those that survived the voyage and a winter in captivity here were liberated in Greenwood Cemetery in Brooklyn the following spring. In something less than a century their descendants, and those of later introduced groups, spread all the way across the continent. Starlings are common as caged pets in European households and no doubt some of them were brought to this country two or three centuries ago. But as a resident wild species they date only as far back as 1890 when sixty imported birds were turned loose in Central Park. The fourth species that calls attention to itself as a part of the life of the big city was native to these parts long before Christopher Columbus made his first westward trip across the Atlantic. That's the abundant Herring Gull (*Larus argentatus*).

Most seaport cities are well furnished with gulls of various kinds, and New York is no exception. Five kinds are common to abundant in our region at different seasons but the Herring Gull, which is found here throughout the year but chiefly as a winter resident, far outnumbers all the other species combined. January probably would find at least 50,000 Herring Gulls on or above land and water within the city limits. The Starlings will outnumber them, but the Herring Gulls will outweigh the total tonnage of the Starlings — and perhaps that of the city

Pigeons, too. These are big birds. The Herring Gull has a wingspread of between 4 and 5 feet and a length of about 2 feet from the tip of the beak to the end of the tail. The average weight is close to 2½ pounds, which means that in winter Father Knickerbocker has more than 60 tons of Herring Gulls in his bailiwick.

These birds are common along the beaches and on the bays, rivers, and reservoirs of the region. They dawdle around sewer outlets and they gather by the thousands at the city dumps. They even descend by the hundreds on such solid ground as parking areas behind beaches to preen their feathers or sun themselves. On many occasions I have counted more than 500 Herring Gulls standing or sitting on the grassy plain and playing field called the Parade Ground in Van Cortlandt Park. They are a part of the sights of the big city and they are also an unpaid part of the sanitation corps through their efficiency as scavengers. Just in case some readers do not know or have been misinformed, the mottled brown gulls are the young ones and the white ones with the bluish-gray backs and wings (called "mantles") are the adults. The young Herring Gulls don the adult plumage in their third year on or above the water.

We have so far mentioned only five species, one of which — the Snow Goose — is decidedly uncommon in the region. There are more than 200 species that a good "birder" would expect to meet within the city limits in the course of a calendar year. There are another hundred species, any one of which he might hope to encounter and many of which undoubtedly he would see if he gave time and energy to the search. Something approaching another hundred species would be rarities or accidental wanderers if reported anywhere on, in or above our territory. The fact is, however, that approximately 400 species have been recorded in the New York City region and all but a scant two dozen or so actually within the city limits. More than 230 species have been recorded from Central Park where it lies surrounded by hotels and apartment houses on crowded Manhattan Island.

We will leave the rarities and the accidentals to the expert ornithologists and the pot-hunters among the keen amateurs who will go to great lengths to add a new bird to the year's list or a life list. The most we can do here is to take notice of the birds that a resident or a visitor might reasonably expect or at least hope to see in the city in the course of a year. We might as well start with the species usually found along the ocean beaches of the city or in the waters offshore. Here we see gulls of different kinds all through the year, shore birds in profusion during the migrating periods, and ducks of many species in winter.

The Herring Gull has been mentioned and is by far the most abundant of the group throughout the colder months of the year, but it does not have the air, the water, or the beaches to itself at any time.   In the winter you will have no trouble picking out the Great Black-backed Gull (*Larus marinus*) among groups of its paler neighbors on the water or along the beaches. The lordly "Burgomaster," a northerly gull, seems to be extending its breeding range southward along the New England coast and is becoming increasingly numerous as a winter visitor in our territory.   Much like the Herring Gull in appearance but definitely smaller in size is the Ring-billed Gull (*Larus delawarensis*) that is a fairly common transient and a regular winter and summer resident in small numbers.   The lovely Laughing Gull (*Larus atricilla*), one of our two black-headed species in the breeding season, may be seen — and heard! — in great numbers in the Upper Bay, on Long Island Sound, and along the Hudson River during the migration months, and some linger through the summer.   Daintiest of the gulls that regularly visit the region in passing from winter to summer quarters or return is the Bonaparte's Gull (*Larus philadelphia*), black-headed like the Laughing Gull in the breeding season but so much smaller that it looks more like a seagoing dove than a gull.

Those are the five gulls that you can count on finding in our territory during the calendar year.   Those who have the patience to go over great flocks of Herring Gulls sitting on the water or ranging over the city dumps in winter will be rewarded now and then by finding a "white-winged gull" that will be either the Glaucous Gull (*Larus hyperboreus*), which is a bit larger than the Herring Gull, or the Iceland Gull (*Larus glaucoides*), which may be the size of the Herring Gull but more often is slightly smaller and trimmer and neater, especially around the head and bill.   Then there is the ocean-loving

Black-legged Kittiwake (*Rissa tridactyla*) that sweeps down from the north offshore in the winter but only occasionally is seen on land or along the shore if it is blown in by great storms.

The graceful terns with their sharp-pointed bills and forked tails are a difficult lot for most of us to unscramble. There are six species that occur with regularity in our region and four of them are so much alike in size, shape, color, and habit as to baffle the ordinary observer at any time and even the expert in some cases after the breeding season is over. These four have black caps, light gray mantles, pure white underparts, and at any distance it is hard to know one from the other as they wing their way steadily over the water or wheel and dive suddenly for the small fish on which they feed. They are largely migrants along our shores and, in some cases, over inland waters. The most abundant is the Common Tern (*Sterna hirundo*) with a rasping voice and a red bill tipped with black in the breeding season. Probably next in abundance, though far outnumbered by the Common Tern, is the Roseate Tern (*Sterna dougallii*) that may be known by its black bill and much sweeter notes. Or it may be that, on migration in some seasons, the Forster's Tern (*Sterna forsteri*) is second in abundance for this quartet over local waters. The least common of the group is the Arctic Tern (*Sterna paradisaea*) that wears an all-red bill in the breeding season and differs slightly in other ways from the other members of this group. It is not seen in our territory in the breeding season, of course, but it does breed as far south as Martha's Vineyard and numbers of such birds must pass through this region either coming or going on migration. Incidentally, the 22,000-mile round trip made by birds of this species that breed in the Arctic and winter in the Antarctic is the avian record for annual travel.

We have two other terns that put in an appearance regularly in this region, and happily there is no difficulty whatever in recognizing them when they are here. One is the almost toy-sized Least Tern (*Sterna albifrons*) that breeds sparingly in the general area along the ocean front, and in the breeding season has a bright yellow bill and a white patch on its forehead below its black cap. This little tern has a length of only 9 inches. The Black Tern (*Chlidonias niger*), which isn't much larger, breeds far inland but regularly appears — sometimes by the hundreds — in New York Harbor from about mid-August through September. Most terns dive headlong into the water when feeding but Black Terns as a rule merely swoop down close to the surface and daintily dip for food without wetting their feathers. They can be recognized at a distance by this butterfly type of flight.

We have occasional visits from larger terns that breed to the southward just as we have random visits from that magnificent offshore bird the Gannet (*Morus bassanus*) that breeds on the sheer faces of rocky cliffs along the shores of Newfoundland and Nova Scotia, but these can no more be counted upon than the rare glimpses of shearwaters, jaegers, or phalaropes from our ocean beaches. Such birds generally are storm-driven strays. I must mention, however, the Northern Phalarope (*Lobipes lobatus*) that, to my astonishment, I saw spinning about and dabbing rapidly for food in the water at the lower end of the Van Cortlandt swamp one day. Mostly they migrate far offshore. Among phalaropes the ordinary roles are reversed. The females do the courting and the males the housekeeping. That is, the males incubate the eggs and bring up the young.

About five years ago the Department of Parks gave a great lift to Nature Study in the city with the establishment of the Jamaica Bay Wildlife Refuge, a wide and watery area well suited for the entertainment of migrants of many kinds and a perfect place for summer residents that require marshy or sandy nesting sites. Within two years of the opening of the refuge Superintendent Herbert Johnson had under his watchful eye, among many other breeding birds, a colony of Black Skimmers (*Rynchops nigra*). These are colorful creatures that feed by flying close to the surface of the water with their lower bills actually cutting the water and acting as scoops or runways up which the food can be rushed into the gullet. This southern species has been extending its range northward in recent years and there were breeding records for Long Island, but this colony at the refuge was the first that I had heard of within the city limits.

But before we become enmeshed in the marsh birds that breed in the refuge we must take another look about the sea beaches and the waters offshore. If a loon is found on a beach it is either a sick bird or a dead one. Loons are not fitted for life on land. But offshore we can see the Common Loon (*Gavia immer*) and the Red-throated Loon (*Gavia stellata*) in the colder months. The Common Loon is almost abundant at times as a migrant and it appears in the Hudson River as well as on some of the larger lakes and reservoirs in the city. The Red-throated Loon sticks pretty well to salt water in our territory and fewer individuals linger through the winter. But there may be weeks in autumn when you will find more Red-throated Loons than Common Loons swimming offshore at Rockaway.

Of the grebes, or "hell-divers," the most common through the colder six months of the year is the Horned Grebe (*Podiceps auritus*) that can always be found along the coast or on Pelham Bay and other such waters from mid-October to mid-April. It is also a regular visitor to park lakes and city reservoirs. The little Pied-billed Grebe (*Podilymbus podiceps*) almost has the rank of permanent resident. It certainly nested within the area before the human population reached its current level and possibly it still does breed in some secluded watery nook within the city limits. It is common on park lakes and reservoirs and some individuals linger there until such bodies of water are frozen over, in which case they may take to salt water or move further south. However, the Pied-billed Grebe is most abundant as a migrant and I have seen a dozen or more of them at a time on the Van Cortlandt lake.

The Red-necked Grebe (*Podiceps grisegena*), which for years was called Holboell's Grebe and honored as a distinct species before it was reduced to the rank of a race of the Red-necked Grebe, is much less common than the Pied-billed and the Horned Grebe in the region but it is a regular migrant and usually sticks to salt water. It is seen more often in autumn than in spring and sometimes a few spend the winter in city waters. It is easily distinguished from its more abundant relatives by its larger size and longer and noticeably yellow bill. Other grebes wander in from the West now and then but the three mentioned are the only members of the group that can be counted on to be on hand with regularity as migrants or winter residents.

We have cormorants as common-to-abundant migrants and a few as winter residents. The debate centers around the comparatively few that spend the winter in these parts. The Double-crested Cormorant (*Phalacrocorax auritus*) that has large nesting colonies as far south as the coast of Massachusetts is the species commonly seen as a migrant and occasionally as a stray bird in summer or winter. However, the Great Cormorant (*Phalacrocorax carbo*), a larger bird that is common in Europe and breeds as far south as Nova Scotia on this side of the Atlantic, is the common wintering cormorant along the Massachusetts coast and undoubtedly some individuals reach our region. In fact, competent observers have identified such birds in city waters but, with some of these visitors in immature plumage to add to the confusion, this is a matter to be left to the experts. The cormorants that can be seen on rocks far out in Pelham Bay in winter are distinguishable as to species only by those who know both species well and can get near enough by boat, or telescope, to make a decision.

An odd thing about our petrels — the Mother Carey's Chickens of seafaring folk — is that the Leach's Petrel (*Oceanodroma leucorhoa*), which breeds on islands off the coast of Maine in late spring and early summer, is a rare sight over our waters whereas the Wilson's Petrel (*Oceanites oceanicus*), which breeds in the Antarctic and "winters" here in our summertime, is of regular occurrence offshore along the city's ocean beaches and often invades the bay. Bathers along the Rockaway beaches occasionally may see hundreds of these dark little birds with white rumps swirling and skittering over the surface of the ocean beyond the line of breakers. On scattered trips to Staten Island I sometimes saw single birds or small flocks sweeping swiftly and erratically over the waters of the Upper Bay, but that was because I was on the watch for them. They are so small, dark, and swift in flight over the dark background of the water that it's difficult to catch sight of them even when you are looking for them. Few ferry riders have any idea there are any such birds in the offing.

As a matter of fact, most ferry boat riders to and from Staten Island read newspapers all the way and wouldn't notice a flock of swans overhead or on the water. Not that we have swans there to be seen. But on quieter waters within the city limits we occasionally encounter the Mute Swan (*Cygnus olor*) of European origin and a bird of such notable longevity that Tennyson, in "Tithonus," put it in these words:

> Man comes and tills the field and lies beneath,
> And after many a summer dies the swan.

This is the species so often domesticated as a decorative feature of lakes and ponds on private estates or in public parks. What often happens on private estates is that the great white birds produce dark cygnets in such numbers in a few years that the owner finds himself with more swans than he bargained for, and the excess birds take to the wild with the full permission — or perhaps to the great relief — of the erstwhile owner. Wild Mute Swans of this kind are quite common on Long Island Sound, Great South Bay, and lakes and inlets around the Hamptons at the eastern end of Long Island. Wanderers from these and other flocks in the general area often turn up on

Pelham Bay, Jamaica Bay, the Hudson River, and other watery precincts of the city. Three Mute Swans lingered for a week in winter in the Harlem River Ship Canal where it broadens out toward Isham Park and the Columbia University boathouse. But our native Whistling Swan (*Olor columbianus*) of North America, which winters in numbers on Chesapeake Bay not far to the south, migrates west of the Hudson and is a rare sight indeed in our territory.

The Canada Geese that nest within the city limits, not always successfully because of marauders, are wanderers from the Bronx Zoo and other kept flocks in the region. I have seen as many as seven goslings grow to maturity out of one brood hatched in the Van Cortlandt swamp. But the wild birds merely rest on city waters in passing or fly overhead without stopping. Their smaller relative, the Brant (*Branta bernicla*), was scarce as a migrant or winter visitor for years when the Eelgrass failed along the Atlantic Coast, but now that the Eelgrass has returned to its ancient haunts, the birds have appeared on schedule again as migrants over or winter visitors on the coastal waters of the city. I have seen as many as a thousand or more at a time on the water within the confines of the Jamaica Bay Wildlife Refuge.

As for ducks, the supply on the premises depends upon the season. In winter we are overwhelmed with them. In summer we are poverty-stricken. The only one that can be relied on as a permanent resident is the Black Duck (*Anas rubripes*) and even this species breeds only sparingly within the city limits. The only other regular breeder is the beautiful and gentle Wood Duck (*Aix sponsa*) that has an uninterrupted breeding record in the Van Cortlandt swamp from as far back as anybody has kept record. Even when the WPA vandals of the Great Depression Era of a quarter of a century ago went through the swamp cutting down all the dead trees just to make work for idle hands, the Wood Ducks somehow managed to bring off a brood or two in the area. Even the motor parkway construction and the more recent intrusion of five golf holes of the public links on terrain that used to be swampland has not discouraged them. Every year I see in the swamp or on the nearby lake a mother Wood Duck with attendant ducklings.

Some thirty years ago, in what was then the upper part of the swamp but is now an open basin beside the Henry Hudson Parkway, I saw a female moving slowly down the little stream with fifteen ducklings trailing behind her, the ducklings so small that they couldn't have been long out of the shell. On another occasion I saw a mother with twelve ducklings. Wood Ducks have bred elsewhere within the city limits and perhaps they still do, but the Van Cortlandt swamp is the best known and the never failing breeding ground of the species within the confines of New York City. I have seen Wood Ducks there every month in the year but ordinarily they are summer residents that arrive in late March and depart in October or early November. I could write indefinitely of these charming and beautiful birds and tell of the broods over which I watched anxiously and of their "moving accidents by flood and field" but, to spare the reader and the printer, I desist.

Our other ducks come to us either as migrants or winter residents, often in great numbers. The "tip-up" or dabbling ducks prefer fresh water, of course, and the Van Cortlandt swamp and nearby lake provide them with food and safe harborage on their migration flights. Here in the fall and again in the spring we have goodly numbers of American Widgeon (*Mareca americana*), with just an occasional European Widgeon (*Mareca penelope*) among them. The Mallard (*Anas platyrhynchos*), which formerly was scarce, is seen in increasing numbers each season, but these are few to the hordes that pour along the westerly flyways of the continent. The Gadwall (*Anas strepera*), also a westerner like the Mallard, is being reported fairly frequently in our territory now and perhaps would be reported more often if more persons knew it when they see it. The elegant and graceful Pintail (*Anas acuta*) is a common

Mallards in Central Park

migrant and an occasional winter resident but I never have seen any numbers of this species on the lake at Van Cortlandt at any one time. Like all the other ducks of this group, it will take to salt water when the fresh water reaches are frozen over.

Those smallest of our ducks, the Green-winged Teal (*Anas carolinensis*) and the Blue-winged Teal (*Anas discors*), often pitch into the lake or pop up suddenly out of the swamp in small flocks of half a dozen or so birds. Once, on a park lake in the Borough of Queens, I saw a European Teal (*Anas crecca*) — over there they simply call it "the" Teal — that wears a horizontal white stripe above its wing and thus is easily distinguished from our Green-winged Teal of much the same appearance but with a vertical white mark in front of its wing. That, at least, is the way the males present themselves in their wedding garments, but females and immatures and the males in eclipse plumage are something else again. A good field guide to birds is the only answer to the problem of sorting them out. I used to find small flocks of teal — the Green-winged more often than the Blue-winged — in the Van Cortlandt swamp as late as December, but they always disappeared when the area froze over.

Long Island is a fine place to go duck hunting with field glasses. The Riverdale–Van Cortlandt region is much better for spring warblers. On that basis Edwin Way Teale and I exchanged visits for some years. In February or March I would meet him at his home in Baldwin, Long Island, and we would spend the day looking for ducks on ponds, lakes, ocean inlets, and the waters offshore. In revenge, he would join me in Van Cortlandt Park in mid-May and together we would check over the throngs of warblers passing through the area. It was mutually profitable, aside from the companionship. He saw spring warblers in Van Cortlandt Park that he might have missed if he had stayed at home, and I saw waterfowl on Long Island that I have yet to see on the Van Cortlandt lake or the adjacent swamp. Always on the Long Island expeditions I saw the Shoveler (*Spatula clypeata*) — sometimes as many as four or five — and never yet have I encountered this brightly colored, shovel-billed duck in the Van Cortlandt swamp or on the lake, though either would make a good stopover for it on migration. Like the Mallard and Gadwall, it is largely a western duck, but it appears regularly in small numbers in our general region on migration and I have not given up hope yet of finding it in my favorite swamp.

The diving-duck group is the one that provides our rivers, bays, and ocean front with great rafts of waterfowl each winter. The most abundant by far on city waters is the Greater Scaup (*Aythya marila*) that winters by the hundreds in the Hudson River and by the thousands on Pelham Bay, Flushing Bay, Jamaica Bay, the Lower Bay, and other such stretches of salt water within the city limits. The Lesser Scaup (*Aythya affinis*), which is slightly smaller and has a purple instead of a green sheen on its head, is just as regular in attendance as its larger relative but it occurs in much fewer numbers and it favors fresh water instead of salt. It never fails to visit Van Cortlandt lake and usually lingers until ice drives it off in late December or January. It appears again when the ice goes out in late winter or early spring. The same thing may be said for the Ring-necked Duck (*Aythya collaris*), which is found more often on our park lakes and reservoirs than on the salt-water reaches of the region.

As far back as 1914 I saw the Redhead (*Aythya americana*) and the Canvasback (*Aythya valisineria*) on the Jerome Reservoir in the Bronx, but since then they seem to have shifted winter quarters to a great extent. Canvasback now winter by the hundreds in Pelham Bay and Little Neck Bay and the Red-head I have not seen for years in the area, though I have been told it occurs sparingly and irregularly. "Whistler" is really a good name for the chunky but beautifully marked Common Goldeneye (*Bucephala clangula*) that is a regular winter resident with us in large numbers. It is no trick at all to identify Gold-eneyes in flight without bothering to look at them, so distinctive is the sound made by their wings in beating the air. They appear "all over the place" in the colder months. You can find them along the ocean front, in the bays, on the rivers, and, unless they are frozen over, on the reservoirs and park lakes.

Much the same thing can be said for the dainty little Buffle-head (*Bucephala albeola*), except that it doesn't favor the open ocean nor does it occur in such numbers in the depth of winter. On the other hand, the almost piebald and notably long-tailed Oldsquaw (*Clangula hyemalis*), whose queer gabble has earned the duck the name of "South Southerly" among hunters on Chesapeake Bay, loves to swim offshore and doesn't seem to mind wild winds and breaking waves. It is common along the ocean front in winter but less common on our quieter waters. I once saw a female King Eider (*Somateria spectabilis*) in the Hudson River near the Riverdale railroad and on another note-worthy occasion a male Harlequin Duck (*Histrionicus histrioni-cus*) on an inlet at Far Rockaway, but these were mere strays, though they were obliging enough to remain around for days and give many observers a chance to add two more distinguished visitors to their city lists. There is nothing strange, however, in seeing the Ruddy Duck (*Oxyura jamaicensis*) in the region in round numbers in the colder months. They prefer fresh water to salt water, and quiet water to rough water, which often is much the same thing. I have seen as many as sixty at a time on the Jerome Reservoir and I am told that others have seen more than a hundred there in a day.

The scoters are largely or almost entirely salt-water addicts with us and spend the winter in bays and on the ocean off our beaches. Now and then a few of them turn up on reservoirs or one of the larger park lakes but the best places to look for scoters is offshore beyond the surf line. By all odds the most abundant with us is the White-winged Scoter (*Melanitta deglandi*) that sometimes can be counted by the thousands from Coney Island to Far Rockaway. Far fewer in number is the Surf Scoter (*Melanitta perspicillata*) that is often called "Skunkhead" for the black and white pattern of its head fore and aft. Even less common but regular as a migrant or winter resident is the — paradoxically in our region — Common Scoter (*Oidemia nigra*), our only scoter (our only diving duck, for that matter) with completely black plumage.

Patience, reader! We are almost out of the water. We have only the Coot (*Fulica americana*), the Common Gallinule (*Gallinula chloropus*), and our three fish-eating ducks, the mergansers, to consider before we reach solid ground. The "white-nosed" Coot, often called the Marsh Hen, is a regular transient through our region, though I never have seen it in any great numbers at one time. It prefers fresh water to salt water. In autumn I have seen as many as five or six Coots lingering for days on the Van Cortlandt lake and some hardy individuals will linger until really cold weather sets in. Incidentally, hunters and fishermen usually refer to the scoters as "coots" or "bay coots" and often are hard to convince that the true Coot, of which salt-water gunners and fishermen see little, is quite a different bird.

On the morning of April 29, 1933, I was walking along what was then Riverdale Avenue and now is a segment of the Henry Hudson Parkway when, at about 250th Street, I picked up a large dead bird from the sidewalk. Just then a police prowl car came along with two officers aboard. I hailed the car and showed the corpse to the minions of the law. They stared at it. Never had seen anything like that before, they vowed. What was it — some fancy kind of chicken? I told them that it was a defunct Common Gallinule that seemed to have suffered a broken neck through hitting one of the telephone wires overhead while migrating at night. The officers were astonished that such things happened on their beat.

These large and rather tame birds bred year after year in the Van Cortlandt swamp and often I saw a clucking mother, looking very much like a dark-bodied, red-nosed, seagoing hen, leading a brood of half a dozen or more young along the edge of the cattails or across an expanse of lily pads in the lower section of the marsh. But apparently they were too tame for their own good and were easy targets for rowdies with stones picked from the railway ballast providentially at hand. The last brood I noted in the marsh was in 1940. Perhaps they still breed somewhere else within the city limits but of that I have no knowledge. All the birds I have seen in recent years in the area were transients.

The mergansers, or sheldrakes, may not be good eating but they certainly are good-looking. At least, the males are strikingly handsome in their courting costumes. The Red-breasted Merganser (*Mergus serrator*) is an abundant migrant and common winter resident on the salt-water reaches within the city limits, whereas the Common Merganser (*Mergus merganser*) prefers fresh water and occurs in respectable numbers on the larger park lakes, the city reservoirs and the Hudson River from the George Washington Bridge northward. The lower section of the river is too crowded with traffic for comfort and the bay is too salty for its taste. The lovely little Hooded Merganser

Common Mergansers

(*Lophodytes cucullatus*), with the white-centered erectile crest as the feature of the well-dressed male, is a regular migrant in small but increasing numbers on the ponds, lakes, and reservoirs of our territory. It has no fondness for salt water but I have seen it on the Hudson River at Riverdale. More often I found it on the lake or in the swamp in Van Cortlandt Park or on the Jerome Reservoir, but never more than a few at a time. Yet on Playland Lake in Westchester I have seen half a hundred that stayed on the premises for weeks in late autumn. It's good to know it occurs in such numbers in the metropolitan region.

Now we are definitely out of the water and on the beach. Here on the sands and on the mud flats of the bays and inlets at low tide we find shore birds of many kinds in abundance during migration and at least a few species at any time of year. The inevitable beach bird of the area is the Sanderling (*Crocethia alba*). It is technically a migrant and, running in and out with each retreating and advancing wave, pours along our beaches in a steady stream of peak volume northward in late May and southward the last week in August. For all that, I have seen occasional small flocks of Sanderlings along our ocean front during every month of the year.

Another smaller, darker, and less hardy beach bird that feeds at the water's edge in running and flitting flocks is the Semi-palmated Sandpiper (*Ereunetes pusillus*) that probably is our most abundant shore bird. This is one of the four species of small sandpipers that are loosely grouped under the name of "Peeps." Probably they all look exactly alike to persons who do not make a habit of scanning the flocks carefully at close range with field glasses to pick out details such as the black legs of the "Semipals," the greenish or greenish-yellow legs of the slightly smaller Least Sandpiper (*Erolia minutilla*), the white patch near the base of the tail that easily betrays the slightly larger White-rumped Sandpiper (*Erolia fuscicollis*), and the heavier bill with the slight downward curve at the tip by which the Western Sandpiper (*Ereunetes mauri*) may be known from the "Semipal" it otherwise so much resembles. The Least Sandpiper, the smallest of our shore birds, prefers the mud flats to the ocean beaches as a feeding ground. Both the White-rump and the Western Sandpiper are scarce in our region as spring migrants but they turn up regularly in the autumn, usually arriving a little later than the much more abundant Least Sandpipers and "Semipals."

An early migrant in spring and a truly late migrant in autumn is the Dunlin (*Erolia alpina*), which, as veteran birders know, is the old Red-backed Sandpiper traveling under the new name conferred upon it by the hierarchy of American ornithology. During the fall migration this chunky sandpiper with the bill bent down at the tip doesn't put in an appearance on our beaches and mud flats until most of the other shore birds have departed for the South. It regularly lingers into December and, if the weather doesn't turn too cold, some individuals winter here. Even hardier than the Dunlin is the Purple Sandpiper (*Erolia maritima*) that comes to us only as a winter visitor in small numbers. The place to look for it is on weed-covered rocks that are exposed as the tide goes out. At high tide it may be found resting on rocks along the shore or jutting out of the water, or perhaps on stone jetties or breakwaters.

If they are passing out new names again perhaps the Purple

Sandpiper should be rebaptized the Rock Sandpiper. By the
same token, perhaps the Pectoral Sandpiper (*Erolia melanotos*)
might become the Grass Sandpiper. Though it does feed on
mud flats with other sandpipers it is frequently found in grass-
covered sections of the marshes and even in wet meadows.
Often I have found Pectorals poking about during migration
in shallow rain pools on grassy flatlands. The straight line
that cuts off the stripes on its breast gives it a neat appearance.
It is a fairly common migrant through our territory but it never
bunches up in platoons or battalions like the Short-billed
Dowitcher (*Limnodromus griseus*) on the mud flats of our salt
marshes in late July. The first southbound Dowitchers usually
appear wearing most of the rich brown garb of the breeding
season, but as the weeks wear on the color gradually fades to
the dark gray and white of the winter plumage.

The Knot (*Calidris canutus*) is another shore-bird migrant
that starts back in late July or early August with breast patches
of reddish-brown left over from its spring finery that long ago
earned it the nickname of "robin snipe." Late birds of the
season, however, wear a smooth and almost snowy gray costume. We must not overlook the only "shore bird" — it also
is quite at home along inland rivers, lakes, and ponds — that
stays with us throughout the warmer half of the year and breeds
regularly in our region. That's the familiar Spotted Sandpiper (*Actitis macularia*) or Teeter-tail, as it is often called because of the way it keeps swaying its hindparts up and down.
The real inland sandpiper is the Solitary Sandpiper (*Tringa
solitaria*) that prefers fresh water to salt and is a common
migrant through our territory on its way to and from its breeding grounds around the lakes and along the rivers of Canada.

Long ago on a rainy April night I was standing on the sidewalk at Columbus Circle, hoping that an empty taxi would
come along, when down through the drizzle and the darkness
above the myriad lights of that city circus came a familiar and
delightful sound that I had heard more often by day in far

lonelier places. It was the clear, mellow, triple whistle of a Greater Yellowlegs (*Totanus melanoleucus*) that was migrating overhead in the inky atmosphere. These birds we have in fair numbers in spring and greater numbers during the fall flight, mostly on coastal marshes and mud flats, but a few always put in an appearance on the Van Cortlandt lake or in the swamp. The Lesser Yellowlegs (*Totanus flavipes*), exactly like the Greater except that it is on a smaller scale and has a shorter and less melodious call, is scarce in the spring with us but common to abundant on the southward journey in August and September.

Willets, curlews, and godwits might be ranked as tall and distinguished visitors along our ocean front but they turn up in such scant numbers during most seasons that, for most of us, meeting with any one of them within the city limits would have to be counted a stroke of luck. We shall leave them and some of our rare sandpipers to the experts who know where and when to look for them and are persistent on patrol. But the Woodcock (*Philohela minor*) and the Common Snipe (*Capella gallinago*) are fairly common on fresh-water marshes and in swamps during their migration periods and it's possible that a few breed on the premises. It is certain that they breed regularly on the outskirts of the city. Often in the deep dusk over the breeding grounds you can hear the winnowing flight of the Snipe and the harsh *beep-beep-beep* of the Woodcock on the ground before it flutters aloft to drop its thin little cascade of bubbling notes over the wet meadow or alder swamp on its downward flight.

Of the half-dozen rails that occur in the fresh- and salt-water marshes of the region the most common is the little Virginia Rail (*Rallus limicola*) that almost deserves the rank of permanent resident. I frequently have seen these birds in the Van Cortlandt swamp in winter and at almost each fresh fall of snow you can see the tracks they made crossing the golfers' causeway that cuts the lower marsh. The King Rail (*Rallus elegans*), which is an "elephant edition" of the Virginia Rail in color and pattern, has nested in the region — Allan Cruickshank recorded a successful nesting in the Van Cortlandt swamp in 1927 — but its visits to my favorite swamp have been irregular and infrequent of late years. The less colorful, slightly smaller, and much noisier Clapper Rail (*Rallus longirostris*) prefers the salt marshes and breeds in Jamaica Bay and similar areas. Some Clapper Rail linger through the winter and the species is logged regularly on the Christmas Census.

The snub-nosed Sora (*Porzana carolina*) is a summer resident with a strong preference for fresh-water marshes and it can be seen — or more often heard — in the cattail region at the lower end of the Van Cortlandt swamp and the upper end of the lake. I never have seen the tiny Black Rail (*Laterallus jamaicensis*) within the city limits (it's no bigger than a sparrow and very difficult to flush) but it has been recorded from the salt marshes along the ocean front and quite possibly breeds there. The Yellow Rail (*Coturnicops noveboracensis*) turns up more often dead than alive in our territory. It isn't much bigger than the Black Rail and is just as secretive but, given a chance, it would be much easier to recognize because of its yellow plumage and a white wing-patch that shows in flight. However, most of the local records are of birds that were picked up dead as a result of striking obstacles when migrating at night. One such Yellow Rail corpse was picked up at the base of the wire fence along the golfers' causeway across the Van Cortlandt marsh. I never have seen the bird alive in the region but the fallen bodies prove that it does pass this way with some regularity and therefore we should be on the watch for it.

Of the plover group the familiar and colorful Killdeer (*Charadrius vociferus*), which is well named in both English and Latin, is a fairly common summer resident on bare open ground in all five boroughs of the city. It is also found in the depths of winter in the Pelham Bay region and on the flat plains of Queens and Brooklyn along the ocean front. The only other member of the group that deserves the rank of sum-

Killdeer

mer resident is the pale and plaintive Piping Plover (*Charadrius melodus*) that, even at a short distance, fades into the background of sand of the upper beach where it feeds and breeds. Its nest is a mere depression in the sand and the four eggs it usually lays are astonishingly large for such a small bird. The Piping Plover is by no means abundant and only scattered pairs are found here and there, mostly on the upper step of the ocean beaches. It is, of course, a regular transient in greater numbers along the same ocean beaches.

The American Golden Plover (*Pluvialis dominica*), noted for the length of its migration flights, the Black-bellied Plover (*Squatarola squatarola*), and the little Semipalmated Plover (*Charadrius semipalmatus*) are regular transients along our shores and tidal flats. The Semipalmated Plover, commonly called Ringneck, is abundant and the Blackbellies often appear in considerable numbers but the Golden Plover is rare in our region in spring and in the autumn is outnumbered at least twenty to one by the Blackbellies among which it often travels. In their fall traveling costumes the Blackbellies and Golden Plover are much similar in appearance when on the ground but in flight the dark tails of the Golden Plover stand out in contrast to the white (seemingly — they are actually finely barred) tails of the Blackbellies. The only other member of the group that is common in the region is the short-legged, orange-footed, and highly colorful — especially when on the wing — Ruddy Turnstone (*Arenaria interpres*) that usually sticks to the tidal stretches during migrations. It prefers rocky headlands and pebbled beaches to pure sand or mud flats but, on migration at least, a bird has to settle for what it finds along the way, which is why you may encounter the Turnstone anywhere along the edge of salt water on its trips through our territory.

The tallest bird regularly visiting our marshes and swamp-lands is the Great Blue Heron (*Ardea herodias*) that sometimes carries its head 4 feet or more above its usually water-covered toes. It is more frequently seen along the coast than inland but it does turn up in local swamps and around the edges of ponds and park lakes. Never a year passes without a Great Blue Heron or two dropping into the Van Cortlandt swamp to sample the food supply there for a few hours or a few days. On our salt marshes it is common as a transient and regular as a winter resident in small numbers.

On July 16, 1916, three tall white birds were found feeding quietly in one of the little canals that were a feature of the "Dutch Garden" then maintained in the southwest corner of Van Cortlandt Park. They were seen by Dr. Samuel Harms-worth Chubb of the American Museum of Natural History, identified by him as Common — or as they were then called, American — Egrets (*Casmerodius albus*), and the photographs he took of the birds were reproduced in a story about the whole affair in the *New York Times*. The substance of the feature story was that here were egrets from the Everglades spending the summer (they did stay for weeks) within sight and sound of a subway terminal in a New York City park. Thousands of persons came to stare at them and hundreds photographed them.

But in twoscore and two years the egret situation has had a drastic change for the better. Under protection by law from the pirates of the feather trade, egrets have increased greatly in numbers over their entire range in the United States and also have been extending their breeding range northward.

Now the Common Egret that caused such a stir on a long ago visit to Van Cortlandt Park actually breeds within the city limits at the Jamaica Bay Wildlife Refuge and so does the smaller and daintier Snowy Egret (*Leucophoyx thula*) that once was a rarity in the region. Since the young of the Little Blue Heron (*Florida caerulea*) appear frequently in our region in their first-year plumage of pure white, that gives us three tall white birds that may be met in our swamps or on our marshes after midsummer, which is generally the time when the Little Blue youngsters begin to appear. There is no trouble, however, in distinguishing one from the other at any reasonable distance. The Common Egret has a yellow bill and is a foot taller than the others. The Snowy Egret's sharp black bill and black legs — its yellow toes may be out of sight under water — are in decided contrast to the coarser and paler bills and legs of the young Little Blue Heron.

Putting any stress on these white waders in our waters is pure swank. The humble little Green Heron (*Butorides virescens*) is the only common to abundant summer resident and breeder of the group. It is not a colony nester like most of its relatives. Pairs go off to nest by themselves and they prefer low branches extending out over the water if they can find such a site. The bulky Black-crowned Night Heron (*Nycticorax nycticorax*) breeds in the Jamaica Bay Wildlife Refuge but many of the adults that are seen flying over or feeding in our marshes and swamps during the warmer months must come from rookeries beyond the city limits on Long Island and in Westchester and New Jersey. Certainly the wave of mottled immature birds that hits the city in the late summer must come from the outside. Since many hardy individuals winter in our salt marshes, we have Black-crowned Night Herons with us every month of the year.

Though there are breeding records for the Yellow-crowned Night Heron (*Nyctanassa violacea*) to the north of us, its real range is southward, and over a span of fifty years I have seen it less than a dozen times in the Van Cortlandt swamp. However, others have reported random birds somewhere on or over city territory every year, so it must be set down as a regular summer visitor in small numbers. As for that hollow-booming bird with the upward look when at rest, the American Bittern (*Botaurus lentiginosus*), I find it every spring and autumn in the Van Cortlandt swamp and sometimes two or three birds lingered until a hard freeze came to spoil their feeding ground. On several occasions in the spring I have seen it give off its "pumping" notes, a most ludicrous performance during which the odd bird seems to be bent desperately on clearing its throat or even emptying its stomach. I believe it formerly bred in the swamp but if it has bred in the area lately it has escaped my notice.

The delightful little Least Bittern (*Ixobrychus exilis*) enables us to end this chapter on a happy note. When I last looked it was still breeding in that same swamp and quite possibly in other favorable locations within the city limits. It's a small bird and doesn't need a great feeding ground. You can see it almost any day from mid-May to mid-September if you stand still long enough on the stretch of railroad track separating the marsh at the lower end of the Van Cortlandt swamp from the little section of marsh at the upper end of the lake. Sooner or later a Least Bittern will lift itself above the cattails and flap slowly in the clear before dropping down out of sight again. It may even fly across the track from one cattail area to the other. All you need is patience. And if you have read this far in this book, you have not only patience but endurance. Surely you will see the lovely Least Bittern.

Chapter 14

The Upland Birds

Now we have emerged from the marshes, those "haunts of coot and hern," and we shall stick to solid ground as we attempt a survey of the upland birds of our region, those we find in the city parks and cemeteries and what other parcels and patches of greenery there remain within the city limits. As a matter of fact, this is no small matter. The Department of Parks alone offers some forty square miles of grass and trees to resident or transient upland birds and there are private estates and "undeveloped acreage" in the outlying sections of the city to add to the park property as a lure or a refuge for birds. We have, indeed, so many kinds of upland birds with us in the course of a year that, to maintain any semblance of order in going even lightly over the field, we shall follow as closely as possible the family lines as set down in systematic arrangement in the latest *Check-list* issued by the American Ornithologists' Union.

Thus we shall start with the birds of prey and a lyric line from Kipling: "The wild hawk to the wind-swept sky." From time immemorial and in many languages, men have made the hawk a symbol of wildness. Yet one of the fiercest and fastest of North American hawks frequently is seen plunging through the canyons of midtown Manhattan or perched moodily on a skyscraper ledge in the Wall Street district. This is the heavy-shouldered, sickle-winged Peregrine Falcon (*Falco peregrinus*) of medieval song and story, the favorite falcon of royalty in the age of chivalry. At least it's the American cousin of the famed European bird. For long years on this side of the Atlantic we called it the Duck Hawk but, since our bird is merely a subspecies or geographical race of the European species, the older English name is now official in this country.

Under either name, this bird of a mere 18 inches or so of body length is a swift and fearless warrior on the wing. No other bird of our skies can match it in boldness or speed and there is good evidence that it can dive on its prey at a speed of better than one hundred miles an hour. It lives almost exclusively on other birds that it overtakes and captures or strikes down in full flight. Its favorite nesting place is a ledge high up on the face of a sheer cliff but it has nested in the eaves and cornices of business buildings or spired churches in bustling cities. In our region it nests regularly on the face of the Palisades, but a pair successfully nested and raised two young just under the roof of a Brooklyn office building and another pair didn't give up an attempt to nest on the roof of the St. Regis Hotel in midtown Manhattan until they were captured with nets and carried protesting from the premises. The reason for the eviction was that the prospective nesters struck fiercely at the tenants of the adjacent penthouse on the St. Regis roof every time the hotel patrons attempted to go in or out of their lofty lodgings.

The main reason for the repeated appearances of these wild birds in a big city is the abundance of Pigeons that they can

capture with ease and dine on at leisure. More than once I looked out of the window of an office I occupied on the twenty-eighth floor of 444 Madison Avenue and saw a Peregrine cruising over the rooftops stretching toward the East River. Now and then a Peregrine picked a favorite perch, where it could be seen at intervals every day for a number of weeks before it moved to other quarters. On one occasion — I remember it was a rainy morning in early April — I helped lower a falcon enthusiast, Richard Herbert, on a rope over the edge of the roof of a forty-story apartment house on Central Park West because he suspected that a Peregrine had a "scrape," or nest, on the metal shelf of a ventilator just under the roof of the building. The bird had been loafing around the shelf for several weeks. However, she proved to be a deceitful female. Our friend at the end of the rope found no eggs or nesting material. But to this day the newspaper offices of the city receive occasional phone calls telling of "pigeon hawks" in action around downtown buildings. The informants know the birds are "pigeon hawks" because they have just seen one catch a Pigeon, and perhaps they add that the hawk has perched nearby and is calmly devouring its prey.

In this way we know that there may be a Peregrine or two somewhere in or over the city at any time, but we must remember that a few Peregrines go a long way. They are never plentiful anywhere at any time, even in the wilderness. Our true Pigeon Hawk (*Falco columbarius*), which is about the size of a Pigeon, is a transient through our region. It is regular and sometimes fairly common along the coastal strip on its southward migration in September but is scarce inland and often slips by unrecognized. The one falcon that many city dwellers see and know is the handsome little Sparrow Hawk (*Falco sparverius*), a permanent resident of all five boroughs and a self-advertiser through its *killy-killy-killy* cries and its habit of perching on telephone poles, treetops, television antennae, or other such exposed positions. It nests in holes in trees or buildings or even in openings in the brickwork of apartment houses.

A bird that is mentioned only with bated breath, even by experts, is the Gyrfalcon (*Falco rusticolus*), the giant of the group and an Arctic resident that occasionally puts in an appearance along the city's ocean front in winter. It is truly a rare bird in our region, which means that it's a great day for a watcher who sees one. Compared to the Gyrfalcon, eagles are ordinary sights in our territory. At least it is true of our national bird, the Bald Eagle (*Haliaeetus leucocephalus*), that is a winter visitor of regular occurrence in fair numbers along our waterways. When the Hudson River is full of ice floes and the tide is running out, anyone who stands on the Spuyten Duyvil or Riverdale shore is almost sure to see at least one Bald Eagle if he sweeps the river with field glasses and looks for a big black blob amid the floating ice. I have seen as many as six on the ice at one time. When the outgoing tide carries them down near the George Washington Bridge, however, they take off and fly up the river again. The Golden Eagle (*Aquila chrysaetos*) must migrate through our region in limited numbers but it is only rarely reported, possibly because it is not distinguished from the immature Bald Eagles in their all-dark plumage.

It's curious that the Turkey Vulture (*Cathartes aura*), which is occasionally seen in flight over city territory, rarely sets foot on the ground in any of the five boroughs. A logical place for it would be at the city dumps and almost certainly it will become common there in the future, because it is steadily increasing as a breeding species in New York, Connecticut, and Massachusetts. As far back as when I was a boy it nested regularly in Dutchess County, where I often saw it during my vacation days on a farm. But in all my years of looking for birds within the city limits, I saw the Turkey Vulture only once and then it was soaring high over Riverdale and drifting steadily toward New Jersey.

Of the Accipiters, the short-winged hawks that give the soaring and beneficial hawks a bad name in farming country, the rate of occurrence varies inversely as the size. The smallest, the Sharp-shinned Hawk (*Accipiter striatus*), is a common transient and not long ago bred sparingly in the outlying wooded sections of the city. The next larger bird of the group, the Cooper's Hawk (*Accipiter cooperii*), is not such a common transient as the little "Sharpie" but a few individuals are more likely to spend the winter in the region. The largest of the trio, the strong and fierce Goshawk (*Accipiter gentilis*), is no more than an occasional winter visitor when the season northward is particularly severe. But don't count on finding a Goshawk on the premises, even if the mercury drops below zero and a wild snowstorm is whirling out of the North.

Of the Buteo or soaring hawk group of much persecuted but truly beneficial birds, three are common and often abundant transients in autumn migration. These are the familiar Redtailed Hawk (*Buteo jamaicensis*), the equally familiar Redshouldered Hawk (*Buteo lineatus*), and the smaller Broad-winged Hawk (*Buteo platypterus*). All three species bred regularly in three of the five boroughs — Queens, Richmond, and the Bronx — within the past twoscore years but unquestionably only a scant few now find nesting sites within the city limits. The Redtail, however, is a regular winter resident in small numbers and the Redshoulder an occasional one. The fourth member of this soaring group, the Rough-legged Hawk (*Buteo lagopus*), breeds in the Far North and is only a transient or winter visitor anywhere in the United States as a rule. It is "logged" regularly in small numbers by observers checking our salt marshes and ocean front during Christmas counts but it is rare elsewhere in the region. My journals contain only one record for the Riverdale sector — a dark bird on a dark February day in 1951 hunting an open slope along the bank of the Hudson River.

It should be mentioned that the skies over the city are a regular hawk highway during autumn migration in September and October and, when wind and sun are favorable, the flights can be spectacular. There were days when I sat on a ridge in the eastern section of Van Cortlandt Park — and even on the upper porch of my Riverdale home — and watched an endless succession of hawks pass high overhead from the northeast to the southwest. One late October afternoon, while sitting in the west stand at Baker Field at the northern tip of Manhattan Island watching Columbia and Navy play football, I noticed some hawks working westward in circles over the playing field. After that, being armed with field glasses, it was easy for me to keep score of the hawks aloft as well as of the game below me on the gridiron. Before the game ended in a Navy victory I had run up a score of eighty-eight hawks, some so high that they were mere specks in the sky. All that were low enough to be identified were either Redtails or Redshoulders, with Redtails predominating.

This, however, verges on the commonplace. It was a baseball game between New York University and some collegiate rival on Ohio Field above the east bank of the Harlem that resulted in a real ornithological record for New York City. About thirty and a few-odd years ago a group of lively young fellows formed the Bronx County Bird Club and often I heard and saw them going "a-whoopin' and a-hollerin'" through the cattail region of the Van Cortlandt marsh, clapping hands loudly at the same time. The din was supposed to — and frequently did — stir up rails that might otherwise be left unseen amid the cattails and marsh grasses. Three members of that lively group were Roger Tory Peterson, now internationally famous as a painter-naturalist, Dr. Joseph J. Hickey, for some years now an ecologist and ornithologist on the staff of the University of Wisconsin, and Allan Cruickshank, noted bird photographer and Audubon Society lecturer. On the afternoon of April 30, 1928, the then redheaded Joe Hickey, student at N.Y.U. and track athlete who won the outdoor intercollegiate one-mile championship in the Harvard stadium, had Allan Cruickshank with him at the ball game at Ohio Field when they looked up and saw a Swallow-tailed Kite (*Elanoides forficatus*) wheeling about in spectacular flight above the diamond and the competing baseball teams. So far as I know, this is the only record for that more southern and western bird within the city limits.

We have only two more of the hawk tribe that are regularly seen in the area. One is the graceful Marsh Hawk (*Circus cyaneus*) that might be ranked a common transient and an uncommon permanent resident of the salt-marsh sectors of the city. At least, Marsh Hawks are seen sweeping over such marshes methodically through all the months of the year, though they are decidedly scarce in summer. Since breeding records within the city limits have dwindled almost to the point of disappearance, perhaps these summer birds are non-breeders or foragers from some nesting site beyond the legal boundaries of the city. A few individuals comb the cattail marsh in Van Cortlandt Park each year during migration, but the place to look for the low-flying harriers is along the tidal marshes and the dunes behind the ocean beaches.

The last of the tribe is the Osprey (*Pandion haliaetus*), often called the Fish Hawk for the best of reasons, since it lives entirely on fish it catches in spectacular feet-first plunges into the water. Of all the birds of land, sea, and air, this is the most widespread species. It ranges the shores of the larger bodies of water everywhere in the world except in the Arctic and Antarctic. It breeds to the south and to the north of us, and is locally common as a breeder at the eastern end of Long Island, but within the city limits it is now only a fairly common transient, mostly along the ocean front and tidal-flat areas. However, I have seen it lift a fish — just in passing — from the Hudson River off Riverdale and it has even condescended to plunge into the Van Cortlandt lake for prey on occasion. Indeed, one Osprey discovered it was so easy to pick up a living there that it lingered by the lake for several weeks in the autumn of 1954.

Here the *Check-list* would have us delve into the pheasants, quails, doves, and cuckoos but, since we have been at grips with birds of prey, we might better continue in that department and round up those winged predators that hunt mostly at night and are more often heard than seen, the owls of the region. It is difficult to check on resident or transient owls but it is well established that the little Screech Owl (*Otus asio*) still breeds in the parks and in the outlying sections of the city and often is heard giving its hollow tremulous call in the deep twilight or just before dawn. There are also recent nesting records for the very valuable but rather nasty-tempered Barn Owl (*Tyto alba*) and that mighty hunter with talons as strong as steel and as sharp as ice picks, the Great Horned Owl (*Bubo virginianus*). However, such nesting Barn Owls and Great Horned Owls are few and far between and always the fear is that the latest brood will be the last on record for the city proper.

The famous Hemlock Grove in the New York Botanical Garden in the Bronx is a popular resort for transient or wintering owls, the Barred Owl (*Strix varia*) in particular, though the Long-eared Owl (*Asio otus*) turns up there regularly, too. These last are quite gregarious and I have seen half a dozen sitting silently and solemnly within a few feet of one another some thirty feet above ground in evergreens in late February and early March. The delightful and strangely tame little Saw-whet Owl (*Aegolius acadicus*), which sometimes can be picked gently off a perch by hand, is what might be called an irregular winter wanderer in our area. The Short-eared Owl (*Asio flammeus*) is an odd character among its fellows in that it steers clear of evergreens, prefers open territory such as moors and marshlands, and has no objection to hunting by daylight, at least on overcast days. Indeed, I have seen it sweeping the tidal flats like a Marsh Hawk during the colder months of the year.

In that same tidal region and along the ocean beaches we might keep a sharp eye out for the Snowy Owl (*Nyctea scanaiaca*) on a winter day. Not every year, however. It depends on an irregular cycle to the northward. When the Snowy Owl population is high and the lemming population is low on the arctic

tundra, these beautiful black-flecked white birds move southward by the hundreds in search of food, and there have been
winters during which they invaded the New York region in
force. One brisk January day I approached a couple of car-
penters who were repairing a bulkhead on the beach at Coney
Island and asked them whether or not they ever had seen a
white owl. The spokesman for the pair gave me a firm denial
and an incredulous look to boot. I merely pointed down toward the edge of the water. Said the spokesman, "That's a
piece of white paper." I suggested that he walk down and take
a closer view. He did so and the "piece of white paper," when
he was halfway down the beach slope, took wing and flew off.
The two workmen were amazed. "Think of that!" said the
spokesman. Occasionally I do.

So much for our birds of prey. Now for some birds that are
quite likely to be preyed upon at times by hawks, owls, and
other predatory creatures. One is the introduced Ring-necked
Pheasant (*Phasianus colchicus*) of Asian ancestry that within the
past fifty years has become a settled resident of the region in
goodly numbers and, in particular, is quite common in the
Spuyten Duyvil–Riverdale–Van Cortlandt Park section. How
they manage to bring off broods where there are so many un-
leashed dogs and hunting house cats is a mystery to me but I
regularly find young birds as well as adults in the neighborhood
and I am inclined to think that they actually have increased in
numbers in the past decade despite all the new buildings in
the area.

On the other hand, the new buildings and the increased
human population certainly drove out an old inhabitant, the
Bobwhite (*Colinus virginianus*), whose melodious calls were familiar sounds in the fields and orchards of the area when I was
a boy. As the local farms were cut up for residential or business purposes and new streets were opened through what had
been hayfields and pastures, the Bobwhite population began to
fall away fast. By 1940 there were only some scattered sur-

vivors in the Van Cortlandt swamp and the remnants of what had been a flourishing bevy in Spuyten Duyvil. Early in the warm and sunlit morning of April 24, 1942, I set out on my neighborhood rounds and as I approached the southern tip of Spuyten Duyvil I first heard and then saw a Bobwhite calling repeatedly from a low branch of a tree in what was then an open field where Kappock Street runs down to meet Palisade Avenue. A pleasant sound and a lovely sight of a fine spring morning. That was the last time I ever heard or saw a Bobwhite in the neighborhood. A massive apartment house now masks the spot from everything except memory.

It is a pleasure to add that Bobwhites have been seen more recently in the far reaches of the Borough of Queens and, even if the resident population should fail, there is always the chance of infiltration from farther down Long Island where the birds are resident in increasing numbers as the distance from Times Square increases in the direction of Montauk Point. Thus we may hope to have the chubby and cheerful Bobwhite as a resident of at least one section of the city for many years to come.

It is also a pleasure to chronicle the fact that the Mourning Dove (*Zenaidura macroura*) of slim form, sedate walk, gentle ways, and plaintive voice still breeds in a few outlying sections of the city, including our neighborhood. It is, to be sure, more common on migration and there are occasional reports of individuals or small flocks staying throughout the winter. Except that they leave us before cold weather sets in, our cuckoos have much the same status as the Mourning Dove in our area. Both the Yellow-billed Cuckoo (*Coccyzus americanus*) and the Black-billed Cuckoo (*Coccyzus erythropthalmus*) breed sparingly in some of the outlying sections of the city. They are much more often seen as transients, especially the Yellow-billed, which some years is almost abundant in autumn migration.

A regular but mostly unseen and unheard bird of passage through our territory is the Whip-poor-will (*Caprimulgus vociferus*). Best known for their vibrant and repeated calls of *whip-*

poor-will at dusk or early dawn in rural regions, these birds rarely utter a sound on migration and it is only occasionally that a walker in the woods will catch sight of a Whip-poor-will, either by flushing it from the ground or by finding it resting lengthwise on the branch of a tree overhead. In all my years of scouring the Riverdale and Van Cortlandt area, I doubt I saw more than half a dozen Whip-poor-wills; yet they must occur in goodly number on migration because they are common summer residents in the farming country to the north of us.

A near relative, the Common Nighthawk (*Chordeiles minor*), we often see on migration, sometimes in astonishing numbers, and possibly it may be found breeding on the flat roof of some building within the city limits. In recent years I have seen and heard it — the buzzing *pe-e-ent* is unmistakable — hawking in the twilight in the Woodlawn section of the city throughout the breeding season, which would imply nesting somewhere in the vicinity, though possibly over the city line. On its breeding grounds it prefers to hawk for insects in the twilight but on migration it travels by days, often in flocks of fifty or more. As they swirl around in swift flight far overhead, they look like great dark swallows with white wing-patches that readily identify them as Nighthawks. They are early migrants and are rarely seen in our skies after September.

The chattering Chimney Swift (*Chaetura pelagica*), of course, is a common summer resident in the outlying residential sections of the city and a familiar sight as it circles overhead looking for all the world like a "flying cigar." They, too, are early migrants and often gather in huge flocks for their southward flights. Still another early migrant is the smallest of our summer residents, the Ruby-throated Hummingbird (*Archilochus colubris*). It's true that the nest of the species is rarely found within the city limits but they are rarely found anywhere over its range because they are so small and inconspicuous. If you ever have tried to track the parent birds to a suspected nest, you will know the difficulties involved. The birds dart so quickly that it is hard to follow their flight and the neutral gray nest shaped like a shallow cup and glued to a small branch of a tree or shrub is only 1½ inches in diameter. The parent birds may come day after day to feed among the flowers along a brook or in a garden, but finding the nest will require either a little luck or great persistence and patience.

For a change we now offer the Belted Kingfisher (*Megaceryle alcyon*), which is not an early migrant; it is a permanent resident. Perhaps that should be qualified. This rattling "high-hatted" bird may be found within the city limits throughout the year, but it is more common as a summer resident around the lakes, ponds, and streams of the region. When these freeze over, the hardy individuals who winter with us have to take to the tidal marshes to find open water and a food supply.

This brings us to the woodpecker tribe, of which group only two deserve full grade as permanent residents. These are the Hairy Woodpecker (*Dendrocopos villosus*) and its smaller and more abundant counterpart, the Downy Woodpecker (*Dendrocopos pubescens*). The Downy is found in all our parks of any size but the Hairy is scarce in such places except in winter when it moves in to take advantage of feeding stations set up by official or unofficial hands. However, the Hairy still breeds regularly on Staten Island and in the outlying sections of Queens and the Bronx but it sticks pretty well to the woods, whereas the friendly Downy is practically a dooryard bird in the residential areas adorned with trees and shrubs — and feeding stations.

The handsome, dashing, and somewhat noisy Yellow-shafted Flicker (*Colaptes auratus*) — it really is noisy only in the warmer months — is abundant as a summer resident in some of the larger parks and all the open sections of the city, and there are individuals that winter in the region, chiefly in the shoreward sections of the city. Thus the bird might be ranked as a permanent resident but there is such an influx in spring and such an exodus in autumn that the great impression of the bird is as

Downy Woodpecker

a rollicking summer resident. The individuals I find lurking about the sumac clumps or the swamps in winter usually are glum and silent, not at all like the gay blades of summer greenery.

The Yellow-bellied Sapsucker (*Sphyrapicus varius*), the bird responsible for the encircling rows of holes in the bark of apple trees and other trees as well, is a more or less common transient through our territory but it often passes unnoticed because on migration it rarely utters more than an occasional sharp call that might easily pass for the inquiring note of a Downy or Hairy Woodpecker. On its breeding grounds to the northward it calls as often and as loudly as any woodpecker and its voice has something of a whine to it that makes it easy to distinguish at any distance within earshot.

I can remember — it was as late as 1920 — being awakened in our Riverdale home by the loud and repeated calls of the Red-headed Woodpecker (*Melanerpes erythrocephalus*) in the early morning. I think the Spuyten Duyvil–Riverdale region was the last stronghold of the species east of the Hudson River. Or perhaps it was only a foothold that this more southerly and westerly bird had gained and then lost in our territory. In the past twenty years I have seen only two individuals in the neighborhood. One was an adult along the river road in Spuyten Duyvil and another was an immature bird on the hillside west of the Van Cortlandt swamp. It is a casual adventurer throughout New England and might turn up within the city limits at any time, but as a breeding species of the Riverdale region it is only a fond memory. There are occasional visits from northerly woodpeckers to such choice spots as the Hemlock Grove in the New York Botanical Garden, but the Flicker, the Hairy, and the Downy are the only woodpeckers that are on the premises for twelve months of the year and the Yellow-bellied Sapsucker is the only regular transient through the region.

Although we have no flycatchers that stay with us through the winter, we have six species that breed regularly within the city limits and two other species that are regular transients. Each breeding species has its own taste in nesting sites and nest architecture. The Eastern Kingbird (*Tyrannus tyrannus*), a shrill-voiced busybody that watches over the open fields and loves to heckle passing hawks, likes to nest near the top center of an apple tree or some tall thick shrub. The Eastern Phoebe (*Sayornis phoebe*) of the wagging tail and the monotonous voice, insists on nesting just over doorways or windows or in protected corners of porches — any sheltered place under a roof of any kind will do for this dooryard bird of the larger parks and the outlying sections of the city.

The Least Flycatcher (*Empidonax minimus*), popularly known as the "Chebec" through its sharp two-syllabled call, is a farmyard and barnyard bird by preference, which means that it can find the rural atmosphere it requires only in the outlying sectors of the city and even there the desired locations are thinning out year by year. It will build in the crotches of the smaller branches of dooryard trees or tall shrubs and never make a porch nuisance of itself as the Phoebe so often does. The Eastern Wood Peewee (*Contopus virens*) is strictly a woodland bird that frequently utters its last name in a plaintive voice and usually builds a beautiful little nest saddled perfectly on a horizontal branch well above the ground.

Possibly the little Traill's Flycatcher (*Empidonax traillii*), formerly known as the Alder Flycatcher, had been a summer resident or a regular transient in my home territory for many years but the first I heard of it in the vicinity was on May 26, 1946, when, of a fine sunny morning, a small bird perched on the top branch of a low tree in the Van Cortlandt swamp kept uttering cries that sounded to me like *Whit-gam! Whit-gam!* The sound has been translated differently by other listeners but we are all agreed on the identity of the bird producing it. It is a pleasure to report that the individual heard this May morning was the forerunner of a steady succession of summer residents of the same species. It has not failed as a breeding bird in the swamp since 1946 and I have found as many as four pairs in separated nesting areas in the swamp throughout a single breeding season. Ancient records prove that it bred regularly among these same alders a century ago. The return of a native is always a cause for rejoicing.

The Great Crested Flycatcher (*Myiarchus crinitus*), whose crest really isn't anything to boast about but whose hoarse cries are distinctive, is the bird that almost invariably adds a cast snakeskin to the lining of the nest it builds in the hollow of a limb or trunk of a tree. There are still enough remnants of orchards and wooded terrain in the region to provide nesting sites for the Great Crested Flycatcher in the outlying sections of the city, but it is becoming scarcer year by year and may be only a transient in the near future.

Those of the tribe that hold rank as regular transients now and have for many years past are the Olive-sided Flycatcher (*Nuttallornis borealis*) and the little Yellow-bellied Flycatcher (*Empidonax flaviventris*) that has an even softer note than the Wood Peewee. The richly colored underparts make the Yellow-bellied Flycatcher easy to identify as it drifts through in migration — sometimes in fair numbers — but the Olive-sided Flycatcher is a stumper for inexpert eyes. On its breeding ground it advertises its presence by taking a prominent perch such as a dead limb or the top of a tree and giving a loud three-syllabled cry that is variously translated. One interpretation is "Quick, three beers!" But ears are no help in our territory because it usually goes through without making any sound except the snap of its bill when it catches an insect in flight. Thus it regularly passes through our region unnoticed except by the experts. To me it looks much like a larger and stockier Wood Peewee doing its flycatching from a perch high up in the open.

Of one of our larks I have an almost incredible tale to tell. Since we regularly have two races, or subspecies, of one recognized or official species in our territory, we have to resort to the trinomial form to distinguish one from the other. Incidentally, they are not always as easily distinguished in the field as they are in print. But in cold weather we have the Northern Horned Lark (*Eremophila alpestris alpestris*) running over flat open ground, feeding largely on weed and grass seed. You will find it at the airports, on golf links, along the upper edges of ocean beaches, and even on college football fields when they are not in use. I always find these birds in fair numbers on the Van Cortlandt Parade Ground in November and usually they remain there until a heavy snow drives them farther south. If it is a mild winter, many of them remain in the general area. In March and April they may overlap with the similar but paler Prairie Horned Lark (*Eremophila alpestris praticola*) that in recent years has come to breed sparingly in our general region. It's the Prairie Horned Lark of which I have a tale to tell.

The Parade Ground in Van Cortlandt Park actually was used as a drill ground and encampment location for National Guard troops as late as World War I but since that time it has been changed into a playing field for baseball, football, soccer, cricket, and other sports. There are sets of grilled backstops for baseball diamonds and on weekends in spring and summer there are so many teams on the field that the outfielders in different games are intermingled. The confusion is fearful and wonderful and, with all the hitting and running and throwing the ball about, anybody who attempts to cross the Parade Ground on such occasions has to be very much on the alert to keep from being hit by a ball or knocked down by some player in pursuit of one. Yet right out there in the open, in what must have been outfield territory for several different games, a Prairie Horned Lark found a nesting site, laid four eggs, and raised three young. However, there was an element of luck in it. There had to be. As an accomplishment it was almost incredible.

It rained on Sunday, June 3, 1956. That was the beginning of the luck. Saturday had been a bad day, too. The playing field had no tenants on either day but it was on this Sunday morning that a Prairie Horned Lark ran out from under my feet as I crossed the Parade Ground on the way to the swamp. The way the bird acted made me suspect a nest and I finally discovered it in a tuft of grass. It was so well concealed that the next time I went to check on it I was forced to go over the ground repeatedly before I could find it. After that I put down markers to guide the way to the exact spot. Since it was June, it must have been a second nesting. Possibly an earlier nest had been trampled underfoot. It seemed impossible that the nest I found could escape being stepped on by some baseball player or bystander over the next weekend.

On Friday, June 8, a clear warm day, I found three nestlings and an unhatched egg in the nest. The next two days would decide the fate of the brood. The weather was wonderful. It drizzled all day Saturday. Sunday was overcast, with occasional showers. Bad for baseball; good for larks. When the nestlings were still safe and sound on Monday morning I knew they had a chance of survival because these birds mature quickly. I was sure they would be able to leave the nest by the time the baseball crowd arrived on the field the following Saturday morning. I removed the unhatched egg — it was addled — to give the nestlings more room and I checked on their progress each morning. By Wednesday the head and throat pattern was clearly marked on the young birds. By Thursday they had sprouted wing feathers of respectable size. By Friday they were ready to leave if an emergency arose. Now I knew they were safe, and my vigil was over. But as I walked away I still thought it was remarkable that such a thing could happen in such a place.

Prairie Horned Larks came into our territory without any formal invitation, but Purple Martins (*Progne subis*) were deliberately lured in by a man who spent years trying before he made a success of the project. The man was — and is — Howard Cleaves, the Staten Island naturalist, nature photographer, and lecturer. It's quite possible that Purple Martins were regular summer residents hereabout when Indians ruled the region, because old accounts have it that the Indians liked to have the birds around and put up empty gourds in which they could nest. But there was no breeding record for modern times until Howard Cleaves hopefully put up a martin house in his yard at Prince's Bay, Staten Island, in 1917, and drew a pair of Purple Martins that brought off a brood successfully.

Although this takes rank as the first actual breeding record on city territory, it turned out to be a false start. The following year the Cleaves family moved to a new home several miles distant from their former location. They took the martin house with them, but the birds didn't follow. Then Howard Cleaves himself left Staten Island for an extended period and, for one reason or another, many years elapsed before he made another and greater effort to persuade Purple Martins to become regular summer residents of Richmond County. From 1946 through 1950 his proffered rent-free houses drew no lodgers of the Purple Martin species. In 1951 two pairs moved in and produced eggs, but the young did not survive. There were no tenants in 1952, and the project began to look like a vain effort. But in 1953 six pairs settled down to raise eighteen young that took the air successfully and every year since; with more houses put in different localities at their disposal, Purple Martins have been breeding in greater numbers on Staten Island. In 1958 the count ran to forty-six breeding pairs, which suggests a bright future for the birds as summer residents of the Borough of Richmond — and perhaps other boroughs if anybody there will take as much interest in the project as Howard Cleaves did on his home ground.

As for our other swallows, the Barn Swallow (*Hirundo rustica*) still breeds regularly in the Riverdale region and doubtless in a few other outlying sections of the city and so does the Rough-

Barn Swallows

winged Swallow (*Stelgidopteryx ruficollis*). Even when the young take to the air, they still clamor for food from the parents. Every summer I see old birds feeding "young beggars" that sit with open mouths and quivering wings on the telegraph wires along the railroad track where the Van Cortlandt swamp drains into the lake. There also, particularly during the spring migration, I find the Tree Swallow (*Iridoprocne bicolor*) that usually is the leader of the swallow tribe on the northward trek and sometimes winters in small flocks in the seaward sections of the city. The Bank Swallow (*Riparia riparia*) and the Cliff Swallow (*Petrochelidon pyrrhonota*) are regular migrants in limited numbers through our region. There are warm sunny days in spring when I can pick out five of our six species of swallows — all but the Purple Martin — either swirling above or skimming low over the waters of the lower marsh and adjacent lake in Van Cortlandt Park. But the Bank and Cliff Swallows require special sites for their little nesting colonies and apparently our neighborhood has nothing to offer that is up to their specifications.

The Blue Jay (*Cyanocitta cristata*) has quite different tastes. It will nest almost anywhere near the center of a tree or a thick shrub and it will eat almost anything, including the eggs and young of smaller birds, wherefor it is often indicted as a common criminal. Even so, it has some strong points in its favor. It is bold and handsome. It stays with us — or at least some individuals do — throughout the year. If it is a thief, it is also a watchman and more than once a posse of Blue Jays has led me to the permanent homes or temporary lodgings of hawks and owls in our neighborhood. It is a dooryard as well as a woodland bird with us and, though hundreds of Blue Jays may be seen heading southward on a single autumn day, those that remain or arrive from the north to spend the winter with us are a sore trial at neighborhood feeding stations, where they overawe and drive off the smaller birds for whom the provender has been set out. Many a man's hand — a woman's, too — is against it, but the Blue Jay remains in residence, dashing and defiant.

Though only those who are interested in birds know about it, we have two resident crows in New York City. One is the Common Crow (*Corvus brachyrhynchos*) that sometimes arouses the wrath of farmers, particularly just after the corn has been planted, but nevertheless probably does more good than harm on farms and in gardens. Our other crow is the Fish Crow (*Corvus ossifragus*), which is slightly smaller but otherwise almost an exact copy of its larger relative. Both birds are permanent residents and the cries of young crows demanding to be fed are common enough in our wooded areas in June and July. Except when the young crows give voice in juvenile tones, it is fairly easy to distinguish the Common Crow from the Fish Crow by the calls. In fact, it is almost the only way because, unless a Fish Crow is standing beside a Common Crow, it is almost impossible to distinguish them by size in the field. But when there are no young crows to add to the confusion, the Fish Crow's *caw* — to me, at least — sounds higher and weaker than that of the Common Crow and very often the Fish Crow gives it in two syllables as *ca-ha* instead of the firm and loud *caw* of the larger and more abundant species. Incidentally, the Common Crow has a variety of other utterances among its vocal resources, including a long-drawn-out creaking sound and a rendition of three liquid notes in quick succession with almost a yodeling effect in the delivery.

It is a big drop in size from the Common Crow to the Black-capped Chickadee (*Parus atricapillus*) that is a common permanent resident of the region and a favorite at feeding stations in cold weather. We have occasional visits of other chickadees from the north and south but the familiar Black-capped Chickadee is by all odds the one you may expect to meet in the woodlands in summer and to find in your dooryards in winter. The Tufted Titmouse (*Parus bicolor*), which is common to the south and west of us, is reported to be a permanent resident in small numbers in some outlying sections of the city, but I encountered it only as a wanderer in the Riverdale region. It is said to be increasing in numbers in our territory, which is good news because it is just as cheerful and friendly as its uncrested and more abundant relative, the Black-capped Chickadee.

The White-breasted Nuthatch (*Sitta carolinensis*) is a permanent resident of our territory and, in winter, is a faithful attendant at dooryard feeding stations where suet, raisins, sunflower seeds, and perhaps other tidbits are on the menu. Like the Black-capped Chickadee, with which it often travels on foraging expeditions, it is largely a woodland bird in the breeding season. Its smaller and more colorful relative, the Red-breasted Nuthatch (*Sitta canadensis*) is a regular migrant in numbers that vary considerably from year to year. Sometimes only a comparatively few birds are noted passing through and at other times, as the saying goes, "the woods are full of them." A few usually remain in the region as winter residents. It shares the family trait of apparently defying the law of gravity in being able to move steadily down a tree trunk head first.

On the other hand, there is the Brown Creeper (*Certhia familiaris*) that always works its way upward on a tree trunk, usually on a spiral path, as it searches for insects or their eggs or larva in or under patches of bark. When it finishes its hunt for food in one tree, often fairly close to the top, it pitches down on a slant to the base of another tree and begins another upward spiral trip. It is a regular migrant through our region and a winter resident in small numbers but because it is small and dull-colored and goes about its work quietly in the woods, it is often overlooked. It is socially inclined to the extent that as a migrant or winter resident it is often found in company with little foraging groups of chickadees, nuthatches, or kinglets.

Almost everybody knows the House Wren (*Troglodytes aedon*) with its bubbling little song, busy little ways, and habit of building its nest in the oddest kinds of places in and around houses, dooryards, barns, barnyards, gardens, and orchards. A knothole in the side of a house will serve as an entrance. An old boot in a corner of a barn will do for a nesting site. A neighbor in Riverdale discovered that a House Wren had built a nest in a clothespin bag that had been left hanging on a wash-line. The line worked on pulleys and, during the incubation period, the bag went back and forth as the wash was hung out and taken in, all without any apparent damage or even concern to the parent birds. Perhaps they enjoyed the rides. Whatever their feelings, they brought off the brood successfully.

The House Wren is a common summer resident in some of

the larger parks and all the outlying sections of the city. In some residential areas you will find wren houses set up on posts or fastened to branches of trees in dooryards or gardens, an open invitation to the birds to nest on the premises. But we have other wrens in the region that receive less attention and happily are left to their own devices in less public haunts. One is the tiny and finely barred Winter Wren (*Troglodytes troglodytes*) that is a regular migrant through our region and a winter resident in small numbers. It slips quietly along old stone walls in the woods and loves to lurk about brush heaps, often uttering sharp little chips as it pokes about in search of food.

The largest and handsomest of the group, the Carolina Wren (*Thryothorus ludovicianus*) with its loud, clear, and ringing three-syllabled song, is unfortunately uncommon within the city limits though it does occur regularly and has been recorded every month in the year. I remember one that wintered in a gully in Spuyten Duyvil and a pair that nested in a tangle on park land in Riverdale. The species always turns up on the Christmas count and it has bred as far north as Maine and Ontario, Canada. Even so, it isn't every day that you can see or hear a Carolina Wren within the city limits even by the most diligent search, and to find a nesting pair would be a stroke of luck.

But if it's the Long-billed Marsh Wren (*Telmatodytes palustris*) that you would like to see, I can guarantee a dozen or so any day from mid-May through the summer in the cattail marsh at the lower end of the Van Cortlandt swamp. In the winter you can invade the marsh and find dozens of their nests with entrances on the sides fastened to stiff and drying cattail stalks. Of course, this doesn't mean that a pair of birds made use of each nest. For some reason, Long-billed Marsh Wrens have a habit of building two or three nests, or even more, and only one is put to use. But through the late spring and summer there will be Marsh Wrens uttering their loud and rattling calls until they moult and grow a new set of feathers to serve as a traveling costume on southward migration. A few individuals are occasionally seen in the region in cold weather — more often on the salt marshes than elsewhere — but by and large the Long-billed Marsh Wren is strictly a summer resident and only locally common in a few places like the Van Cortlandt marsh. As for the Short-billed Marsh Wren (*Cistothorus platensis*), the wet meadows in which it breeds have just about disappeared within the city limits — and the birds with it, except for the few that are regularly recorded as migrants by experts who know how and where to look for them.

Now we come to some larger and really gifted singers, three members of a melodious family: the Mockingbird (*Mimus polyglottos*), the Catbird (*Dumetella carolinensis*), and the Brown Thrasher (*Toxostoma rufum*). To be frank, we really have little claim on the famous Mockingbird as a native New York City songster. Though it has bred as far north as the Canadian border and even beyond, it is largely southerly in distribution and, despite the fact that it has been recorded at all seasons, it is hardly more than a stray within the city limits. I remember seeing one of a summer day along what was then Spuyten Duyvil Parkway and is now the West Side Highway or Henry Hudson Parkway, and even more vividly I remember seeing one clinging to the ivy on the side of a house in Riverdale during a January snowstorm. Both birds seemed out of place. Indeed, the one in the driving snowstorm was complaining bitterly about the weather in our neighborhood. At least, that's the way I interpreted the loud squawks it was uttering.

The Catbird and Brown Thrasher are regular summer residents in suitable locations in our territory. The Brown Thrasher is the louder and clearer singer and usually goes through its vocal efforts on a lofty perch where it is easily seen. For this reason everybody who knows the bird at all considers it a fine songster, which it is. But there are many persons who know a Catbird by sight and still think that all it ever utters is the catlike mewing note that accounts for its common name.

That's because the Catbird, which is more numerous in the area than the Brown Thrasher, frequently runs through its musical repertoire while concealed in a thick shrub or a tangle of vines. More than once I met with cold stares from incredulous friends when I identified an unseen songster as a Catbird.

There is no doubt about our thrushes, however. All of them have good voices and the fact is rather generally realized by many persons who do not know one thrush from another except the one that everybody knows under another name, the abundant, familiar, and friendly Robin (*Turdus migratorius*). I have counted as many as 200 Robins on the Van Cortlandt Parade Ground on a mid-April day. Of course, most of these birds are migrants but the Robin is certainly one of our most abundant summer residents and a common breeder in all five boroughs. The Wood Thrush (*Hylocichla mustelina*), with its fluted two-phrase song, and the Veery (*Hylocichla fuscescens*), whose ringing notes spiral downward, also are regular summer residents, but in far fewer numbers than the Robin and in less public places. The Wood Thrush lives in the shade of tall trees or massed shrubbery and the Veery is a bird of the swamps, and there is only a limited amount of that kind of territory remaining within the city limits.

What used to be called the Olive-backed and is now officially the Swainson's Thrush (*Hylocichla ustulata*) is a common migrant through our region and on the northward trip in spring it frequently favors us with its song, which is very much like that of the Veery except that it spirals upward instead of downward. The Gray-cheeked Thrush (*Hylocichla minima*) is a regular transient in smaller numbers and often slips through unrecognized — except by the experts — because it is the most difficult of our thrushes to identify with certainty at a quick glance and, furthermore, usually it is silent on migration. I never have heard the bird sing in our territory. It prefers the woodland or shaded ground but occasionally it ventures into the open. One October

morning I looked down from my bedroom window in our Riverdale home and saw a Graycheek standing quietly on the rim of
the bird bath on the lawn below me.

If there is one bird of North America that might be mentioned in the same breath with the Nightingale of Europe it is
the shy brown bird of our northern woods and swamps in summer, the Hermit Thrush (*Hylocichla guttata*). The delicate
quality of its upward-drifting, flute-like notes, heard most
frequently in the early dawn or the deepening twilight, is impossible to put in words. But perhaps its song shouldn't even
be mentioned here because, as a transient through our territory,
it rarely utters any sound other than a hoarse, croaking call
note all out of keeping with its wonderful singing voice. The
Hermit Thrush is an early migrant in spring and a late migrant
in fall and always we have a few individuals that spend the
winter in sheltered spots in our area.

Our Eastern Bluebird (*Sialia sialis*) is a hole-nesting thrush
and for this reason the bird, once an abundant summer resident
of the region, is now largely a transient in what — to borrow a
fit phrase from Longfellow — we might call mournful numbers.
In my boyhood days in Kingsbridge the Starlings were just
starting their ouster proceedings against the local Bluebirds.
There were farms and orchards in the area at the time and
Bluebirds, adult and young, were common around dooryards
and barnyards and several broods a year came out of most
nesting holes. But the Starlings increased rapidly in numbers
and the less robust Bluebirds were shouldered roughly away
from their old nesting sites as the newcomers moved in and took
possession. The last nesting Bluebirds I saw in the region
raised a brood in a hole in a telegraph pole along the railroad
that skirts the Van Cortlandt swamp. That was some years
ago. Since then I have seen a fair number of transients and
have heard many more passing overhead in early spring and
late autumn, but their doom as residents was sealed when the
Starlings moved in.

We are on the northeastern fringe of the breeding range of the little Blue-gray Gnatcatcher (*Polioptila caerulea*). There is always the chance of seeing one or two of these sprightly birds with tiny bodies and comparatively long tails throughout the warmer months of the year. Some years I have seen as many as five in a season and other years I missed them entirely. They might be set down as regular warm-weather visitors in small numbers. Both the Golden-crowned Kinglet (*Regulus satrapa*) and the Ruby-crowned Kinglet (*Regulus calendula*) are common to abundant transients through our region and a few always spend the winter in the more sheltered nooks within the city limits. The Golden-crowned is the handsomer little bird but my favorite is the Ruby-crowned, not only for the little red flag it raises on its crown when courting or fighting but because, on migration in spring, it pours out a delightful little roulade of bubbling notes that skitter gaily down the scale. The Golden-crowned Kinglet only rarely gives us any more than a string of beady little notes.

What we used to call simply "the Pipit" is now, by imperial ornithological decree of 1957, the Water Pipit (*Anthus spinoletta*). The change in name has made no difference in the bird's habits and travels. With us it is a regular transient, locally abundant at times, and frequently a winter resident in small flocks in the seaward sections of the city such as the ocean beaches and the salt-marsh areas. Like the Northern Horned Lark, with which it is often found during migration, it likes flat ground and short grass and the best places to seek it in season are on airfields and golf courses. I meet it regularly as a migrant — more numerous in the autumn than in the spring — on the Van Cortlandt Parade Ground, where I have seen as many as several hundred at a time walking about calmly and feeding on grass seed. Only a few of our small birds walk about in this leisurely fashion; most of them run or hop.

Apparently there are no general laws or local ordinances that govern the presence or absence of the Cedar Waxwing

(*Bombycilla cedrorum*) in our territory. It bred regularly in former years and possibly still does in some outlying sectors but beyond this the only local label that could be put on the bird is the bizarre one of "irregular resident," since it may be encountered alone or in small flocks on any day of the year in any one of the five boroughs. Some days we might have a dozen Cedar Waxwings sitting on clotheslines in the backyard and then months would pass before another one would be sighted. I have seen Cedar Waxwings in summer and winter, in fall and spring, usually flying overhead in small flocks and dropping a series of beady little notes in passing.

Next to this quiet and gentle little bird, a model of modesty, we have on the systematic list a definite contrast in the shrikes or "butcher birds," of which two species occur in our territory with some regularity but never any abundance. The Loggerhead Shrike (*Lanius ludovicianus*) is a regular migrant in small numbers and is more often seen in the autumn than in spring; this is natural enough since the young of the year are added to the adult population of any species at that time. The larger and fiercer Northern Shrike (*Lanius excubitor*) is a more or less regular but by no means common winter visitor and where it appears it often takes a station in a swamp and hunts the area for weeks. Many persons dislike shrikes because they kill birds and hang their bodies on thorns by way of storage, but they also destroy small mammals and some of the large injurious insects. Ecologists tell us that, if the account is fairly balanced, shrikes must be considered beneficial birds.

There is no such difference of opinion about our vireos, all of which are looked upon as well-behaved and helpful little birds that comb our shrubs and trees and rid them of many insect pests in one form or another. We have four vireos as summer residents and two that are regular transients. The most common of the summer residents is the Red-eyed Vireo (*Vireo olivaceus*) whose song, consisting of an endless repetition of disjointed warbling phrases, is heard throughout the summer wherever there are shade trees in the area. No other vireo approaches the Red-eyed in numbers in our territory but the Warbling Vireo (*Vireo gilvus*) still breeds regularly in some out-lying sections of the city and its song, sweeter and smoother than that of the Red-eye, can always be heard on warm sunny days in the Van Cortlandt swamp.

To my ear, the sweetest singer of the group is the Yellow-throated Vireo (*Vireo flavifrons*) that usually feeds, sings, and nests high up in the shade trees of the quieter stretches within the city limits. Its notes have a husky rich quality and its short phrases have a leisurely tempo that befits the woods in late spring or summer. The Yellow-throated Vireo is by no means common in the region but in recent years I could always count on finding two or three pairs somewhere in the Spuyten Duyvil–Riverdale region and the wide expanse of Van Cortlandt Park. One nest I located in a tree on the edge of the swamp was at least sixty feet above ground.

The perky little White-eyed Vireo (*Vireo griseus*) is a regular transient through our swamps, wet thickets, and hedgerow tangles but it has fallen away sadly as a summer resident, and in the past ten years I knew of only one breeding pair in the Riverdale–Van Cortlandt region. We still have some suitable terrain for the bird within the city limits but it nests fairly close to the ground and such sites are subject to continuous disturbance by roaming dogs and hunting cats on the outskirts of the city. The Solitary Vireo (*Vireo solitarius*) is a regular transient in fair numbers. Usually it is the first of the vireos to appear in spring and it moves through our region silently, which is too bad because it is a pleasing singer on its breeding ground to the north. Its song is somewhat like that of the Red-eye, but a little slower and a little sweeter. The really un-common bird of the group is the Philadelphia Vireo (*Vireo philadelphicus*) that is regularly reported as a transient but always in limited numbers. Possibly it often goes unrecognized because its song is much like that of the Red-eye and in appear-

ance it is much like a Warbling Vireo with a yellow tinge to the underparts. If you scan carefully every singing Red-eye and every silent Warbling Vireo in the region, sooner or later one of them will prove to be a Philadelphia Vireo.

This brings us to the warblers, where really we are swamped. Whole books could be, and some have been, written on the wood warblers of North America, a group of — for the most part — dainty and beautiful little insect-eating transients and summer residents. They are a delight to the heart and the eye but, despite the group name, no great shakes to listen to. In most cases the best thing about the song is that it identifies the species "sight unseen," which is often a big help in the case of a small bird in a big tree or a thick tangle of vines and shrubbery in wet ground. There are more than fifty species listed for the United States. On the bird card I use for convenience in checking on field trips there are thirty-seven species and two hybrids listed. I have seen every one of the thirty-seven species within the confines of New York City, some only two or three times in forty years, some in abundance each year. I never had the luck to find either hybrid on city territory, though I have encountered both in New England.

I honestly believe that Van Cortlandt Park — from the swamp on the west to the oak woods on high ground on the east — is as good a place to find spring warblers as any area of similar extent in any part of North America. In the eastern section alone, a half-mile strip of oak woods with wet undergrowth and a roar of traffic on both sides, I have found twenty-six species of warbler in one spring season. But for all this boasting, I must admit that only a scant half-dozen species remain to nest in the same general area. At least this is all that I found year after year in the Spuyten Duyvil–Riverdale–Van Cortlandt Park region.

Probably the little black-masked Yellowthroat (*Geothlypis trichas*) is our most common resident warbler in summer. There must be a dozen pairs nesting in the Van Cortlandt swamp area each season. There also you can find the Yellow Warbler (*Dendroica petechia*) and the Chestnut-sided Warbler (*Dendroica pensylvanica*), and an occasional nesting American Redstart (*Setophaga ruticilla*), though more often I find the Redstart in the woods. For that matter, the Chestnut-sided Warbler is common in the upland shrubbery and the Yellowthroat's *witchery* song is frequently heard where the undergrowth is heavy in the wet woods. On a little firmer ground in wooded sections we find the Ovenbird (*Seiurus aurocapillus*) walking around and turning over dead leaves in search of food. It flies up to a branch now and then to give its *teacher-teacher* song that keeps its presence in any region from being a secret.

Where the trees are scattered or a hillside is dotted with shrubbery you will hear on warm sunny days the lazy *zee-zee* of the Blue-winged Warbler (*Vermivora pinus*), though this species doesn't compare with the others mentioned for total numbers in the region. I would estimate the Blue-wing summer population at about one pair per square mile of open woods and fields. Occasionally I come upon the Black-and-White Warbler (*Mniotilta varia*) in our summer woods and I suspect it may breed there, but I never count on it as I do the others that have been listed. Some years ago the Worm-eating Warbler (*Helmitheros vermivorus*) bred in the Bronx and I know it breeds regularly across the Hudson River in New Jersey as well as in Westchester, but I never have found any as summer residents of my home territory in recent years.

The most abundant of the migrant warblers through the region is, by all odds, the Myrtle Warbler (*Dendroica coronata*) that some days seems to be everywhere in the branches of our trees and shrubs. It also has the distinction of being a winter resident of the area in small numbers where there are stands of Bayberry bushes in sheltered places. The only other warbler I ever found on the premises in winter was an Orange-crowned Warbler (*Vermivora celata*) that I saw flitting about a dooryard fruit tree in mid-December, 1953. Unlike the Myrtle, the

Orange-crowned Warbler is uncommon in our region at any time. Or perhaps the truth is that it often goes unrecognized on migration because of the lack of any striking color or pattern in its plumage. When there are no other warblers about, its actions show that it belongs to the Warbler Family and then it is easy to clinch the identification.

About mid-April the warblers begin to appear in numbers and, in addition to the Myrtles, among the early arrivals are the Pine Warbler (*Dendroica pinus*) and the Yellow Palm Warbler (*Dendroica palmarum hypochrysea*), to which we have to give that triple Latin name because it is only a recognizable subspecies or race of the more westerly Palm Warbler (*Dendroica palmarum palmarum*) that occurs sparingly in our region in spring and is common during the autumn migration. Another early migrant is the shy Louisiana Waterthrush (*Seiurus motacilla*), whose finer song and white eye line distinguish it from the otherwise very similar Northern Waterthrush (*Seiurus noveboracensis*) that has a yellowish eye line and comes along a bit later in considerably larger numbers.

These and a few other early adventurers may be seen in April but May is the month of madness for bird-watchers. By the tenth day of the month the resident warblers are on the scene and the transients are arriving in bewildering waves when conditions are favorable. There are warblers everywhere you look, from ground level to treetop. One fine morning in mid-May I counted eleven different species of warbler in a big White Oak standing on the lawn of a neighbor in Riverdale. There is no doubt that oak catkins are favorite feeding grounds for many warblers, but there will be low feeders flitting about the undergrowth in the woods and the shrubbery along stone walls. On a warm bright morning at the high tide of the invasion you might expect to see — and hear, too — the Nashville Warbler (*Vermivora ruficapilla*), the delicately tinted Parula Warbler (*Parula americana*), the dashing and flashing Magnolia Warbler (*Dendroica magnolia*), the husky-voiced Black-throated Blue

Warbler (*Dendroica caerulescens*) with its neat black and white weskit, and the Black-throated Green Warbler (*Dendroica virens*) that "drops a stitch" in its oft repeated song.

High overhead amid the still-young foliage you may catch sight of the flaming orange throat of the Blackburnian Warbler (*Dendroica fusca*) and low in the undergrowth in the wet woods you might find the Hooded Warbler (*Wilsonia citrina*) with its striking headdress or the Canada Warbler (*Wilsonia canadensis*) with its necklace of black pearls draped across its yellow breast. There also, but much less frequently, you might find the Mourning Warbler (*Oporornis philadelphia*) of lively liquid voice but almost somber costume. From a tangle of vines along an old stone wall at the edge of a field may come an assortment of hollow mocking notes and jeering calls. Whether you catch sight of the talented singer or not, that will be the Yellow-breasted Chat (*Icteria virens*). Perhaps in the shrubbery along the same wall you might see the sprightly little Wilson's Warbler (*Wilsonia pusilla*) in all-yellow plumage except for the tiny black Eton cap or "beanie" on top of its head. From a shrub or small tree in the open field beyond you are almost sure to hear a Prairie Warbler (*Dendroica discolor*) running up the scale in a thin wiry voice.

A return to the oak grove certainly should produce the Bay-breasted Warbler (*Dendroica castanea*) all aglow in vernal chestnut hue and the almost colorless Tennessee Warbler (*Vermivora peregrina*) with the vibrant chattering song. A little luck might bring into view a Cape May Warbler (*Dendroica tigrina*) that somehow is scarce in its beautiful striped suit of spring finery but quite common in autumn in a more subdued costume. Perhaps some short wiry notes high up in a tree will lead to a glimpse of a Golden-winged Warbler (*Vermivora chrysoptera*), a bird rather strangely scarce within the city limits considering that it is a common summer resident to the north and northeast of us. To top off the list you are bound to see the Blackpoll (*Dendroica striata*) that represents the rear guard of the regular army of migrating spring warblers. It usually feeds high in the trees and, though it is often abundant for a week or more, in the thickening foliage it is more often heard than seen. But when the Blackpoll appears, you know that the parade is almost over.

There's more to it than that, however. The warblers already mentioned are merely the expected transients and regular summer residents of our region, all of which you could count on seeing at some time during the year. There are occasional surprises to enliven a day or make a season memorable. Twice on April days in different years I saw the glowing Prothonotary Warbler (*Protonotaria citrea*) feeding and singing intermittently in the branches of trees overhanging water. On the first occasion this southern bird appeared on the fringe of a private swimming pool in Riverdale and remained in the area for almost a week. Two years later I came upon one flying from one bank of the Bronx River to the other in the New York Botanical Garden. Twice, in successive years, I found the Cerulean Warbler (*Dendroica cerulea*) in Riverdale toward the end of the spring migration and, strangely enough, in the same oak tree on Dodge Lane each time. This is a rare bird on city territory. So, too, is the Kentucky Warbler (*Oporornis formosus*), a bird that breeds sparingly in Westchester County to the north of us. Three times in thirty years I have met the Kentucky Warbler on my home ground. Two were singing males feeding low in the woods during spring migration and one was a silent bird that peered at me at eye level in the deep shade of the midsummer greenery of an oak grove that since has been buried under a mass of masonry.

I have very good ears. They have been most helpful to me in finding birds in the field. They serve well elsewhere, too. At this moment, for instance, I can almost hear the reader muttering: "Is the man mad? Is there no end to his romancing about wandering warblers he met on city property?" The good news is that the warbler story is almost ended. I have just two more members of the family to present.

It was misty at dawn on Sunday, May 2, 1954, but by 7:30

A.M., at which time I was watching warblers feeding in an oak tree on the west edge of the Van Cortlandt swamp, the sun had broken through and the day was perfect. Suddenly, at the outer tip of a low branch of the oak, I saw a bird that at first glance looked like a Black-and-White Warbler with a bright yellow throat. I didn't recognize the species. A bird on my home ground that I didn't know? That was a stunner! Then I realized I had seen the bird before — in Florida. It was a Yellow-throated Warbler (*Dendroica dominica*), an occasional and very distinguished visitor from its ordinary range to the south of us. Finally there is the sober and — in our territory — silent Connecticut Warbler (*Oporornis agilis*) that migrates up the Mississippi Valley in spring and regularly drifts southward along the Atlantic Coastal Flyway in scant numbers in autumn. It is a bird of unstreaked plumage and subdued colors: dull yellow, olive, and bluish gray. It has to be seen clearly to be distinguished from certain other species much like it in fall plumage. A fleeting glimpse, such as might easily distinguish many other species, will not do with this bird. To find it during the autumn migration requires either great persistence or extraordinary luck — or both. My last view of one was on October 2, 1954, in a Riverdale garden. Indeed, I doubt that a search of my records would turn up more than five or six Connecticut Warblers on city property in the past twenty years. It's the uncommon bird, difficult to detect, that gives the real thrill to the eager searcher when it is found.

We have not done justice to all our wonderful warblers but, even so, we must get along to other birds. The next one on our list is the Bobolink (*Dolichonyx oryzivorus*) that commonly nested in our wet meadows years ago, but recently I have known it only as a regular spring migrant in small numbers and an abundant fall migrant in August and September. To hear the bubbling song of the bright-backed male in June, I have to visit the lush hayfields of Westchester, Putnam, or Dutchess County to the northward. Day or night in September I can

stand on my home ground and hear the liquid *chink* of Bobo-
links migrating overhead, and often I have seen flocks of a
hundred or more, in fall plumage, drop into or rise up out of
the reeds in the Van Cortlandt marsh. The Eastern Meadow-
lark (*Sturnella magna*) can be found every month in the year in
the seaward sections of the city but in the open sections of the
Bronx it is mostly a common migrant, more abundant in the
spring than in the fall, and a local summer resident in diminishing numbers. The familiar Redwinged Blackbird (*Agelaius
phoeniceus*) has about the same status except that it is with us in
greater numbers in the summer, when it breeds in all our
marshes. Anybody who wades out into the Van Cortlandt
marsh in late May or early June will find a dozen or more Red-
wing nests containing eggs or young birds. The cheerful *konkaree*
of the early migrating males in February is a joyous sound in
the marshes at that bleak time of year. These birds with their
bright two-toned epaulettes are hardy heralds of spring.

It surprises some persons to learn that our orioles are related
to our blackbirds, but such is the case. The family is called the
Icteridae and it includes the Bobolink, all the blackbirds, and
our orioles. We have two orioles that are registered as summer
residents of New York and New England but one of them has
vanished from my sight in recent years. That's the Orchard
Oriole (*Icterus spurius*) I once knew as a regular migrant and
summer resident in small numbers. I haven't heard of a breeding pair in my neighborhood in many years and the last individual of which I have record on the premises was a black-
chinned, yellow-plumaged, second-year male that was calling
repeatedly from the top of a Tulip-tree on a Spuyten Duyvil
hillside on June 2, 1943. Even when it was a summer resident
it was only on a part-time basis, since parents and young went
southward before the end of July. Others have seen the species on scattered occasions within the city limits since that time,
but to me the bird at this moment is only a memory.

We still have the beautiful, friendly, and melodious Balti-

more Oriole (*Icterus galbula*) as a regular summer resident of our larger parks and practically all the residential sections of the city where there are shade trees and scattered patches of woods. It doesn't seem to be disturbed by auto traffic and often hangs its pear-shaped woven nest directly above a roadway in the outer branches of a shade tree, preferably an American Elm but any tree with drooping branchlets and broad leaves will do as a nesting site. Baltimore Orioles come to us in early May and usually disappear in September. Life in a great city appears to suit them well enough and I am sure we shall have them with us for untold summers to come.

The creaky-voiced Rusty Blackbird (*Euphagus carolinus*) is a regular migrant through our swamps and fresh-water marshes, sometimes in flocks of considerable size, and a few individuals remain as winter residents. On occasion I have found flocks of five or six feeding around open water in the Van Cortlandt swamp in January, but the spring rush comes in late March and the autumn migrants are most numerous in late October or early November. The long-tailed Common Grackle (*Quiscalus quiscula*) — we shall leave the subspecies to the experts — is not only a common summer resident but a common nuisance in some sections of the city, particularly when hordes of migrants pour through our territory in March and November and stalk about the park lawns and the branches of trees, all the while filling the air with rasping discordant chatter. Harassed householders of quiet residential sections often appeal to the police or the mayor of the city to put a stop to the racket and drive the invaders from the scene.

I approach the Brown-headed Cowbird (*Molothrus ater*) with mixed feelings. I regret that each young Cowbird of the year represents the loss of a complete brood of some usually smaller and far more attractive birds but the parasitic habits of the Cowbird and the cunning with which the female deposits its eggs in the nests of what are to become the foster parents of Cowbird foundlings fills me with amazement almost amounting to awe. Possibly that's because the whole process and end product run counter to everything we know of human customs and experiences. Most of us are what we are because of our upbringing, our early family life and training. We speak the language of our parents and conform to the customs of those who surround us in childhood. But the young Cowbirds that are reared by vireos, warblers, and sparrows never acquire a single vireo, warbler, or sparrow note for utterance, never absorb anything from their foster parents except food, and, when they are full-grown, go off to join up with other birds they never before have seen in their young lives—other Cowbirds similarly reared in an extraordinary variety of foster homes and now all looking alike, acting alike, and sounding alike! It's an astounding sequence.

As far as its status in the city goes, the Brown-headed Cowbird is a common summer resident, a rare or at least uncommon winter resident, and an abundant migrant in the autumn when flocks of several hundred at a time may be found walking about and feeding on flat open ground. It is often found in mixed flocks of Starlings, Grackle, and Redwings.

One of our handsomest birds and most persistent singers is the male Scarlet Tanager (*Piranga olivacea*) that we still have with us as a common migrant and a regular summer resident in fair numbers in the outlying wooded areas of the city. Scarlet Tanagers usually arrive in early May and then the brilliant plumage of the male stands out amid the light greenery of the woodland foliage at that time. But the yellowish-green female usually goes unnoticed and, for that matter, so does the male in autumn when it has changed to a similar dull hue. In the spring I often receive phone calls from excited friends who tell me that they have just seen a Scarlet Tanager, as though it were startling to find a bird like that in our neighborhood. I receive no such calls in late summer or early autumn when it is obvious that we have more Scarlet Tanagers as residents or migrants than we do in spring, because we have the young of the year added to the adult population. Furthermore, anyone who knows the song of the Scarlet Tanager or its *chip-burr* call notes can find it any day in our summer woods, where it vies with the Red-eyed Vireo for sustained singing throughout the hot season. The Summer Tanager (*Piranga rubra*), the male of which species has all-red plumage and is reported almost every year from somewhere in our territory, is a mere wanderer from the south or west and not an integral part of our local birdlife.

But the flaming red Cardinal (*Richmondena cardinalis*) and its less gaudy mate, accomplished whistlers both, have definitely moved into the city and settled down as permanent residents. When I was a boy a Cardinal would have been a sensation in the neighborhood. In one recent season I located three nesting pairs in the Spuyten Duyvil–Riverdale region alone. Not only that, but they have been extending their range northward into New England and wherever they settle down they make a habit of turning up regularly at window or dooryard feeding stations in cold weather. With their loud whistles and friendly ways, coupled with the fact that the male keeps its bright color throughout the year, Cardinals do not long go unnoticed wherever they make themselves at home.

Since I still see and hear the beautiful and melodious Rose-breasted Grosbeak (*Pheucticus ludovicianus*) in the woods and the shade trees of Riverdale and Van Cortlandt Park throughout the summer, I believe it remains as a breeding species in small numbers. Possibly it breeds in other outlying sections of the city. I never have found a vireo's nest that wasn't a model of design and execution. I never have seen a Rose-breasted Grosbeak's nest that wasn't a scanty and almost inadequate shallow bowl of twigs and grass. In particular, I remember one that was placed about twelve feet above ground in the fork of a shrubby Nannyberry tree that stood in a thicket along Palisade Avenue in Riverdale. I could stand underneath and actually see the four eggs — and daylight — through the bottom of the nest. To me it was a wonder that it lasted long enough to serve its purpose; but it did, though it was only a shapeless handful of scraggly twigs when the young birds were old enough to leave. Since I have mentioned this, I must add in fairness that another of my favorites, the Scarlet Tanager, is also a miserable architect.

The Indigo Bunting (*Passerina cyanea*) is a summer resident in small numbers in the outlying sections of the city. I can always count on a singing male in our neighborhood on the hillside sloping down to the Hudson and sooner or later I find the mottled female and pin-feathered youngsters chipping and sputtering in a tangle of blackberry bushes at the roadside. The glittering male sings loudly from an elevated perch to which it frequently returns throughout the day. I have also heard and seen singing males during the breeding season in the easterly high ground in Van Cortlandt Park and have no doubt that it breeds sparingly in other suitable locations within the city limits.

Since I have seen the Dickcissel (*Spiza americana*) no less than three times in Van Cortlandt Park in the past few years, it would be well to be on the watch for this wanderer from the West in the fall and winter. Then there is that larger and much more brightly colored wanderer from the north, the Evening Grosbeak (*Hesperiphona vespertina*), flocks of which occasionally descend on dooryard feeding stations in our region and consume almost incredible quantities of sunflower seeds. Such birds, however, are not to be counted on. But we can always watch for the Dickcissel in autumn, and hope for the Evening Grosbeak in winter.

I have a complaint against the Purple Finch (*Carpodacus purpureus*) in that it breeds within fifty miles of the city in all directions but is only a somewhat erratic transient and irregular winter visitor in our five boroughs. That is unfortunate for us because it is in best voice and color on its breeding grounds. During the spring migration we are favored occasionally with a rich rolling warble from a raspberry-tinted male but our autumn migrants and winter wanderers, most of them dull-colored, utter only sharp little clicks or "ticks" that serve as call notes. For the ordinary citizen who takes an interest in birds that are about the dooryard and garden, the Purple Finch problem may soon be complicated by the fact that the House Finch (*Carpodacus mexicanus*), which is native to the western part of the country and quite similar in general appearance to the Purple Finch, was introduced into Long Island not long ago and in 1958 was reported breeding not only on Long Island but in Westchester and Connecticut. Since House Finches are well named and wherever they appear nest confidingly in dooryard shrubbery and porch vines, we may soon expect to find them in the outlying residential sections of the city. However, familiarity with the newcomer will lead to ready recognition of the differences in voice and markings between it and the Purple Finch.

I have met the Pine Grosbeak (*Pinicola enucleator*) on winter trips to New England and I have come upon it as far south as Westchester County, but I never have seen it on city property. Others have been luckier and it is a matter of record that it has appeared here a number of times. As for other winter finches, the Common Redpoll (*Acanthis flammea*) and the Pine Siskin (*Spinus pinus*) are sometimes with us in considerable numbers, occasionally in mixed flocks; some seasons I have missed them entirely. The Siskin probably is a little more regular in attendance than the Redpoll but there have been winters when I never laid eyes on a Siskin in the area. There have been other seasons when they came as early as October in abundance, thinned out in January and February, added to their numbers again in March, and didn't go north until mid-April. I rarely see Redpolls in the area until during or after the first real driving snowstorm of the winter. During such a storm I have seen a Black Birch on a Riverdale lawn filled with Redpolls dining on the little seed cones (or strobiles, to be technical). Sometimes I find the American Goldfinch (*Spinus tristis*) mixed with flocks of Siskins and Redpolls but with us this friendly, cheerful,

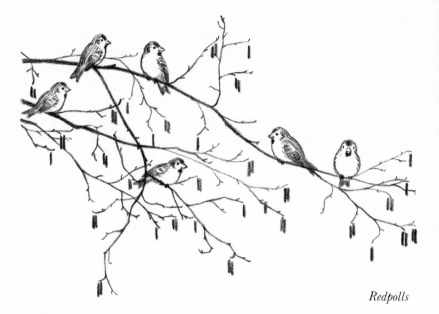

Redpolls

and beautiful little bird is largely a summer resident in the larger parks and the open residential sections of the city. Many persons call them "wild canaries" when they find them feeding on dandelion seeds on park or private lawns.

Long ago repeated attempts were made to introduce the European Goldfinch (*Carduelis carduelis*) into this country and for a time — around the beginning of this century — it bred over much of our city territory, including Central Park. Then the population failed except for a small number of survivors on Long Island. In recent years the Long Island population has increased steadily though slowly, and nesting reports have been received over a widening range. I have heard of no nesting records on my home ground, however, and in the past thirty years I have seen just three European Goldfinches that were chance wanderers in the neighborhood. If they are moving in on us, it will be an enjoyable invasion. They are friendly birds, even more colorful than our American Goldfinch.

Probably the rarest or at least the most irregular of the birds repeatedly visiting the region are the Red Crossbill (*Loxia curvirostra*) and the White-winged Crossbill (*Loxia leucoptera*) that look something like miniature parrots with malformed mandibles or beaks. I have met them only on rare occasions within the city limits. Once I found a flock of about two dozen Red Crossbills extracting seeds from the cones of a Scotch Pine on a lawn at the Frances Schervier Home in Spuyten Duyvil. On another occasion, while I was looking for Long-eared Owls in the little spruce grove at Orchard Beach on Pelham Bay, I heard a strange note above me. Just as I located the bird that was uttering the soft call note, it flew off toward the north-west, still calling. I knew there was a pine grove in that direction and I hurried off to it, just a few hundred yards away. There I heard the note again and finally located the bird when it came crawling around the tip of a Red Pine branchlet like a mouse to feed on the exposed cones. It was a White-winged Crossbill, and my first meeting with the bird on city property.

That brings us down to the last great group of birds of the region, the sparrows and their allies, the largest and most familiar of which is the Rufous-sided Towhee (*Pipilo erythroph-thalmus*), a formidable name for such a common and friendly summer resident. You may call it the Chewink if you please. Both the male and female often announce themselves by utter-ing something approximating that name. Because of the dark head and chestnut flanks of the male and the way the birds scratch for food in dead leaves on the floor of woods and thickets, some persons call them Ground Robins. It's curious how much noise they can make scratching among the leaves.

Other common summer residents are the cheerful and musi-cal Song Sparrow (*Melospiza melodia*), the Swamp Sparrow (*Melospiza georgiana*), the Chipping Sparrow (*Spizella passerina*), and, in fewer numbers, the Field Sparrow (*Spizella pusilla*). The Song and Swamp Sparrows are permanent residents to the extent that they may be found every month in the year; even a few Field Sparrows may spend the winter in our territory.

As far as I know, these are the only species breeding regularly in the Spuyten Duyvil–Riverdale–Van Cortlandt Park sector and I believe they are just as numerous as summer residents over similar terrain in other parts of the city. But we have no tidal marshes in our neighborhood, nor do we have the rural sections that still remain on Staten Island. I suspect that Richmond County is the summer home of more species of sparrow than any other city division can boast because it has both tidal marshes and upland woods and fields. Only the salt-marsh species nest in the grasses of Jamaica Bay, Flushing Bay, and Pelham Bay. But whether it be on Staten Island, in the Long Island sections of the city, or the East Bronx, there are half a dozen more breeding species that must be added to our list of summer-resident sparrows. They are the Savannah Sparrow (*Passerculus sandwichensis*), the Grasshopper Sparrow (*Ammodramus savannarum*), the Henslow's Sparrow (*Passerherbulus henslowii*), the Vesper Sparrow (*Pooecetes gramineus*), and those two skulkers that dodge in and out of the dark aisles made by the stiff stalks of the salt-marsh grasses, the Sharp-tailed Sparrow (*Ammospiza caudacuta*) and the Seaside Sparrow (*Ammospiza maritima*). Of that group the only one whose song is worth listening to is the Vesper Sparrow, which, to my ears, sounds like a much improved Song Sparrow with a touch of melancholy added for artistry. The vocal offerings of the Savannah, the Grasshopper, the Sharptail, and the Seaside Sparrows could pass as beady and buzzy insect notes. As for the short and ridiculous song of the Henslow's Sparrow, it sounds as though the bird were attempting to stop a dribble.

That about completes the list of our summer sparrows, to which we must add the roster of our regular migrants and winter residents or visitors. One of the most abundant of our migrants and one also fairly common as a winter resident is the friendly little Slate-colored Junco (*Junco hyemalis*) with dark upper parts and white outer tail feathers that show plainly as the bird flits about lawns and roadsides. It usually puts in an appearance about the first of October and within a few weeks it is everywhere on the ground in the region — in the woods, along the roadsides, on lawns, and in the shrubbery of the parks and private estates. About the beginning of December the big rush is over and we have with us only the scattered flocks that wander about the region throughout the winter. Many of them turn up at dooryard feeding stations. The northward traffic begins in late winter, reaches a peak in April, and May finds only a few lingerers or belated travelers.

Next in abundance as a migrant and in regularity as a winter resident is the handsome White-throated Sparrow (*Zonotrichia albicollis*), the "Peabody Bird" of Canada. Even more handsome but far fewer in numbers as a migrant and more or less accidental in winter is the White-crowned Sparrow (*Zonotrichia leucophrys*). An artist friend once remarked to me that he wished he were rich enough to give up painting magazine covers and spend the remainder of his life painting sparrows. He said they were the most beautiful of all our birds. I didn't debate the point but I'm sure the White-crowned Sparrow was not the least of the tribe on his mind when he made the remark. It must be that the Whitethroats outnumber the White-crowns by at least 200 to 1 on migration through our region, and yet anyone who keeps his eyes open will have little difficulty in finding White-crowns in our territory in October (one reason is that they seem to prefer cleared ground and lawns to underbrush for feeding purposes and thus are more readily observed).

The Ipswich Sparrow (*Passerculus princeps*) is a late autumn migrant and an early spring migrant along the ocean front and through the salt marshes that are the summer home of the Sharp-tailed and the Seaside Sparrow, and a few occasionally are turned up as winter residents. Farther inland the Lincoln's Sparrow (*Melospiza lincolnii*) regularly moves through the region in small numbers that for the most part go undetected or at least unrecognized by many watchers of the wild. Except for a buffy band across the breast that often is difficult to see, they look much like Song Sparrows and they are masters at dodging out of sight over a wall, into a tangle of vines, or down low in thick shrubbery before you can get a look at them. The

Ipswich Sparrows are more obliging. Occasionally they move sedately around the outside of a patch of grass by a tide pool and sometimes the pace is so leisurely that they actually walk, which is a strange gait for a sparrow. But the Ipswich Sparrow is a strange bird. It breeds only on Sable Island, Nova Scotia, a narrow strip of land only twenty miles long, and it winters along the Atlantic Coast from Massachusetts to Georgia. In other words, its summer range is twenty miles and its winter range is something over a thousand miles. It's called the Ipswich Sparrow because the first specimen was collected at Ipswich, Massachusetts, in 1868.

You are lucky if you see either the Lincoln's Sparrow or the Ipswich Sparrow on migration through our territory, but you should not miss the large, reddish-brown, well-spotted, and sweet-singing Fox Sparrow (*Passerella iliaca*) that is a late autumn and early spring migrant in flocks of fair size and a regular winter resident in small numbers. For a sparrow it is really a distinguished vocalist and its spring aria, though short, is a fancy bit of warbling or whistling. One more of the tribe that we have on the premises each year in round numbers is the handsome and cheerful Tree Sparrow (*Spizella arborea*) that I always expect to arrive about the first of November to settle down for the winter in the Van Cortlandt swamp and other favorable localities. Snowstorms, high winds, and low temperatures apparently have no effect on the blithe spirits of these neatly marked and delicately tinted sparrows and many a cold gray day in January has been lightened for me by meetings with flitting flocks of them going briskly about their business to the musical accompaniment of their tinkling call notes.

I look for Tree Sparrows in the Van Cortlandt swamp each winter and never have they failed me. I look for the Lapland Longspur (*Calcarius lapponicus*) and the Snow Bunting (*Plectrophenax nivalis*) whenever I cross the nearby Parade Ground on my way to the swamp and not more than a dozen times in thirty years did I find them. These residents of the Arctic are regular winter visitors in our territory and they like the same kind of terrain on which Horned Larks occur. Indeed, they often travel in company with Northern Horned Larks. But Northern Horned Larks are regular and sometimes abundant feeders on the Parade Ground in cold weather, whereas Lapland Longspurs and Snow Buntings are merely occasional visitors. December 19, 1951, remains a notable day for me, because on that morning I found seventeen Snow Buntings

Snow Buntings

there. In our general region the Longspurs and Snow Buntings favor the ocean beaches and flat areas nearby when they come down from the north in November. Search for them on parking lots behind the ocean beaches. What may look like hard bare ground to you may well be covered with wind-blown grass and weed seeds on which they can feed. Seaside golf courses and airports are favorite landing strips for them. I live in hope that someday an inspired enthusiast will chalk up on the bulletin board at Idlewild International Airport: "Now arriving from Labrador: Lapland Longspurs and Snow Buntings!" It could easily be true any day in late autumn or early winter.

This completes the list of birds one might fairly expect or reasonably hope to see within our city limits as residents, migrants, or seasonal visitors in the course of a year. Many additional species, to be sure, have been recorded in the area. Tropical birds have been whirled up this way by hurricanes; birds of northern Europe have reached here by way of Greenland and Labrador; unexpected oceanic birds have been blown along our ocean front by great winds at sea; and many western land birds have wandered this way on migration. Such arrivals are interesting but our city has no real claim on such birds, nor, if a touch of parochial pride may be pardoned, any need of them. The birds that belong here add up to an astonishing and fascinating group. Here in this city of millions of human inhabitants, of famous skyscrapers, of Wall Street, of Broadway, of Harlem and Coney Island, of arriving and departing ocean liners, of great bridges and tunnels, of chaotic traffic, crowded sidewalks and noisy subways, we also have wild birds in great numbers at all seasons, many species that are "native and to the manner born" and many more that come to us from farms and forests far away, from offshore islands and the arctic tundra. So it is, though comparatively few persons view the great metropolis in such a light, that New York City is a most fertile field in which to pursue the absorbing science of ornithology or the gentle art of bird-watching.

Chapter 15

The Four Seasons in the City

CITY LIFE IS notoriously fast. Or so runs the report in the rural districts. But we have been dealing with nature within our city gates and, whether in a crowded metropolis or a desolate wilderness, nature's pace is always the same: slow, steady, relentless. Our changing seasons, of course, are due to the tilt of the earth's axis of rotation at an approximate angle — it varies slightly from year to year — of 23° 27′ 8″ from the vertical to the plane of its orbit. At the equator the effect of this tilt is negligible. At the poles it is the difference between day and night — the six-month Arctic and Antarctic days and nights.

We are, so to speak, in the middle. At our latitude the difference between summer and winter is striking, and the light greenery of spring is not at all like the riot of color that surrounds us in autumn. But the change from one season to another is slow, gradual, almost imperceptible. From the Gulf of Mexico to the Canadian border a man could walk northward with the spring and not fall a day behind it. If this pace seems slow as to miles per day, the onward march of seasons is even slower if we measure it by the time clock of the stars.

Overhead of a clear night in July you will see the bright star Vega. As far back as 5000 years ago the high priests of Egypt and of Ur of the Chaldees knew as well as we do that the stars follow the same apparent courses across the heavens year after year. Thus when we look up of a clear summer night and see Vega shining like a lovely jewel against a dark velvet background, we know that if the skies are clear we will see it there again tomorrow night — with one slight but important difference. Tomorrow night Vega will reach that same point in the sky 3 minutes 55.9 seconds earlier than the moment at which we see it there tonight. This is the measured pace at which our four seasons move along and merge one into the other in succession as this spinning planet goes on its long trip around the sun that we call a year.

Just for good measure, we can add a touch of speed by viewing the matter in another light. As earthbound creatures, we are carried along on this annual trip around the sun. It is a journey of nearly 600,000,000 miles through space that we make at a speed of approximately 18½ miles per second. But we have no feeling about the matter and seldom give it a thought. The rotational speed of the earth doesn't bother us, either, nor the other rotational and orbital speeds to which we are subjected. Our sun is a star revolving around the center of a rotating galaxy that is itself on the move toward another point in space. All these motions that we do not feel add up to an amazing total. A young man may say with regret that he never has traveled, but if he is twenty years old he has traveled well over 10,000,000,000 miles within our own little solar system, not to mention the far greater distance in galactial rotation at a speed of roughly 175 miles per second. And never a single mile of this amazing journey retraced!

We shall now come back to earth. These vast distances and great speeds have no perceived influence on our daily lives. But we do feel the change of seasons and we can see the constellations march across the night skies in the course of a year. In this way we can measure our daily lives against the nightly change in the stars above us. Call it approximately four minutes a day. Nothing can hurry it. Nothing can stop it. For us, this is the cosmic clock. This is the stream of Time in which, by his own account, Thoreau went a-fishing. He was a man who felt most at home outdoors and never lacked for good company when he was alone with his thoughts on a woodland path.

There is never a day, even in the depths of winter and the confines of the city, when there isn't something stirring outdoors. A walk in the winter woods always yields a good harvest. Except for the evergreens, we see the trees naked and unadorned and can better appreciate the strength of the oaks, the gracefulness of the birches, the rough coat of the Shagbark Hickory, and the smooth silvery bark of the Beech. At a distance we can recognize the Sour-gum by its short horizontal branches and the White Ash by its stubby branchlets that are almost bleak against the cold sky. Now is the time to look at the leaf scars on the twigs and, under a magnifying glass, study these "fingerprints" of the different species. On tree trunks and rotting stumps and fallen logs we find fungus growths of different colors, shapes, and sizes. Here's a whole field of study in itself. Then there are catkins to inspect on various shrubs and trees, and cocoons to collect. Now the Muskrat houses stand out in the cattail marsh and in the undergrowth of the swamp the three-angled seed pods of the Wild Yam are clinging in little bunches to the endless stems that twine about the shrubbery. Only a foot or so above the ground is the last summer's nest of a Yellowthroat. How dainty it is; how soft. As soon as I touch it, out jumps a mouse — a "wee, sleekit, cowrin', tim'rous beastie" to which I meant no more harm than

Robert Burns did when his November plowing turned one out of house and home on his Mauchline farm in Ayrshire long ago.

There are some birds about, to be sure, but this is not the best place in the city to look for birds in winter. When the park lakes and the ponds are frozen, the tidal reaches and the ocean front are the areas that have an alluring collection of birds to put on view. This is the time to explore the Brooklyn and Queens waterfront, to look over the gulls in the Upper Bay and in the Narrows, to find out what fish the hardy anglers are hauling in at the Coney Island piers, to scan the ocean beaches for Horned Larks, Snow Buntings, Lapland Longspurs, and possibly a Snowy Owl, to visit the Aquarium at the ocean's edge, to turn binocular seaward to discover what scoters, grebes, or loons are loafing or feeding offshore, and, most fruitful of all, to check over the thousands of ducks and whatever geese may be found in the Jamaica Bay Wildlife Refuge that is maintained by the Department of Parks of the city.

Even the hardest winter begins to creak at the joints during warm spells in late February. Broken ice floes coming down the Hudson often carry Bald Eagles as passengers as far south as Dyckman Street. The staminate catkins of the hazels and alders are beginning to soften and lengthen. On Washington's Birthday I scrape away a thick matting of wet leaves around the roots of a Red Maple in the Van Cortlandt swamp and uncover the first flowers of the year, a Skunk Cabbage in multiple bloom under the protection of its thick curved hood with fancy striping. March is the Indian giver, the month that promises much and then tries to take it all back. We have a spell of warm sunny days. The Field Garlic has turned green in the low meadows and the wet woods. The Redwings are calling in the cattail marsh and the Grackles are stalking noisily about the Parade Ground. There are Robins and Dandelions on the park lawn and the Coltsfoot is in yellow bloom on sunlit banks. The Spring Peepers tune up in the hush of a calm twilight and the whole frog chorus increases as the light grows

less. You can plainly see that the dark buds of the elms are swelling and the Red Maple is getting ready to burst into bloom. A neighbor reports Bluebirds in his yard and a Mourning Cloak butterfly was seen in the woods. Then we have either a heavy fall of snow or a paralyzing ice storm. The wind is raw; the footing is treacherous; considering the date, the landscape is an appalling sight! We are informed by the newspapers that the sun has moved into Aries and officially it is spring, but the season seems to be moving backward instead of forward.

April puts an end to all that. It's a cantankerous month of good, bad, and indifferent days, but snow and ice are quickly put to rout. Spring begins to assert itself. The Red Maples are in colorful bloom and Marsh Marigolds open to pave the floor of the swamp with gold. The lake now harbors a pair of Wood Ducks, a Coot, two male Ring-necked Ducks, three Pied-billed Grebes, and a pair of Pintails of aristocratic bearing. The Horsetail stalks stand a foot high along the railroad track and a little Garter Snake, moving among them, pauses to stick out its tongue at us. No offense is intended on either side. Insect hatches are coming off the water and little clouds of midges gyrate over our heads in the sunlight. On a half-sunken log at the edge of the cattails eight Painted Turtles are sunning themselves in a row. Now the shore birds are beginning to drift northward along our ocean beaches and tidal flats and the Laughing Gulls have returned to the Hudson River.

This is the month of sparrows and swallows. The transients are going through and our summer residents are settling down for the season. The shad nets are up in the Hudson River. The early warblers are in the evergreens and the opening foliage of the shrubbery. The trees are still bare of leaves but there are insects on the wing in the woods and little butterflies of the group called "Blues" flutter across the woodland paths. On the steep sides of moist glens there are patches of Dutchman's Breeches for the children to gather and there are early violets open for inspection. By the last week in April there is no doubt about the season. Definitely it's spring.

The rush of late April becomes a runaway in May. We can't keep up with the arrival of birds and the opening of buds. Dogwood comes into stunning bloom. Spring Beauties, Wild Geraniums, and other lovely flowers make gardens of the floors of the wet woodlands. Ferns of a dozen species are unrolling their curved fronds. The oaks are draped with their strings of staminate flowers and warblers of many species and bright colors are flitting about among them. This is the high tide of the warbler migration. In the small but famous shaded patch of ground called The Ramble in Central Park, as many as twenty-nine species of warbler have been observed on a single day in May. This is fifteen minutes by subway from Wall Street, the financial center of the world. Now the shade trees reach the stage of full foliage and the inchworms, the iniquitous geometrids, go into action, munching and crunching and making sickly skeletons of what had been broad green leaves.

We move forward into June, which is the month of brides and butterflies. It is also the month of roses and of White Daisies in the hayfields. It is the time of the nesting of birds and the flowering of the Tulip-tree, the Catalpa, the Horse-chestnut, and the Black Locust with its drooping clusters of creamy flowers of overwhelming sweetness. Now the Linden is odorous and audible as the honeybees gather to the feast that it offers in profusion. Now the female Snapping Turtle hauls herself up the bank above the lake or pond to scratch a hole in the dirt, deposit therein a dozen or two — or three! — round white eggs with tough but flexible shells, cover the clutch with dirt, lumber down to the water again, and leave the eggs either to hatch by themselves or furnish a meal for a marauding Skunk, Raccoon, or Fox.

The summer solstice passed unnoticed. Our hottest weather is ahead but by our time clock of the stars the year is on the wane. Everything quiets down in the heat of July. Everything except the dazzling dragonflies and damselflies darting about in spectacular flight over the quiet ponds and pools of the area. It's fascinating to watch them sowing their eggs in the water or, with curved bodies, inserting them into the plant stems rising out of the shallows along the edges of the ponds. Look closely at these amazing creatures with transparent wings and burnished bodies. To me they are the precious jewels of the insect world. Even so, we must not linger or the south-bound shore birds will get past us before we know it. By mid-July the movement is well started and in August the ocean beaches, the tidal mud flats and the low wet meadows are the feeding grounds or rest areas for retreating shore birds of many and often confusing species in their autumn plumages. In August, too, some of the more cautious upland birds are in retreat, with warblers in the van. For that matter, the tower-ing Tulip-tree, with numerous golden leaves dappling its great green crown, also is in retreat. We notice that twilight comes much sooner now than it did in June.

The almanac has it that autumn doesn't start until the sun moves into Libra on or about September 23 but all of us know better than that. Labor Day is the turning point. The shut-ters go up at camps in the mountains and on shacks at the seashore. The children are made ready for school. As far as the residents of this city are concerned, summer is over. September is the month of the southbound warbler flight and the gradual turning of the leaves to red and gold. The fields and roadsides are bright with goldenrods and asters. The nights are cooler and the crickets slow down the tempo of their incessant chirps in the dark. By the time autumn takes over officially the Red Maple is aflame in the swamp and the Sour-gum is a crimson banner on the hillside. Somehow it always seems that spring comes slowly but summer departs in haste.

October is our finest month. The fields, the woods, the hill-sides, are a riot of glorious color and, for the most part, the days and nights are crisp, clear, and altogether wonderful.

You can see flocks of birds migrating by day and you can hear them passing overhead at night. Robins, Redwings, Grackles, and Blue Jays like to travel by day and usually go in companies like pilgrims going to Canterbury. Bluebirds drift lightly across the sky, dropping musical murmurs as they go. Any time after the middle of the month we can look for a big hawk flight when conditions are right, meaning a blue sky dotted with snowy islands of cumulus clouds and a fair wind from the northwest to help things along. Each cloud is the cottony cap of a rising current of warm air that condenses when it reaches the colder upper air. The hawks, soaring in circles, are carried upward on these rising currents of warm air and thus gain altitude without effort. Then off they glide on a downward slant to the south or the southwest toward another helpful rising air current to repeat the effortless progress of such a southbound trip. A hilltop in the Bronx is a good perch from which to watch such hawk flights, but the roof of an apartment house in Flatbush will do just as well on occasion.

On a lower level we have Juncos, Whitethroats, and Swainson's Thrushes in the shrubbery. Chickadees and Whitebreasted Nuthatches are returning to familiar dooryard feeding stations to find out whether or not suet, peanut butter, and sunflower seeds are on the free list again. The nights are frosty now. Overhead is the Great Square of Pegasus. A little to the northeast a keen-eyed observer should be able to spot the little round haze that is the Great Nebula in Andromeda, but some of us need binoculars to see this faint glow that, traveling toward us at a speed of 186,000 miles per second, has taken some 1,500,000 years to reach our retinas. It is, we are further told, the nearest of the great extra-galactic spiral nebulae in our skies. This is too large a subject for us. We had better come back to earth and our little affairs.

Now on our walks we find the Witch-hazel bravely bearing its yellow flowers along its bare branches in the woods. No other native shrub or tree dares to bloom this late in the year.

The ground is carpeted brilliantly with the mingled reds and yellows of the fallen leaves. The first driving rain in November will strip most of the trees of the last vestige of summer clothing. This is the time of year that stirred William Cullen Bryant to write

Oh, Autumn! why so soon
Depart the hues that make thy forests glad,
Thy gentle wind and thy fair sunny noon,
And leave thee wild and sad.

Wild and sad, perhaps, in the eyes of a poet, but still beautiful in the eyes of an artist. The swamp and the hillside are rich with subtle shades of brown. This is what I call "the Blakelock period" in the changing landscape of the year. It has beauty combined with rugged strength. It has readied itself for on-coming winter.

But before winter moves in and settles down all around us, we usually are granted a short reprieve in the form of a mild spell called Indian Summer, a few days or a week of warm hazy weather in late November or early December. Some-times Thanksgiving Day has the benefit of this soft touch so late in the year, but it is by no means guaranteed for any given calendar day, week, or year. What is certain is that on or about December 22 the sun will enter Capricornus and winter will rule the region for the next three months. Even so, let nothing stop us from our self-appointed rounds. Warm cloth-ing, waterproof footwear, binocular, and a pocket magnify-ing glass are all we need to find pleasure and profit in our winter walks around the frozen lake, over the snow-clad hills, or along the windswept sea beaches. No man ever will live long enough to learn all there is to know about the wildlife that exists in this great city. And from the boardwalk at Coney Island, quite as well as from any Arcadian cliff overlooking the Ionian waves, a lover of Nature may always hope to

Have sight of Proteus rising from the sea;
Or hear old Triton blow his wreathèd horn.

Reference Books

IN THE somewhat disputed field of scientific nomenclature I have followed, for the most part, the authorities listed here:

American Ornithologists' Union, *Check-list of North American Birds*. 5th edition. N.p., 1957.

William H. Burt and Richard P. Grossenheider, *A Field Guide to the Mammals*. Boston, 1952.

Boughton Cobb, *A Field Guide to the Ferns*. Boston, 1956.

Roger Conant, *A Field Guide to Reptiles and Amphibians*. Boston, 1958.

David Starr Jordan, Barton Warren Evermann, and Howard Walter Clark, *Check List of Fishes of North and Middle America*. Washington, D.C., 1955 reprint.

Alexander B. Klots, *A Field Guide to the Butterflies*. Boston, 1951.

Frank E. Lutz, *Field Book of Insects*. New York, 1935.

Roy Waldo Miner, *Field Book of Seashore Life*. New York, 1950.

George A. Petrides, *A Field Guide to Trees and Shrubs*. Boston, 1958.

Frederick H. Pough, *A Field Guide to Rocks and Minerals*. Boston, 1953.

In the chapter on flowers I accepted the authority of *The New Britton and Brown Illustrated Flora of the Northeastern United States and Adjacent Canada*, by Henry A. Gleason and others and published by the New York Botanical Garden (New York, 1952), quite possibly because of the imprint that closely associates it with happy memories of many hours spent within the confines of the New York Botanical Garden in Bronx Park.

J.K.

Index

Index

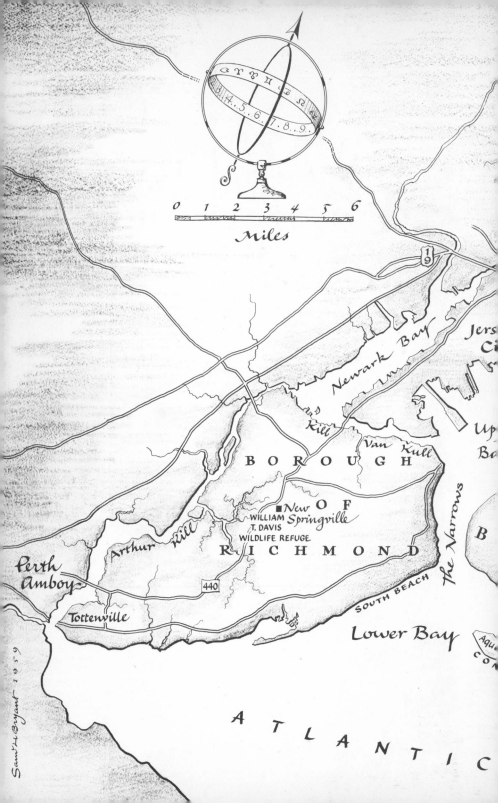

Miles

0 1 2 3 4 5 6

Newark Bay

Jers.
Ci

Kill

Van Kull

Up
Ba

B O R O U G H

O F

■ New Springville

WILLIAM
T. DAVIS
WILDLIFE REFUGE

R I C H M O N D

The Narrows

B

Perth
Amboy

Arthur Kill

440

Tottenville

SOUTH BEACH

Lower Bay

Aqu
Co

A T L A N T I C

Sam'l Bryant 1959